BETWEEN YESTERDAY AND TOMORROW

BETWEEN YESTERDAY AND TOMORROW

German Visions of Europe, 1926–1950

Christian Bailey

berghahn
NEW YORK • OXFORD
www.berghahnbooks.com

Published in 2013 by
Berghahn Books
www.berghahnbooks.com

©2013, 2016 Christian Bailey
First paperback edition published in 2016

All rights reserved. Except for the quotation of short passages for the purposes of criticism and review, no part of this book may be reproduced in any form or by any means, electronic or mechanical, including photocopying, recording, or any information storage and retrieval system now known or to be invented, without written permission of the publisher.

Library of Congress Cataloging-in-Publication Data

Bailey, Christian.
  Between yesterday and tomorrow: German visions of Europe, 1926–1950 / Christian Bailey.
      pages cm
  Includes bibliographical references.
  ISBN 978-1-78238-139-6 (hardback) -- ISBN 978-1-78533-197-8 (paperback) -- ISBN 978-1-78238-140-2 (ebook)
  1. Europe--Politics and government--1918-1945. 2. European federation--History--20th century. 3. Europe--Politics and government--1918-1945. 4. Germany--Politics and government--1918-1933. 5. Germany (West)--Politics and government. 6. Civil society--Germany--History--20th century. 7. Civil society--Europe--History--20th century. 8. Socialism--Europe--History--20th century. 9. Democracy--Europe--History--20th century. I. Title.
  D1060.B237 2013
  943.087--dc23

2013022505

British Library Cataloguing in Publication Data

A catalogue record for this book is available from the British Library

ISBN 978-1-78238-139-6 (hardback)
ISBN 978-1-78533-197-8 (paperback)
ISBN 978-1-78238-140-2 (ebook)

For my parents, and for Suzanne

Contents

Acknowledgements	ix
Abbreviations	xii
Introduction	1

Chapter 1
Making the Case for Europe: Transnational Organizations and
Cultural Journals — 23

Chapter 2
The Defence of Europe in *Merkur: Deutsche Zeitschrift für
Europäisches Denken* — 54

Chapter 3
The *Internationaler Sozialistischer Kampfbund*: From World
Revolution to European Federalism — 86

Chapter 4
The Rise and Fall of a Socialist Europe: The ISK and the SPD
in Opposition — 115

Chapter 5
'An Island Surrounded by land': Das Demokratische Deutschland
in Switzerland — 145

Chapter 6
'Europe our Fatherland, Bavaria our Heimat!' Das Demokratische
Deutschland and the Post-war Trajectories of European Federalism — 172

Conclusion	198
Bibliography	211
Index	241

Acknowledgements

The chaplain of my old undergraduate college, Michael Chantry, used to say that God had given him nothing that he wanted, and everything that he needed. As a (still) young historian, I have often felt the same way about the academic world. The need to slowly develop one's skills – to write, revise, re-revise and to teach (often outside one's 'comfort zone') – can, at times, feel like a gruelling apprenticeship. Yet, a great compensation through all of this has been the people I have met as teachers and as colleagues.

I would like to thank some of those people now. First, I owe thanks to my doctoral supervisor, Ute Frevert, who expertly steered me through the PhD process. Since then she has been a conscientious, challenging and supportive mentor whose own work has served as a(n unattainable!) model of innovative scholarship. I was also lucky to have benefited from the help of other gifted historians at Yale. Jay Winter was always ready to offer thoughtful advice when asked and read through various drafts of my written work, offering, alongside John Gaddis and Seth Fein, penetrating analyses of this project. Since finishing my studies at Yale I was lucky enough to work as a Postdoc at the Max Planck Institute for Human Development in Berlin, again under the directorship of Ute Frevert. I am extremely grateful to all of my colleagues at the MPI for what they taught me about the craft of researching and writing through their professionalism and collegiality. Yet, I have to single out a couple of them. Jan Plamper read through this manuscript and various iterations of related article drafts. He has always been extremely generous with his time and his prodigious abilities. Similarly, Pascal Eitler took the time to offer me encouragement and friendship over our daily coffees, at which he listened patiently to my mangled German. I have learned an immense amount from what he had to say and how he said it.

Beyond Berlin, I have been lucky enough to receive much help from other academic friends and mentors. Ever since my undergraduate days, Martin Conway has encouraged my interest in history and helped me in countless ways whenever I have asked (which has been a lot). Anyone who knows him will no doubt share my wonder at how he manages to give so freely of his time and his many gifts as a colleague, writer and teacher. In the case of this book, he read a number of the chapters and offered insightful and valuable guidance. Similarly, Paul Betts, through his teaching and writings inspired me to study German history in the first place, when I was still sure I was going to dedicate my life to writing about the Victorians. More recent colleagues at Balliol College, Oxford and at The Open University have been wonderfully supportive. I am particularly grateful to David Vincent of The OU for reading through this manuscript and offering a number of helpful suggestions.

As for the writing of the manuscript, this would not have been possible without the support of various funding bodies. Apart from generous help from its Graduate School, I received grants from the Whitney and Betty MacMillan Center for International and Area Studies at Yale University. I was particularly fortunate to receive a Fox Fellowship to the Free University of Berlin through the MacMillan Center, which was also funded with the support of the Max Kade Foundation, New York. Similarly, I am indebted to the International Security Studies Program at Yale, which awarded me Olin and Smith Richardson Fellowships. In addition, I would like to thank the Connecticut–Baden-Württemberg Exchange Program, which funded a number of preliminary research trips to the University of Tübingen. Finally, I would like to thank my colleagues at the Modern European History Research Centre at the University of Oxford where I was a Visiting Researcher.

The staff at Berghahn Books, especially Marion Berghahn, Ann Przyzycki DeVita and Charlotte Mosedale, have been wonderful. I would particularly like to thank the anonymous peer reviewers whose detailed and searching feedback greatly improved the manuscript.

I would also like to thank the librarians and archivists at the Bundesarchiv, Berlin; the Politisches Archiv des Auswärtigen Amts, Berlin; the Archiv der sozialen Demokratie at the Friedrich Ebert Stiftung, Bonn; the Deutsches Literaturarchiv, Marbach; the Institut für Zeitgeschichte, Munich; the Archives de l'Occupation française en Allemagne et en Autriche, Colmar; the Modern Records Centre, University of Warwick; the Bodleian Library, University of Oxford; and the National Archives, College Park, Maryland. Their expertise was invaluable.

Finally, I turn to the members of my family, who have helped me in innumerable ways. My sister has always been willing to help me, not least taking me on a number of greatly appreciated breaks when graduate studies seemed overwhelming. As for my parents: they have made many sacrifices – of time, of money, of energy – to prioritize my education. It must be one of the strange things about encouraging a child's education – you never know to what ends they will use it. I cannot be sure they pictured things turning out quite as they have but I thank them for continuing to encourage me on this path and for making an academic career possible in the first place. Their belief in education and in their children has been an inspiring example to me. This leaves only my wife, Suzanne, to thank. As rather more people than I would like already know, I lied to her about my age and sporting abilities when we first met. Yet, since then, she's stuck with me when reality – so much reality! – asserted itself. To quote Michael Chantry again, she has always been a 'strong arm to reach out for in the dark' and, as anyone who knows us can testify, the writing of this book could not have happened without her supporting me in every possible way. Her presence in my life sustains me and spurs me on; she will always have my gratitude and love. I dedicate this book to my parents, and to her.

LIST OF ABBREVIATIONS

ACUE	American Committee on United Europe
AdsD	Archiv der sozialen Demokratie (Archive of Social Democracy), Friedrich Ebert Stiftung
ADGB	Allgemeine Deutscher Gewerkschaftsbund (Association of German Trade Unions)
AOAA	Archives de l'Occupation en Allemagne et en Autriche, Colmar (Archive of the French Occupation in Germany and Austria)
BDI	Bundesverband der Deutschen Industrie (Federation of German Industry)
BHE	Bund der Heimatvertriebenen und Entrechteten (League of Expellees and Deprived of Rights)
BP	Bayernpartei (Bavarian Party)
BVP	Bayerische Volkspartei (Bavarian People's Party)
CCF	Congress for Cultural Freedom
CDU	Christlich Demokratische Union Deutschlands (German Christian Democratic Party)
CIA	Central Intelligence Agency
CMEA/ COMECON	Council for Mutual Economic Assistance
COMISCO	Committee of the International Socialist Conference
CSU	Christlich-Soziale Union Bayern (Christian Social Union Bavaria)
DEVA	Deutsche Verlagsanstalt
DFG	Deutsch–Französische Gesellschaft (German–French Society)
DDP	Deutsche Demokratische Partei (German Democratic Party)
DLA	Deutsches Literaturarchiv (German Literature Archive)
EC	European Community
ECSC	European Coal and Steel Community
EDC	European Defence Community
EEC	European Economic Community
EM	European Movement

EPC	European Political Community
EPP	European People's Party
ESV	Europäische Schriftsteller Vereinigung (Association of European Authors)
EU	European Union
EUCD	European Union of Christian Democrats
FDP	Free Democratic Party
GDR	German Democratic Republic
IfZ	Institut für Zeitgeschichte (Institute for Contemporary History)
IJB	International Youth Association
ILP	Independent Labour Party
ISK	Internationaler Sozialistischer Kampfbund (International Socialist Vanguard)
ITF	International Transport Federation
IWUSP	International Working Union of Socialist Parties
KPD	Kommunistische Partei Deutschlands (Communist Party in Germany)
KPO	Kommunistische Partei – Opposition (Communist Party in Germany – Opposition)
LSE	London School of Economics
LSI	Labour and Socialist International
MRC	Modern Records Centre, University of Warwick
MRP	Mouvement Républicain Populaire (French Popular Republican Movement)
MSI	Militant Socialist International
NATO	North Atlantic Treaty Organization
NEC	National Executive Committee of the Labour Party
NEI	Nouvelles Equipes Internationales (New International Teams)
OEEC	Organization for European Economic Cooperation
OMGUS	The Office of Military Government, United States
OSS	Office of Strategic Services
PID	Political Information Department
PWE	Political Warfare Executive
RSK	Reichsschrifttumskammer (German Government Chamber of Literature)
RSÖ	Revolutionäre Sozialisten Österreichs (Revolutionary Socialists of Austria)
SAI	Sozialistische Arbeiter-Internationale (Labour and Socialist International)
SAP/D	Sozialistische Arbeiterpartei Deutschlands (Socialist Workers' Party of Germany)
SER	Sender der Europäischen Revolution (Radio of the European Revolution)

SFIO	Section française de l'Internationale ouvrière (French Section of the Workers' International)
SIPDIC	Secrétariat International des Partis Démocratiques d'Inspiration Chrétienne (International Secretariat of Christian-inspired Democratic Parties)
SKVP	Schweizerische Konservative Volkspartei (Swiss Conservative People's Party)
SOE	Special Operations Executive
SPD	Sozialdemokratische Partei Deutschlands (German Social Democratic Party)
SPÖ	Sozialistische Partei Österreichs (Austrian Socialist Party)
SPS	Sozialdemokratische Partei der Schweiz (Swiss Social Democratic Party)
SVG	Socialist Vanguard Group
UdM	Union der Mitte (Union of the Centre)
UEF	Union Européenne des Fédéralistes (Union of European Federalists)
UNESCO	United Nations Educational, Scientific and Cultural Organization
USG	Unabhängiger Sozialistischer Gewerkschaft (Independent Socialist Trade Union)
WAV	Wirtschaftliche Aufbau-Vereinigung (Economic Reconstruction Association)
WCC	World Council of Churches
WEU	Western European Union
WIS	Working Group of International Socialists

Introduction

Without knowing what lay in the future, the late 1980s may have seemed as good a time as any to review the history of European integration. In 1987, two years before Europe's Cold War barriers would unexpectedly collapse, the historian Wilfried Loth took stock of this history in the preface to a documentary account of European integration. This volume was commissioned by the European University Institute, a European Community (EC) venture nestled in the hills above Florence. According to Loth, such a project could help the EC, 'too often seen in purely technocratic terms', to acquire 'an historical self-awareness and consequently … a political identity'. The signs were good: seeing 'so many workers from different countries and universities' commit themselves to this shared endeavour led Loth to believe 'that Europeans are approaching agreement about the history of their integration'.[1] Expressing such a desire for scholarly and even broader social consensus about history may seem an unusual goal for a prominent historian to espouse. Yet, Loth was doing what many other intellectuals have done over the course of the twentieth century: he was envisioning a version of Europe – Europe as an integrated whole – with the ambition of bringing it to life. By spotlighting this Europe, defining it, narrating its history, explaining its growth and noting its shortcomings, he and his fellow historians were telling Europeans to 'become what you are': members of an ideal unified Europe that until now had only ever partially existed in its historical manifestations.

It is no peculiarity of historians of European integration to recognize that the historical context they establish will frame how individuals and societies interpret their present and approach their future. Yet, these historians of the European project did seem to be predominantly looking forward rather than back – an uncomfortable position for historians to maintain for any extended period of time. They were, of course, by no means alone in this regard. As the launching of the federalist Spinelli Group of leading European politicians and intellectuals in September 2010 suggests, many European leaders continue to work towards the ideal of a fully fledged federal Europe, even if their efforts may, as yet, have failed to inspire many of their fellow European citizens, who seem less inclined to vote in European elections or to provide retrospective validation in referenda for the decisions taken by their leaders.[2]

By contrast, the purpose of this book is to move away from teleological histories and understandings of European integration; to do so not by seeking to debunk the desires for unity felt by many Europeans across the twentieth century, but by taking them seriously in their historical diversity. The book does this by focusing on the activities of, and debates between, politicians and intellectuals who sought to create a united Europe from the interwar period to the early post-Second World War years. The Europes with which this book is concerned are primarily, therefore, those which never happened – what could be called lost Europes.[3] They were very different in their contours and characters from those more commonly associated with European integration. In particular, they were the work, most often, of outsiders: individuals who by their ideology and choices stood outside the mainstream of interwar political debate. Many of these individuals were also exiles. Their common European experience of exile afforded them a comparative perspective on the factors that united and divided Europeans and the loyalties that were shared across national borders.[4] Similarly, their experience of the First World War, as well as of National Socialist aggression demonstrated that individuals' security and prosperity were not only affected by ideological conflict occurring at a national level but also by international clashes that affected all Europeans. Beginning this study in the interwar period therefore highlights not only the support for European integration that grew among groups acutely affected by national and ideological rivalries and war, but also how these groups became Europeanized by their experiences.[5]

By focusing on such a time period, the book seeks to problematize what, I will argue, is a foundational myth of integration as a linear and solely post-war process. It will do this by demonstrating the variety of formulae for European integration that existed in the early post-Second World War years, which, in turn, had their roots in pre-existing debates and discourses about Europe. As will be shown, support for European integration was not simply a reaction to the divisions and enmities destructively evident during the Second World War. Instead, it grew out of longer traditions of internationalist thought and intersected with deep-rooted dissatisfactions regarding the reconfiguration of Europe after Versailles and more broadly concerning the growth of nation-states from the nineteenth century onwards.[6] These longer-standing discourses did not fit easily with the definition of European integration that came to the fore during the post-war years. The ways of talking about Europe, and imagining its political future, that emerged in the preceding decades had been based predominantly on rejection of the political status quo. In contrast, the European integration that occurred in the 1950s and 1960s was focused primarily on stabilizing the nation-state structure of Europe, and the democratic structures on which it was based.[7] This book's concern with lost Europes thus orientates it away from a concern with the origins of the new Western Europe of the post-1945 years and points attention back towards mid-century plans for integration, often designed to address the problematic post-First World War redrawing of the European map alongside the weaknesses of interwar democracy. Yet, examining the variety of blueprints for new Europes, which never came into being but which were formulated by many prominent intellectuals and politicians in the mid twentieth century, also has the effect of forcing us to recognize afresh the contingent nature of the Europe that developed after 1945.[8]

It may seem quite easy to argue that historians of integration should extend their focus back further than 1945; it is perhaps not so obvious why a study such as this should not look further forward than the early 1950s. However, much can be gained by focusing on the early post-war years when both Eastern and Western German states had been created, and when various versions of European integration had already been realized. These forms of integration included the founding of a European parliament; the forming of the Organization for European Economic Cooperation (OEEC), which established a supranational European authority to administer Marshall Plan aid; the signing of the Brussels Defence Pact; and the formulating of the Schuman Plan, which laid the foundations for the European Coal and Steel Community (ECSC).[9] Moreover, debates within civil society about how to integrate Europe were in some ways at their most vibrant during this period, particularly as party orthodoxies had not yet been enforced at the national level and the Cold War divisions had not been firmly set. For instance, the German pressure group Europa Union was said by 1951 to have eleven thousand members and three hundred local circles in Western Germany and formed part of a wider Union of European Federalists (UEF) that by 1950 numbered two hundred thousand members across Europe. Similarly, journals with a European agenda enjoyed an unprecedented popularity at this time.[10] Transnational organizations such as the Nouvelles Equipes Internationales (NEI) grouping of Christian Democrats also convened some of the most important high-level meetings between the European leaders who went on to be the architects of the European Union (EU) during these years.[11] Such initiatives are important for understanding how European politicians became persuaded of the merits of integration and how they could legitimize the early measures of post-war integration in the eyes of national electorates. Yet, they are often passed over quickly in wide-ranging histories of integration that concentrate on the major treaties and thus range from 'Rome to Maastricht' or from 'Paris to Lisbon' and may serve to reinforce the impression that integration was merely a series of negotiations concluded between national statesmen.[12]

The histories foregrounded in this book thus serve to complicate the largely diplomatic, institutional and economic histories that have dominated the recent historiography of European integration. As will be argued, European integration cannot be adequately grasped as a series of negotiations by a small number of national politicians and technocrats; nor can it be seen as the result of a collective Damascene experience by Europeans after 1945.[13] By contrast with histories such as those by Alan Milward and Andrew Moravcsik, which only begin with the plans devised during the later Second World War or post-war years, this history illustrates the social and ideological sinews that tied the post-war period to the interwar. It does this while acknowledging that the changes in post-war European nations such as Germany were decisive as they took the 'long road West' and embraced parliamentary democracy and peaceful coexistence with their neighbours.[14] Indeed, as this history will show, the process of European integration should not be dismissed as a series of happy accidents retrospectively justified by self-interested national politicians who decided to cover themselves in federalist camouflage.[15] Rather, it was influenced by the self-awareness and political identities of leading political and intellectual groups, whose ideas of Europe and plans for European integration helped to create a 'permissive consensus' behind the measures of European integration enacted by political leaders.[16]

While many of the issues addressed above have resonance in a variety of national contexts, this is a book concerned first and foremost with German views of Europe, or more exactly with the visions of Europe articulated by German-speaking (and -writing) intellectuals in Europe from the late 1920s to the 1950s. The definition of being German in this period was, of course, somewhat elastic. Many of the people with whom this work is concerned were not formally German, either by birth or by citizenship. Many were exiles from Germany, while others formed part of the more long-standing Central European diaspora of German-speaking intellectuals who had proved so influential during an era of educational and political modernization. Indeed, one of the goals of this work is to illustrate how debates about the make-up of Europe in the mid twentieth century refracted competing ideas about the extent (or limits) of the German community – ideas that were often formulated by intellectuals and politicians in Austria and Switzerland who felt marginalized from the predominant version of German national community represented by the Prussian state and its successors. As will be shown, ideas for unifying Europe were often made by German-speaking intellectuals who saw European integration as a means of recovering a more all-embracing, European version of a German community.

Another reason that the book focuses on Germany is that the 'German problem' has often been seen as the main incentive for post-war European integration, although Germany's role as 'good European' after 1945 has also been subject to varying, often critical, interpretations.[17] This book seeks to explain how this country moved from practising aggressively nationalist politics in the 1930s and early 1940s to advocating a pooling of national sovereignty within an integrated Europe in the post-war period, without falling back on a *Stunde Null* or Zero Hour thesis.

Europe from the Perspective of Civil Society

Accordingly, the analysis offered in this book is not primarily of the actions performed by the major national political players and technocrats (Milward's ironic European 'saints') who negotiated treaties for European integration. Rather, it is more concerned with the shaping of public opinion in and beyond Germany, provided we understand public opinion not as some numerical construct of individual views but as a more malleable and complex phenomenon composed of the way in which opinions are formulated and channelled in response to the influences of a wide variety of actors.[18] In particular, I will focus on the associations – some connected to media production, others feeding into political parties – that make up civil society as a particularly important type of opinion former. By focusing on such civil society bodies, I will offer a perspective on whether European integration can be assessed from the viewpoint of an emerging European society and not merely as a series of negotiations between national politicians. I look at the intellectual activities of a variety of civil society organizations, such as their publishing of journals and their taking part in international conferences, as important ways in which individuals worked to integrate Europe, and, in turn, integrated themselves within European networks and institutions.

Before I go any further, it is probably necessary to give a clearer definition of what I mean by civil society. The term in German – *Zivilgesellschaft* – emerged in the seventeenth and eighteenth centuries and suggested a kind of association between individuals that disrupted the hierarchical relationships characteristic of absolutist and corporatist states. Yet, it faded in the nineteenth century, only regaining currency in the 1980s, via its use in an Anglo-American context.[19] As Konrad Jarausch has commented, this term enjoyed a 'surprising revival', not least because of the role played by civil society organizations in bringing democratization to the former Soviet bloc in Eastern Europe.[20] However, the term has also been used to describe the associational life that constituted an important intermediate space in the nineteenth and twentieth centuries between the private sphere of family life and the institutions of state, within which the interests of like-minded individuals could emerge and take on political significance.[21] As historians of post-war Germany and of post-communist Eastern Europe have shown, civil society activity has been valorized as a way of schooling people's political sensibilities, of encouraging them to argue, lobby, and disagree, all with a degree of civility.[22] It has also been encouraged by European policy-making elites in recent years, due to their concern about the 'democratic deficit' that appears to be widening in Europe, as national populations apparently fail to legitimize the decisions of European politicians through referenda and voting in European elections.[23] These moves on the part of policymakers and bureaucrats towards conceptualizing and encouraging a European civil society have, in turn, led political scientists to reconsider European integration from the perspective of such European associations, organizations and movements. However, their studies rely on a slender historical record.[24] This book attempts such an analysis for the mid twentieth century, with particular reference to Germany, assessing how the civil society organizations that flourished in the interwar and early post-1945 periods did or did not help to integrate Europe.

As will be argued, it is important to understand how groups operating in this intermediate space between private life and government mobilized opinion behind, or against, forms of European integration. This should not, nevertheless, mean rehabilitating a Whiggish history of integration by uncritically emphasizing the activity of such associations. Indeed, these associations did not always function as the 'consensus-building little republics' that Alexis de Tocqueville described when he characterized them as the bedrock of democracy.[25] Indeed, rather than functioning as a 'transmission belt' between individuals and politicians, many of the organizations that worked to promote European integration lobbied against the democratic constitutions in the post-1918 nation-states. They appealed to earlier forms of supranational community such as the Austro–Hungarian Empire, which they claimed protected European communities from the ideological and nationalist enmities that engulfed post-First World War Europe.[26] Similar organizations in the early post-1945 period also agitated against, rather than simply supporting, the early democratic institutions in the Federal Republic. For instance, they rallied opposition to the creation of centralized institutions in the Bizone/Trizone, questioned the reconfiguration of the political parties and lobbied against Konrad Adenauer's policy of *Westbindung* or alignment with the West. Yet, for all this, the engagement of political associations, not least in the area of European integration, was an important part of the history of how democracy was reintroduced into western Germany and of how European integration policies were formulated by democratically elected governments and approved by national electorates.

The groups focused on in this book make up a range of civil society associations. The first group was based around *Merkur: Deutsche Zeitschrift für europäisches Denken*: a journal and, although the subject of political and commercial patronage, thus a venture functioning within the 'literary-political field'.[27] The second group is the Internationaler Sozialistischer Kampfbund (ISK), an association active in leftist politics that was a significant producer of journals and other works through its publishing company. However, it was primarily active in a party-based political sphere and its leaders sought to work chiefly through the Sozialdemokratische Partei Deutschlands or Social Democratic Party of Germany (SPD) in the postwar period. Similarly, the third group, Das Demokratische Deutschland was a collection of politicians and intellectuals who were active in the Christian Democratic and Social Democratic parties and in transnational party alliances, having attempted to influence Allied policymakers during wartime through internal communications rather than via publicly published materials.

The different ways in which these organizations sought to bring about political change raises methodological considerations, particularly concerning how one approaches groups with such different goals and effects, and whether these groups can be analysed together within one study. Certainly, groups active in the political field aimed to make a different contribution to those active in the literary field and this should be recognized when reading sources.[28] As this book will illustrate, political actors, particularly when working within political parties, sought to advance policy proposals within ideological packages that commanded consent and support from large groups of the population and competed with rival parties. By contrast, organizations within the literary, even literary–political, field, sought primarily to provide commentary. Whatever critiques or suggestions they made and whatever political influence they sought to exercise, their utterances did not made the same claims as a politician's: to provide a mandate to effect change or exercise authority by taking control of the instruments of state on behalf of those addressed. There is therefore something of a division between the way in which *Merkur* is analysed and the study of the more directly political groups, the ISK and Demokratisches Deutschland. Nevertheless, as will become apparent, the line between associations active in the public sphere and parties and government agencies is a porous one, with individuals moving between these bodies. Indeed, the history presented here illustrates how the revival of a more open political life in Germany was achieved by the interaction of new and revived associations with a refashioned party-political sphere.

Narratives of European Integration

Approaching the history of European integration from the perspective of civil society therefore addresses a notable gap in the historiography and makes a distinctive contribution to this history. This is not to say that the pre-existing literature has not served to advance our understanding of European integration. Indeed, European integration history has been a source of vibrant debates, which have refracted some of the most significant recent methodological controversies about which sources to consult and which kinds of political, economic and social developments to prioritize when writing history.

For instance, debates in the 1980s and 1990s pitted the federalist account advanced by Walter Lipgens, among others, against the neo-realist or rational choice interpretation best represented by Alan Milward. The first generations of post-war historians of integration such as Lipgens focused on post-1945 Western Europe and told an admiring intellectual history of the heroic first steps taken by European federalists.[29] These persecuted and marginal figures in fascist Europe had gone into exile and the underground resistance and went on to argue for a far-reaching federation of Europe. This would break up the state system in Europe in favour of a multi-level structure of governance with a mixture of 'self-rule' by the regions plus 'shared rule' at a European level.[30] Lipgens's far-reaching documentary history of European integration included the plans of a wide variety of political and civil society pressure groups, including National Socialist groups. Yet, the reception of Lipgens's work by neo-realists has tended to view his narrative as constructing a grand litany of European 'saints'. This litany starts with interwar luminaries such as Richard Coudenhove-Kalergi, founder of the Paneuropa Union, and Aristide Briand, the author of a plan for European integration laid before the League of Nations in 1930, and climaxes with the European Movement that emerged out of the wartime resistance movements headed by Ernesto Rossi and Altiero Spinelli.[31]

Turning away from intellectual history and towards political and economic history, neo-realists such as Alan Milward found that the groups profiled by Lipgens, whatever their popular support (which was often quite limited), had a negligible effect on the national politicians and bureaucrats who negotiated the early measures of European integration. These individuals – Jean Monnet, Robert Schuman, Alcide de Gasperi, Konrad Adenauer and others – envisaged a much more limited form of intergovernmental union than the federalists. Their approach to integration led Milward to conclude that European integration was less the institutional realization of wartime plans by visionaries who had glimpsed the future beyond the nation-state, and rather a process of negotiation between national leaders, whose economic self-interest prompted them to sacrifice elements of national sovereignty in order to preserve their nation-states from a more radical crisis.[32] Milward's focus on the economic causes of integration was taken up by prominent political scientists such as Andrew Moravcsik, whose *Choice for Europe* also stressed the continuing role played by national actors for whom integration was the best way of ensuring the economic viability of their nation-states in Europe.[33]

The neo-realist analysis has thus disenchanted the study of European integration and illustrated the economic rationale behind this process (which predated 1945). Nevertheless, after more than sixty years of deepening integration, it appears doubtful that the European project can be adequately analysed at only the level of short-term decisions by individual statesmen and events such as the European treaties. When viewed across the *longue durée* European integration appears instead to be a rather more profound development than a mere series of feats of crisis management, as the various European treaties appeared according to the neo-realist account.[34] To deal with the causes of European integration, a number of historians have recently suggested that we need a reconsideration of the cultural and intellectual history behind the phenomenon of European integration. They have stressed that such a cultural and intellectual history approach can also take European integration history out of its ghetto and link this process with more wide-ranging historiographical trends observable in the mid twentieth century.[35]

One way in which recent histories have attempted to do this is to connect the growth in support for an integrated Europe with what has been described as the Westernization of Europe after 1945. By Westernization, historians such as Anselm Doering-Manteuffel have referred to a process akin to Americanization, stressing, however, that such a process was not merely marked by cultural transfer from the United States to Europe but represented the multiple entanglements between peoples from both continents.[36] These historians of Westernization have focused on measures such as the Marshall Plan, which saw $25 billion of aid being provided for European reconstruction in the decade after the war and created the first supranational institutions within which Europeans worked together, planning their economies and allocating resources.[37] They have also illustrated how the contribution of the United States has been greater than the sum of any such treaties. For instance, exiled German intellectuals and politicians helped to 'Westernize' German political discourse and practice after 1945, often elaborating schemes for the reconstruction of Europe conceived within American organizations and then transmitted back to their home countries via Allied governments or the Allied-controlled post-war media.[38]

Historians have also recognized that supporters of European integration could be agents of Westernization but could alternatively seek to resist the increasing Americanization of Europe. They could do this by advocating a more unified political community based on pre-national traditions in Europe, such as the Holy Roman Empire. Seeking to reconstruct how ideas of an integrated Europe were formulated in Germany in the twentieth century, historians from the Westernization school largely identified two versions of integrationist thought: a liberal, pro-Western tradition (discussed above) and an *abendländisch* tradition. The *abendländisch* model of integration was formulated by predominantly conservative groups who sought to offer an alternative vision of Europe to the post-Versailles European settlement. They appealed to an Occidental, pre-nationalist Europe with its roots in a Christian culture that had supposedly unified the aristocratic states of the Holy Roman Empire from 1648 to 1806. These groups referred to this Europe as the *Abendland*, the most literal translation of which is Occident, yet which had a much greater currency in German than this equivalent has ever possessed in English. While this term was sometimes used to mean simply 'the West', it was also employed to contrast a West with its heart in the Central European *Kulturländer* with a West with its centre in the *Zivilisationen* of the United States or Britain and France.[39]

As the early histories of the *abendländisch* movement illustrate, this conception of Europe as *Abendland* had an extended life beyond 1945, in many ways predominating over more liberal conceptions of a 'Western', Anglo-Americanized Europe, until the early 1960s. However, while *abendländisch* academies and journals propagated plans for integration into the 1960s, such models of European integration waned in influence during this decade as Germany became established as a successful member of the U.S.-dominated Western European bloc. This argument suggests that, although many intellectual and political groups were sceptical about allying with the United States and about reviving parliamentary democracy in Europe, their anti-Bolshevism prompted them to make common cause with pro-democratic groups in order to wage a 'fight for freedom' against the Soviet Union. Accordingly, they became committed to the Western bloc, largely because the Cold War forced such either/or decisions upon political groups, and ultimately dropped their plans to reshape Europe along the lines of the *Abendland*.[40]

The histories of the *abendländisch* case for Europe have thus tended to offer a picture of a westernizing Germany, even if this process has been described as non-linear and abbreviated. Yet, a number of historians have further complicated this picture, recovering a variety of alternative plans formulated by Germans throughout the late nineteenth and twentieth centuries. These include the attempts made by Germans to establish their country as the leading member within a

Mitteleuropa, composed of a community of nations from East Central Europe. This entity was valorized as a way of negotiating the tensions between a German statehood(s), a greater German nationality and the presence of Germany within a wider central European region with a profoundly mixed ethnic make-up.[41] The influence of such a German-centric vision of European unity was significant, and provided much of the underpinning for the ideas articulated by German political leaders during the First and Second World Wars. For instance, figures such as Friedrich Naumann formulated plans for a union between Germany and the Habsburg Double Monarchy as the first step towards creating a *mitteleuropäisch* community that would form the basis of a German-French Empire that could rival the British.[42] Leaders such as Kaiser Wilhelm II and Hitler could build on such plans, claiming that by bringing together the peoples of Central Europe around some form of German-led federation, their empires could offer an effective defence against the non-European forces of East and West, as well as providing a new form of political organization.[43] Similarly, conservative politicians and businessmen proved receptive to Nazi plans for a commercial *Mitteleuropa* because Germany had already become a dominant trading partner in this region during the interwar period, with Poland, Austria and Czechoslovakia proving to be one of the largest areas for German exports after France, Belgium and the Netherlands.[44] Such plans for a *Mitteleuropa* also appear to have receded in the post-Second World War period. Nevertheless, it will be suggested in what follows that these schemes for Central Europe reemerged in albeit altered form periodically throughout the mid and late twentieth century, as the numerous references in post-war histories to 'rediscoveries' of Central Europe have illustrated.[45]

Accordingly, one of the major contributions of recent histories of European integration has been to expand our horizons when considering how European integration was theorized and popularized in Europe during the twentieth century. In so doing these histories have, at least partially, decentred the story of the EU-ization of Europe, illustrating how the post-war European project emerged out of a constellation of competing visions for a unified Europe. Furthermore, they have enriched the study of European integration from an earlier narrower focus on diplomatic or institutional histories.

The history outlined in this book also seeks to offer a broader perspective on European integration history. It approaches integration as something more profound than a mere series of negotiations between diplomats and politicians, regarding integration rather as a process of encounter, interaction, competition and cooperation between Europeans that occurred as part of everyday experiences, such as travelling, conducting business, fighting wars, and sharing technology.[46] As will be shown, these experiences informed and changed Europeans' beliefs about themselves and their neighbours, their visions of the past and future, their habits, and their political allegiances and actions.

Towards a New Intellectual History of European Integration

Seeking to make a contribution to a broader social and cultural history of European integration, this book focuses on people's ideas of Europe as they interacted with one another. It therefore claims that the ideas people formulated offer insights into, as well as having had a profound impact upon, their lived experience. This argument thereby suggests that intellectual history should be seen as a vital part of the social and cultural history of European integration.[47] One implication of this claim is that the ways in which Europeans conceived of an integrated Europe and communicated these ideas to one another, in the process not only travelling through each other's countries and consuming each other's cultural goods but also creating organizations and institutions that linked Europeans to one another, were among the most important ways in which Europe became integrated. As a consequence, the intellectual history presented here involves analysing how ideas emerged out of particular communal, institutional and political constellations. It also assesses the role these ideas played in deciding how communities, intellectual organizations and political parties were structured and how they interacted and competed with one another.[48] As will be shown, the inherited meanings that attached and clung to concepts such as Europe profoundly shaped the ways in which individuals and societies explained the political events they confronted. These concepts of Europe were thus a force that could influence people to form into organizations or break away from them, seek to construct peace or make war, or to offer their support to, or withhold their backing from, parties.[49]

Narrating such an intellectual history of European integration nevertheless presents many challenges, as it involves assessing the role played by ideas of Europe in a variety of political debates and discourses. For instance, reconstructing plans for European integration entails exploring people's ideas about cultural and political geography, political systems, history, religion and revolution, among many other things. These elements served to give Europe content – as place, historical civilization and political community – and gained their own meaning as features of the European 'rhetorical topography'.[50] I now examine each of these aspects in turn.

As the historiographical review above has made clear, concepts of Europe had a geographical dimension. Individuals and groups formed mental maps of Europe, for instance, locating Europe in the West or the *Abendland* (with Asia starting East of the Elbe or of Vienna's Landstrasse depending on your perspective) or describing a core Europe in a *mitteleuropäisch* community that would rival and overtake the nations on Europe's Western fringes.[51] These mental maps were highly value laden, with the West either appearing as the height of civilization or as decadent while the East often featured as primitive and wild. Such perspectives have been illustrated by Vejas Liulevicius whose work profiled the German *Drang nach Osten* (drive toward the East), whereby Germans and Austrians sought to fulfil their Hegelian 'world-historical task' to settle and civilize the East.[52] As I will argue, Germans were rarely content to simply think about their relationship with or within the West but conceived their role as being a Central European power that could unite the Western and Eastern components of the *abendländisch* civilisation. As such, the argument presented here will take issue with the subsuming of debates about European integration within an overarching Westernization thesis. Instead, I contend that an integrated Europe was usually presented in the mid twentieth century as a future goal, and as a recovery of a lost federalist past, which would be achieved via a Western alliance but would be distinct from it. This suggests that the rather one-sided focus on *Westbindung* predominant in the historiographical literature can obscure the more deep-rooted attachment of many Germans to a Europe more like the *mitteleuropäisch* Holy Roman Empire and more like the Central Europe within which Germans had been dominant for much of the first half of the twentieth century, than a Western Europe still regarded as merely a torso by politicians such as Helmut Kohl as late as the 1980s.[53]

One of the corollaries of the Westernization thesis is that those who sought to bind the Federal Republic and the nations of Europe within a transatlantic Western alliance also sought to democratize its political culture. They therefore conceived of Europe not only as a geographical space but also as a political system. Indeed, this implication is clear for advocates of the Westernization thesis who see the winning over of West Germans to liberal democracy to be the most conclusive evidence of the Westernization of Germany.[54] However, if we focus instead on those who advocated tying German reconstruction into a broader project for European integration, can we argue that such attempts at Europeanization also constituted an attempt to democratize the new West German state? If so, what kind of democracy did they aim for? As Martin Conway has argued, the type of democracy that became the predominant form of government in Europe between the late 1940s and the mid 1960s was a 'constrained' form of democracy, 'in which decision-making was largely remote from the people'.[55] The argument advanced in what follows will suggest that groups across the ideological spectrum conceived of European integration precisely as a means of constraining, rather than extending, the kind of parliamentary democracy they believed had stirred up partisan enmities and delivered nationalist demagogues during the interwar years. Furthermore, it will be argued that this constrained form of democracy was regarded as more viable than the interwar version of democracy which was often excoriated as an Americanized Wilsonian import. For many, the interwar version was regarded not as having protected individual and minority freedoms and rights so much as having entrenched 'mass rule' through the rise of increasingly radical mass-membership parties, which led to the dominance of one ideological faction over another and of majorities over minorities.[56]

In the analysis of Europe as political system that follows, it will be suggested that the Westernization thesis cannot do justice to the variety of ideas current among Germans in the mid twentieth century concerning what sort of political system an integrated Europe should represent. For instance, the creation of states according to what was seen as a Wilsonian right to national self-determination in 1918 had, in many Europeans' eyes, brought about a de-integration of Europe by increasing the numbers of borders within Europe and restricting the movement of peoples and goods around the continent.[57] Furthermore, rather than Wilson's ideas serving to Westernize Europe, they appeared to provide an ethnic basis to nationalism. This was particularly problematic given Europe's ethnic make-up and conflicted with, for instance, other Western ideas of constitutional nationhood such as those formulated by the French.[58] By contrast, advocates of European integration argued that a unification of Europe would not only reunite Europeans who had been divided as citizens of rival nations, but would also see power devolved again to the regional and local levels, thereby reviving an earlier form of *abendländisch* order, based on the looser federal arrangement of the Holy Roman Empire.

Implicit in such arguments in favour of European integration was a scepticism about how parliamentary democracy functioned in Europe, particularly with regard to the role of parties. Advocates of an integrated Europe that would be led by a supranational elite and made up of largely self-governing regions, believed that such an institutional framework would limit the power of centralized national political parties first to divide nations and then to claim to speak and act in the name of these nations. This did not mean that such advocates of European integration dispensed with the language of democracy; however, they all sought to avoid a recapitulation of the democratization ushered in by the post-1918 settlement. In common with many groups that had sought to defend democracy and resist dictatorship in the 1930s and 1940s, they advocated a radical refashioning of what appeared to be a terminally compromised parliamentarianism in the interwar period.

As these discussions of democratic reform in Europe suggest, plans for European integration also involved offering rival interpretations of European history. We will see that support for integration was tied to a long-standing tradition of federalist sentiment within Germany, which, as Maiken Umbach has argued, 'never disappeared from the German political imagination' and provided rival narratives of German development to a Prussian nationalist one.[59] Indeed, the arguments advanced by the groups featured in this book suggest that we may have misunderstood how incompletely regionalism in Germany was overcome by the Bismarckian unification of 1871. Rather, instead of German unification replacing regionalism with nationalism, the constitutional settlement of 1871 – whereby sovereignty lay with the Bundesrat, the representative of the aristocratically ruled states established by the Vienna Settlement of 1815 – meant that regional sentiments continued to shape political discourse into the twentieth century and provided much of the impetus behind support for further measures of federalism in Germany and Europe.[60] According to this argument, instead of a new unitarist consensus being established in Imperial and post-Imperial Germany, the dominance of one region – Prussia – over the others, continued to inflame regionalist loyalties, particularly in the southern states, through into the Weimar period.[61] As a result, the federalist sentiment of Germans, who could look back with nostalgia to the Holy Roman Empire, could be mobilized to ensure support for the federalist reforms proposed in the late 1940s at a German and European level.[62]

Taking account of such historical narratives offers us a new way of understanding support for integrating Europe as a Third Way, which was advocated by federalists in the late 1940s and 1950s as a means of keeping European nations out of a future war between the United States and the Soviet Union.[63] While the following account recognizes the importance of the Cold War to Third Way sentiment, it also looks for the latter's deeper roots. It suggests how support for a move away from the nation-state could have a particular persuasiveness in parts of Germany (and Austria) that had experienced the birth of the nation-state as more a process of partition than of unification. In these regions power was delocalized and centralized in a Prussian government that went on to separate Germans from one another by means initially of military victory and subsequently by military defeat.[64] From this vantage point, the emerging superpowers in the post-1945 period were fitted into a longer-standing trajectory of dominant nations imposing their political authority on European localities and regions. Thus, the United States to some extent and the Soviet Union to a far greater extent appeared as the imperialist heirs of the nationalist spirit of the nineteenth century. This impression was garnered through the post-war settlement of 1918 and seemingly confirmed by the bloc-building these powers initiated at Potsdam.[65]

Groups that lamented the post-Second World War dominance of godless mass polities such as the United States and Soviet Union often cited the falling away of religion as a cause of European decline, as had the similar groups that bemoaned the post-1918 reconstruction of Europe. Both sets of groups hearkened back to a supposedly more united Europe or *Abendland* that had been, so the story went, unified through the rise of Christianity and the formation of the Holy Roman Empire. This appeal to a medieval, or at least, pre-nineteenth-century Europe may sound fantastically nostalgic but was nevertheless widespread in Germany and Austria in the early twentieth century. Such conceptions of Europe as *Abendland* were formulated by initially Catholic but increasingly ecumenical religious and political groups who produced journals such as the influential *Hochland* and *Abendland*.[66] These groups aimed to counteract the feared *Untergang des Abendlandes* (decline of the West) envisaged by Oswald Spengler among others through a re-Christianisation and reunification of the continent.[67]

Although such groups often existed in a tense relationship with the Catholic Church's hierarchy, they argued that obedience to the universalist Catholic Church (with its local authority figures, the priests in every parish) or at least to the universalist tenets of Christianity would reunite Europe's masses. According to these arguments, the masses had been divided by the nationalist movements of the nineteenth century, and radicalized as members of ideologically profiled political parties, which encouraged them to see ideological enemies at home and abroad. Such *abendländisch* groups, particularly during the interwar period, contrasted religious forms of community and hierarchy with democratic types and worked against the democratic order in the European societies of their time. Yet, as we will see, not only *abendländisch* groups on the Right but also liberal and social-democratic advocates of European integration who had witnessed a National Socialist 'sacralization of politics' advocated versions of religious revival or of religiously inflected politics in Europe as a means of relativizing the claims of the political sphere in post-Second World War Europe.[68] Thus, while the analysis offered here will trace the rise of Christian democracy and the embracing of democracy by the Christian churches in the post-Second World War period, it will also show how Christianity was used as a depoliticizing force in the democracies of this era.

This focus on the role that religion played for advocates of European integration might lead us to believe that such advocates were typically war-weary quietists. As we will see when looking at groups on both the Right and Left, this was certainly not always the case. Rather, agitating for European unity could, and often did, involve calling for radical and even revolutionary change in Europe between the 1920s and 1950s. This agenda for European (re)unification could be styled as a conservative revolution, as it was by right-wing groups active during the interwar period. They envisaged overthrowing the established order in the various European nations and threatening the sovereignty of nations that encompassed minority populations made up of co-nationals from a neighbouring state. Similarly, European unity could be conceived of as the goal of a socialist revolution. This kind of revolution would, according to socialist theorists, dismantle the transnational economic forces that sustained the increasingly dictatorial political regimes in the various European nations during the interwar period. Indeed, as socialists in interwar and wartime Europe became disillusioned with the neo-imperialism practised by the Soviet Union but equally disenchanted by the apparent unsustainability of parliamentary democracy in Europe and by the Machiavellian foreign policy of Western European statesmen, they believed that a unified revolutionary movement would rise up in Central Europe and bring about the withering of the (nation-)state.

Such a focus on the revolutionary aspirations of advocates of European integration may appear surprising given that European integration was conceived by post-Second World War leaders as a means of avoiding the revolutionary upheaval of the post-First World War period. Certainly it is true that mainstream politicians and parties converged around an agenda for European unity that sought to minimize ideological strife within and between nations. Nevertheless, the arguments that such politicians made for European federation involved advocating radical change, including the kind of radical personal transformation that personalists among the early federalist and Christian democratic movements believed necessary.[69] Similarly, social-democratic advocates of European integration, even if they did not advocate Marxist revolution, contended that, only if radical economic reforms could be carried out on a European level, could parliamentary democracy be practised safely within the nation-states. Further than that, they looked to more direct forms of democracy and self-management, suggesting their abiding ambivalence about parliamentarianism and anticipating many of the New Left arguments advanced in the 1960s.

These themes will recur in what follows. For now, I move to an outline of the chapters, summarising how the argument develops as the three groups cited above are studied in greater depth.

The Structure of the Book

This book analyses three groups in three sections with two chapters devoted to each group. While each section moves chronologically from the 1920s to the 1950s, the book as a whole juxtaposes the interwar, wartime and post-war experiences and projects of the groups across the same timeframe. Each section is relatively self-contained, although instances of communication and cooperation between the featured groups are highlighted.

The first two chapters of the book are focused on a cultural journal, *Merkur: Deutsche Zeitschrift für europäisches Denken*, founded in the French Zone in 1947 and still thriving, having attracted contributions from some of the most prominent names in cultural and political life in Germany and Europe after 1945. The book begins by focusing on how such a cultural journal made the case for an integrated Europe. It does this because, before political parties were allowed to function again in Germany and at a time when book production was low, cultural journals were licensed by occupation authorities, attracting circulation figures usually in the tens of thousands and gaining the most highly regarded intellectuals of the day as contributors and readers.[70] Chapter 1 outlines the interwar background to the founding of this journal, highlighting how cultural journals also thrived in the interwar years, emerging out of the flourishing associational life evident in Germany during this period.[71] This chapter and chapter 2 show the continuities between influential civil society groups in the interwar and post-1945 periods and the ways in which they sought to mobilize support for European integration. They illustrate how concerns about the growth of American and Soviet power, as well as a fear of the rise of democratic nation-states and the mass politics practised within them, animated much of the *abendländisch* support for Europe across this period. They therefore offer a nuanced perspective on the Third Force agenda for Europe, excavating its roots in the politics of the interwar period rather than seeing it solely emerge out of the resistance movements.[72]

The remaining chapters focus on two groups that were influential in the forming of the post-war political parties in Germany. As Wolfram Kaiser has illustrated, the Christlich Demokratische Union Deutschlands or Christian Democratic Union of Germany (CDU) and the SPD were among the primary agents in shaping how European integration was advanced, negotiated, criticized and extended after 1945, both at a domestic and transnational level.[73] The research presented in the following chapters will suggest that the history of the two major parties' European policy was shaped not only by short-term competition between them and by the short-term interests promoted and defended within diplomatic negotiations. Rather, the European policy of these parties was greatly influenced by debates about European (dis)unity in predecessor organizations during the interwar and wartime periods. Thus, the approach of the major parties towards integration can be usefully historicized by analysing such groups as the ISK and Demokratisches Deutschland, both of which developed proposals for European integration not only in conversation with Western Allied governments but also with ideological colleagues from across Europe.

Chapters 3 and 4 concentrate on the ISK, an interwar splinter group from the SPD whose members went into French and British exile, and whose leader, Willi Eichler, became one of the SPD's most important theorists as the major author of the Godesberg Programme of 1959. Chapter 3 describes the founding of the ISK and its flight into exile after 1933, focusing particularly on how its internationalist ideology shifted during these years towards an advocacy of European integration. Chapter 4 describes the reintegration of its members within the SPD after 1945, illustrating how its leaders went on to shape the SPD's policy towards European integration. These chapters contextualize the supposedly 'nationalist' European policy of Kurt Schumacher. They suggest that the SPD's commitment to European integration as a means of reforming parliamentary democracy and of pursuing an internationalist agenda that would reunite East and West has been misunderstood in much of the pre-existing historiography. The chapters also highlight the existence of transnational debates between exiled socialist groups that complicate the traditional narratives of international cooperation (or lack of cooperation) between European socialist parties after 1945.[74]

The final two chapters are concerned with Das Demokratische Deutschland, a cross-party coalition of exiles from Nazi Germany that formed in wartime Switzerland and whose members went on to be influential in CDU and SPD politics. The organization was a rival to the Freies Deutschland group that was established in that country as part of a broader Soviet-sponsored Freies Deutschland popular front of German exiles that issued some of the early salvos in the Cold War. The leaders of Demokratisches Deutschland went on to assume leading positions in post-war European federalist movements and in post-war party politics in Germany. Chapter 5 focuses on the ideas for European integration formulated by the group's leaders as they worked with Allied secret services and foreign ministries to plan for post-war reconstruction, offering rival proposals to the Freies Deutschland group. It highlights the federalist orientation of the largely southern German leaders of the group who conceived of European integration as a means of shifting the balance of power away from northern states such as Prussia and recreating a Central European community with its heart in the Catholic, southern Germanic states. Chapter 6 spotlights the post-war careers of the group's leaders, showing how figures such as Wilhelm Hoegner sought to increase the autonomy of the southern German states within a 'Europe of the regions'. These chapters, taken together, illustrate how European integration intersected with a broader Cold War agenda but also suggest that, in many ways, European integration was conceived as a way of keeping European nations out of the

Cold War. They therefore show some of the deep continuities in federalist sentiment in Germany but also how such sentiment was Europeanized after 1945.

The Conclusion offers an overview of the central themes of the book, highlighting the elements of continuity and change across the period between 1926 and 1950. It also looks beyond these dates, assessing how support for a Third Force Europe fed into the *Ostpolitik* initiatives of the 1950s and 1960s. Reviewing the policies of leading German politicians towards Eastern Europe throughout the twentieth century, it argues that while these leaders continued to push forward measures of European integration within the 'Western' European Community they never stopped seeking to increase West Germany's influence and trade presence in the East Central European region as well as to reunify East and West Germany. The Conclusion finishes by offering further suggestions for rethinking some of the concepts used by historians to describe European integration and the history of mid-twentieth-century Europe in the light of the research presented in this book.

Notes

1. W. Loth, 'Preface', in W. Loth (ed.), *Documents on the History of European Integration, Volume 3: The Struggle for European Union by Political Parties and Pressure Groups in Western European Countries 1945–1950* (Berlin: de Gruyter, 1988) pp. viii–ix.
2. For more on the efforts of intellectuals to foster European integration, see J. Lacroix and K. Nicolaïdis (eds), *European Stories: Intellectual Debates in National Contexts* (Oxford: Oxford University Press, 2010).
3. Thanks to Martin Conway for help with this point.
4. J.M. Palmier, *Weimar in Exile: The Antifascist Emigration in Europe and America* (London: Verso, 2006).
5. M. Conway and J. Gotovitch (eds), *Europe in Exile: European Exile Communities in Britain, 1940–1945* (New York and Oxford: Berghahn Books, 2001).
6. For a recent discussion of some of these longer-term internationalist perspectives, see M. Mazower, *Governing the World: The History of an Idea* (London: Allen Lane, 2012).
7. A. Milward, *The European Rescue of the Nation-State* (London and New York: Routledge 2nd ed., 2000) pp. 18–39; M. Conway, 'Conclusion', in M. Conway and K.K. Patel (eds), *Europeanization in the Twentieth Century: Historical Approaches* (Basingstoke: Palgrave, 2010) pp. 271–77.
8. Thanks to David Vincent for help with this point.
9. See D. Bark and D. Gress, *A History of West Germany. Vol. 1: From Shadow to Substance* (Oxford: Blackwell, 1989) p. 258; W. Loth, *Die Teilung der Welt: Geschichte des Kalten Krieges 1941–1955* (Munich: dtv, 2002) pp. 216, 258, 263.
10. V. Conze, *Das Europa der Deutschen: Ideen von Europa in Deutschland zwischen Reichstradition und Westorietierung* (Munich: Oldenbourg, 2005) p. 305; M. Dedman, *The Origins and Development of the European Union 1945–2008: A History of European Integration* (London and New York: Routledge, 2nd ed. 2010) p. 10.
11. W. Kaiser, *Christian Democracy and the Origins of European Union* (Cambridge: Cambridge University Press, 2007).

12. A well-executed example of such an approach is J. Young, *Britain and European Unity, 1945–1992* (Basingstoke: Macmillan 2nd ed., 2000). For a critique of such an approach see W. Kaiser, B. Leucht and M. Rasmussen, 'Origins of a European Polity: A New Research Agenda for European Union History', in Kaiser, Leucht and Rasmussen (eds), *The History of the European Union: Origins of a Trans- and Supranational Polity 1950–1972* (London and New York: Routledge, 2009) pp. 1–11.
13. However, a number of autobiographies by leading statesmen record how they became converted to the cause of Europe. See for example J. Monnet, *Memoirs* (New York: Doubleday, 1978) esp. chapter 12; W. Martens, *Europe: I Struggle, I Overcome* (New York and Heidelberg: Springer, 2009).
14. H.A. Winkler, *Der Lange Weg nach Westen. Zweiter Band. Deutsche Geschichte vom "Dritten Reich" zur Wiedervereinigung* (Munich: Beck, 2000).
15. This is the interpretation offered by T. Judt in his *A Grand Illusion? An Essay on Europe* (New York: New York University Press, 2011) esp. pp. 3–24.
16. On this concept of 'permissive consensus', see V.O. Key, *Public Opinion and American Democracy* (New York: Knopf, 1961).
17. For a useful discussion of Germany's role as post-war 'good European', see K. Dyson and K.H. Goetz, 'Living with Europe: Power, Constraint and Contestation', in Dyson and Goetz (eds), *Germany, Europe and the Politics of Constraint* (Oxford: British Academy/Oxford University Press, 2003).
18. For a discussion of the difficulties inherent in, and the possibilities for, analysing popular opinion, see I. Kershaw, *Popular Opinion and Political Dissent in the Third Reich, Bavaria 1933–1945* (Oxford: Oxford University Press 2nd ed., 2002) esp. pp. 4–10; P. Laborie, *L'Opinion française sous Vichy* (Paris: Seuil, 1990); M. Conway and P. Romijn, *The War for Legitimacy in Politics and Culture 1936–1946* (Oxford: Berg, 2008) esp. pp. 5–8.
19. J. Kocka, 'Civil Society in Historical Perspective', in J. Keane (ed.), *Civil Society: Berlin Perspectives* (New York and Oxford: Berghahn Books, 2006) pp. 37–38.
20. K. Jarausch, *After Hitler: Recivilizing Germans, 1945–1995* (New York: Oxford University Press, 2006) pp. 12–17.
21. N. Bermeo and P. Nord (eds), *Civil Society before Democracy: Lessons from Nineteenth-Century Europe* (Lanham: Rowman and Littlefield, 2000); J. Keane, 'Introduction', in J. Keane (ed.), *Civil Society and the State: New European Perspectives* (London: Verso, 1988) p. 19.
22. See Jarausch, *After Hitler*, pp. 12–17 and J. K. Glenn, *Framing Democracy: Civil Society and Civic Movements in Eastern Europe* (Stanford: Stanford University Press, 2001).
23. D. Friedrich, *Democratic Participation and Civil Society in the European Union* (Manchester and New York: Manchester University Press, 2011) pp. 13–15. EU institutions themselves have increasingly sought to cultivate dialogue with the associations that make up civil society, with an 'open and structured dialogue between the [European] Commission and special interest groups' being launched in 1992 and intensified by a series of measures between 1996 and 1998, which has led to biennial meetings being convened between the Commission and a Social Platform made up of Non-Governmental Organizations (NGOs). Friedrich, *Democratic Participation*, p. 90.
24. Few historians have heeded Wolfram Kaiser's and Hartmut Kaeble's calls for studies of European integration from the perspective of a historically emerging European society. See Kaiser, 'From State to Society? A Historiography of European Integration', in M. Cini and A. Bourne (eds), *From State to Society? The Historiography of European Integration* (Basingstoke: Palgrave, 2006) pp. 190–208; and H. Kaelble, 'Das Europäische Selbstverständnis und die Europäische Öffentlichkeit im 19. und 20. Jahrhundert', in H. Kaelble, M. Kirsch, A. Schmidt-Gernig (Hg.), *Transnationale Öffentlichkeiten und Identitäten im 20. Jahrhundert* (Frankfurt am Main: Campus, 2002) pp. 89–90.

25. P. Nord, 'Introduction', in Bermeo and Nord, *Civil Society before Democracy*, pp. xiv–xv, xxiii–xxviii.
26. K. Tenfelde, 'Civil Society and the Middle Classes in Nineteenth-Century Germany', in Bermeo and Nord, *Civil Society before Democracy*, p. 102. On civil society associations as a 'transmission belt', see J. Steffek and P. Nanz, 'Emergent Patterns of Civil Society. Participation in Global and European Governance', in J. Steffek, C. Kissling and P. Nanz, *Civil Society Participation in European and Global Governance: A Cure for the Democratic Deficit?* (Basingstoke: Palgrave, 2007) p. 3.
27. M. Reitmayer, 'Kulturzeitschriften im intellektuellen Feld der frühen Bundesrepublik' in D. Münkel and J. Schwarzkopf (eds), *Geschichte als Experiment: Studien zu Politik, Kultur und Alltag im 19. und 20. Jahrhundert* (Frankfurt am Main: Campus, 2004) p. 64.
28. The concept of a field is taken from P. Bourdieu. See his *Language and Symbolic Power* (Cambridge MA: Harvard University Press, 1991) pp. 171–203 and *The Field of Cultural Production* (New York: Columbia University Press, 1993) pp. 34–45.
29. For details of how this federalist perspective continues to attract support particularly in Italy, see D. Pasquinucci, 'Between Political Commitment and Academic Research: Federalist Perspectives', in W. Kaiser and A. Varsori (eds), *European Union History: Themes and Debates* (Basingstoke: Palgrave, 2010) pp. 66–84.
30. This is a paraphrase of the political scientist, Daniel Elazar. See M. Burgess, *Federalism and European Union: the Building of Europe, 1950–2000* (London and New York: Routledge, 2000) p. 26. For more of the social science literature on federalism, see A. Heinemann-Grüder, *Federalism Doomed? European Federalism between Integration and Separation* (New York and Oxford: Berghahn Books, 2002); and C. Jeffery and R. Sturm (eds), *Federalism, Unification and European Integration* (London and New York: Routledge, 1993).
31. W. Lipgens (ed.), *Europa-Föderationspläne der Widerstandsbewegungen, 1940–1945* (Munich: Oldenbourg, 1968); W. Lipgens, *A History of European Integration, vol. 1: 1945–1947* (Oxford: Clarendon Press, 1982); Lipgens (ed.), *Documents on the History of European Integration*, vol. 2, *Plans for European Union in Great Britain and in Exile, 1939–1945* (Berlin, 1986); W. Lipgens and W. Loth (eds), *Documents on the History of European Integration*, vol. 3, *The Struggle for European Union by Political Parties and Pressure Groups in Western European Countries, 1945–1950* (Berlin: de Gruyter, 1988).
32. See the Introduction to Milward, *European Rescue of the Nation-State*.
33. A. Moravcsik, *The Choice for Europe: Social Purpose and State Power from Messina to Maastricht* (Ithaca: Cornell University Press, 1998).
34. G. Brunn, *Die Europäische Einigung: Von 1945 bis heute* (Bonn: Bundeszentral für politische Bildung, 2004) p. 16.
35. T. Risse, 'Social Constructivism and European Integration', in A. Wiener and T. Diez (eds), *European Integration Theory* (Oxford: Oxford University Press, 2004) pp. 166–71.
36. A. Doering-Manteuffel, *Wie westlich sind die Deutschen? Amerikanisierung und Westernisierung im 20. Jahrhundert* (Göttingen: Vanderhoeck und Ruprecht, 1999) esp. pp. 15, 71.
37. M. Hogan, *The Marshall Plan: America, Britain and the Reconstruction of Western Europe, 1947–1952* (Cambridge: Cambridge University Press, 1987) p. 22; and Pindar, 'Europe in the World Economy, 1920–1970', in C. Cipolla, *The Fontana Economic History of Europe: Contemporary Economies Part One* (Glasgow: Collins, 1976) pp. 349–50.
38. A. Schildt, *Zwischen Abendland und Amerika: Studien zur westdeutschen Ideenlandschaft der 50er Jahre* (Munich: Oldenbourg, 1999); Conze, *Europa der Deutschen*; Doering-Manteuffel, *Wie westlich sind die Deutschen?* esp. pp. 12–13; A. Söllner (ed.), *Zur Archäologie der Demokratie in Deutschland: Analysen politischer Emigranten im amerikanischen Geheimdienst* (Frankfurt am Main: Europäische Verlagsanstalt, 1982 (2 vols.)); Söllner, *Deutsche Politikwissenschaftler in der Emigration: Studien zur ihrer Akkulturation und Wirkungsgeschichte* (Opladen: Westdeutscher, 1996); C.-D. Krohn and P. von zur Mühlen (eds), *Rückkehr und Aufbau nach 1945: deutsche Remigranten im öffentlichen Leben Nachkriegsdeutschlands* (Marburg: Metropolis, 1997);

C.-D. Krohn and A. Schildt (eds), *Zwischen den Stühlen?: Remigranten und Remigration in der deutschen Medienöffentlichkeit der Nachkriegszeit* (Hamburg: Christians, 2002).
39. O. Köhler, 'Abendland', in Görres-Gesellschaft (ed.), *Staatslexikon: Recht, Wirtschaft, Gesellschaft in 5 Bänden*, vol. 1 (Freiburg/Basel/Vienna: Herder 7th ed., 1985) pp. 1–6.
40. Schildt, *Zwischen Abendland und Amerika*, pp. 67–75; Conze, *Europa der Deutschen*, pp. 312–23.
41. P. Stirk, 'The Idea of Mitteleuropa', in P. Stirk (ed.), *Mitteleuropa: History and Prospects* (Edinburgh: Edinburgh University Press, 1994) pp. 1–16; P. Krüger, 'Europabewusstsein in Deutschland in der ersten Hälfte des 20. Jahrhunderts', in R. Hudemann, H. Kaelble and K. Schwabe (eds), *Europa im Blick der Historiker* (Munich: Oldenbourg, 1995) pp. 33–34.
42. J. Elvert, *Mitteleuropa! Deutsche Pläne zur europäischen Neuordnung (1918-1945)* (Stuttgart: Franz Steiner, 1999) pp. 9–13.
43. V. Liulevicius, *War Land on the Eastern Front: Culture, National Identity and German Occupation in WW1* (Cambridge: Cambridge University Press, 2000) pp. 22–26; M. Mazower, *Hitler's Empire: How the Nazis Ruled Europe* (London: Penguin, 2008) pp. 31–52.
44. Elvert, *Mitteleuropa*, pp. 9–13, 99–108; R. Spaulding, *Osthandel und Ostpolitik: German Foreign Trade Policies in Eastern Europe from Bismarck to Adenauer* (Providence RI and Oxford: Berghahn Books, 1997) pp. 477–78.
45. See, for instance, G. Delanty, *Inventing Europe: Idea, Identity, Reality* (Basingstoke: Palgrave, 1995) esp. pp. 132–38.
46. This formulation recalls the definition of Europeanization offered by K.K. Patel and U. von Hirschausen in their 'Introduction', in Patel and Conway, *Europeanization in the Twentieth Century*, pp. 1–7.
47. On this, see B. Cowan, 'Intellectual, Cultural and Social History: Ideas in Context', in R. Whatmore and B. Young (eds), *Palgrave Advances in Intellectual History* (Basingstoke: Palgrave, 2006) esp. pp. 171–80.
48. L. Raphael and H.-E. Tenorth, *Ideen als gesellschaftliche Gestaltungskraft im Europa der Neuzeit: Beiträge für eine erneuerte Geistesgeschichte* (Munich: Oldenbourg, 2006).
48. R. Koselleck, 'Linguistic Change and the History of Events', *The Journal of Modern History* 61/4, (1989) 649–66.
50. This phrase is taken from P.T. Jackson, *Civilizing the Enemy: German Reconstruction and the Invention of the West* (Ann Arbor: University of Michigan Press, 2006) p. xi.
51. On the theme of mental maps, see S. Casey and J. Wright (eds), *Mental Maps in the Era of Two World Wars* (Basingstoke: Palgrave, 2008). The reference to Asia starting on the Landstrasse is Metternich's and to Asia starting standing at the Elbe is Adenauer's. See Judt, *A Grand Illusion*, p. 47; and Loth, *Der Weg nach Europa: Geschichte der europäischen Integration 1939-1957* (Göttingen: Vanderhoeck und Ruprecht 2nd ed., 1991) p. 42.
52. Liulevicius, *The German Myth of the East: 1800 to the Present* (Oxford: Oxford University Press, 2009) p. 198.
53. Kohl was quoted in U. Kessler, 'Deutsche Europapolitik unter Helmut Kohl: Europäische Integration als 'kategorische Imperativ'?', in G. Müller-Brandeck-Bocquet et al., *Deutsche Europapolitik: Von Adenauer bis Merkel* (Wiesbaden: VS 2nd ed., 2010) p. 132. On *Westbindung* see R. Granieri, *The Ambivalent Alliance: Konrad Adenauer, the CDU/CSU and Westbindung* (New York and Oxford: Berghahn Books, 2003).
54. On this see Jarausch, *After Hitler*, pp. 103–5.
55. Conway, 'Democracy in Postwar Western Europe: The Triumph of a Political Model', in *European History Quarterly* 32/1, (January, 2002) 65–66.
56. For more on the many critiques of democracy current in interwar Europe, see M. Mazower, *Dark Continent: Europe's Twentieth Century* (New York: Vintage, 1998) pp. 14–27.
57. J. Wardhaugh, R. Leiserowitz and C. Bailey, 'Intellectual Dissidents and the Construction of European Spaces 1918-1988', in Conway and Patel, *Europeanization in the Twentieth Century*, pp. 28–43.

58. On this see R. Brubaker, *Citizenship and Nationhood in France and Germany* (Cambridge MA: Harvard University Press, 1992); A. Smith, *The Ethnic Origins of Nations* (Oxford: Blackwell, 1986).
59. M. Umbach, 'Introduction: German Federalism in Historical Perspective', in M. Umbach (ed.), *German Federalism: Past, Present, Future* (Basingstoke: Palgrave, 2002) pp. 4–5. On this see also D. Langewiesche, *Nation, Nationalismus, Nationalstaat in Deutschland und Europa* (Munich: Beck, 2000).
60. A. Nicholls, 'German Federalism in History: Some Afterthoughts', in Umbach, *German Federalism*, p. 206.
61. A. Gunlicks, *The* Länder *and German Federalism* (Manchester and New York: Manchester University Press, 2003) pp. 29–31.
62. J. Waley, 'Federal Habits: the Holy Roman Empire and the Continuity of German Federalism', in Umbach, *German Federalism*, pp. 15–35.
63. On this, see Loth, 'Léon Blum und das Europa der Dritten Kraft', in R. Hohls, I. Schröder and H. Siegrist (eds), *Europa und die Europäer. Quellen und Essays zur modernen europäischen Geschichte* (Stuttgart: Franz Steiner, 2005) esp. pp. 442–46.
64. D. Blackbourn, *History of Germany 1780–1918: The Long Nineteenth Century* (Oxford: Blackwell, 2003) p. xvi.
65. U. Frevert, 'Europeanizing Germany's Twentieth Century', in *History and Memory* 17/1, (2005) 87–116. See also Wardhaugh, Leiserowitz and Bailey, 'Intellectual Dissidents and the Construction of European Spaces, 1918–1988', in Conway and Patel, *Europeanization in the Twentieth Century*, pp. 28–43; M. Grunewald and U. Puschner (eds), *Le Milieu Intellectuel Catholique en Allemagne, sa Presse et ses Réseaux (1871–1963)* (Berne: Peter Lang, 2006).
66. On this, see particularly D. Pöpping, *Abendland: Christliche Akademiker und die Utopie der Antimoderne 1900–1945* (Berlin: Metropol, 2002); Conze, *Europa der Deutschen*, Schildt, *Zwischen Abendland und Amerika*.
67. O. Spengler, *Der Untergang des Abendlandes. Umrisse einer Morphologie der Weltgeschichte* (Munich: dtv, 17th ed., 2006).
68. The phrase 'sacralization of politics' is taken from E. Gentile, *Politics as Religion* (Princeton: Princeton University Press, 2006).
69. For more on Personalism, see M. Caciagli, 'Christian Democracy', in T. Ball and R. Bellamy (eds), *The Cambridge History of Political Thought* (Cambridge: Cambridge University Press, 2002) pp. 172–80; J.O. Bengtsson, *The Worldview of Personalism: Origins and Early Development* (Oxford: Oxford University Press, 2006); H.S. Hughes, *The Obstructed Path: French Social Thought in the Years of Desperation* (New Brunswick: Transaction, 2002) esp. pp. 65–101; R. Papini (trans. by R. Royal), *The Christian Democrat International* (Lanham: Rowman and Littlefield, 1997).
70. Reitmayer, 'Kulturzeitschriften', in Münkel and Schwarzkopf, *Geschichte als Experiment*, p. 72; M. Grunewald and H.-M. Bock (eds), *Der Europadiskurs in den deutschen Zeitschriften (1871–1955) (Vols. 1-4)* (Berne: Peter Lang, 1996–2001).
71. F.S. Saunders, *Who Paid the Piper? The CIA and the Cultural Cold War* (London: Granta, 1999); M. Hochgeschwender, *Freiheit in der Offensive? Der Kongress für kulturelle Freiheit und die Deutschen* (Munich: Oldenbourg, 1998).
72. An interest in federalism emerging out of 'the spirit of resistance' has been revived in recent years, see F. Niess, *Die europäische Idee – aus dem Geist des Widerstands* (Frankfurt am Main: Suhrkamp, 2001).
73. Kaiser, *Christian Democracy and the Origins of European Union*, p. 8.
74. For more on these traditional narratives, see T. Imlay, '"The Policy of Social Democracy is Self-consciously Internationalist": The SPD's Internationalism after 1945', *The Journal of Modern History* (forthcoming).

Chapter 1

MAKING THE CASE FOR EUROPE
Transnational Organizations and Cultural Journals

Walking through the foyer of the Titania Palace cinema in Berlin-Steglitz today, it might be hard to imagine the 'hunger for culture' felt by Germans in the immediate aftermath of the Second World War or how this venue satisfied it. Yet this present-day Cineplex, which escaped the effects of the bombing that destroyed much of central Berlin, was the site of the first post-war concert of the Berlin Philharmonic orchestra, given in May 1945 and attended by over one thousand audience members who came on foot or by bike.[1] Listening to Mendelssohn's *Midsummer Night's Dream* Overture or Tchaikovsky's Fourth Symphony, it might have been possible for the audience to forget briefly the signs of decay and poverty visible in defeated and occupied Berlin. However, such events were not merely well-judged distractions from the degradations of daily life. Instead, they formed part of what many saw as a remarkable 'resurrection of culture' in Germany, as an otherwise sceptical Theodor Adorno recounted in a review of the early post-war scene.[2]

An area in which this resurrection of culture was particularly noticeable was the print media. Newspaper production soared, with the Allies granting 150 licences in the first four years of occupation.[3] Very significant growth was also witnessed in the production of cultural journals, which not only attracted circulation figures of over fifty thousand before the currency reform of 1948 but also secured contributions from the leading intellectuals and politicians of the day.[4] Daily newspapers were reintroduced by occupation authorities who either wanted them to be part of an impartial, information press after the American model or a political-party-aligned press, similar to that functioning in Britain.[5] By contrast, cultural journals, which usually appeared monthly, primarily sought neither to report nor to advance a party-political agenda but to revive a culture of discussion and argument among the public, and thus to reinvigorate civil society. As the Heidelberg philosopher Karl Jaspers put it, explaining the founding of one such cultural journal: 'Because we can [now] talk freely with one another, the first task is to really talk to one another ... Through public discussion we want to become aware of the connections that allow us to live together.'[6] However, this model of an argumentative but peaceful civil society was recognized as more an ideal than a reality by some editors: as *Merkur's* founder and chief editor, Hans Paeschke, acknowledged, it was a great challenge to connect readers to one another across political and professional boundaries, which required publications to appear above political or interest-group concerns.[7]

This chapter highlights how what came to be known as 'a culture of discussion' (*Diskussionskultur*) was fostered in Germany, and across Europe more widely, in the interwar period before being revived in the early post-war years. The focus will be on the civil society associations that multiplied across Europe during this period, often serving as the sponsors of the burgeoning cultural journals in which a discussion culture was fostered and performed. Taking the case study of *Merkur* and its predecessor journals, the *Europäische Revue* and the *Neue Rundschau*, we will see how a Franco-German exchange was developed in the interwar years through a transnational network of associations and their journals. These networks did not necessarily promote peaceful, pro-democratic sentiment across the continent and thus we are presented with a different sort of Franco-German rapprochement to that represented by the Locarno Treaties of 1925 and the Briand Plan of 1929. The chapter also goes on to shift attention away from Franco-German relations and towards the growth of associational activity and networks across Central Europe, illustrating how anti-democratic conceptions of *Mitteleuropa* and of a revived *Abendland* came to be advanced during the interwar period and revived after 1945. Such a focus should offer us a new vantage point from which to view Third Force politics in Germany and Europe after 1945, and allow us to refine theories of post-war Westernization.

Post-War Journals in Germany – Reviving an Interwar Agenda

Those responsible for cultural journals in post-war West Germany did not only wish to reconnect Germans with one another but to bring together Europeans whose opportunities to interact and engage freely with one another had, in many cases, been drastically curtailed in recent years. Thus, among the most renowned of the post-war journals, the topic of European reconstruction and cooperation became a constant preoccupation. This was made explicit in *Merkur*, which was subtitled *German Journal for European Thought*, and which featured contributors from across Europe, particularly those in French- and German-speaking countries. However, it was also crucial to the mission of other journals such as *Die Wandlung*, which was founded by a group of Heidelberg-based philosophers including the editor, Dolf Sternberger; Alfred Weber, the brother of Max Weber; and Karl Jaspers, a colleague of Martin Heidegger and Hannah Arendt.[8]

In these journals, the issue of reintegrating Europe represented the concerns of German intellectuals who had felt cut off during National Socialist years and who wished to reengage with their colleagues from across Europe. In others, such as the American-sponsored *Der Monat*, many formerly exiled intellectuals, who had already lived in a pan-European microcosm in American or British exile, were reproducing arguments they had advanced while abroad. And yet, as will be suggested here, some of the arguments for European integration presented in journals such as *Merkur* represented a different kind of European intellectual engagement, often performed by conservative intellectuals and politicians such as Ernst Jünger, Bertrand de Jouvenel and others who sought to revive a conservative interwar agenda for integrating Europe, and to further discussions in which they had secretively engaged during wartime.

While most post-war cultural journals sought to profile themselves as above party politics, some were less coy than others about revealing their ideological leanings. Alongside the purportedly non-ideological publications cited above, more obviously leftist publications also addressed questions of European unity, particularly the *Frankfurter Hefte*, which was edited by a former Buchenwald inmate, Eugen Kogon. This journal advanced a left-wing Catholic agenda, seeking to sketch out a Third Way politics in an integrated Europe that would avoid the authoritarianism of the Soviet Union and the excesses of unrestrained capitalism as epitomized in the United States.[9] Another more short-lived leftist publication devoted to European issues was *Der Ruf*, the self-styled socialist voice of 'Young Europe', edited by former communists and prisoners-of-war in the United States Hans-Werner Richter and Alfred Andersch. These individuals fell foul of the American authorities due to their withering critiques of occupation policy and were replaced in 1948 by a more pliant editor, Erich Kuby, although they went on to found Gruppe 47, the leading literary circle in the post-war Federal Republic. In addition to such nominally home-grown publications, another major journal that contributed to a European discourse in the early post-war period was *Der Monat*, edited by a Polish-American military officer, Melvyn Lasky. This journal was covertly funded by the CIA-backed Congress for Cultural Freedom (CCF) that was largely composed of ex-Communists who went on to be some of the most combative wagers of the cultural Cold War.[10]

Among this group of influential post-war cultural journals, *Merkur* is one of the few to have survived and thrived until today. While its circulation figures dropped from close to fifty thousand before the currency reform of 1948 to around fifteen thousand throughout its early decades, it has continued to attract many of the leading intellectuals from Germany and beyond including Theodor Adorno, Jean Améry, Hannah Arendt, Gottfried Benn, Ralf Dahrendorf, T.S. Eliot, Jürgen Habermas, Martin Heidegger and Jean-François Lyotard, among many others. In early decades it won plaudits from such luminaries as Clement Greenberg, editor of the American cultural journal, *Partisan Review*, who lamented the lack of a comparable organ in the English-speaking world.[11] It has continued to attract praise, winning the German Critics' Prize in 1990, but it has also courted controversy, particularly in a special edition of 2003, 'Capitalism or Barbarism', which was interpreted by some as advancing a 'Clash of Civilizations' thesis between the Western and Arabic worlds.[12] However, its place among German and international cultural journals seems assured, as a *New Left Review* article by Perry Anderson makes clear. Anderson commented:

> Since the war, Germany's leading journal of ideas has been *Merkur* ... Its remarkable founding editor Hans Paeschke gave it an interdisciplinary span–from the arts through philosophy and sociology to the hard sciences–of exceptional breadth, canvassed with consistent elegance and concision. But what made it unique was the creed of its editor ... Averse to any kind of *Syntheselei*, he conceived the journal socratically, as a dialectical enterprise, in keeping with the dictum *Der Geist ist ein Wühler*. Spirit is not a reconciler, but a trouble-maker.[13]

Although *Merkur* editors have long been proud of the journal's ideological eclecticism from its early days as a forum for 'all shades of uncorrupted thought',[14] Paeschke agreed in a radio-interview retrospective of 1982 that there was a conservative flavour to the journal in its early years. Yet he also said in other interviews that the journal moved from 'liberal conservatism to national liberalism to left liberalism' from the 1940s to the 1970s.[15] Certainly there were a greater number of contributors to the journal in the 1940s and 1950s that belonged to the political Right. Moreover, when Paeschke explained how important it was that *Merkur* was called 'German Journal for European Thought' rather than just 'Journal for European Thought', he emphasized that its authors did not want to 'say goodbye to our German history'. Here he was reiterating the arguments of conservative 'inner émigrés' who sought to present Nazism as a radical departure from more healthy German political traditions that could be revived. He even went as far as to quote Arnold Bergstraesser, a German conservative who found wartime exile in the United States, when he commented that he had been 'chased out of a land of sadism and returned to a land of masochism'.[16] The following section describes the intellectual origins of this (at least initially) conservative journal, and, rather than waving goodbye to its German history, focuses on its predecessors, the *Europäische Revue* and the *Neue Rundschau*.

Predecessor Journals and a Franco-German Rapprochement

Merkur was founded in 1947, in the French Zone, by Paeschke, a former counter-espionage agent who had been active with the German military defence division in southern France during the later war years. Paeschke had already been engaged by the French occupation authorities in the immediate post-war period to produce a cultural journal, *Lancelot*, which was designed to bring a message to the German people from France and to aid the reconciliation of the two countries. *Merkur* thus fits into a context of significant cultural supervision and patronage by the occupation authorities. Nevertheless, this immediate context, which will be focused on in chapter 2, can be better understood with some knowledge of the pre-1945 history, which helps to illuminate the journal's agenda and explain how it came to thrive and exert influence in German and European public life. For, although the early post-Second World War period might appear as especially vibrant in terms of its print media, particularly when compared with the censored media landscape of National Socialist Germany, it was not so unprecedented when viewed against the background of a similarly vibrant print culture in Weimar Germany. Moreover, journals dedicated to questions of European unity were similarly prominent in the late 1920s and early 1930s in Germany. They emerged in response to such initiatives as the Locarno Treaties of 1925 that were concluded between the former First World War enemies in order to promote Franco-German reconciliation and provide peaceful means of altering the boundaries in Central and Eastern Europe established at Versailles in June 1919.[17]

In order to understand *Merkur's* agenda, it is necessary to look particularly at two journals regarded by the editors, Hans Paeschke and Joachim Moras, as its predecessors: the *Neue Rundschau* and the *Europäische Revue*. These were not only edited by the two *Merkur* editors but were the main forums in which the early *Merkur* contributors came to prominence, although they wrote during the National Socialist period and were never free from National Socialist interference.[18] The *Neue Rundschau* and the *Europäische Revue* were two of many publications spanning a broad ideological spectrum in the interwar period that discussed, debated and sometimes advocated European integration. Many of these journals were also not altogether self-contained ventures: they usually functioned as the primary outlets for the work of political and cultural organizations that provided funding, readers and authors for the publications, but which also sought to make a political impact through other channels – for instance, by convening conferences, establishing informal networks and exercising influence 'behind the scenes'.

As Pierre Bourdieu has suggested in his work on the 'field of cultural production', many journals gained their respected position within the field by claiming independence from political interests and from the needs of the market, styling themselves as publications made for other cultural producers rather than for consumers.[19] This was particularly the case in Weimar Germany where unaffiliated daily newspapers modelled on the late-nineteenth-century *General-Anzeiger* rapidly gave way to papers backed by political- and industrial-interest groups.[20] Furthermore, the need for independent voices in the press appeared all the more urgent as it became clear that semi-official media associations, often working in conjunction with the state propaganda ministry, the Reichszentrale für Heimatdienst, were feeding news to the press, particularly regarding contentious political issues such as the French seizing control of the Ruhr in 1923.[21] As a result, intellectuals and 'literary journalists' sought to work collectively within journals to provide an 'objective' and detached perspective on the seemingly ever greater plurality of news, which was too great for any individual to absorb as a whole.

Of course, such intellectuals were linked not only by a common loyalty to their profession but also by a coincidence of other factors such as region, religious affiliation and cultural orientation.[22] However, such groups of intellectuals should not be understood as being narrowly tied to political parties, even if they advanced an ideological agenda, particularly because major political parties did not function as magnets for political and cultural groups in Germany as they had done in countries such as Britain. Therefore, while this and the following chapter focus on the politics of cultural journals and the milieux responsible for their production, they analyse the journals and intellectual communities as 'optional communities' within civil society, rather than as projections of party-political agendas. Although it should also be said that these optional communities were not operating in an ideal, Habermasian public sphere but one in which government agencies and political parties were active, if sometimes concealed, actors.[23]

The Neue Rundschau *and Pro-integration Groups on the Left*

The *Neue Rundschau* fitted this model of a publication with its roots in civil society, having been linked with the Freie Bühne Verein in the 1890s, and, since 1918, largely providing a venue for literary authors signed to the renowned Fischer publishing house, such as Alfred Döblin, Heinrich and Thomas Mann, Stefan Zweig and many others. Indeed, the journal continued to guard its independence, as well as any publication could during the Third Reich, creating space for over one hundred blacklisted authors.[24] In the 1920s, this preeminent literary journal, nevertheless, followed a cultural agenda that was not without political significance. It provided space for supporters of European unity such as the Pan-Europeanist Richard Coudenhove-Kalergi, and it was a consistent proponent of Franco-German rapprochement, being described by Michel Grunewald as a 'precursor to the "spirit of Locarno"'.[25] The journal devoted particular attention to works by French authors in its reviews, published reports by Germans on French cultural and political life and made room for the novels, letters and journalistic reports of French writers such as André Gide.[26] At times this cultural mission became more pointedly political, as when the French army reoccupied the Ruhr under orders from Prime Minister Raymond Poincaré, after his government had refused to accept a delay in reparations payments from Germany. While popular opinion in Germany turned strongly against the French, the *Neue Rundschau* in July of 1923 sought to argue against any resurgent nationalism directed against France, opening with Heinrich Mann's *Europa, Reich über den Reichen* and following with a German translation of Gide's *L'avenir de l'Europe*. Such a decision reflected the outlook of the *Rundschau* editor, Samuel Saenger, who was a friend of Czechoslovak President Thomas Masaryk, and a pupil of Friedrich Naumann. Saenger consistently advocated the integration of Europe, having laid the blame for Germany's defeat in the First World War on German industrialists rather than on the French.[27]

This journal's attempts to repair damaged relations were some of the many initiatives launched in both countries to bring French and German elites closer again. A number of publications including *Europe, revue mensuelle; L'Europe nouvelle; La Revue européenne; Europäische Gespräche;* and *Paneuropa* sought to recreate a European unity out of a renewed Franco-German friendship during the early-to-mid interwar period.[28] Such initiatives were not just carried out in print, but also within wider civil society: for instance the professor and journalist Paul Desjardins had already in 1922 revived yearly meetings of French and German cultural elites at the Burgundian commune of Pontigny, which had previously taken place between 1910 and 1914.[29] Similarly, during the early-to-mid-1920s, other Franco-German ventures were launched, including a Deutsch-Französische Gesellschaft (DFG), for which Paeschke worked and which attracted many of the liberal-conservative intellectuals and politicians also drawn to the Europäischer Kulturbund, the organization responsible for the production of the *Europäische Revue*. Such attempts at rapprochement were by no means the exclusive preserve of the Right, as leftist organizations such as the Deutsche Friedensgesellschaft and the French-initiated Liga für Menschenrechte were among the first such organizations established in the early interwar years.[30] Furthermore, leftist intellectuals who participated in such ventures as the journal *Europe* supported international organizations like PEN International (Poets, Essayists and Novelists) and various anti-fascist committees that formed in the 1920s and 30s, seeking to reinforce the international solidarity of intellectuals in the face of the increasingly hostile policies of their governments.[31]

The cultural rapprochement between France and Germany is, according to many historical accounts, typified by the founding of the Paneuropa Union by Austrian Count Richard von Coudenhove-Kalergi in Vienna in 1926. This brought together European (not least French and German) elites and inspired its honorary President, Aristide Briand, to lay out a plan or 'Memorandum on the Organization of a System of European Federal Union', before the League of Nations in May 1930.[32] The Plan envisaged 'a permanent [European] political council' which would work for a 'customs policy' that moved Europe 'towards the ideal end goal: establishing a common market'. It also, nevertheless, suggested combining policies on transport, postal services, radio, telephones and telegraphs, rulings on social questions, emigration and immigration of workers, and advocated cooperation between universities and academies and a centralization of scientific research.[33] Due to scepticism from imperial Britain and fascist Italy and the world economic crisis following the Wall Street Crash of autumn 1929, Briand's proposal garnered insufficient support in the League. In spite of its lack of success, this Plan, and the federalist sentiment supposedly animating it, have been regarded as the result of elite cooperation between Europeans such as occurred in the Paneuropa Union and which waned in the later 1930s but which could be revived in the post-1945 period. Coudenhove-Kalergi's Paneuropa Union was, however, merely one pro-integration initiative among many in the interwar period, not all of which were designed to cultivate a democratic, federalist Europe. I now focus on one such initiative, the Europäischer Kulturbund and its journal, the *Europäische Revue*.

The Europäische Revue *and Pro-integration Groups on the Right*

Probably the most important cultural organization in the interwar period in Central Europe, the Europäischer Kulturbund was founded to create a new European community with a centre in *Mitteleuropa* and a political culture rooted in pre-democratic, aristocratic traditions. It was established in 1922 by an Austrian Prince, Karl Anton Rohan, who was urged to advance the cause of European unity by Austrian statesmen such as Joseph Redlich, who had worked with the Austrian Emperor Karl to manage the post-1918 transition.[34] Rohan decided to make France an early focal point of the organization, not least because it was the ancestral home of his aristocratic family but also because he wished to avoid giving the impression that the Kulturbund was a revanchist project put together by the war's losers. Starting out from his base in Vienna, Rohan established chapters in France, Spain and Portugal in the winter of 1923, and held an international congress in Paris in November 1924, designed to illustrate the extent of post-war Franco-German rapprochement. This meeting attracted significant figures from France's cultural elite including Marie Curie, the authors Georges Duhamel and Paul Valéry, and a representative of the Archbishop of Paris.[35]

The organization started to publish a journal, the *Europäische Revue*, in 1925 as a means of publicizing its activities and of rallying intellectuals behind its vision of an 'alternative' integrated Europe. The journal represented a Kulturbund that, in the words of Guido Müller, stretched from Portugal to the Baltic, with a 'membership list [that] … reads like a *Who's Who* of European celebrities'. With annual meetings attended by three hundred members, and regular local meetings in more than fifty branches across Europe, the Kulturbund became 'the most important intellectual network on the continent', and its journal maintained a readership of around seven thousand, and a faithful of two to two and a half thousand subscribers.[36] Once German chapters were set up from September 1926, they secured the membership of prominent German intellectuals, politicians, artists and industrialists, such as Heidelberg academics Alfred Weber, Arnold Bergstraesser and Ludwig Curtius, the Catholic jurist Carl Schmitt, Thomas Mann, Cologne mayor Konrad Adenauer and Lilly von Schnitzler-Mallinckrodt, the wife of an I.G. Farben executive.

While the membership of the Kulturbund was ecumenical and pan-European, the organization and its journal nevertheless represented the reassertion of a political Catholicism that had been on the retreat in Germany since the *Kulturkampf*. In some senses anti-Catholicism appeared a German peculiarity, where the leadership of all political parties in Germany except the SPD and the Centre Party had been Protestant and where the majority of press censorship laws of the early 1870s had been used against Catholics rather than socialists. However,

Kulturkampf legislation aimed at curbing the power of the Catholic Church was passed in Switzerland, Austria, Spain, Belgium, the Netherlands and France between 1860 and 1890. This led many Catholics to believe that Germany was on the same liberal nationalist path as other countries – a path that led to the erosion of Christian traditions in Europe.[37] Therefore much of the support for a united Europe among centre-right groups in the interwar period emerged from newly assertive French, German and Austrian Catholic groups, which also produced daily newspapers and advanced their cause within national political parties.[38]

The cultural elites that practised a fledgling form of European civil society at Kulturbund meetings also contributed to interest groups such as the German Catholic Academic Association (CAA). They similarly supported the Rhineland Catholic publication, *Abendland. Deutsche Monatsheft für europäische Kultur*, which was financially backed by the aristocrats and business figures behind the *Kölnische Zeitung*, the largest circulation newspaper of the (Catholic) German Centre Party, with a readership of seventy thousand in 1933.[39] The editors of this publication were closely tied to the founders of the *Europäische Revue*, and the two publications shared a number of Catholic contributors, including Austrian Chancellor and priest Ignaz Seipel, and Friedrich Schreyvogl, editor of *Abendland*. However, these publications rallied and reflected a growing ecumenical, conservative, Christian politics, which was increasingly palatable to Protestants writing for other *abendländisch* publications such as *Hochland*. These Protestant authors explained that the connection between Protestant churches and the state had been eroded by the revolutions and parliamentary regimes that had reconfigured political life in Europe in recent decades.[40]

The *Europäische Revue* did not merely address religious communities though; it could rely on support from a more broadly based political elite in Germany. Through such individuals as Wilhelm Heinrich Solf, a member of the liberal Deutsche Demokratische Partei (DDP), ambassador to Japan and Chairman of the *Revue*'s board, the publication was well known among diplomats and others in the Foreign Ministry as well as liberal-conservative politicians more generally. Solf also belonged to the SeSiSo Club of the leading hundred or so centre-right German politicians in the interwar period. Alongside the Deutsche Gesellschaft 1914, this club linked politicians and intellectuals with bankers and industrialists such as Robert Bosch (a liberal who went on to be an opponent to Hitler), Alfred Hugenberg (a national liberal who joined Hitler's first cabinet) and French industrialists such as Henri de Peyerimhoff, a leading member of the Deutsch-Französische Studienkomitee.[41] Such elite clubs were particularly important sources of anti-republican sentiment, within which senior civil servants made alliances with conservatives, who preferred such traditional elites over the prospect of a politicized civil service made up of pro-republicans. These predominantly conservative civil servants often had more impact on government policy than elected politicians, remaining in their jobs while coalitions changed rapidly.[42] Thus the journal sought to exercise influence on such policy shapers. Its authors were particularly eager to exert influence on leading diplomats in the 1920s as the predicament of Germany, Austria and other European nations was so obviously shaped by foreign affairs, with European politicians and businessmen having to react to a post-war situation in which European nations owed money to the United States and thus demanded reparation payments from Germany. The next section illustrates how entangled such intra-European concerns as those addressed above became with global issues such as debt and ideological conflict.

Europe 'between the Colossus of the West and the Leviathan of the East'

While what I have covered so far may have implied the distinctiveness of leftist and rightist agendas for uniting Europe, when it came to analysing threats to Europe from beyond its borders, groups across the ideological spectrum often offered similar perspectives. Writing within the pages of the *Europäische Revue*, the liberal intellectual, Alfred Weber, positioned Europe in an ever-tighter space between 'the Colossus of Western civilization', the United States and 'the second Leviathan, of the East', the Soviet Union. Weber believed that the results of the First World War offered the prospect of Europeans as either 'slaves of the East or West' or as living in 'a battleground between the two'.[43] This position was also represented by French contributors to the *Revue*, including the future Vichy minister Lucien Romier, an advocate for the antiparliamentarian *Redressement français* and the author of *Who Will be Master, Europe or America?* and Pierre Drieu La Rochelle, a member of Jacques Doriot's fascistic Parti Populaire Française and enthusiastic supporter of the Nazi occupation of northern France, who addressed the Russian threat in his *Geneva or Moscow*.[44]

Neue Rundschau contributors echoed such fears, with the sociologist and later co-founder of the 'University in Exile' in New York, Emil Lederer, worrying about Russia's growing importance as 'the capital city of Asia for the young generation'. He argued that Europe had revived itself enough to resist the Bolshevik threat, but only with the equally fatal assistance of the United States. Referring to the benefits brought about by the Dawes Plan of 1924, which advanced credit to Germany for the payment of reparations and was delivered only on the condition that France abandon its 'aggressive military policy', Lederer commented, 'For the first time, in dramatic form, the supremacy of foreign bank capital over a world power became visible.' Somewhat paradoxically, he went on to contend that all of the measures designed to entrench peace in Europe such as the Dawes Plan and the Locarno Treaties would eventually leave Europe weaker and less able to repel an invasion from Russia anyway. Such international agreements reduced armaments, limited the sovereignty of European nations and 'reduced the likelihood of an offensive against Russia'.[45]

As unfair as Lederer's charges might seem, they reflected a belief common among Europeans that Wilson's vision for the 'self-determination of peoples' had not, and could not be realized in Europe.⁴⁶ Not only did the sizeable ethnic minorities in the new states in Eastern Europe make this clear; so too did the economic interdependence of such nations. Criticizing the rise in nationalism and economic protectionism that accompanied the growth of small nation-states in post-1918 Europe, the economist and communist sympathizer Robert Kuczynski explained in a contribution to the *Neue Rundschau* that '[e]conomic nationalism driven on by political nationalism' that sought to make the new nations 'independent' from foreign powers often actually went against their real economic interests.⁴⁷ Here he was reflecting on a post-First World War situation that had seen a continent with 26 customs areas and 13 monetary systems before 1914, emerge after 1918 with 35 customs areas and 27 monetary systems as well as an additional six thousand metres of customs barriers, as Carlo Sforza recalled in an article written in the journal *Europe* in 1937.⁴⁸

The debates aired in the *Neue Rundschau* and *Europäische Revue* reflected the political and economic tensions in Germany and Europe throughout the 1920s and early 1930s. While any threat from the Soviet Union was difficult to assess, as its support for exporting revolution appeared to fluctuate throughout the period, political commentators nevertheless regarded sovietism as one of the 'ideologies of the future' that would replace the temporary expedient of parliamentarianism in countries such as Weimar Germany.⁴⁹ Such a perspective seemed plausible given the rapid pace of urbanization and industrialization being forced through by communist leaders in the Soviet Union. Furthermore, discontent surrounding the toppling of the 1918 revolution in Germany and the increasingly hostile divisions between social democrats and communists were exacerbated by the inflammatory rhetoric employed by an ever more assertive Soviet-led Comintern.⁵⁰ Lucien Romier summed up this perspective, arguing that while 'Asiatic' peoples such as the Russians might at present stand behind Europeans in terms of economic and cultural development, they would increasingly master European technology and use it towards their own ideological ends, thereby bringing Europeans into their sphere of influence.⁵¹

Whereas the Soviet Union might present Europe with one possible course, the United States appeared to offer an alternative future, with American-style capitalism already appearing more modern than European varieties to commentators such as Pierre Drieu La Rochelle.⁵² For instance, as such European commentators were aware, the pace of American manufacturing growth greatly outstripped the speed of European development and its steel production topped that of Britain, France and Germany together by fifty-one per cent, exceeding the production of the whole of Europe.⁵³ Furthermore, the United States appeared to be exporting not only goods but, like the Soviet Union, an ideology. The post-war settlement, supposedly the creation of President Wilson, had divided Europeans from one another as members of nation-states and accelerated the rise of partisan politics and class antagonism. Indeed, this settlement was characterized as fundamentally un-European: the product of a levelling

American political culture that had little respect for European traditions. As one contributor, Heinz Ziegler, commented, American leaders at Versailles had supported a form of democratic nationalism that had amputated European traditions and communities from one another. 'Wilson [was], as a result of his nation-state democratism, an enemy of international law.' What remained was 'the war between sovereign nations', which was, 'in principle, unending'.[54]

Despite the help that the U.S. provided for Germany in the post-war era, through the Dawes Plan of 1924, the Young Plan of 1929, and the Hoover-initiated moratorium on German reparations, it also seemed increasingly clear to many Germans that the financial world was ill-served by a predominant United States. From 1924 to 1930 Germany borrowed a total of 7174 million *Reichsmarks*, sixty-two per cent of this sum coming from the United States, meaning that when many of the short-term loans issued after 1928 were recalled in the wake of the Wall Street Crash, the economic hardships experienced in Germany, such as unemployment figures of over three million by August 1930, were in part blamed on the U.S.[55] Indebtedness to the United States was hardly a uniquely German condition in the interwar period: however, the Allies' debit balance with the United States of twelve billion dollars between 1918 and 1931 led them to squeeze Germany ever tighter for reparations repayments.[56] European economists furthermore pointed out that unlike Britain, which had maintained free trade from 1848 to 1916, the United States adopted the Smoot-Hawley Tariff Act of 1930, although the World Economic Conference of 1927 had recommended a tariff truce, and the American President, Herbert Hoover, had received more than thirty formal protests from other countries and contrary advice from over one thousand economists.[57] As the French economic commentator, C.J. Gignoux, remarked in the *Revue*, the masses in Europe could thus not understand how Americans could raise tariffs and act in such protectionist ways at the same time as trying to develop their presence in the European market.[58]

The fear of the Soviet Union and the United States that was expressed in such publications as the *Neue Rundschau* and *Europäische Revue* merged with fears about trends such as urbanization and the 'rise of the masses' in Europe. On the one hand, Germany was experiencing a growing population and the concentration of young people in cities. This meant that excessive demands were made on the labour and housing markets and gave plausibility to *Volk ohne Raum* (people without space) arguments that Germany was overcrowded and lacking 'living space', particularly once it had lost its colonies after the First World War. On the other hand, the population in Europe was ageing, especially in comparison with the youthful populations in the United States and the Soviet Union. Furthermore, Germany was still as much an agricultural as an industrial society with only around a third of the population living in cities, an equal number still in the countryside. Thus, debates about the culture of Germany seemed particularly urgent as the country appeared to be on the cusp on decisive demographic change.[59]

Such debates about modernity were not unique to Germany, however. Authors such as the Spanish philosopher and author of *The Revolt of the Masses*, José Ortega y Gasset, worried about the role of elites across Europe in an age of mass politics. Since nationalist movements in the nineteenth century had urged the masses to become sovereigns of their nations, it appeared that the communities of Europe had been broken up into national majorities which had become politicized through the dominance of political parties. These developments were greatly intensified by the post-1918 settlement, which had enshrined the right of national self-determination and thus swept away the empires and hierarchies that had existed for much of the nineteenth century. Bemoaning the 'nationalist splintering of the spirit' that occurred in the nineteenth century and saw the masses influencing the elite rather than the reverse, Gasset looked forward to a return of 'the cosmopolitanism of the best'. However, this cosmopolitan community of elites seemed unlikely to return to frontline politics during an era characterized by the 'barbarity [of] ... the unexceptional individuals'. Instead, as Gasset argued, such cosmopolitan intellectuals must first work within civil society and concentrate on creating new principles for the future conduct of politics.[60]

Developments such as those described by Gasset were also regarded by many authors in both publications as trends much more advanced in non-European countries such as the United States and the Soviet Union, where it appeared that the masses, either through democracy or communism, had come to dominate political life. Such a concern for Europe's elites, accompanied by fears that Europe was emulating the example of its Eastern and Western neighbours, was widespread in German and more broadly European cultural journals as well as among cultural and political organizations across the Continent.[61] This is, perhaps, unsurprising as the elites that made such arguments had in many ways been marginalized by the recent changes in Europe's political geography: transnational empires had been replaced by nation-states within which populations were ruled not necessarily by aristocrats but primarily by politicians claiming popular approval and the backing of democratic political parties.[62] Much of the support for such publications as the *Europäische Revue* thus came from aristocrats who sought to find ways to overcome the division of Europe into democratic nation-states, and to revive a transnational elite capable of leading a reunited continent.[63]

This background to interwar attitudes to the United States and Soviet Union in Europe offers a new perspective on the roots of Third Force sentiment in Europe, which clearly preceded the onset of the Cold War and resonated with long-established fears of American and Soviet predominance over Europe. What is particularly striking, in light of the supposed later Westernization of Germany, is how Franco-German elites, represented by figures such as Rohan, Romier and Drieu La Rochelle, sought to sharply distinguish European political cultural from American as well as Soviet culture. As Rohan commented in an article on 'Western Europe', what appeared promising in the interwar years was how growing numbers of intellectuals and politicians in France appeared eager to move away from the values of the Enlightenment and the political rationalism of the Revolution, and return to Catholicism and pre-revolutionary traditions in Europe.[64] Thus, for Rohan, the old division between a western *Zivilisation* – represented by France, Britain and the United States – and a *Kultur* – typified by the Germanic states – was breaking down, with the countries of Europe forming a distinct bloc with its heart in Central Europe. I turn now to ideas for this *Mitteleuropa* as formulated in such journals as the *Europäische Revue*.

A Third Force Mitteleuropa?

It would not be accurate to say that most authors writing in the *Neue Rundschau* and the *Europäische Revue* believed that the United States and the Soviet Union were equally antithetical to European political cultures. The majority shared Luigi Valla's opinion that the 'European spirit' was evident in the United States in a way that it was not in the Soviet Union.[65] Nevertheless, they were equally eager to locate the centre of European culture in the *Kulturländer* of *Mitteleuropa*, such as Germany and Austria, and thereby distinguish between Europe and the Western, Anglo-Saxon countries. As will be suggested in this section, such a perspective reflected not just the historical (and lost) influence of the Austrian Empire in Central and Eastern Europe. It also illustrated the political mobilization of German minorities in the region and the increasing trade presence of Germany in a part of Europe that had lost its dominant state power. A study of the arguments for the integration of *Mitteleuropa* should thus show how consistently Germans looked East during the interwar years, and apply a corrective to a one-sided focus on a western Franco-German axis as the basis for any moves towards integration even before 1945.[66]

Such a *mitteleuropäisch* perspective emerged in both the *Neue Rundschau* and the *Europäische Revue*. It should be no surprise that this was the case in the *Neue Rundschau*, as the political editor and author of the political 'Junius' column, Samuel Saenger, was a pupil of Friedrich Naumann and a friend of Czech President Thomas Masaryk.[67] However, the case for *Mitteleuropa* was more consistently made in the *Revue*, not least because ideas of *Mitteleuropa* were more common among right-wing political communities in the interwar years, but also because the *Neue Rundschau*'s contributions were weighted towards belletristic writings rather than political commentary. Therefore, this section will focus on articles published in the *Europäische Revue*.

Some of the contributions in the journal of the late 1920s and early 1930s advocated the limited goal of greater economic integration in the Central European region. These contributions represented the positions of the influential private interest groups with commercial interests in Central Europe that were able to lobby politicians in Weimar Germany due to its corporatist structure and the 'behind-the-scenes' bargaining that went on between parties within the shifting coalition governments. However, the influence of such private interest groups also meant that governments were hampered in their efforts to conclude trade agreements with neighbouring countries such as Poland and Czechoslovakia, as they were subject to competing pressures from rival sectors. Accordingly, economic commentators increasingly called for the links between Central European economies to be formalised so that trade policy would not become the subject of such jockeying for influence on the part of various economic groups.[68]

In spite of Germany's dominant position as export power within the East-Central European economy, many of the politicians and economists writing in the *Revue* did not advocate integrating only the economies of East-Central Europe. Richard Riedl, an Austrian economist working at the International Chamber of Commerce, argued in 1930 that the predominantly agricultural lands of East-Central Europe needed to be integrated with the industrial lands of the western parts of Central Europe (as he referred to France, Belgium and Switzerland) as well as Germany and Austria, in order for any economic integration to be mutually beneficial.[69] Such authors often sought to position their proposals as alternatives to the Briand Plan, conceiving them in the same spirit of Franco-German reconciliation. Others however, described how France had sought, and continued to seek, to organize *Mitteleuropa* in its own image so as to minimize German influence in the region. The journal's founder, Prince Rohan, was particularly concerned at the attempts by the French to construct alliances with Central European nations such as the Little Entente directed against the Germans and the Austrians.[70] As a result, calls were issued, with a grand rhetorical flourish, for a 'mitteleuropäisch[e] ... Monroedoktrin' that would prevent the interference of countries outside of the region.[71]

As can be seen, there was hardly unanimity among authors about the precise dimensions of any *mitteleuropäisch* economic or political community or about how it would interact with countries beyond its borders. What nevertheless became clear was that calls for integration between the German and Austrian economies and polities became increasingly consistent in the late 1920s and early 1930s, both within the journal and among political elites more generally. As a response to the economic problems encountered by the war's losers, particularly after the Wall Street Crash of 1929, German and Austrian politicians conceived plans for a customs union, with German Foreign Secretary Julius Curtius putting one such scheme before the League of Nations at the request of the British in 1931. This proposed union attracted much support, particularly from the Austrian side, with many intellectuals publishing supportive essays in favour of an *Anschluss*, and businessmen suggesting that Vienna could thrive as the 'Hamburg of the East'.[72]

The motivation for proposing such a union was not merely economic, at least not among the contributors to the *Revue*. The Austrian editors and leading lights of the journal, such as Prince Rohan, were among those who particularly favoured a neo-Habsburgian arrangement for twentieth-century Germany and Central Europe, advocating a renewal of the conservative spirit and the overcoming of the nationalisms of the nineteenth century with the *Reichsidee* or idea of a new Holy Roman Empire.[73] Of course they were not alone as Austrians dissatisfied not only with the post-1918 settlement but also with wider nationalist trends since the mid-nineteenth century: the founder of the Paneuropa movement, and another Austrian aristocrat, Richard Coudenhove-Kalergi, similarly sought to overcome nationalism in interwar and post-war Europe. However, his Paneuropa ideas were rejected by Rohan as they would make a 'Switzerland of Europe', rather than the neo-imperial arrangement in Central Europe he preferred, which would have a Greater Germany at its heart.[74]

Columnists, including Rohan and the Czech-born German Heinz Ziegler, therefore advocated a German *Anschluss* of Austria as the first step towards this greater *mitteleuropäisch* unity, speaking for Austrians who 'strive[d] for the returning home to the Greater Germany [*Großdeutschland*], from which they have been shut out for the last sixty years'.[75] This version of the *Reichsidee* appealed not only to Austrians who had been marginalized by the Prussian-led unification of the late nineteenth century; in addition, it continued to garner support among Germans in the south-western states, and in Bavaria, who had been similarly marginalized and who agreed with Rohan when he suggested that the creation of an Austrian crown by Metternich and of a Berlin crown by Bismarck were revolutionary acts that desacralized the *Kaiserkrone*.[76]

Such revisionist sentiments clearly had deep roots in the political settlements of the nineteenth century and suggest that Germans in the South and in Austria had not altogether reconciled themselves to the nationalist projects of this period. However, the revisionist case could also appeal to many of the ten to twelve million ethnic Germans living outside of Germany and Austria in the 1920s.[77] These German minorities made up a sizeable proportion of the European minority populations that had existed throughout Europe for centuries but whose status as citizens had become increasingly problematic as the relationship between the nation – understood as an ethnic or cultural community – and the state – regarded as the constitutional authority exercising sovereignty over a particular territorial realm – shifted in the late nineteenth century, and again after 1918.[78] With the rise of nationalist movements and the creation of nation-states modelled on Wilson's principle of the 'self-determination of peoples' after the First World War, states were increasingly understood as the embodiment of a national community, thus rendering the presence of minorities within a national body politic problematic. As a result of the discrimination faced by national minorities, leaders from groups including the Baltic Germans, East-Central European Jewish communities and the Hungarian minorities established a European Nationality Congress in October 1925 that continued to meet until 1939.[79] This body initially sought to exist as a civil society initiative, advocating the interests of those not represented in inter-state negotiations and seeking to establish legal safeguards for minorities across Europe. However, by the early 1930s, it became dominated by ethnic Germans. It also became increasingly financially dependent on the German Foreign Ministry, which believed it could help push forward a revisionist policy in East-Central Europe, arguing for policies that would help ethnic Germans to be reunited with other members of their *Volksgruppe* in the German 'homeland'.[80]

Many of the arguments articulated within this Congress were also aired in the *Europäische Revue*, with two of the leading Baltic Germans, Paul Schiemann, a Latvian politician, and Werner Hasselblatt, a German lawyer from Estonia, writing about the 'minority problem' in its pages. While Schiemann was a liberal politician, eager to achieve a synthesis for Europeans between belonging to a state and a national community, he was equally concerned with ensuring that the Baltic states be safeguarded from Russian incursions by the protection of a great state such as Germany.[81] He argued in 1926 that the independence of the Baltic states should be guaranteed by Germany, not least because Russia did not, and could not ever, form part of the *abendländisch* community.[82] In some respects, his arguments echoed those of Hasselblatt, who was eager to regain much of the autonomy ethnic Germans had enjoyed before the Russification policies of the late nineteenth century in the Baltic states.[83] But his arguments went further, suggesting that the Germans in East-Central Europe could look to their co-nationals as guardians, implying some sort of quasi-imperial relationship between Germany and states with sizeable German populations.

This issue became a significant enough concern for the *Revue* authors that the editor, Rohan, even published a 'Design for a Minorities Statute' in June 1930, which he had written together with representatives from Austria, Germany, Romania, Hungary and Czechoslovakia. This document aimed to protect the right of national minorities to organize associations that functioned within nation-states and served to establish networks of co-nationals across state borders. It also envisaged the guaranteeing of community schools for minorities, within which the major language of instruction would be that spoken by the national group.[84] While such proposals could certainly be read as merely firming up long-held traditions of protecting the cultural autonomy of minorities, they could also be read as ways of cultivating forms of associational life and civic activism that would work to destabilize the ruling order in the nations of East-Central Europe. Certainly, other writings by Rohan around the same time, give the impression that a revisionist policy was being pursued. Writing about 'Western Europe' and 'Future Questions for German Foreign Policy' in 1929, Rohan made clear that Germany should take the lead in *Mitteleuropa* as the 'leading cultural people in Central Europe [*führendes Kulturvolk in Mitteleuropa*]', arguing further that 'the German problem of this century is to organize Central Europe' as the region was chaotic and disorderly and 'Only a people … [that is] ruled [beherrschte] … can be trusted by others.'[85]

Rohan's and others' proposals could be interpreted in many ways, with Rohan suggesting that a new Empire in Central Europe could be like the old Holy Roman Empire, within which the Emperor would play more the rule of judge in a supranational 'order of right', rather than the 'embodiment of genuine power'.[86] However, the appeal to creating a new Empire also conjured up images of a turn away from a Europe of democratically ruled nation-states towards a more authoritarian form of rule. This advocacy of a 'post-democratic Europe' was certainly a feature of the writings in the *Revue* and represented a significant disenchantment with parliamentary democracy on the part of the elites that made up the Europäischer Kulturbund. I will now look at some of the ideas for reforming political practice in Europe as they were developed in the *Revue*.

A Post-democratic Europe?

From its earliest issues, the *Revue* welcomed the fascist movement as a reinvigorating force in Europe, particularly saluting its celebration of youth. This regard for fascism and its exultation of youth reflected a generational solidarity advocated by former wartime soldiers such as the *Revue*'s editor, Prince Rohan, who believed that Europe's youth had been strengthened by their shared *Fronterlebnis* or experience of the front during the War. As numerous contributions to the journal made clear, the basis for the Franco-German rapprochement witnessed by many Europeans in the mid-1920s was said to be the shared experience of the War, when a new generation of soldiers emerged, united by their common (if opposing) commitment to their nations. However paradoxical it may sound, this argument for reconciliation and indeed European unity out of shared nationalisms was an argument made by a wide variety of French and German intellectuals, many of whom, for example Pierre Viénot and Arnold Bergstraesser, had seen wartime action. Such an argument also appealed to the many young German aristocrats who would have looked forward to promising careers in the military but whose opportunities after 1918 were severely limited by the reduction of the German army to one hundred thousand.[87]

Due to the supposed brotherhood between battle-hardened European youths, which had been stifled by Versailles provisions that had only exacerbated national tensions, the journal's founder, Rohan, greeted fascism 'as the first great movement of the young generation', 'the first step out of the decline of the European present towards a constructive future'. Furthermore, Rohan saw fascism in Italy as a potential model for a European community; for in Italy people could feel 'brotherly' because they had been freed from 'democracy' and the 'cultural liquidation' that was a product of the 'terror of equality'.[88] Rohan's argument was not pitched exclusively at Italians however, but also at the growing numbers of anti-republicans in Germany and at the military circles in France in the 1920s that went on to provide much of the support for the Ordre Nouveau and *Jeune Droite* Catholic and often anti-republican movements of the 1930s.[89] The Kulturbund was committed to cultivating a new European elite, and a number of its leading members, including Rohan, participated in the Volta Congress held in Rome in 1932 to discuss the topic of uniting Europe from a fascist perspective. This event was conceived not simply to provide a fascist alternative to Briand's plans for European integration; it marked an important milestone for Asvero Gravelli, one of the architects of fascist Italy's 'youthful revolution'.[90] During this year, Rohan also commissioned a special issue of the *Revue*, celebrating ten years of fascist rule, presenting it as the first successful counter-revolution since the French Revolution.[91]

This valorization of fascism was the corollary of the broader critique of parliamentary democracy constructed in the *Revue*. One of the most consistent opponents of parliamentarianism, the future National Socialist jurist and post-Second World War contributor to *Merkur*, Carl Schmitt, offered an image of how democratic practice served to erode the national community. He argued that national parliaments had not transformed the various interest groups existing in European societies into the sort of general will described by Rousseau, but instead had become a 'stock market on which the various pieces of social power are traded'. Such an institutional set-up had, argued Schmitt, led to a complete politicization of public life, whereby citizens identified themselves primarily as members of political parties. As a result, paradoxically, parliament became no longer truly sovereign but merely the hostage of the predominant party at any given time. Furthermore, the competing parties in any democratic polity might not even agree as to the role of the law within the state and a 'plurality of conceptions of legality' might emerge. Under these circumstances, contended Schmitt, it would become difficult to maintain a bureaucracy whose primary loyalty was to the state, and thus a crisis of authority within the state would emerge.[92]

Such scepticism of parties and parliamentarianism was well established in Weimar Germany and grew out of some genuine problems that had beset the German experience of parliaments. For instance, the twenty-two cabinets formed during the fourteen years of the Weimar Republic, with an average period of slightly less than eight months per government, had not proven particularly conducive to the effective implementation of policy. Moreover, backroom deals between coalition partners were common, as parties rarely commanded significant majorities, with the highest vote gained by any one party being the 44.2 per cent achieved by the National Socialists in 1933.[93] The diverse interests of Landtage representing the German states had also frustrated big business leaders with trans-regional interests, such as Hans Luther, whose 'League for the Renewal of the German Reich' or Lutherbund was formed in January 1928 as a pressure group lobbying for an end to regional parliamentarianism.[94] Even the Weimar constitution itself made just one reference to parties, in Article 130, which was negative and warned civil servants against committing themselves to a party. Moreover, constitutional provisions designed to limit the power of parties abounded: an independently elected president equipped with emergency powers was supposed to stand above party politics, and the use of referenda and plebiscites were designed to afford citizens a direct voice in the legislative process and overcome the 'stultifying effect' of party politics.[95]

Writing in the *Revue* in 1926, in an article entitled 'Das junge Europa', Rohan suggested that not only Germans and Austrians but many young Europeans therefore looked towards a post-democratic future. He claimed: 'in Versailles Europe reached its democratic high point. At the moment when democratic sentiments experienced their greatest expression in power, their shortcomings were clear to we who were born late. Our generation is post-democratic; the age that we will lead, post-democratic.' Rohan, along with many other aristocrats envisaged the possibility of an aristocratic revival, provided aristocrats made alliances across Europe with the growing New Right movements. Aristocratic *Revue* authors such as Franz Graf Hestadt therefore sought to rally Europe's aristocracy against the 'decadence of democracy' and the 'hypertrophy of the administration', arguing that it could be the 'last saviour of our time against the uniformist movement that equally from New York as from Moscow assaults Europe'.[96]

This shift towards fascism on the part of Europe's aristocracy no doubt had its generational aspect too, with younger members of the nobility denied the opportunities their elders had enjoyed. Furthermore, Weimar politics was dominated by older *Gründerzeit* politicians, adding to the sense of alienation of youths among Europe's elites.[97] As a result, the journal made a more direct appeal to the young, halving its price, in accordance with a new policy initiated by Lilly von Schnitzler, the journal's treasurer and wife of I.G. Farben executive Georg Schnitzler who provided the *Revue* and Kulturbund with funding.[98] The hope was that the increasingly radical students, mobilized by right-wing university associations and facing uncertain employment prospect within the civil service and industry, might provide new impetus for the envisaged conservative revolution.

It seems clear, then, that before 1933, the journal had shifted its orientation towards the New Right and it would continue to follow this trajectory after the Nazi *Gleichschaltung*. What is important about this shift is that as the *Revue*'s contributors became increasingly opposed to the democratic constitutions in their nations, they sought to mobilize those elites active in associational life to work against the democratic order throughout Europe. This development offers further confirmation that an active associational life at a European level did not necessarily draw citizens closer to their politicians, nor increase their sense of investment in the democratic process. That said, such organizations as the Kulturbund clearly profited from the associational freedoms available in democratic interwar Europe and they were to suffer the lack of such freedoms after 1933. My focus now turns to this period.

After 1933: Associational Life and Cultural Production after the *Gleichschaltung*

When trying to entice the renowned poet, Gottfried Benn, into writing for *Merkur* in 1948, Hans Paeschke explained that his assistant editor, Joachim Moras, and he were aiming to 'advance the legacy of [the] two leading German journals' of the interwar period, the *Neue Rundschau* and the *Europäische Revue*. Although Paeschke had been editor of the *Rundschau*, he focused particularly on the legacy of the *Europäische Revue*, in spite of its right-wing orientation before 1933 and its co-optation after the Nazi seizure of power.[99] This perhaps reflects Paeschke's experience as editor of the *Neue Rundschau* during the National Socialist period, when the journal's output was limited to belletristic contributions due to political pressure, being little more than 'a clique economy [for] … too many house poets', as the Bonn literary critic, Ernst Robert Curtius, put it in a letter to Paeschke of July 1947.[100] Indeed, by the time that Paeschke was a leader writer on the *Neue Rundschau* in 1939, it had been forced into a 'shadow existence' after the Fischer publishing company was forced to sell it and retreat from public life in Germany, although a rival publisher, Peter Suhrkamp, upon buying the journal, promised to 'maintain it as the last bastion of free expression in Germany'.[101] Paeschke nevertheless agreed with Curtius's characterization, telling him that *Merkur*, 'strived much more for the characteristic and living diversity that the *Europäische Revue* (in contrast somewhat to the *Neue Rundschau*) alone among the German journals possessed in its early stages and … never completely lost'.[102]

Indeed, in spite of its seemingly enthusiastic embracing of fascism even before 1933, the *Revue* nevertheless remained a mercurial presence on the Right in the early 1930s, continuing to include a wide variety of cultural commentary in its pages, including critical pieces by such authors as Theodor Adorno, who lamented the German 'retreat into military marches and associated symbolism' in his 'April 1933: Farewell to Jazz', published in the May 1933 issue.[103] Perhaps in order to tame the idiosyncrasies of the journal and to profit from its cultural capital, the National Socialist Propaganda Ministry took over its funding from the beginning of 1934. This led to changes in personnel and content with Prince Rohan being forced out of the editorial position in 1934, perhaps because his conception of a European union with its heart in an Austrian-centred *Großdeutschland* did not accord with the neo-Prussianism of the National Socialist regime. Rohan went on to be a member of the illegal Austrian Nationalsozialistische Deutsche Arbeiterpartei (NSDAP) and a Sturmabteilung (SA) brigade, and he opposed the 1938 *Anschluss*, having favoured a Rome-based alliance of fascist Italians, independent National Socialist Austrians and Nazi Germans.[104] He was replaced in 1934 by an NSDAP deputy, Freiherr von Freytagh-Loringhoven, whose revamped publication gave pride of place that year to a Goebbels speech, given before the Hungarian section of the European Kulturbund.[105] From then on the publication became ever more closely aligned with the National Socialist regime and foreign authors were no longer permitted to submit articles that were in any way critical of the German government's foreign policy.[106] The Europäischer Kulturbund also folded in 1934, ostensibly due to disagreements between Hungarian and Czech representatives regarding questions of national minorities but no doubt also due to the supervision that such a supposedly 'open' civil society group could expect to be exercised by its National Socialist backers. Nevertheless, the *Europäische*

Revue continued to be published until 1944, providing space and a livelihood for non-party writers such as future German president Theodor Heuss and his colleague at the formerly left-liberal *Frankfurter Zeitung*, Dolf Sternberger. In the *Revue* they could publish nonconformist cultural commentary, even after they had been forced out of their prominent positions in public life.[107]

Paeschke made clear that he was most influenced by the earlier editions of the *Europäische Revue* before it was policed by the National Socialist regime. A number of the most important contributors to *Merkur* started out with this publication after 1933, however, and their experiences during the years of Nazi rule are not insignificant in explaining the intellectual heritage behind *Merkur*. Certainly Moras and another of the most prominent early contributors to the post-war journal, Herbert von Borch, wrote articles after 1933 that would not have easily fit with a pro-European agenda in the post-1945 period. In an article called 'The Costs of Multilateralism' of September 1935, Moras gave a scornful appraisal of the League of Nations, arguing that its 'only principle of unity is the fiction of a German danger' and that the 'breakdown of the "collective system" had long overwhelmed the elements of a genuine union of Europe'.[108] Of course, interwar Europeanists from across the ideological spectrum, including leftists such as Georges Duhamel criticized the League as the guardian of an unsustainable status quo that masked deep-seated unities and affinities among Europeans.[109] However, Moras went on to contend that with the Flandin Plan of 1936, which advocated a League of Nations Army for Europe and a series of mutual assistance pacts, the French were pushing forward 'the construction of a universal *Überstaat*' and attempting to pour 'the new wine of an European *Lebenswille*' into 'the old, porous wineskins of an imperialistic nationalism'. By contrast, he argued in May of 1937, 'A retrospective of the European politics of the last four years, as presented in this journal, shows how carefully German foreign policy has been developed out of the principle of equal rights and of an honest settlement'.[110] Writing in November 1936 Herbert von Borch echoed such sentiments, criticizing Britain, France and Russia for bringing ideology into foreign policy by speaking up for democracy, when really foreign policy should simply be concerned with securing the 'necessities of life for the peoples'. He contrasted these countries' foreign policies with Italy's in an article of December 1937, 'Risorgimento, Imperium, Europa', in which he defended Italy's new role as the 'good European' arguing that its actions in Abyssinia, first invading the country and then merging it with other Italian colonies in East Africa did not impede it assuming this role. For Italy had 'overcome the injustices of Versailles that have hampered Europe through its own power, by winning colonial *Lebensraum*'.[111]

It is, of course, very difficult to situate such contributions. While it could be argued that they show elements of continuity with what had been written before 1933, we should remember that articles written during the National Socialist period were heavily censored and hardly performed the same function as journal articles that were supposed to publicize the debates and resolutions of civil society associations such as the Europäische Kulturbund before 1933. Therefore, rather than offer a detailed analysis of the output of *Merkur's* editors after 1933, I turn instead to their biographical details from this period, which may offer a more revealing background to *Merkur's* project than post-1933 writings that did not necessarily represent the authors' most meaningful activity at this time.

The Biographies of the *Merkur* Editors after 1933

It should be said that the biographies of both editors after 1933 are murky. This is particularly the case with Joachim Moras, who may have had more to hide than his future colleague, Hans Paeschke. Apart from editing the *Revue*, Moras continued to be active among international networks of intellectuals after 1933, working within the Europäische Schriftsteller Vereinigung (ESV), a kind of anti-PEN organization made up of 'collaborating' writers, although led by the doctor and poet Hans Carossa, who has been counted among the 'inner émigrés' by some experts.[112] It seems that Moras attended the 'Poets' Conference' organized in Weimar in 1941 under the aegis of this group, which received the patronage of Josef Goebbels and his Propaganda Ministry.[113] Moras appears to have firmed up connections with authors such as Ernest Gimenez Caballero, a minister in Franco's government whose work he promised to publish and who represented a southern European form of fascism, more Catholic than the German version.[114] Thus, Moras's connections may imply his presence among the 'imagined community' of inner émigrés that was made up of intellectuals, conservative politicians and industrialists who collaborated or at least offered no direct opposition to Nazi rule. However, one might argue that his presence among ESV members was to be expected given the political orientation of *Revue* journalists even before 1933.

Paeschke's biography is somewhat more visible although again does not allow for easy interpretation. Paeschke had worked as secretary to Otto Grautoff, editor of the *Deutsch-Französische Rundschau* and founder of the Deutsch-Französische Gesellschaft (DFG), an organization later taken over by Otto Abetz from 1932 to 1934 and regarded by Guido Müller as one of the most important civil society groups in interwar Europe alongside the Europäische Kulturbund.[115] This organization was responsible for a number of important civil society initiatives in interwar Europe, not least facilitating letter-writing exchanges between fifteen thousand schoolchildren, school exchanges for over a thousand pupils and university exchanges for hundreds of students between 1928 and 1932.[116] It was also an arena within which Paeschke would have met many of the liberal and conservative intellectuals and politicians engaged in Franco-German rapprochement who were often connected with the *Europäische Revue* and who went on to contribute to *Merkur* in the post-war years. These included some of Paeschke's closest associates such as Arnold Bergstraesser and Ernst Robert Curtius but also renowned writers and politicians from across Europe including Paul Valéry, André Gide, Karl Jaspers and Richard Coudenhove-Kalergi.[117]

Paeschke was never a prolific writer despite having worked since 1936 as a journalist, going on to edit the *Neue Rundschau* between 1939 and 1944. Between 1937 and 1941 he was a member of the Reichsschrifttumskammer (RSK) – a part of Josef Goebbels's Board of Culture (Reichskulturkammer) that controlled intellectual life in Germany – as were most German authors who wished to publish. However in 1941, he seems to have taken advantage of a provision that allowed occasional writers to remain outside of this organization, as a letter from the President of the RSK reveals. As his lapidary entries in the RSK *Fragebogen* (questionnaire) and an accompanying curriculum vitae attest, he also never joined the National Socialist Party.[118] He did, nevertheless, serve in the Second World War in Toulon, although little is known about his experiences there.[119]

Yet, a number of clues suggest that his loyalty to the regime was less than wholehearted. He was a member of the notoriously unreliable Abwehr (German military intelligence service), whose mercurial director, Admiral Canaris, emerges in recent historiography as a consistent saboteur of the German war effort. It appears likely that Canaris leaked details of Operation Sealion, Germany's planned land invasion of Britain in 1940; failed to notify High Command when he learned of the Allies' Operation Torch landing in North Africa in late 1942; and misled Hitler regarding Italian Prime Minister Badoglio's intentions to stay in the war after Mussolini's overthrow, with the effect that the Italian battle fleet was turned over to Britain rather than Germany.[120] Paeschke's chief within the *Spionageabwehr* or Abwehr III (espionage division) was Colonel Egbert von Bentivegni, a traditionalist Prussian officer, who conspired with Colonel Erwin von Lahousen and Canaris in the 20 July assassination attempt that led to Canaris's gruesome execution.[121] It seems reasonable to assume, then, that Paeschke, having sought employment with one of the least loyal military organizations in the Third Reich, shared the aristocratic, officer-class distaste for the Nazis widespread among Abwehr operatives: an impression supported by Kurt Scheel, the current assistant editor of *Merkur* and a colleague and friend of Paeschke's.[122] Indeed, Paeschke's nonconformism saw him briefly transferred to the Eastern Front: his decision in wartime to marry a Frenchwoman, a naturalized noble Russian émigré no less, causing his superiors great alarm.[123]

That Paeschke was chosen, furthermore, in 1946, to be the editor of the predominant French cultural magazine in the German language, *Lancelot. Der Bote aus Frankreich* suggests that he had made a favourable impression on French contacts during the war years.[124] It appears likely that Paeschke was well connected among the same French circles that had been prominent in the Franco-German cultural exchanges of the interwar period, and which shared a common anti-republicanism with their German counterparts. Although an atheist, Paeschke told the journalist and author Paul Assall that he had been influenced by the *renouveau catholique* (Catholic renewal) movement in France in the early 1930s rather than supporting the Popular Front movement. This movement, as suggested earlier in the chapter, gave birth to various forms of political activism, some of which were decidedly hostile to the republican political authorities in France and Europe during the interwar period.

Thus, Paeschke should not be characterized as a supporter of the French Republic, defending it against the National Socialist government, as German exiles on the left had done in the 1930s. However, he did not need to be to find congenial company among French intellectuals and politicians active in associational life in the interwar and Second World War periods. As Julian Jackson has shown, the Republic had 'few friends' by 1940: not only Vichy politicians but also resisters including General De Gaulle refused to identify themselves with it.[125] As the next chapter will suggest, much of the impetus for post-Second World War European integration emerged from groups that had not only been anti-Nazi during the war years but which were also long-term opponents of the political settlement in interwar Europe. These groups sought to revive a European unity they believed split apart by the proliferation of democratic nation-states after 1918. Again, then, they suggest that civil society organizations worked for European unity before 1945 but not necessarily for a liberal democratic united Europe.

*****

Viewed against the background of the post-1933 scene, it may appear that the resurrection of culture that was commented upon in West Germany after the Second World War was remarkable. However, as has been suggested, it built on a vibrant interwar print media culture not only evident in Weimar Germany but across Europe. This media culture was not merely nationally organized but, in cases such as the *Europäische Revue*, addressed a transnational audience based around the Europäischer Kulturbund, whose members were conceived as a fledgling European civil society that met at international congresses and interacted via reciprocal invitations issued between local Kulturbund branches. As we will see, many of the connections formed in the interwar period via such organizations endured through the war years, or were revived after 1945, and provided the basis of post-war co-operations between European elites.

This history details important aspects of the interwar cultural and intellectual history that lay behind the surge in support for European integration evident in civil society and in the print media after the Second World War. Certainly European unity and disunity, integration and de-integration were topics not only discussed after 1945 but debated widely between 1918 and 1933. However, whereas pro-European groups have often been described as having their roots in a wartime resistance movement, which sought to overthrow the dictatorships making war in 1940s Europe and replace them with democratic regimes, we have seen, and will continue to see, that support for European integration had a longer and more complicated intellectual heritage. For, the organizations focused on here were civil society groups that agitated for European unity, yet their members were not uncomplicatedly pro-democratic. Rather, these members outlined visions of Europe that, they hoped, would restructure the mass societies they encountered in interwar Europe. They looked for a new form of political leadership not rooted in the parliamentary democratic mandate granted to national political parties but rather exercised by a self-selecting elite of aristocrats, intellectuals and those whose leadership abilities were proven by military experience.

As has been stressed, such arguments for Europe were not peculiar to Germany but rather had a wide currency in a variety of European states during the interwar period. Indeed, they were developed chiefly through transnational conversation and encounter. Such a(n open) dialogue between Europeans was often not possible after 1933 as people's freedoms to travel and socialize were curtailed. Nevertheless, as the preceding section has suggested, certain networks endured, which facilitated cooperation between Europeans who wished to work for an integration of their continent. The following chapter traces how these conceptions of Europe developed during the war and post-war years, again through a variety of transnational networks that operated largely secretively between 1939 and 1945 and more openly after 1945, particularly via media such as the resurgent genre of cultural journals.

Notes

1. D. Bark and D. Gress, *A History of West Germany, Vol. 1: From Shadow to Substance 1945–1963* (Oxford: Blackwell, 1989) p. 141. See also E. Janik, '"The Golden Hunger Years": Music and Superpower Rivalry in Occupied Berlin', in *German History* 22/1, (2004) 76–89; L. Freede, '"Botschafter der Musik": The Berlin Philharmonic Orchestra and the Role of Classical Music in Post-War German Identity', in *Modern Humanities Research Association Working Papers*, 2, (2007) 23–24.
2. T. Adorno, 'Auferstehung der Kultur in Deutschland?', in *Frankfurter Hefte* 5/5 (1950) 469–77.
3. Bark and Gress, *History of West Germany*, p. 156.
4. See U. Puschner, '*Der Ruf*. Deutschland in Europa (1946–1949)', F. Beilecke, 'Von Europa der Dritten Kraft zur Weltregierung. Ursprünge und diskursive Ausprägungen der Europa-Thematik in *Die Wandlung* (1945–1949)', M. Grunewald, 'Die *Frankfurter Hefte*: Eine Stimme der europäischen Föderalisten', T. Keller, '*Der Monat*. Zwischen Verwestlichung und Europäisierung', in M. Grunewald (ed.), *Der Europadiskurs in den deutschen Zeitschriften (1945–1955)* (Berne: Peter Lang, 2001). Also M. Hochgeschwender, 'Congress for Cultural Freedom' in J. Spalek, K. Feilchenfeldt and S. Hawrylchak, *Deutschsprachige Exilliteratur seit 1933*, Vol. 3, *USA*, part 3 (Berne and Munich: Francke, 2002).
5. S. Schoelzel, 'Pressepolitik in der französischen Zone' in F. Knipping et el (eds), *Frankreichs Kulturpolitik in Deutschland, 1945–1950* (Tübingen: Attempto, 1987) pp. 195–96.
6. Quoted in M. Reitmayer, 'Kulturzeitschriften' in D. Münkel and J. Schwarzkopf (eds), *Geschichte als Experiment: Studien zu Politik, Kultur und Alltag im 19. und 20. Jahrhundert* (Frankfurt am Main: Campus, 2004) p. 66.
7. Deutsches Literaturarchiv (DLA), Marbach, A: Merkur, TNL Paeschke, H. Paeschke, 'Exposé zur Situation des Merkur', 1955.
8. Beilecke, '*Die Wandlung*', in Grunewald, *Europadiskurs in den deutschen Zeitschriften*, pp. 121–48.
9. For more on the *Frankfurter Hefte*, see M. Miller, *The Origins of Christian Democracy: Politics and Confession in Modern Germany* (Ann Arbor: University of Michigan Press, 2012); A. Lienkamp, 'Socialism out of Christian Responsibility. The German Experiment of Left Catholi-

cism', in G.-R. Horn and E. Gerard (eds), *Left Catholicism: Catholics and Society in Western Europe at the Point of Liberation* (Leuven: University of Leuven Press, 2001) pp. 196–227.
10. See Puschner, '*Ruf*', Grunewald, '*Frankfurte Hefte*', and Keller, '*Der Monat*', in Grunewald, *Europadiskurs*, pp. 105–121, 219–44, 245–82; S. Mandel, *Group 47: The Reflected Intellect* (Carbondale and Edwardsville: Southern Illinois University Press, 1973); S. Parkes and J. White, *The Gruppe 47 Fifty Years On: A Re-Appraisal of Its Literary and Political Significance* (Amsterdam: Rodopi, 1999); F.S. Saunders, *Who Paid the Piper? The CIA and the Cultural Cold War* (London: Granta, 1999).
11. DLA, Redaktionsarchiv des *Merkur* Zeitschrift, D: Merkur, Letter to Hans Paeschke of 16 June 1952.
12. See for instance, Enno Stahl, 'Merkur im freien Fall' at: www.satt.org/gesellschaft/03_12_merkur.html
13. P. Anderson, 'A New Germany?', in *New Left Review* 57 (May–June, 2009) 5–40, esp. 29–33.
14. H.-M. Bock, 'Die fortgesetzte Modernisierung des Konservatismus: *Merkur: Deutsche Zeitschrift für Europäisches Denken* 1947 bis 1957', in Grunewald, *Europadiskurs*, p. 150.
15. Paeschke, *Kontinuität und Wandel: 35 Jahre Zeitschrift "Merkur": Erfahrungsbericht*, (Marbach, 1983), Audio Recording, DLA; A: Merkur, Teilnachlass (TNL) Paeschke, 'Zeitgenossen: Hans Paeschke and Paul Assall'. As the list of contributors from Habermas to Lyotard cited above suggests, the journal clearly became a forum for intellectuals from across the political spectrum.
16. DLA, D: Merkur, 'Zugehörige Materialien', Paeschke, 'Rundfunkmanuskript' and Paeschke, *Kontinuität und Wandel*, Audio Recording.
17. Grunewald, 'Deutsche Intellektuelle als Vorläufer des "Geistes von Locarno". Die *Neue Rundschau* und Frankreich zwischen 1919 und 1925' in *Recherches Germaniques* 18 (Summer, 1988) 66–83.
18. Bock, '"Das Junge Europa", Das "Andere Europa" und Das "Europa der weißen Rasse". Diskurstypen in der *Europäischen Revue* 1925-1939', in Grunewald and Bock (eds), *Der Europadiskurs in den deutschen Zeitschriften (1933–1939)* (Berne: Peter Lang, 1999) pp. 324–26.
19. P. Bourdieu, *The Field of Cultural Production: Essays on Art and Literature* (New York: Columbia University Press, 1993) pp. 38–39.
20. J. Wilke, *Grundzüge der Medien- und Kommunikationsgeschichte. Von den Anfängen bis ins 20. Jahrhundert* (Cologne: Böhlau, 2000) pp. 266, 343–53.
21. C. Ross, *Media and the Making of Modern Germany: Mass Communications, Society, and Politics from the Empire to the Third Reich* (Oxford: Oxford University Press, 2008) p. 227.
22. Grunewald and Bock, 'Zeitschriften als Spiegel intellektueller Milieus. Vorbemerkungen zur Analyse eines ungeklärten Verhältnisses' in Grunewald and Bock (eds), *Le Milieu Intellectuel de Gauche en Allemagne, sa Presse et ses Réseaux (1890–1960)* (Berne: Peter Lang, 2002) p. 24.
23. Grunewald and Bock, 'Zeitschriften als Spiegel intellektueller Milieus', in Grunewald and Bock, *Das linke Intellektuellenmilieu in Deutschland*, pp. 24–31.
24. F. Schwarz, 'Literarisches Zeitgespräch im Dritten Reich: Dargestellt an der Zeitschrift *Neue Rundschau*', in *Börsenblatt für den deutschen Buchhandel* 27/51, (1971) 1409–1508.
25. Grunewald, '*Neue Rundschau* und Frankreich', in *Recherches Germaniques*, 83.
26. F. Beilecke, '"Austausch zwischen den Geistern Frankreichs und Deutschlands". Die Berliner "Neue Rundschau" und das französischer Kulturleben in der Weimarer Republik', in Bock (ed.), *Französische Kultur im Berlin der Weimarer Republik. Kulturelle Austausch und diplomatische Beziehungen* (Tübingen: Narr, 2005) p. 222.
27. Grunewald, '*Neue Rundschau* und Frankreich', 69, 77–78.
28. J. Wardhaugh, R. Leiserowitz and C. Bailey, 'Intellectual Dissidents and the Construction of European Spaces', in M. Conway and K.K. Patel (eds), *Europeanization in the Twentieth Century: Historical Approaches* (Houndmills: Palgrave, 2010) p. 32.

29. I.U. Paul, 'Konservative Milieus und die *Europäische Revue* (1925–1944)', in Grunewald and U. Puschner (eds), *Le Milieu Intellectuel Conservateur en Allemagne, sa Presse, et ses Réseaux (1890–1960)* (Berne: Peter Lang, 2003) p. 515.
30. I. Belitz, *Befreundung mit dem Fremden. Die Deutsch-Französische Gesellschaft in den deutschfranzösischen Kultur- und Gesellschaftsbeziehungen der Locarno-Ära. Programme und Protagonisten der transnationalen Verständigung zwischen Pragmatismus und Idealismus* (Frankfurt am Main: Peter Lang, 1997), p. 97; Bock, 'Weimarer Intellektuelle und das Projekt Deutsch-Französischer Gesellschaftsverflechtung', in R. Hohls, I. Schröder and H. Siegrist (eds), *Europa und die Europäer. Quellen und Essays zur modernen europäischen Geschichte* (Stuttgart, Franz Steiner, 2005) pp. 422–24.
31. Wardhaugh et al, 'Intellectual Dissidents', p. 26.
32. E. Wistrich, *The United States of Europe* (London and New York: Routledge, 1994) pp. 21–22.
33. F. Niess, *Die europäische Idee – aus dem Geist des Widerstands* (Frankfurt am Main: Suhrkamp, 2001) pp. 24–5, 27; and W. Loth, *Der Weg nach Europa: Geschichte der europäischen Integration 1939–1957* (Göttingen: Vanderhoeck und Ruprecht 2nd ed., 1991) p. 13.
34. G. Müller, *Europäische Gesellschaftsbeziehungen nach dem ersten Weltkrieg* (Munich: Oldenbourg, 2005) p. 316.
35. Ibid., pp. 327–40.
36. See G. Müller, 'France and Germany After the Great War: Businessmen, Intellectuals and Artists in Nongovernmental European Networks', in J. Gienow-Hecht and F. Schumacher (eds), *Culture and International History* (New York and Oxford: Berghahn Books, 2003) pp. 102–4; and G. Müller, 'Von Hugo von Hofmannthals 'Traum des Reiches" zum Europa unter nationalsozialistischer Herrschaft – Die "Europäische Revue" 1925–1936/44', in H.-C. Kraus (ed.), *Konservative Zeitschriften zwischen Kaiserreich und Diktatur. Fünf Fallstudien* (Berlin: Duncker und Humblot, 2003) pp. 162–3 for subscription figures. Readership based on Paeschke's estimates in DLA Marbach, D: Merkur, Letter to E.R. Curtius, 30 July 1948.
37. H.W. Smith, *German Nationalism and Religious Conflict: Culture, Ideology, Politics, 1870–1914* (Princeton: Princeton University Press, 1995) pp. 19, 34–40, 63.
38. D. Pöpping, *Abendland: Christliche Akademiker und die Utopie der Antimoderne 1900–1945* (Berlin: Metropol, 2002) pp. 15, 66–70, 171–72.
39. V. Conze, *Das Europa der Deutschen: Ideen von Europa in Deutschland zwischen Reichstradition und Westorientierung* (Munich: Oldenbourg, 2005) p. 348.
40. Pöpping, *Abendland*, pp. 143, 171–72.
41. I.U. Paul, 'Konservative Milieus und die *Europäische Revue* (1925–1944)', in Grunewald and Bock, *Le Milieu Intellectuel Conservateur*, pp. 517–29; Müller, *Europäische Gesellschaftsbeziehungen*, p. 445.
42. H. Mommsen, *From Weimar to Auschwitz: Essays in German History* (Cambridge: Cambridge University Press, 1991) pp. 82–83.
43. A. Weber, 'Der Deutsche im geistigen Europa', ER II/11 (February, 1927) 277–78.
44. L. Romier, 'Europäische Solidarität' in ER II/7 (October, 1926); P.D. La Rochelle, 'Kapitalismus, Kommunismus und europäischer Geist', in ER III/1 (April, 1927). See also J. Jackson, *France: The Dark Years 1940–1944* (Oxford: Oxford University Press, 2001) pp. 53, 78, and 205; M. Beale, *The Modernist Enterprise: French Elites and the Threat of Modernity 1901–1940* (Stanford: Stanford University Press, 1999).
45. E. Lederer, 'Russland in der Weltpolitik', in *NR* 37/1, (1926) pp. 566, 570.
46. U. von Hirschhausen, 'From Minority Protection to Border Revisionism: The European Nationality Congress, 1925–38', in Conway and Patel, *Europeanization in the Twentieth Century*, p. 87.
47. R. Kuczynski, 'Wirtschaftlicher Zusammenschluss Europas', in *Die Neue Rundschau*, 37/1, (1926) 541–42.

48. Wardhaugh, Leiserowitz and Bailey, 'Intellectual Dissidents', in Conway and Patel, *Europeanization in the Twentieth Century*, p. 33.
49. See La Rochelle, 'Kapitalismus, Kommunismus, und europäischer Geist', in *ER* III/1, 67.
50. K. McDermott and J. Agnew, *The Comintern: A History of International Communism from Lenin to Stalin* (New York: St. Martin's Press, 1997); R. Daniels (ed.), *A Documentary History of Communism and the World: From Revolution to Collapse* (Hanover: University of New England Press, 1994) pp. 25, 32–34, 60–63.
51. L. Romier, 'Die Zukunft Europas', in *ER* 1/2 (1925) 211.
52. La Rochelle, 'Kapitalismus, Kommunismus, und europäischer Geist', *ER* III/1, 67.
53. J. Pindar, 'Europe in the World Economy 1920–1970', in Carlo Cipolla (ed.), *The Fontana Economic History of Europe. Contemporary Economies Part One* (Glasgow: Collins, 1976) pp. 326–27.
54. H. Ziegler, 'Nation und Politik', *ER* 2/7 (October, 1926) p. 41.
55. H. James, *The German Slump. Politics and Economics 1924–1936* (Oxford: Clarendon Press, 1986) p. 138.
56. D. Aldcroft, *From Versailles to Wall Street 1919–1929* (Berkeley: University of California Press, 1977) p. 93.
57. C. Kindleberger, *The World in Depression 1929–1939* (Berkeley: University of California Press, 1973) pp. 139, 293–4.
58. C.J. Gignoux, 'Frankreich-Amerika und die Vereinigten Staaten von Europa', *ER* V/5, (August, 1929) 337.
59. D. Peukert, *The Weimar Republic: The Crisis of Classical Modernity* (New York: Hill and Wang, 1989) pp. 7–11.
60. J.O. y Gasset, 'Kosmopolitanismus', in *NR*, (1926, Vol. 2) 5–6.
61. P.M. Lützeler, *Plädoyers für Europa. Stellungnahmen deutschsprachiger Schriftsteller 1915–1949* (Frankfurt am Main: Fischer, 1987).
62. U. Frevert, 'Europeanizing Germany's Twentieth Century', in *History and Memory* 17.1/2 (2005) 87–116, esp. 94–98.
63. S. Malinowski, *Vom König zum Führer. Soziale Niedergang und politische Radikalisierung im deutschen Adel zwischen Kaiserreich und NS-Staat* (Berlin: Akademie, 2003) pp. 305–06.
64. Rohan, 'Westeuropa', *ER* V/5, (August, 1929) 308–9.
65. L. Valla, 'Sinn und Begriff Europas', in *ER* IV/3 (June, 1928) 161.
66. This, of course, is not to suggest that excavating the variegated pre-1945 history of the Franco-German 'axis' is not valuable and necessary work. See C. Fischer, *Europe between Dictatorship and Democracy: 1900–1945*, (Chichester: Wiley-Blackwell, 2011) pp. 329–30.
67. Grunewald, 'Neue Rundschau', *Recherches germaniques*, 67.
68. R. Spaulding, *Osthandel und Ostpolitik: German Foreign Trade Policies in Eastern Europe from Bismarck to Adenauer* (Providence and Oxford, 1997) pp. 477–79.
69. R. Riedl, 'Die Wirtschaftliche Neuorganisation Europas', *ER* VI/4 (April, 1930) 256.
70. See Rohan, 'Zukunftsfragen deutscher Aussenpolitik', *ER* V/6 (September, 1929) 368–69 and 'Europa und der Donauraum', *ER* VIII/5 (1932) 266.
71. M. Clauss, 'Europäisches Triumvirate', *ER* V/11 (November, 1929) 388.
72. J. Elvert, *Mitteleuropa! Deutsche Pläne zur europäischen Neuordnung (1918–1945)* (Stuttgart: Franz Steiner, 1999) pp. 106–7, 119–21.
73. Müller, 'Europäische Revue', in Kraus, *Konservative Zeitschriften*, p. 158.
74. Ibid., p. 159.
75. H. Ziegler, 'Nation und Politik', *ER* II/7 (1926) 39. See also P. Wust, 'Die Krise der westeuropäischen Humanitätsidee', *ER* I/2 (1926); Rohan, 'Zukunftsfragen deutscher Außenpolitik' in *ER* V/6 (September, 1929) 375

76. Rohan, 'Glosse des Herausgebers: Österreich', in *ER* I/12 (1926) 413; Rohan, 'Vom Mythos der Totalen Nation im Dritten Reich', *ER* IX/4 (1933) 195; Malinowski, *Vom König zum Führer*, p. 256.
77. Peukert, *Weimar Republic*, p. 201.
78. On this see A. Smith, *The Ethnic Origins of Nations* (Oxford: Blackwell, 1986); R. Brubaker, *Citizenship and Nationhood in France and Germany* (Cambridge MA: Harvard University Press, 1992).
79. Hirschhausen, 'From Minority Protection to Border Revisionism', in Conway and Patel, *Europeanization in the Twentieth Century*, p. 103.
80. Ibid., pp. 90–100.
81. P. Schiemann, 'Nationalitätenprobleme', *ER* IV/6 (1928) 460.
82. Schiemann, 'Das Randstaatproblem', *ER* II/9 (1926) 162–67.
83. W. Hasselblatt, 'Der Baltische Deutsche in der Nationalitätenfrage', *ER* III/6 (1927) 424.
84. 'Entwurf eines Minderheitenstatuts', *ER* VI/6, (1930), 456–61.
85. Rohan, 'Zukunftsfragen deutscher Außenpolitik', 369; Rohan, 'Westeuropa', 317.
86. Ibid., p. 372.
87. Malinowski, *Vom König zum Führer*, p. 201.
88. Rohan, 'Fascismus und Europa' in *ER* II/2 (1926) 122.
89. Müller, *Europäische Gesellschaftsbeziehungen*, p. 377.
90. R. Griffin, 'Europe for the Europeans: Fascist Myths of the New Order 1922–1992', *Occasional Paper No. 1,* Humanities Research Centre, Oxford Brookes University, 1993.
91. Müller, *Europäische Gesellschaftsbeziehungen*, p. 452.
92. C. Schmitt, 'Die Wendung zum totalen Staat' in *ER* VII/4 (April, 1931) 248–49.
93. E. Haas, 'The Late Flowering and Early Fading of German Nationalism', in J. Brady, B. Crawford and S. Wiliarty (eds), *The Postwar Transformation of Germany: Democracy, Prosperity and Nationhood* (Ann Arbor: University of Michigan, 1999) p. 300.
94. James, *German Slump*, p. 74.
95. M. Richter, 'From State Culture to Citizen Culture: Political Parties and the Postwar Transformation of Political Culture in Germany', in Brady et al., *Postwar Transformation of Germany*, pp. 125–26.
96. F.G. Hestadt, 'Der aristokratische Kulturbegriff' in *ER* V/9 (December, 1929) 632–33.
97. Peukert, *Weimar Republic*, p. 16.
98. Müller, *Europäische Gesellschaftsbeziehungen*, p. 445.
99. Paeschke to G. Benn, 1 July 1948, in G. Benn, H. Paeschke and J. Moras (ed. H. Hof), *Briefe Band VII. Briefwechsel mit dem Merkur 1948–1956* (Stuttgart: Klett-Cotta, 2004) p. 7.
100. DLA, D: Merkur, Letter from Ernst Robert Curtius to Paeschke, 28 July 1947.
101. S. Voss, 'Sich auf hohem Niveau unterhalten lassen', in *Börsenblatt für den Deutschen Buchhandel* 46/7 (23 January 1990) 218–19.
102. DLA, D: Merkur, Paeschke to Curtius, 17 August 1947.
103. Paul, '*Europäische Revue*', in Grunewald and Bock, *Le Milieu Intellectuel Conservateur*, p. 536.
104. Müller, 'Europäische Revue', in Kraus, *Konservative Zeitschriften*, pp. 174–78.
105. Bock, '*Europäische Revue*', in Grunewald, *Europadiskurs*, pp. 324–26.
106. Ibid., pp. 324–25.
107. Ibid., pp. 324–29.
108. J. Moras, 'Kosten des Multilateralismus', in *ER* XI/9 (1935) 607, 611.
109. See Wardhaugh, Leiserowitz and Bailey, 'Intellectual Dissidents', in Conway and Patel, *Europeanization in the Twentieth Century*.
110. Moras, 'Kosten des Multilateralismus', 611; 'Zwischen Nil und Rhein', in *ER* XII (1936) 341; 'Besinnung', in *ER* XIII (1937) 398.
111. See H. von Borch, 'Die Ideolisierung der europäischen Außenpolitik', in *ER* XII (1936) 907–08 and 'Risorgimento, Imperium, Europa', in *ER* XIII (1937) 998.

112. See E. Klee, *Das Kulturlexikon zum Dritten Reich. Wer war was vor und nach 1945* (Frankfurt am Main: Fischer, 2007).
113. F.-R. Hausmann, 'Kollaborierende Intellektuelle in Weimar – Die 'Europäische Schriftsteller-Vereinigung' als 'Anti-P.E.N.-Club", in H. Seemann (ed.), *Europa in Weimar. Visionen eines Kontinents* (Göttingen: Wallstein, 2008) pp. 399–422.
114. Hausmann, *"Dichte, Dichter tage nicht!". Die Europäische Schriftsteller-Vereinigung in Weimar, 1941–1948* (Frankfurt am Main: Vittorio Klostermann, 2004) pp. 75–76.
115. Bock, 'Modernisierung des Konservatismus', in Grunewald, *Europadiskurs*, pp. 153–54; Müller, *Europäische Gesellschaftsbeziehungen*, p. 468; DLA Marbach, A: Merkur, TLN Paeschke, 'Zeitgenossen: Paeschke and P. Assall'.
116. Belitz, *Befreundung mit dem Fremden*, p. 164.
117. Ibid., p. 131.
118. Bundesarchiv (BA), Berlin-Lichterfelde, Reichsschrifttumskammerakte, R 56 – V/16. See Paeschke's Mitgliedausweis, Lebenslauf and the letter from the Präsident der Reichsschrifttumskammer of 18 March 1941.
119. The files kept by the National Socialists on Paeschke and now housed in the Bundesarchiv do not mention his duties in France. Nor do Paeschke's literary remains located at the German Literature Archives in Marbach or the records at the Archives of the French Occupation in Colmar.
120. R. Bassett, *Hitler's Spy Chief: The Wilhelm Canaris Mystery* (London: Weidenfeld and Nicolson, 2005) pp. 194–45, 247; and D. Johnson, *Righteous Deception: German Officers Against Hitler* (Westport CT: Prager, 2001) pp. 19–20.
121. Bassett, *Hitler's Spy Chief*, p. 111; and J. Waller, *The Unseen War in Europe: Espionage and Conspiracy in the Second World War* (London and New York: I.B. Tauris, 1996) p. 334.
122. Scheel stated that National Socialism was regarded by Paeschke as *'Pöbelherrschaft'* in an interview with the author, June 2007.
123. Scheel, interview, June 2007.
124. Bock, '*Merkur*', in Grunewald, *Europadiskurs*, p. 154.
125. Jackson, *The Dark Years*, p. 43.

Chapter 2

THE DEFENCE OF EUROPE IN MERKUR: DEUTSCHE ZEITSCHRIFT FÜR EUROPÄISCHES DENKEN

Baden-Baden has long been feted as 'Europe's Summer Capital' or the 'World Spa in the Black Forest'.[1] However, in the late 1940s, it did not seem such a playground for European elites to easily intermingle. The head of the French occupation forces, General Pierre Koenig, could enjoy the still excellent facilities on offer at his base in the Brenner's Parkhotel. Yet most Germans in the town were struggling to find enough food, failing until autumn 1948 to secure the 1550 calories per day set by the occupation authorities as a minimum requirement. With the French military requisitioning apartment blocks and enforcing gestures of submission such as saluting from the local population, the spa town did not look like an ideal case study of harmonious cooperation and co-existence between European neighbours.[2]

As the centre of the French Zone in Germany, Baden-Baden was, nevertheless, also an employment hub. It offered opportunities for the political figures who formed the early anti-fascist committees and revived party organizations after December 1945, as well as for former German military figures such as Walter Bargatsky, a member of the Nazi Party who had served with the German military in Paris and who became Baden-Baden's Police Chief in October 1945. He, like *Merkur's* editor, Hans Paeschke, was identified as being connected to the military opposition to Hitler and was valued by the French, having sought to prevent France's cultural treasures being brought back to Germany by the troops.[3] Indeed, a wide variety of Germans were employed by the French authorities to help with reconstruction and re-education, not least in the cultural sector. Perhaps the most famous employee in this capacity was Alfred Döblin, the expressionist author of *Berlin Alexanderplatz* and Catholic convert from Judaism who arrived out of Californian exile as a French cultural officer, even wearing the French uniform.[4] Others such as Paeschke were recruited because of their language skills and long-standing links with French and German cultural circles, as highlighted in the previous chapter. Paeschke was initially employed in 1946 as an editor of the bilingual *Lancelot* journal, which carried the 'Message from France' and was one of a number of high-circulation review journals including *Wort und Tat, Umschau* and *Dokumente* established in the early post-war period.[5] However, the ideological constraints of such contracted work were disagreeable to Paeschke, who left *Lancelot* to found *Merkur* in Baden-Baden in 1947, having received one of the first licences granted by the French for such an independent publishing venture.[6]

This chapter analyses the immediate post-war context in Germany, highlighting not only how German intellectuals sought to revive civil society associations after the fall of the Nazi dictatorship but also how the cultural policy of the occupying forces shaped the kind of civil society activity initiated in the German states. The focus is on the founding of *Merkur: Deutsche Zeitschrift für Europäisches Denken* as a case study of how a 'free press' was revived, of how civil society associations sought to exercise political influence, particularly regarding the issue of European integration, and of how European elites reestablished connections after the rupture of the war years. As will be argued, the European conversation developed in *Merkur* was rooted in the transnational European connections cultivated in the interwar years, particularly among liberal and conservative groups. These groups had often worked to overturn various forms of democratic 'mass rule' within the European nations and went on to collectively rework their positions in such publications as *Merkur* in the post-war period. Yet they continued to advocate European unity as a means of restraining what they saw as the innately divisive tendencies within democratic nation-states. I will draw attention to how conservatives' arguments for European integration changed, as the prospects for a neo-Habsburgian arrangement of Central Europe receded and the Cold War segmented the continent into East and West. However, I will also note the continuities between interwar agendas for *Mitteleuropa* and the abidingly Central European perspective of many conservatives, who, it will be suggested, were among the early architects of an *Ostpolitik* from the Right.

Denazification and the Revival of Cultural Life in the French Zone

The recruiting of Paeschke and the licensing of his journal by the French military authorities suggests that sympathies and networks existed between figures in the German and French militaries, in spite of the predominant atmosphere of hostility between the wartime enemies. Certainly numerous French leaders were aware of the reluctance with which certain senior German military officials had followed the orders of their National Socialist masters, not least because figures in the army such as Ernst Jünger had conveyed this impression to French cultural elites.[7] Jünger was not alone in his scepticism of his National Socialist superiors; rather his sentiments were shared by a number of senior military officers in France such as the Generals Speidel, Stülpnagel and Rommel who were implicated in the 20 July 1944 plot to assassinate Hitler. Indeed, as early as October 1943 Jünger had shared his *Der Friede* (*The Peace*) with these figures, outlining a peace plan within the frame of a united Europe.[8] Of course, not all of the French occupation forces would have been sympathetic to such conservative (if not Nazi) figures in the German military. Yet there was sufficient ideological breadth among French leaders – reflecting the chequered ideological background of 1930s and 1940s France – to enable cooperation between a variety of German and French groups and individuals, and not merely between members of the Resistance on either side. For the French military government boasted everything from communist- and socialist-inclined officials from the Resistance to those who were connected to the Christian Democrat MRP (Mouvement Républicain Populaire), Gaullists and even right-wing radicals who had served in high positions in the Vichy administration.[9]

These divisions on the French side perhaps informed the occupying power's denazification policy, which was never carried as far as in other zones because the French were wary of drawing the hard-and-fast distinction between guilty and innocent that, for instance, the Americans were outlining in their zone.[10] Moreover, French policy had to be improvised, due to the army's late arrival in the field. It was also deliberately anti-centralist, reflecting the long-held belief of French officials that southern and western Germans retained a more democratic outlook than northern Germans and, moreover, that a federal Germany would pose less of a threat than a centralized nation-state.[11] The initiative was thus handed to local French officials, who were supposed to grant licences to individuals rather than organizations or institutions.[12] This policy meant that personal contacts were all-important, allowing sympathies to develop between French officials and those Germans eager to contribute to a new, post-National Socialist public life. As the British General Consul explained, writing to the British Foreign Secretary, Ernest Bevin, at the start of 1948: 'there is a distinct tendency among senior French officials to work independently and individualistically without filing an account of what they are doing. This applies not just for the relations between the Zone and Paris, rather also for matters that play out between Baden-Baden and the provincial governors.'[13] The wilfulness of individual French officials seemed to go beyond even what the anti-centralist French military leaders desired, with Raymond Schmittlein, the General Director for Cultural Affairs in the French Zone complaining in a report of 30 January 1948 that: 'the *délégués supérieurs* at the moment do not seek to represent French decisions with regard to the Germans, rather – in which they make themselves the spokesmen of German objections – the German views against the French administration.'[14]

One result of the anti-centralist policies of the French occupying forces was that many Germans who would not have found publishing opportunities in the U.S. Zone were able to revive their literary careers in the French Zone. As the *New York Times* reported in October 1945, at least twenty-seven Germans dismissed from posts in the American Zone received employment in the French Zone.[15] Although the French claimed that this was largely due to clerical errors, it is not insignificant that two of those who resettled in the French Zone, having failed to get employment in U.S. or U.K. zones, were Konrad Adenauer and Carlo Schmid. They were significant players in Christian Democratic and Social Democratic politics who had not, however, left Germany as political exiles during the National Socialist years.[16] Indeed, Hans Paeschke recognized how much he benefited from the eclecticism of the French military government when in a 1982 interview he commented that *Merkur* might have been censored in the American Zone, as another cultural journal, *Der Ruf*, was in 1948.[17]

The successful establishment of *Merkur* was due to more than the mercurial nature of French officials on the ground though. As the first chapter illustrated, Paeschke had cultivated relationships with French cultural and political leaders since the early 1930s as Secretary to the Deutsch-Französische Gesellschaft and (probably) then as a counter-espionage agent in Toulon during the war years. Thus, when he launched *Merkur* as a venture that would restart a conversation between European cultural and political elites, he emphasized the role of a Franco-German rapprochement in this process. He made this clear in a letter requesting financial support from the High Commissioner of the French Zone, André François Poncet, within which he requested French help so that the journal could remain independent of party-political, religious or military interference.[18] It is not clear if Paeschke and Poncet knew one another from their shared time in Berlin in the 1930s, when Poncet was French Ambassador to Germany. Irrespective, as a centre-right politician and author who had written about German issues in the interwar period and who was well connected to diplomatic elites across Europe, Poncet moved in similar circles to Paeschke. He is thus likely to have been familiar with the sort of cultural enterprise Paeschke had in mind.[19] As I move through the chapter, I will seek to show how cooperation between certain Franco-German elites, not least those who had worked together in such conservative interwar civil society organizations as the Europäische Kulturbund, shaped debates about European integration after 1945.

The Policing and Sponsorship of Culture in the Post-war Period

The granting of a licence to Paeschke took place against a background of cultural rapprochement between the French and the Germans. A whole raft of cultural initiatives was introduced in the two years between the end of the war and the publication of *Merkur*. In 1946, university summer courses were held in Tübingen and Freiburg, with six hundred students from Germany, France and other nations attending. The same summer an exhibition called 'A Message from the French Youth' was sent around Germany by French youth groups and was visited by 120,000 Germans. Summer camps were held in the French Zone, which were attended by members of church and political groups, of whom 1,035 were French. French universities were persuaded to take a number of German students and French Institutes were founded at Freiburg, Tübingen, Mainz and Trier. Eight major exhibitions were held, including one illustrating the ties of Baden with France. Towns started twinning, mostly as a result of organizations such as the Franco-German Union in Ludwigshafen. Perhaps most importantly, in the context of the founding of *Merkur*, the International Bureau of Liaison and Documentation, set up in 1945 in Offenburg in Baden and staffed by a group of Catholics and Protestants, tried to increase understanding between the two nations by publishing a bilingual cultural journal called *Dokumente/Documents*.[20] As Paeschke recalled in a 1982 interview, *Merkur* was conceived in this spirit, the French originally intending the journal to be *Merkur der France*.[21]

The many initiatives launched by French and German politicians and citizens were part of a broader politicization of the cultural sphere within western Germany and across Europe. International congresses for intellectuals and artists abounded, as did government funding for cultural organizations and exhibitions. The United Nations Educational, Scientific and Cultural Organization (UNESCO) was established in 1946, under whose auspices intellectuals from either side of the emerging Cold War divide argued fiercely about the role of culture at the World Congress of Intellectuals in Wrocław in 1948.[22] The United States government was particularly concerned to promote its view of Western culture, which was, it contended, both the root and flower of a liberal democratic polity. Its State Department sponsored the 'Advancing American Art' exhibition that toured Europe and South America from 1946, and various American government agencies funded the Congress for Cultural Freedom (CCF) that was founded in 1950 in Berlin at a meeting which 118 intellectuals from twenty countries attended.[23] This organization, after receiving funding from the Central Intelligence Agency (CIA), opened offices in thirty-five countries and was supported by editors such as Lasky and Kogon, as well as pro-European politicians such as Carlo Schmid.[24] It functioned as an agent of the soft power of the United States, with its members publicizing the freedom of expression enjoyed by Western intellectuals and the censorship prevalent in the Soviet spheres of influence.

The existence of such cultural organizations as the CCF and the sponsorship they received suggests that cultural producers were particularly prized for their role in justifying the new democratic forms of government introduced by the allies and in cultivating the consent of the governed. This perhaps suggests that civil society had become as politicized as it appeared in the interwar analysis of Antonio Gramsci, who believed civil society elites formed part of a society's superstructure, within which hegemonic ideologies could be hatched.[25] However, as Pierre Bourdieu has argued, cultural producers often needed to assert their independence from political pressures as well as from commercial concerns in order to win influence, as their voices were only respected so long as they appeared to be above political and economic interests.[26] Editors such as Paeschke jealously guarded what they believed to be their editorial independence from political or financial masters. More than this, such editors advertised their publications as uniquely capable of achieving distance and perspective on day-to-day events in the political and cultural spheres. This did not mean they believed culture should not be politically engaged; quite the reverse, as Paeschke made clear at the opening conference of the Southwest German Cultural Circle arguing: 'that the accountability of the intelligentsia is an integral part of the public life of a nation, that intellect has a duty before society, and that the worst consequences of the denial of this function of the ""public spirit" ... is for all to see in Germany today.'[27] Nevertheless, for *Merkur* to be an effective voice in the contemporary 'pluralist society split up into interest groups', Paeschke argued that the journal had to be, 'free from connections to parties, churches and state institutions and also independent of the specific interests of publishing companies'. Here he was outlining his idealistic vision of a politically engaged but independent European civil society, made up of public intellectuals, 'who through their names and works [that were of] genuine European quality, would self-evidently represent accuracy and breadth', rather than narrow party or national loyalty.[28]

Staying Independent and Securing Funding: *Merkur* and Big Business

Paeschke's aspirations for the journal to be a disinterested and independent forum for cultural conversation may have been designed to set it apart from competitors such as the CIA-funded *Monat*, the left-Catholic *Frankfurter Hefte* and *Die Wandlung*, which was tied to Heidelberg academic circles. Paeschke argued that, whereas other journals 'propagated a programme of political and spiritual renewal in the form of theses and appeals (new federalism, new democracy, new Europe, World State),' *Merkur*, 'left [its] readers ... alone with contributions, whose diversity was not tied together around any programme'.[29] *Merkur* nevertheless required funding and therefore paymasters who might have a political agenda, particularly as the journal's editors did not aim for high circulation figures.[30] This proved a problem for them as the journal's complicated financial history suggests. *Merkur* started out being published by the Heller and Wegner Verlag, although Paeschke explained that the journal had bankrolled this organization for one and a half years, while it failed to publish a single book.[31] Paeschke turned to his assistant editor, Moras, to help with fundraising, although owing to Moras's history as editor of the *Europäische Revue*, it was only deemed safe to mention his involvement as assistant editor in the sixth issue.[32] In 1947, Moras, along with another ex-*Revue* contributor, Herbert von Borch, sought out funding from their former colleague at the *Revue* Alfred Weber, who secured support from the Heidelberg Institut für Sozial-und Staatswissenschaften at which another old colleague of Paeschke's and Kulturbund member, Arnold Bergstraesser, had also worked.³³ Through such negotiations, the institutional links between the interwar *Revue* and *Merkur*, and the enduring relationships between contributors at both publications, were reaffirmed.

As a more durable solution, Moras moved *Merkur*'s editorial seat from Baden-Baden to Stuttgart in 1948 and secured a publishing deal that was to last until 1962 with Deutsche Verlagsanstalt (DEVA), the company that had published the *Europäische Revue* until its collapse in 1944 and had also published *Deutsche Zukunft*, another forum for Paeschke's journalistic output in the late 1930s.³⁴ DEVA was a publishing company partially owned by the Bosch family that had also financially assisted the *Europäische Revue*. When one looks at the history of the Bosch Corporation it seems likely that the arrangement of 1948 developed out of relationships cultivated in the interwar period. The Bosch hierarchy appears to have moved in similar cultural milieux to the *Merkur* editors: conservative circles that had supported Brüning and von Papen before 1933 and whose relations with the Third Reich ranged from uneasy compromise and cooperation to non-engagement or even secretive opposition. For instance, Robert Bosch had been a friend of the Paneuropeanist Richard Coudenhove-Kalergi, had channelled money to the Confessing Church via the Lutheran Bishop Theophil Wurm of Württemberg, and found employment for the former Mayor of Leipzig and conservative politician Carl Goerdeler, who worked with the Allies against the National Socialists after he was blacklisted by them in 1937. Indeed, it appears that the Bosch Corporation may have facilitated a significant amount of anti-Nazi activity, with Bosch's successor Hans Walz maintaining links with the Goerdeler Circle and with the American Consul in Zurich Maurice W. Altaffer, who were working to bring down the regime in Germany.³⁵

The connections between Bosch and *Merkur* were one of a number of links between this journal, its predecessor the *Europäische Revue*, and big business. As editor of the *Revue*, Moras had been able to secure funding from Kulturbund members who represented concerns such as I.G. Farben, Bosch, the chemical company BASF, and the Luxembourg steel and iron producer ARBED. Indeed, the Cologne industrialist Otto Wolff, another of the *Revue*'s backers, explained his support for the venture when he asked the journal's founder, Prince Rohan, 'Where is the political idea with which we in Europe can stand up in opposition to Russian Bolshevism?'³⁶ In the late 1940s and early 1950s, Moras was once again an important figure in networks between business and cultural organizations as a member of the Cultural Circle of the Bundesverband der Deutschen Industrie (BDI), editing their *Jahresring: Beiträge zur deutschen Literatur und Kunst der Gegenwart*, and serving as a member of the organization's jury for awarding funding to writers.³⁷

As recent research has suggested, the BDI was a very active pressure group in the early Federal Republic. It drafted legislative proposals and sought to influence the policy-making process, not least in the area of European integration, where it supported the Organization for European Economic Cooperation (OEEC) developed under the auspices of the Marshall Plan, but opposed the European

Coal and Steel Community (ECSC) as excessively statist.[38] However, the Cultural Circle of the BDI also proved to be an eclectic supporter of the arts. It not only supported traditionalist ventures such as the restoration of church organs and the exhibiting of representational arts, but also funded abstract art exhibits and published authors such as Adorno, Andersch, Bachmann, Böll, Grass and Habermas in its *Jahresring* (Yearly Review), alongside the more right-wing authors it tended to favour.[39]

The priorities of such industrialists appeared, in many ways, to match those of the *Merkur* editors. As Jonathan Wiesen has illustrated, after 1945 German business leaders were keen to present themselves as 'nonconformists' who had long prized economic and political freedom against the collectivism and frenzied ideological commitment of mass parties such as the Nazis. Furthermore, even as they found it increasingly profitable to manufacture consumer goods to a mass market, they were eager to show that they did not pander to mass tastes. Instead they wished to educate the taste of the masses and thus to encourage an appetite for the refined goods they wished to produce as inheritors of a proud '*bürgerliche (middle class)* culture'.[40] Indeed, by being such promoters of cultural activity, they hoped they might even finally reconcile the divide between the *Bildungsbürgertum* (educated middle class) and the *Wirtschaftsbürgertum* (economic middle class). If this sounded elitist it was no accident: the director of the BDI in its early years, Gustav Stein, talked of the 'Task of the New Elite' in his work, *Unternehmer in der Politik* (*Entrepreneurs in Politics*) of 1954, which he believed to be the preserving of freedoms won by liberalism against the 'rule of the majority of the masses'. Similarly, the Cultural Circle invited like-minded speakers to its annual meetings, most notably, José Ortega y Gasset, who reiterated his appeal for the cultivation of a new elite after the 'revolt of the masses' (to quote the title of his most famous work) in 1953, and Bundestag President, Eugen Gerstenmaier, who spoke in 1958 'On the Meaning and Fate of the Elite in a Democracy'.[41]

It would appear that the BDI also sought to influence the editorial policy of *Merkur* but was resisted by Paeschke on a number of occasions. Paeschke was pressured to restrain some of his authors, such as the Catholic historian Albert Mirgeler whose work had to be edited because, as Paeschke explained to him, 'we are, in the end, a journal of the Protestant spirit and must exercise restraint with regard to Catholic tendencies'.[42] This would seem to suggest that the journal's backers did not envisage it pursuing the *abendländisch* agenda that had been pushed forward by the *Europäische Revue* in the interwar years and represented something of a revival of political Catholicism in Central Europe. However, Paeschke enlisted influential friends and colleagues to protect the eclecticism and nonconformism of the journal from the ideological dictates of its backers at DEVA. He wrote to thank Ernst Robert Curtius, one of the most influential literary theorists in early post-war Germany, for convincing German President Theodor Heuss to speak to those in control of DEVA who 'dreamed of a purely Christian publisher used for domestic Protestant' concerns, and who wished to prevent André Gide being published in the *Merkur*.⁴³ Nevertheless, in spite of such temporary victories, Paeschke repeatedly sought to establish a *Merkur* Foundation so that the editors did not have to answer to the financial interests within a publishing company.

The interests of business were, even so, easier to accommodate for Paeschke and conservative contributors to the journal than those of the predominantly left-wing and liberal exiles who were represented by the major publishing house Suhrkamp, and whose presence in early post-war German public life was resented by many of the early *Merkur* authors. In a letter to the Austrian author and philosopher Rudolf Kassner, Paeschke expressed his fear that *Merkur* would need the backing of the publishing company Suhrkamp and would be fused with his old journal, the *Neue Rundschau*. Then he 'would have the whole clique from the emigration around my throat'.⁴⁴ Paeschke was expressing a critique of those who left National Socialist Germany made by many conservative, self-styled inner émigrés. As Leopold Ziegler, a revered contributor to both the *Europäische Revue* and *Merkur*, and friend of the conservative Edgar Jung (who was murdered by the National Socialists), argued in a letter to Paeschke upon hearing a speech made by Thomas Mann before the American Public Forum in 1947:

> Why do we still tolerate the arrogance and conceit of these people, who left Germany with a thick chequebook in their pockets [because] it was dangerous to persevere there as an independent spirit, as an unsoiled human being … We who lived with the consequences, all the while night after night lamed by the horror of the executioner of the Third Reich, against which we were pledged and conspired [and] which we knew could find us and lead us to our death or the torture chamber.⁴⁵

From such comments, it is possible to see some of the scepticism of conservatives in Germany towards agents of 'Westernization' such as émigrés like Thomas Mann. As will be shown in the following section, the attempts of journalists such as Paeschke to revive civil society in Europe were conceived as ways of resisting the kind of Americanization that had purportedly occurred after 1918, when democratization and the right of peoples to 'national self-determination' had supposedly been foisted upon Europeans by President Wilson. Indeed, the revival of civil associations and journals was designed to revive a European *Kultur* and reeducate European elites. These elites could then work together to integrate European institutions and prevent the resurgence of the kind of mass-based ideological politics that had provoked warfare in the 1930s.

Civil Society in Europe: A Safeguard against Mass Politics?

The *Merkur* editors believed that 'political unity was always a correlative of cultural unity.' Thus, European unity would develop out of the cultural links that had long existed among European peoples but which had been obscured by recent political history. The first step was that a genuinely European discourse would emerge from a revived art of conversation in which the posing of questions was deemed more important than the propagation of prepared answers.⁴⁶ Therefore the founding of *Merkur* was designed as a contribution to a revival of the civil society they believed had existed in interwar Europe, but which had been stifled by the censorship and restrictions on associational life imposed by regimes in the 1930s and 1940s. The editors sought to collect a circle of European authors together that would not only constitute an elite transnational network but which, through their output, would project an image of this European civil society to a wider public. Contributions were sought and secured from some of the most prominent European intellectuals, including André Gide, T.S. Eliot, Eugenio Montale, Ortega y Gasset and Bertrand Russell, alongside the many German-language intellectuals that featured in the journal.⁴⁷ However, the editors also engaged with other individuals who were institutionally well-connected, including Herbert von Borch, editor from 1950 of one of the premier German foreign policy journals, *Aussenpolitik*, alongside Arnold Bergstraesser, the head of the German Council on Foreign Relations and a number of leading figures in Chatham House (or the Royal Institute of International Affairs) in Britain.⁴⁸

Many of the most important links Paeschke maintained with influential pro-Europeans such as Denis de Rougemont, a Swiss intellectual and one of the most prominent European federalists in the mid twentieth century, nevertheless went back to the interwar period. Rougemont was co-editor of Emmanuel Mounier's *Esprit* journal, the personalist religious politics of which came to influence many European federalists and Christian democrats in the post-war period. Perhaps more significantly in this context, Rougemont had also been well known to members of the Deutsch-Französisches Studienkomitee as an anti-liberal and anti-socialist whose appointment at the University of Frankfurt in 1935 was in no small part due to the lobbying of Otto Abetz, German Ambassador to Vichy France during the war years.⁴⁹ Paeschke was, in general, particularly eager to reengage with German-language writers from Switzerland and Austria who had experienced the National Socialist years from a different perspective, and who could offer commentary free from the burden of German national guilt. He enlisted the services of prominent Swiss liberals and conservatives, including Gonzague de Reynold, and Wilhelm Röpke. Reynold was an authoritarian conservative aristocrat and French monarchist in the 1930s, who had attended the Volta Congress organized by the Italian fascists to provide an alternative to the Briand Plan, while Röpke was an anti-Nazi who came to be celebrated as the founder of the social-market economy and whose ideas particularly influenced Ludwig Erhard.⁵⁰

Paeschke sought such individuals because he was eager to establish a transnational debate within *Merkur* and to include German voices from outside the German state.⁵¹ This latter concern indeed provided the impetus for a *Merkur* compendium – *Deutscher Geist zwischen Gestern und Morgen. Bilanz der Kulturellen Entwicklung seit 1945*, published in 1954. Explaining the rationale behind the project, Moras stated the editors' aim to reestablish a pan-German cultural entity. He believed that Hitler's 'nationalization of Germanness' had left Germans estranged from the living roots of their culture, which had been nourished abroad: Marxism travelled to Russia, existentialism to France and psychoanalysis and Bauhaus architecture to the United States. Moras's own contribution, 'Die Mitte Europas', explained that although Germans were now receiving the benefits of German culture as reimports in the form of reeducation, what was really needed was for the population to understand Germany's spiritual life in its European dimensions.[52] Here Moras projected an alternative vision of a European Germany. He conceded that the Habsburgian proposals of the interwar years were no longer viable as a way of reestablishing this greater Germany at the heart of Europe. Yet he maintained that any European culture could not be divided between East and West as it was during the early Cold War but must emanate from its centre in *Mitteleuropa*.

As well as offering a projection of European civil society in the pages of *Merkur*, the journal's editors sought to work practically within transnational networks. Paeschke, along with the editors of other European journals in Germany, attended numerous cultural congresses; indeed, Paeschke's early articles in *Merkur* included the text of a speech on 'The Responsibility of Culture' that he gave at the Southwest German Cultural Circle in November 1946 and a report on the Rencontres Internationales held in Geneva in September 1946, at which Karl Jaspers and Georg Lukacs offered rival justifications of the role of culture within the emerging Western and Eastern blocs.[53] Paeschke had attended this latter conference with editors of some of the most important cultural journals including Alfred Andersch of *Der Ruf*, Eugen Kogon of the *Frankfurter Hefte* and Karl Jaspers of *Die Wandlung*. Taking part in such civil society ventures, Paeschke saw the potential for a new elite to form across Europe from the groups of intellectuals and politicians who had sought to move beyond ideologies he believed belonged to the preceding century. This was in spite of the clear ideological differences separating such 'Western' and 'Eastern' intellectuals as Jaspers and Lukacs. For Paeschke: 'The most important ideological positions: the proletarian and the bourgeois, the socialist and the capitalist, the revolutionary and the conservative, the romantic and the technological, the collective and the aristocratic – through the constant misuse of world views as platforms for political power … had become almost tautologous.' By contrast: 'In a report on the first meaningful European conversation after the war, the Geneva Rencontres Internationales of 1946, we could show the first examples of a new elite of European minds that was beginning to form and, aware of the taintedness of all existing ideologies, was beginning to think beyond these old oppositions.'[54]

The hope expressed by *Merkur* editors that populations in Europe would no longer be divided by the rival ideologies advanced by political parties but be reunited in civil society was a commonplace among advocates of European unity in the early post-war period. Pro-European groups such as the Europa-Bund – which were among the most popular grassroots political movements in the immediate post-war period, in some cases boasting larger memberships than local political parties – declared themselves 'independent from all party doctrines and party organizations', and advocated Europe being a non-aligned Third Force in world politics.[55] Similarly, members of the German public questioned by The Office of Military Government, United States (OMGUS) between 1946 and 1949 appeared relatively sceptical of party politics. Sixty per cent of respondents to an OMGUS survey preferred a government providing economic security to one guaranteeing democratic freedoms, while half of the respondents asked which rights they would most readily give up expressed their willingness to lose their right to vote for a political party. Between 1946 and 1947 three quarters said they would reject politics as a potential career for their sons, and even by May of 1949 two-thirds believed that political parties advanced their own, rather than voters', interests.[56]

In this regard the population was not, however, so out of line with occupiers and reeducators among the Western Allies. The Allies had sought to limit the power of parties by pushing for all-party governments and grand coalitions, and had established and enforced parity among the parties on public bodies and ensured that interest groups were also represented in these organizations. In addition, press and broadcasting laws were issued that were designed to protect the public from party propaganda. Furthermore, in their endeavours to limit the power of political parties, the Allied Forces were aided by prominent German politicians such as the Bavarian Minister-President, Wilhelm Hoegner, who welcomed the federalist reforms proposed by the occupation leaders as a means of limiting the power of central party organizations.[57] However, not all the Western Allies were as wary of political parties: the Military Governor of the U.S. Zone in Germany, General Lucius Clay, pushed for the early reintroduction of political parties and organized local elections for early 1946, albeit against the advice of a number of colleagues.[58] And the party leaders, Adenauer and Schumacher, were similarly eager that party organizations be revived, with Schumacher proving willing to go into opposition rather than form a coalition with the 'bourgeois bloc' in the late 1940s.[59]

Not just Allied leaders, but also members of Germany's cultural and political elite nevertheless feared the revival of democratic politics and the rise of political parties in post-war Germany. Friedrich Meinecke, in his *Die Deutsche Katastrophe*, published in 1946, feared a return of '*Massenmachiavellismus (Machiavellianism of the masses)*', which he described as a form of popular imperialistic jingoism that had emerged among European nations once the masses had been enfranchised in the late nineteenth century.[60] Similarly, the conservative journalist Winfried Martini argued that, while democracy might be entrenched within the constitution, its practice should be confined to issues of domestic politics such as social policy and should not affect the conduct of foreign policy, where its influence could be dangerous. In academia too, voices warning of the dangers of a renewed democracy were also heard. For instance, Werner Weber, a protégé of Carl Schmitt who taught at the University of Göttingen, outlined his concerns about the Basic Law in his inaugural lecture, arguing that, in the absence of a strong executive, the masses would again be organized by 'oligarchies' such as the parties and trade unions. Accordingly, he pleaded for the creation of a new elite of the few, who could carry the responsibility of ruling on their shoulders.[61]

Thus, intellectuals across Germany argued for the rebuilding of non-ideological elites not least through a revived transnational associational life. They believed that a transnationally socialized elite could act on the international stage to limit the power of national, party-based politicians, while more of domestic politics could be organized at the local level where communities supposedly socialized and worked together across party lines. As will be shown, such proposals to transfer power upwards and downwards from the national level were not post-war inventions. Rather, they represented new ways of articulating those concerns expressed in the interwar period particularly by intellectuals and politicians from the southern states and from Austria, who sought to revive older forms of European community such as the Holy Roman Empire as a means of preserving federal traditions in Germany and Europe against the rise of national party machines.

In spite of their wish not to be identified with any party-political agenda, *Merkur* contributors were eager to engage in politically controversial issues. As Jürgen von Kempski, a former *Europäische Revue* author and Paeschke's 'first horse in the [*Merkur*] stable',[62] argued in a letter to Moras: the contributors should, 'take a stance on fundamental national or international problems', unlike during the Third Reich when they had to, 'shimmer in all the colours of the rainbow, like a chameleon, so one could always say, they were, in reality, something else.'[63] Taking such stances often did give the impression that *Merkur* contributors were advancing an ideological agenda and indeed that the journal's purported non-ideological position was in reality a tactic often adopted by conservatives to vilify leftist groups as excessively ideological.[64] Indeed, even the repeated focus in *Merkur* on reviving civil society rather than reviving party-political life could be read as an argument for local and private initiatives, rather than statist solutions. As Paeschke commented in his first article for *Merkur*, 'The Responsibility of the Spirit':

> In the broadest terms *Mittlertum* means the correspondence between the near and the universal, between the smallest and the largest world. Its instruments are charity, the fantasy of the heart, the trust in the far-reaching effects of what is accomplished in the smallest circle of life and therefore the limiting of our practical responsibility to this sphere. Goethe's word can serve as a leitmotif, that everyone should order the things of his own immediate environment, when he wants to improve the orders of the universal.[65]

The *Merkur* editor combined his enthusiasm for local activism with a scepticism of party-political democracy arguing: 'When a beginning again in the smallest circles in this sense is spoken of, it should be understood that our lesson in democracy does not have to start with party democracy, as in 1918 ... Parties embody the rules of the game in democracy quasi in abstract form and presuppose a regulation of the sociological and spiritual forces, that we have to newly develop.'[66] No doubt largely due to the assault on freedoms of association in National Socialist Germany, such a focus on the small units of civil society was common to many of the cultural journals in the post-war period, regardless of their ideological differences. The editor of the left-Catholic *Frankfurter Hefte*, Eugen Kogon, who had, in the interwar period, been a member of right-wing *abendländisch* circles, also worried about 'the atomization of society' within modern democratic polities and the 'disassociation of the individual from the natural bonds and natural duties of the human-sized membership and pressure groups – of the family, of the small community … of the cultural circles, of the church'.[67]

What had to be countered in post-war Europe was, Kogon argued, the individual's 'subsumption in mass parties' and 'the emphasis on the majority'. For 'the majority can sublimate liberalism and direct it towards a dictatorship – to the dictatorship of one, who gives the majority its voice, or the dictatorship of a minority, who the majority at first follows freely, or to the no less objectionable dictatorship of the majority over all minorities'. Kogon also advocated a revival of 'civil society', which 'dissolves the masses, places … the individual in the centre of the gradually rising levels of self-government through immediate civic participation … limits the role of parties as great political interest groups under the influence of rules of superior general interests and eliminates each concentration of power'. It was thus 'the internal equipoise of democracy'.[68] Kogon's position might well represent the stance of post-war German intellectuals described by Jan-Werner Müller as being 'post-post-liberal'.[69] While German intellectuals, not least those who had suffered at the hands of the Nazis, recognized that the authoritarian post-liberal solutions of the interwar years proved far worse than the political settlement they had replaced, they nevertheless continued to believe that popular sovereignty posed a threat to the freedoms of the individual. The following section illustrates how these intellectuals turned to an integrated Europe as a means of preserving these freedoms, which they believed had been crushed by the post-liberal interwar order.

Reforming Democracy: The European Agenda of the German Right

As we have seen then, the calls to revive civil society issued within *Merkur* and its rival cultural journals contained within them a critique of democratic political culture. Indeed, political participation in parliamentary democracy, whereby large groups of citizens were mobilized within political parties, was said to have brought about a lowering in standards of political discourse and to have decreased individuals' ability to cooperate in society as fellow citizens. As Julius Overhoff wrote in *Merkur*, he was concerned about the contemporary situation that caused: 'a group of people [to become] a mass ... through the sinking of the level of quality below the average level of the individual, whereby the strangely unitary reactions of the masses emerge.' This situation arose because traditional intermediate institutions and communities such as 'family and marriage' had been eroded and the state had come to 'resemble God'. Once such social and political developments had occurred, individuals came to identify with rival political parties that competed to operate the levers of state and engaged in a 'struggle over the distribution of positions of power ... [and] the efforts to administer "raw materials" and society', which was 'made without any scruples'.[70]

The case for a revived European civil society made in *Merkur* thus constituted an attempt to cultivate cultural and political elites. These elites would then reorder the democratic political culture that had degenerated in the interwar period as political leaders had sought to mobilize a mass electorate behind ideological programmes and nationalist and racial causes. While the ill-advised alliances concluded between German aristocrats and New Right movements in the 1920s and 1930s had decisively curtailed the political role of a German and European aristocracy, *Merkur*'s editor nevertheless maintained that a new elite must fill its role. This was because a nationally-based party-political elite was destined to become dictatorial or a threat to its neighbours.[71] Paeschke explained this argument when corresponding with Leo Matthias, a German professor who had emigrated to the United States. The latter had submitted an article arguing that South American nations had better integrated their varied races than the United States had theirs, due to their Catholic and transnational hierarchy. Paeschke disagreed. He maintained that aristocracy had been a more important factor, as the aristocracy, 'because of its tradition and education, achieved the correct distance and methods of handling people'. By contrast: 'every democracy is ultimately nationalist and only capable of existing as such. If it wishes to embrace different peoples, races and traditions, it encounters the arrogance of race – or the merciless dictatorship of a Stalin ... [In order to survive] every supranational element must be guided by the elements of distance and of aristocracy.'[72]

Jürgen von Kempski, a former student of Carl Schmitt's and one of the most prominent contributors to early issues of *Merkur*, similarly doubted the capabilities of party-political figures to unify society. He urged instead the cultivation of local and European-wide elites, advising Paeschke: 'One ought not to forget that our middle class politicians are on the whole indistinguishable from cretins, a lamentable heap of interests'. Moreover, Kempski was rejecting Germany's early experience of democracy: 'hitherto all constitutional things in Germany have developed as they may under no circumstances now develop, started by the right to vote. A parliament called into being by a general vote would cobble together a constitution that would only distinguish itself from the Weimar version by being worse.'[73]

Wilhelm Röpke echoed Kempski's elitist attitude, when he decried the 'Nationalization of the Peoples' in *Merkur*.[74] He criticized the 'educational Jacobinism that struggled against humanist culture as aristocratic and thereby assiduously slit the spiritual cord that had bound the elite of the European nations for a thousand years'. In Röpke's opinion, this Jacobinism was ironically practised by the 'advocates of the same progressive ideology ... that endeavours to build a European or planetary unity'. At the root of Röpke's critique was a conviction that the masses were more likely to be xenophobic than a cosmopolitan elite. He argued that: 'xenophobia is no aristocratic weakness but a passion of the masses located in the deep recesses of the soul'. The great threat for Röpke was that politicians appealed to such xenophobia in order to win votes: '[I]t corresponds to the essence of the modern mass democracy, that the new sovereign, the people, are flattered and pandered to, in a way that has no parallel even in the time of absolutism.' For the development of a genuinely international spirit, what was needed was the kind of encounter with another culture that only members of an elite, benefiting from a humanist education, could experience: 'In order to really empathize with the characteristics of another nation, one needs more than a superficial broadness and a degree of culture that can be expected only in an elite, as the fruit of a traditional schooling and general social and cultural conditions that the modern mass democracy is ever less able to offer.'[75]

For a number of *Merkur* authors, both the nationalist and socialist dimensions to National Socialist ideology were to be taken seriously as a threat to the freedom of European peoples. Such an opinion was hardly marginal in postwar Germany, also being aired in such publications as Friedrich Meinecke's *Die deutsche Katastrophe*, published in 1946, which was one of the most influential explanations of the rise of National Socialism until the 1960s.[76] According to *Merkur* authors such as Paeschke, parties like the National Socialists had indeed practised a form of socialism, as they had not only sought to increase the role of the state in economic and cultural life but also to eliminate non-state entities that existed in civil society. Writing in the early 1950s, Paeschke took issue with the leftist critique that saw National Socialism as 'an outgrowth of a Junker and Prussian General mentality rather than also or directly a symptomatic sickness of the socialist idea'. He wrote that he was more concerned to interpret how people 'abandoned themselves to the decline of an already empty and counterfeited democratic ideology'. Paeschke even went so far as to argue that the Right had suffered more under the National Socialists than the Left, paying tribute to 'the best of that German conservatism that shed more blood than the German left, and in the last years of Hitler's Third Reich was decimated'.[77]

Taking further the argument that socialism was inherently nationalist, *Merkur* contributors such as Wilhelm Röpke explained that socialism necessarily encouraged individuals to view each other as national rivals. Röpke went so far as to argue that xenophobia was being channelled into the social policies of trades unions and social democratic parties, contending that:

> This passion of the masses [xenophobia] has united itself with social political considerations, in order everywhere to bring about legislation regarding foreigners and emigration.

This has led to a situation whereby, while on the one hand whole peoples and races can be shipped around like cattle, voluntary international migration has become a celebrated exception and in many countries one cannot become a street sweeper without possessing the requisite documentation.

Röpke singled out trade unions as particularly culpable, practising hyper-nationalism while advocating a theory of internationalism. He cited the recent founding conference of the (non-Communist) International Federation of Trade Unions at which the Anglo-Saxon unions, having set out the basic rights of workers, refused to pass the Italian delegation's suggestions to ease immigration restrictions. Such an attitude was characteristic of peoples who had been 'nationalized' through socialism and had come to rely on the state to provide work and regulate prices, argued Röpke. As he explained:

> The increasing socialization of people means their incremental nationalization, which is tied to the socialization within a society organized by the national state. The last and most explicit escalation of this process is ... reached when not only, as in the welfare state, the profits of the economic process and their distribution are made the business of state, but when the economic process itself becomes directed by the state and the market economy based on the regulatory function of prices is suppressed by the command economy of the state.[78]

As Röpke explained, such a nationalization of the economy and of the citizens was not without its international consequences: 'Economic regulation, stored up inflation, full employment (which should be called overemployment), the politics of "cheap money", the control of foreign currency, the planned economy, state control of foreign trade', all entailed 'bilateralism' as no nation could surrender any of its ever-increasing sovereignty over its citizens. The 'cornerstone of the whole edifice' was the 'control of foreign currencies', which 'more radically separated the peoples from one another'. Röpke concluded: 'When money itself' 'freedom coined' as Dostoyevsky called it – can no longer freely move beyond borders, so is the highest degree of national isolation and international anarchy – or to use some earlier expressions, the national superintegration and the international disintegration – reached.'[79] The liberal economist therefore saw an integrated Europe, bound by laws entrenching freedoms of movement and trade, as a defence against over-mighty nation-states. What was needed, he argued, was not nation-states that claimed to provide all the necessaries for their citizens. Instead, he called for a European community whose legal framework ensured the maximum freedom of individuals to travel and exchange goods and services as economic actors, and to engage with one another as members of a civil society that could function across borders.

Merkur and the National Socialist Plans for Europe

Much of the discussion above highlights how *Merkur* authors contrasted the ideal of an integrated Europe with the post-war Europe of democratic nation-states that was said to be corrosive of individuals' freedoms. But what about the recent context of the 'integration' of Europe effected by the National Socialist conquests? It should be said that the *Merkur* editors made little attempt to analyse National Socialism or its European policy in a sustained way. We can speculate about the reasons for this: Paeschke offered his own appraisal, writing off Nazism as possessing 'no ideology, no philosophers, no literature'. On the one hand, this perspective was that of a German intellectual who interpreted Nazism in narrow terms – as a movement whose comparatively small group of true believers should be distinguished from those, like *Merkur* contributor Martin Heidegger, who made a temporary accommodation with the regime. On the other hand, when asked whether Nazism was a 'pseudo-revolution', Paeschke countered that is was a 'genuine re-evolution', stating that what had occurred after 1945 had been the real 'pseudo-revolution'.[80] Paeschke thus seemed to suggest that while Nazism had genuinely sought to overhaul the unsustainable post-1918 domestic and international institutional framework, the real work of bringing about the necessary decisive and enduring change in European politics had not yet been achieved, even if it had been anticipated by revisionist voices in interwar Europe.

Paeschke, and the contributors he sought out, usually only tangentially touched on Nazi plans for Europe. Instead, they offered more wide-ranging analyses of revisionist agendas for Europe formulated by interwar conservatives and conservative 'inner émigrés' during the Nazi years. For instance, the conservative historian Gerhard Ritter offered a sympathetic review of the 'foreign policy hopes of the 20 July conspirators' in *Merkur* in 1949, dwelling on how plans for eastern border revision formulated by the conservative politician Carl Goerdeler might have won the support of Allied leaders, had this conservative opposition movement managed to overthrow Hitler. Indeed, Ritter suggested, in a passage lamenting the 'loss of our entire East', how the Yalta settlement was only agreed to by Roosevelt out of desperation when he believed that the Allies might not win the war and so was eager to keep the Soviets fighting at all costs.[81] Ritter placed such proposals as Goerdeler's within a wider context of plans for European reconstruction and integration articulated by conservative opposition figures such as Ernst Jünger, whose *The Peace* of 1943 described the war as having 'the shape of a unifying war, not a conquering war', even if the Nazis had not realized it.[82]

Jünger's hopes for the war were shared by significant numbers of Europeans during the war years who wished to see in the Nazi territorial gains more than a colonial-style network of resources and manpower between a Greater German Empire and its European dependents. For instance, in 1943, Hendrik de Man, a socialist former minister in Belgium, heralded a Nazi-led European superstate that would preserve a large degree of autonomy for the nation-states.[83] Similarly, traditional conservative elites in Germany, including those who did not turn against the Nazis, continued to formulate plans for *mitteleuropäisch* communities until the late war years, usually with National Socialist approval. So too did Nazi allies in nominally free Europe such as Vidkun Quisling in Norway, who proved particularly sensitive when it appeared that more obviously imperialist policies were being followed by the Germans in the later war years.[84]

The discussion of post-war European integration in *Merkur* did not simply reflect the agenda of such disgruntled conservatives and revisionists. For instance, the Social Democrat Felix Stössinger interpreted the Schuman Plan of 1951 as the best chance to create the European 'Empire' that the Germans had attempted to fashion between 1914 and 1945. Stössinger's argument was particularly interesting as it was formulated by a Jewish émigré from Prague, who had been forced to emigrate to Zurich faced with the threat of Nazi aggression in East-Central Europe. Thus it was no simple articulation of an unrepentant German imperialism. Rather it contained many of the elements of the socialist case for Europe that will be analysed in the following two chapters and which showed interesting elements of convergence with more conservative projects for European integration. Stössinger identified the French need for security in the face of German industrial might as a long-standing concern, dating back at least to 1918 and providing much of the impetus for France's reparation demands. However, he argued that German dominance could not be halted, but only federated, in post-Second World War Europe. As he explained, Germany was at the heart of the 'industrial core' of Europe, and so was needed by the peripheral countries in Europe, which included not only those in Eastern Europe but also Italy and France, as predominantly agricultural producers. Stössinger therefore identified the possibility for a European 'autarky' to be created, based on a preferential customs network similar to that operating in the British Commonwealth. Furthermore, in Stössinger's scheme it appeared that Germany would indeed play the equivalent role to Britain in the Commonwealth, selling finished and high-tech goods to less industrialized nations, which would furnish Germany with primary goods.[85]

Stössinger's argument was a remarkable form of regionalist sentiment, which he claimed was widespread among intellectuals and politicians of the day. He advanced something similar to a Third Force agenda for Europe, claiming that Europe would not be a Third Force, but a Fifth Force, as what might be referred to as the 'Third World' beyond the Superpowers should itself be divided into three regions.[86] His analysis was thus a striking blending of the backwards- and forward-looking; it saw the possibility for a European federation modelled on the unification of Germany, but also recognized the emerging reality of the Cold War and the rise of the former colonial nations. His attitude of looking back as well as forward, was a constant theme in *Merkur* contributions. This was most strikingly clear in an article of 1948 by Leopold Ziegler who spoke of a new *Imperium Europaeum* not only as a Third Force between East and West but also as a genuine *Dritte Reich* which would also be a third European empire after the

Imperium Romanum and the *Imperium Sacrum*.[87] In the following section, I examine how advocates of European integration writing in *Merkur* blended looking back to a former golden era of European greatness and forward to a period when Europe would again be independent and no longer in the shadow of superpower neighbours. Such a context reveals new insights into the Third Force case made by federalist groups in the early post-war years, which has an intellectual history that extends back beyond the exile politics of the war years.

The Cold War and Europe as *Dritte Kraft*

The European federalist movement that emerged out of collaborations between wartime resistance movements had, by the end of the 1940s, been co-opted by 'unionists', most notably Winston Churchill and his son-in-law, Duncan Sandys. They advocated a more limited form of European cooperation between (Western European) nations, rather than the radically federalist plans proposed by resistance groups in the late-war and immediate post-war years. Federalists were thus marginalized by this new leadership; however, they also encountered resistance among national parties in their own countries. In the case of Christian Democratic parties, the leaderships often supported more limited forms of integration, while reemerging European socialist parties were hampered by the lack of enthusiasm for federation on the part of the dominant European socialist party, the British Labour Party.[88] As Herbert von Borch explained in an article of 1949 in *Merkur*, which described a federalist movement spread out over Eastern and Western Europe:

> [T]he leaders of the European *Résistance* were practically everywhere … squeezed out by the old parties from the state constellations of power, with the consequences that the united European consciousness that emerged in the struggle against the National Socialist dictatorship spread out into a plurality of non-official groups and organizations of a pan-European tendency, which now position themselves as a new European *Résistance* (as they say in their circles) that is opposed to the governments.[89]

While *Merkur* was by no means a mouthpiece for such federalists, the conceptions of Europe advanced within its pages resonated with visions of an integrated Europe proposed by such groups, which were also supported by many influential groups and organizations in civil society and the media. As Alexander Gallus has shown in his important study of neutrality in the early Cold War period, significant sections of German society were far from convinced that a policy of Western alignment and Western integration was the best means of ultimately achieving German or European unity. As is well known, editors of publications on the Left such as the *Frankfurte Hefte* and *Der Ruf* advocated a Third Force Europe in the immediate post-war period.[90] However, other influential media figures such as Richard Tüngel, editor of *Die Zeit* from 1946 to 1955; Rudolf Augstein, founder and editor of *Der Spiegel* from 1947-1969; and Paul Sethe, coeditor of the *Frankfurter Allgemeine Zeitung* from 1949 to 1955 consistently critiqued the pro-Western policy of Konrad Adenauer and the CDU, arguing instead for a neutralism that would allow for German reunification and a limited form of integration between European nations.[91]

As has been suggested, the roots of this Third Force sentiment should not be sought simply in the political programmes of the wartime resistance movements. Third Force sentiment after 1945 had deeper and more variegated roots than the wartime politics of exiled opponents of the Nazis. Much of the agenda for an independent Europe was formulated in interwar *abendländisch* publications, which sought to integrate the European nations as a means of protecting them from the rising power of the United States and the Soviet Union. For instance, *Der Christliche Ständestaat*, a Catholic, Vienna-based journal founded in 1933, had advocated a Catholic-led Christian empire that would serve as a successor to the Holy Roman Empire. Its authors not only contrasted this Europe with the rising powers beyond Europe's borders but also styled it as an alternative to a Europe led by a Greater Germany in the throes of the 'new paganism' of Nazism.[92] One of the *Ständestaat*'s writers, Franz Klein, who was part of the future federalist leader Otto von Habsburg's circle in American exile, returned to journalism in the postwar period, writing a number of articles for *Merkur* under the pseudonym of Robert Ingram. In one such article, he drew explicit links between the American ideology of democracy and nationalism put forward by President Wilson at the Paris Peace Agreements and the Pan-Germanism that had terminated in Nazism. As he argued, by destroying the Habsburg and German empires, Wilson:

> [D]estroyed the Danubian monarchy, which, inhabited by Slavs and Non-Slavs, was a bulwark in Europe against Pan-Germanism and against Pan-Slavism. He therefore made the German *Reich* ripe for the principle of the French Revolution of the *république une et indivisible* that on German soil was totally and utterly unhistorical ... Thus created Wilson the ideal preconditions for the centralist dictatorship and for the establishment of a *Großdeutschland*.[93]

According to this version of history, Americanization did not serve to integrate Europe within a liberal, freedom-loving West but encouraged the sort of ethnic nationalism that had ended in Nazism. While Klein's history may have been tendentious, it was playing on an anti-nationalist, anti-republican trope popular among European conservatives after 1918: that republicanism and nationalism had severed the best European traditions and in their latest versions were harmful imports from outside of Europe. However, such a focus on a deleterious American influence in Europe took on particular significance in the immediate post-Second World War period as the United States, along with the Soviet Union and Britain and France, was again negotiating a European settlement. To such commentators, the upshot of the agreements at Yalta and Teheran was not that Germany would become part of a liberal Western community of nations. Rather, it seemed that much of Germany and indeed much of Europe would be 'Easternized', consigned to the Soviet sphere of influence.[94] Apart from the division of Germany and the loss of its Eastern territories, these agreements also established that the Soviets regained the borders of the Russian Empire of 1914 and indeed added some territory. Furthermore, the Soviets were thereby able to defend their gains and potentially threaten Europe with the largest land army in the world, standing at more than eleven million men at the end of the Second World War and remaining over 2.8 million-strong throughout the Cold War.[95] The agreements concluded at Yalta and Potsdam, refashioning the map of Europe without the participation of resistance groups and governments-in-exile, therefore only reinforced a belief among federalists and others sceptical about the emerging Superpowers that, whichever New Order was reached after the War, it would be a foreign confection force-fed to the peoples of Europe.[96]

Nevertheless, and in common with many of the supporters of European integration, *Merkur* authors greeted American initiatives such as the Marshall Plan for European reconstruction and cooperation with enthusiasm, contrasting the Americans' European policy favourably with that of the Soviets. Alfred Weber, who had written apocalyptically of the threat to Europe from the United States and the Soviet Union in the interwar period, welcomed American aid for European integration when writing in *Merkur*. As he commented:

> I have ... often questioned if there were not opportunities to come to tolerable compromise solutions and to avoid the smooth division of Germany ... But the general line that the Marshall Plan has pursued, and the second, the accompanying ideal line that leads via the European Movement to the European Council – commitment to these lines was absolutely necessary. They are the only way that the economic recovery of the part of Germany that can be saved within the framework of freedom and with the situation being as it is in Europe, can be achieved.[97]

Weber was responding to an evident change in approach from the United States since the post-First World War period. Rather than demanding the repayment of wartime loans, and ignoring the relationship between Allied debt and German reparations, through the Marshall Plan the United States compelled European nations to put together a common recovery plan and even allowed these countries to impose import quotas on goods from outside of Europe.[98] Significantly, the Marshall Plan also facilitated a rapprochement between the French and the Germans, offering incentives to both. On the one hand, the Americans stipulated that ownership of the Coal, Iron and Steel Industries would be decided by a representative of a free German government, while, on the other, the Marshall Plan enabled the French economy to be rebuilt with American credit rather than German reparations.[99] Such initiatives helped push forward a certain Westernization of Western Europe's intelligentsia. This appeared to be confirmed by the founding of such organizations as the (covertly CIA-funded) Congress for Cultural Freedom in 1949/1950, within which intellectuals (including some of the most left-wing) spoke out against the Soviet system and threw their support behind the fledgling western liberal democracies.[100] Such a realignment was perhaps most starkly illustrated by a comment from Bertrand Russell in *Der Monat* in October 1948. He considered the plight of intellectuals in the East and in the West and asked himself if he could imagine Professors in Oxford and Cambridge having to do forced labour in Alaska, like Eastern Europe intellectuals might in Siberia. The answer, he assumed, was clear to all.[101]

Many European intellectuals and politicians even encouraged the Americans to be more active in pushing Europeans towards further integration, as Geir Lundestad has argued in his study of American intervention in Europe, which he described as an 'empire by invitation'.[102] Certainly, even interwar advocates of Europe as *Abendland*, such as Franz Klein writing in *Merkur*, urged the Americans to take a stronger line with Europeans. Klein commented that, 'many observers of the Marshall Aid Programme, particularly many Germans, have already expressed their reluctant surprise at what appears to them as the patience of angels, if not of the lamb [waiting to be slaughtered] displayed by the Americans. America, they believe, can now compel Europeans to genuinely work together … why don't they make use of this one-off opportunity?'[103] Furthermore, while contributors continued to hope to extricate Germany and the European nations from any commitment to either the Americans or the Soviets, they nevertheless maintained that while European nations remained under threat from Soviet military force this would not be possible. As Klein explained, only countries that were militarily protected from the Soviets could afford the luxury of non-alignment; those in the Eastern bloc had no such options. To remain neutral in this situation was to deny the geopolitical preconditions of one's freedom, and 'to equate America and Russia [as] … imperialist disturbers of the peace, which misuse other peoples for their own needs', was to effectively reiterate Soviet 'propaganda'. For: 'One notices that neutralization is never suggested for the countries already gobbled up by the Soviets such as Poland or Hungary. Neutrality is only recommended for those, who are still free enough, to commit themselves to the West.'[104]

Such arguments seem to provide compelling evidence of the Westernization that occurred among intellectuals in the Western zones of Germany in the late 1940s and early 1950s. However, the commitment of such intellectuals to a United States led Western alliance was provisional and geared towards overcoming the status quo from a position of strength. This is evident from the debates that occurred within the pages of *Merkur* over the policies of the SPD and CDU/CSU in Germany, for instance concerning Schumacher's policy of prioritizing German reunification over Western integration versus Adenauer's preference for integration first and reunification second. What is striking about the discussions is that *Merkur* contributors regarded both policies from the perspective of effecting an *abendländisch* 'creative restoration' in Europe, rather than one being presented as representing a decisive shift towards an Atlantic orientation versus the other advancing a Third Force case for Europe.[105] For instance, a report by the Director of Chatham House, Lionel Curtis, who had spoken at the Hague Congress of 1948, highlighted the enthusiasm shown by the predominantly conservative German delegates (including Adenauer) for the integration of the western states into a European federation.[106] Such a move would, it was argued, provide 'a ticket to come out of the German ghetto', as Herbert von Borch put it. But it would also offer the prospect of a new sort of German state, which would recapture the best of the Holy Roman Empire's federal structure and within which the southern and western states could thrive more than they had within the Bismarckian state.[107]

By contrast, although a supporter of federalism against the 'planned union' envisaged by the Americans, Paeschke stated his support for Kurt Schumacher's nationalist position on European integration, in spite of his long-standing opposition to socialism.[108] He argued that, in the instance of the division of Germany and of Europe, *Merkur* must 'emphasize the other Eastern side of the European spirit', which seemed to be 'Schumacher's line' and the 'only possible one'.[109] Thus Paeschke recruited such prominent opponents of *Westbindung* as the journalists Margaret Boveri and Paul Scheffer. They were encouraged to explore the 'lessons from Rapallo', and to assess the prospects for a *modus vivendi* with the Soviet Union in the early 1950s as a means of recovering Germany's economic and political influence in Central Europe.[110] While promoting such early explorations of an *Ostpolitik*, Paeschke nevertheless recognized that both he and those contributors who favoured an initial integration of Western Europe were seeking different ways of achieving a 'reunification with the East' and the 'unification [of East and West] within a European federation'.[111]

Such arguments present a varied picture of the pro-integration sentiment put forward in *Merkur*. The interwar plans for a *mitteleuropäisch* community advanced in predecessor publications, such as the *Europäische Revue*, appeared unrealizable after 1945 when Soviet dominance in the East became an incontestable reality. Yet, as has been shown, the kind of *abendländisch* community evoked in *Merkur* was conceived as an alternative to a Western Europe that would be swallowed up into an American-led Western bloc. It may nevertheless appear that the cultural and political distance between Europe and the United States shrank in light of such American initiatives as the Marshall Plan. This may well have been at least partially the case, not just because Europeans increasingly believed that their idea of a European *Abendland* could be reconciled with American ideas of a Western bloc, but also because Americans had expanded their ideas of Western civilization, clinging less tenaciously to conceptions of American exceptionalism.[112] However, if Westernization does not simply mean Americanization then we might want to consider which other Western influences were impacting upon German intellectuals such as those writing in *Merkur* when they advocated the integration of Europe. Certainly, pro-integration Germans had been strongly influenced by French colleagues, whose approach to European integration provided a quite distinct form of Western ideology, focusing on the uniqueness and wholeness of Europe, whose independence should be guarded against the dominance of either Superpower.[113]

Indeed, the *Dritte Kraft* Europe proposed by *Merkur* contributors such as Kempski proved to be quite palatable to the French censors who scrutinized *Merkur* in the early post-war years. This was not least because the arguments in favour of European federation promised to pool the resources of the German industrial giant. Equally, the arguments for maintaining independence against the United States and the Soviet Union appealed to the French governing classes who had been so marginalized by the other victorious allies, which, particularly in the case of the United States, appeared eager to revive a unified German state. Never mind the sidelining of de Gaulle during the wartime meetings of the Great Powers or the decline in France's economic standing in the early post-war period: just within post-war Germany the French were being asked to submit to the will of an Allied Control Council that was dominated by the American delegation. For instance, Clause Eight of the 'Political Principles' of the Potsdam Agreement of July 1945 stated that there should be some centralized German administrative departments, which would be under the direction of the Central Council, against the wishes of the French. Similarly, Clause Fourteen stipulated that Germany should be treated as a single economic unit; a provision the French rejected, with the result that the decisions reached at Potsdam could not be implemented by the Allied Control Council and each zonal commander enjoyed almost complete autonomy.[114] Again, French elites were eager to work with German counterparts, as in the interwar period, to provide an alternative European settlement to what appeared an American design that would endanger the peace of Europe. This early post-war history provides a vital context to the divide that opened up between 'Atlanticists' and 'Gaullists', concerning Germany's European policy in the later Adenauer years and offers a more variegated picture of what the Westernization of Germany entailed.[115]

Europe between Yesterday and Tomorrow

As this and the previous chapter have argued, much of the impetus for a Franco-German led campaign for an integrated Europe emerged not solely out of the post-war situation described above; it was founded on cooperation between French and German elites, not least conservative and often anti-republican elites during the interwar years. This is certainly an important part of the story of how civil society groups in Germany and Europe worked to integrate Europe in the early post-war years. However, as this chapter has also sought to show, German intellectuals and politicians were eager to remain a people at the centre of Europe and not simply tie themselves to Western Europe, even if this Western Europe was shaped by Germany's western neighbours, as well as the Americans.

As a way of explaining their commitment to a Europe that united East and West, the *Merkur* editors, in their first published retrospective of the early years of the journal, *Between Yesterday and Tomorrow,* identified a symmetry between the spatial and temporal situation of Germany in the 1940s and 1950s: being in the middle between East and West and between the past and the future. Such a situation of being in-between may have seemed like being stuck; however, by transposing the geopolitical predicament of Europe into a temporal framework, the authors were able to imagine possibilities for change as well as reconnect to what they saw as healthy traditions in Europe. This way of thinking in temporal terms of Europe as a goal to be realized rather than as a fixed geographical reality helps to explain the attractiveness of arguments for integrating Europe as they appeared in publications such as *Merkur.* Rather as with the policy of *Ostpolitik* that followed in the 1950s and 1960s, the current political situation, whereby Germany had been reordered by American and other Western allies, could thus be relativized as a temporary state of affairs that could be revised by adopting a long-term strategy for European unity.

Such a way of arguing for European integration was hardly marginal in postwar West Germany but influential in federalist associations and among those writing in the print media. It may also have been rather more widespread among politicians than has been realized. While Konrad Adenauer's policy of pushing forward with West Germany's integration into a West European community and an American-led western bloc might suggest the persuasiveness of a Westernization thesis, enthusiasm for a *détente* between East and West garnered much support throughout the 1950s among politicians and the public at large. This development may be obscured from a historical view by the waning of support for *détente* that occurred once the East German regime consolidated the borders between the two Germanys at the end of the decade and provoked a (short-lived) hardening of relations between the rival German states. Yet before this shift of East German policy, Adenauer was opposed in his pro-Western orientation not only by the leaders of the rival SPD and Freie Demokratische Partei (FDP) but also by his Foreign Secretary (after 1955), Heinrich von Brentano, by Jakob Kaiser, the Berlin leader of the CDU and by rising stars in the CDU/CSU such as Franz Josef Strauss of the Bavarian CSU.[116]

Similarly, the various defence initiatives from the Brussels Pact of 1948 to the abortive negotiations for a European Defence Community (EDC) in 1954 illustrate the eagerness of many Europeans to increase their independence, even within the context of needing American military backing during the early Cold War years.[117] As recent research has illustrated, even Konrad Adenauer's policy of *Westbindung* was ambivalent and appears to have been conceived at least partially as a temporary expedient designed to provide a platform for reunifying Germany and reestablishing a German economic and political presence in Central and Eastern Europe.[118] It would appear that his pro-Western policy stiffened after the Soviet Union's decision to recognize the German Democratic Republic (GDR) in 1955, although he continued to work on plans for a neutralized Central Europe throughout the mid

1950s, responding to alternative plans conceived by United States officials such as George Kennan and the Polish Foreign Minister Adam Rapacki.[119]

The Third Force case for integrating Europe made in *Merkur* can therefore be contextualized alongside a broader Third Force agenda that was widespread in post-war West Germany. However, such a position grew at least partially out of the interwar a*bendländisch* case for Europe, which sought to recapture a form of European unity and federalism that predated the nationalist developments of the nineteenth and early twentieth centuries. This *abendländisch* perspective on Europe appealed to long-held and barely suppressed federalist sentiment in Germany, particularly evident in the southern states, whose advocates could interpret European integration as a recreation of the 'Europe of the regions' that had existed before the rise of nationalist movements in the nineteenth century.[120]

Such a focus on the *abendländisch* roots of support for European integration is not only significant as a context for the kind of Europe that Germans, among others, imagined. *Abendländisch* groups were among the most important organizations active in the civil society having taken shape in the early post-Second World War years and previously during the interwar period. They practised and advocated civil society participation as a means of educating European citizens and providing a counterweight to the politicization of the masses supposedly brought into effect by the activity of democratic political parties. And so a commitment to civil society was one way in which conservative elites ambivalently reconciled themselves to democratic political practice in West Germany. These elites advocated a revival of civil society as a means of stimulating local civic engagement, and of promoting the growth of a European elite, whose presence within federal European institutions would be a vital means of 'constraining' the practice of democracy in the nation-states.[121]

*****

The focus up to now has been on organizations that functioned in civil society, not least because they were able to make political arguments and become politically active before political parties were again formally active. However, as Alan Milward's and Wolfram Kaiser's research has illustrated, for support for European integration to gain traction among policymakers, it had to be mobilized among members of the political parties that acted partially on a transnational basis but primarily in the national political sphere.[122] Accordingly, the remaining chapters are focused on organizations that sought not only to become politically engaged in civil society but furthermore to become influential in the policymaking of political parties. In the following two chapters, I retrace how socialist groups adapted their internationalist perspective of the interwar years to the early post-Second World War period, and came to advance rival conceptions of an integrated Europe to the ascendant Christian Democratic proposals.

Notes

1. www.royal-spas.net/BadenBaden.html
2. K. Hochstuhl, 'Baden-Baden – französische Stadt an der Oos', in K. Moersch and R. Weber, *Die Zeit nach dem Krieg: Städte im Wiederaufbau* (Stuttgart: Kohlhammer, 2008) pp. 40–42.
3. Hochstuhl, 'Baden-Baden', in Moersch and Weber, *Zeit nach dem Krieg*, pp. 42, 47–48.
4. A. Reimer, *Stadt zwischen zwei Demokratien. Baden-Baden von 1930 bis 1950* (Munich: Martin Meidenbauer, 2005) pp. 276–78; A. Döblin, *Schicksalsreise: Bericht und Bekenntnis* (Solothurn und Düsseldorf: Walter, 1993) pp. 305–22.
5. Archives de l'Occupation en Allemagne et en Autriche (AOAA) Colmar, AC 79/7 Affaires Culturelles, Cabinet, Lancelot 1946–1951, Letter from E. Rohmer to Monsieur le Général Commandant en Chef Français en Allemagne, 18 January 1948.
6. DLA Marbach, D: Merkur, Letter from Paeschke to Ernst Robert Curtius, 29 June 1948; S. Schoelzel, 'Pressepolitik in der französischen Zone', in F. Knipping and J. LeRider (eds), *Frankreichs Kulturpolitik in Deutschland, 1945–1950* (Tübingen: Attempto, 1987) p. 199.
7. E. Jünger, *Strahlungen I/II: 2 Bände* (Stuttgart: dtv/Klett-Cotta, 1995).
8. W. Lipgens (ed.), *Europa-Föderationspläne der Widerstandsbewegungen 1940–1945* (Munich: Oldenbourg, 1968) pp. 158–59.
9. K.D. Henke, 'Politik der Widersprüche. Zur Charakteristik der französischen Militärregierung in Deutschland nach dem Zweiten Weltkrieg', in C. Scharf and H.J. Schröder (eds), *Die Deutschlandpolitik Frankreichs und die Französische Zone 1945–1949* (Wiesbaden: Franz Steiner, 1983) pp. 56–57.
10. F.R. Willis, *The French in Germany, 1945–1949* (Stanford: Stanford University Press, 1962) p. 150.
11. E. Wolfrum, *Französische Besatzungspolitik und deutsche Sozialdemokratie. Politische Neuansatze in der 'vergessenen Zone' bis zur Bildung des Südweststaates 1945–1952* (Düsseldorf: Droste, 1991) p. 261; R. Hudemann, 'Kulturpolitik im Spannungsfeld der Deutschlandpolitik. Frühe Direktiven für die französische Besatzung in Deutschland', in Knipping and LeRider, *Frankreichs Kulturpolitik*, p. 20.
12. Schoelzel, 'Pressepolitik in der französischen Zone', in Knipping, *Kulturpolitik*, p. 195.
13. Henke, 'Politik der Widersprüche', in Scharf und Schröder, *Deutschlandpolitik Frankreichs*, p. 66.
14. Ibid., p. 66.
15. Willis, *French in Germany*, p. 161.
16. Ibid., p. 161.
17. DLA, Hans Paeschke, *Kontinuität und Wandel: 35 Jahre Zeitschrift 'Merkur': Erfahrungsbericht*, Audio Recording.
18. AOAA, AC 969/7 1949–1950, Ministère des Affaires Étrangeres, Paeschke to Poncet, undated [1949–50].
19. Willis, *France, Germany, and the New Europe: 1945–1967* (Stanford: Stanford University Press, 1965) pp. 59–61.
20. Willis, *French in Germany*, pp. 177–179.
21. DLA, Paeschke, *Kontinuität und Wandel*.
22. F. Ninkovich, *The Diplomacy of Ideas: U.S. Foreign Policy and Cultural Relations, 1938–1950* (Cambridge: Cambridge University Press, 1981) pp. 94, 160.
23. Ninkovich, *Diplomacy of Ideas*, p. 123; M. Hochgeschwender, 'Congress for Cultural Freedom', in J. Spalek et al (eds), *Deutschsprachige Exilliteratur seit 1933, vol. 3: USA* (Berne: Francke, 2002).
24. R. Pells, *Not Like Us: How Europeans Have Loved, Hated and Transformed American Culture since World War II* (New York: Basic Books, 1997) pp. 70, 74; and F. Stonor Saunders, *Who Paid the Piper? The CIA and the Cultural Cold War* (London: Granta, 1999) pp. 71, 88.

25. See A. Gramsci, 'State and Civil Society', in Antonio Gramsci (eds Q.Hoare and G.N. Smith), *Selections from the Prison Notebooks of Antonio Gramsci* (New York: International Publishers, 1981) p. 259; and N. Bobbio, 'Gramsci and the Concept of Civil Society', in J. Keane (ed.), *Civil Society and the State: New European Perspectives* (London: Verso, 1988) pp. 82–92.
26. P. Bourdieu, *The Field of Cultural Production: Essays on Art and Literature* (New York: Columbia University Press, 1993) pp. 38–39.
27. Paeschke, 'Verantwortlichkeit des Geistes' (speech of 9 November 1946), in *Merkur* 1/1, p. 100.
28. DLA, TNL Paeschke, Paeschke, Konvulut: 'Redaktionelle Notizen und Entwürfe für Aufsätze und Vorträge zur Situation des "Merkur"' and D: Merkur, letter from Paeschke to Ernst Robert Curtius, 17 August 1947.
29. Paeschke, 'Notizen für Aufsätze und Vorträge zur Situation des "Merkur"'.
30. See DLA, D: Merkur, letter from Curtius to Paeschke, 10 October 1947.
31. DLA, D: Merkur, Paeschke to Curtius, 30 July 1948.
32. My thanks go to Kurt Scheel for pointing this out in an interview of June 2007.
33. DLA, D: Merkur, Letter from Alfred Weber to *Merkur*, 13 June 1950. See also H.-M. Bock, 'Modernisierung des Konservatismus', in M. Grunewald (ed.), *Der Europadiskurs in den deutschen Zeitschriften (1945–1955)* (Berne: Peter Lang, 2001) pp. 159, 166; and G. Müller, 'Von Hugo von Hofmannthals "Traum des Reiches" zum Europa unter nationalsozialistischer Herrschaft – Die "Europäische Revue" 1925–1936/44', in H.-C. Kraus (ed.), *Konservative Zeitschriften zwischen Kaiserreich und Diktatur: Fünf Fallstudien* (Berlin: Duncker und Humblot, 2003) pp. 162–63, 166.
34. 'Merkur: Esoteriker Gesucht' in *Der Spiegel* 18 (2nd May, 1962) p. 87; Bock, 'Modernisierung des Konservatismus', in Grunewald, *Europadiskurs*, pp. 152, 158.
35. See U. Siemon-Netto, 'The Legacy of a Philanthropist' in *The Atlantic Times* (July, 2007); K. von Klemperer, *German Resistance Against Hitler: The Search for Allies Abroad, 1938–1945* (Oxford: Oxford University Press, 1992) pp. 51–52; M. Balfour, *Withstanding Hitler, 1933–1945* (London: Routledge, 1988) p. 37.
36. Müller, 'Europäische Revue', in Kraus, *Konservative Zeitschriften*, pp. 162–63.
37. W. Bührer, 'Der Kulturkreis im Bundesverband der Deutschen Industrie und die "kulturelle Modernisierung" der Bundesrepublik in den 50er Jahren', in A. Schildt and A. Sywottek (eds), *Modernisierung im Wiederaufbau. Die westdeutsche Gesellschaft der 50er Jahre* (Bonn: Dietz, 1993) p. 588.
38. W. Bührer, 'Der Bundesverband der Deutschen Industrie und die schweizerische Wirtschaft in den 50er Jahren', in A. Fleury, H. Müller and H.-P. Schwarz (eds), *Die Schweiz und Deutschland 1945–1961* (Munich: Oldenbourg, 2004) pp. 144–45.
39. Bührer, 'Kulturkreis', in Schildt and Sywottek, *Modernisierung im Wiederaufbau*, pp. 587–94.
40. J. Wiesen, *West German Industry and the Challenge of the Past, 1945–1955* (Chapel Hill: University of North Carolina Press, 2004) pp. 160–63.
41. Ibid., pp. 164–70.
42. DLA, A: Merkur, Paeschke to Albert Mirgeler, 15 December 1950.
43. DLA, D: Merkur, Merkur to Curtius, 24 May 1950.
44. DLA, D: Merkur, Merkur to Kassner, 3 August 1948.
45. DLA, D: Merkur, Leopold Ziegler to Paeschke, 27 December 1947.
46. DLA, Paeschke, *Kontinuität und Wandel*.
47. P. Anderson, 'A New Germany?', in *New Left Review 57* (May–June 2009) 29–30.
48. D. Eisermann, *Außenpolitik und Strategiediskussion:Die Deutsche Gesellschaft für Auswärtige Politik 1955–1972* (Munich: Oldenbourg, 1999) pp. 97–99.
49. F. Knipping, 'Denis de Rougemont 1906–1985', in H. Duchhardt et al. (eds), *Europa-Historiker: Ein biographisches Handbuch*, Vol. 3 (Göttingen: Vanderhoeck und Ruprecht, 2007) pp. 159–66.

50. A. Mattioli, 'Gonzague de Reynold 1880–1970', in H. Duchhardt et al. (ed.), *Europa-Historiker: Ein biographisches Handbuch*, Vol. 2 (Göttingen: Vanderhoeck und Ruprecht, 2007) pp. 189–205.
51. DLA, A: Merkur, TLN Paeschke, 'Zeitgenossen: Hans Paeschke and Paul Assall'.
52. J. Moras and Paeschke (eds), *Deutscher Geist zwischen Gestern und Morgen: Bilanz der Kulturellen Entwicklungen seit 1945* (Stuttgart: DEVA, 1954) pp. 443, 445.
53. Paeschke, 'Verantwortlichkeit des Geistes' in *Merkur* 1/1 (1947) 100ff., and 'Das Europäische Gespräch', in *Merkur*, 1/4, (1947) 560–61.
54. Paeschke, Notizen für Aufsätze und Vorträge zur Situation des 'Merkur'.
55. Lipgens, *Die Anfänge der europäischen Einigungspolitik 1945–1950. Erster Teil 1945–1947* (Stuttgart: Ernst Klein, 1977) p. 599.
56. M. Richter, 'From State Culture to Citizen Culture: Political Parties and the Postwar Transformation of Political Culture in Germany', in J. Brady, B. Crawford and S. Wiliarty (eds), *The Postwar Transformation of Germany: Democracy, Prosperity and Nationhood* (Ann Arbor: University of Michigan, 1999) pp. 127–28.
57. Ibid., pp. 127–28. For more on Hoegner, see chapters 5–6.
58. W. Jacoby, *Imitation and Politics: Redesigning Modern Germany* (Ithaca: Cornell University Press, 2000) p. 60.
59. L. Edinger, *Kurt Schumacher: A Study in Personality and Political Behavior* (Stanford: Stanford University Press, 1965) p. 119.
60. K. Lenk, 'Zum westdeutschen Konservatismus', in Schildt and Sywottek, *Modernisierung im Wiederaufbau*, p. 638; F. Meinecke, *Die Deutsche Katastrophe. Betrachtungen und Erinnerungen* (Wiesbaden: Brockhaus 6th ed., 1965) pp. 79–86.
61. Lenk, 'Westdeutschen Konservatismus', in Schildt and Sywottek, *Modernisierung im Wiederaufbau*, pp. 639–42; D. Moses, *German Intellectuals and the Nazi Past* (Cambridge: Cambridge University Press, 2007) p. 88.
62. DLA, D: Merkur, Paeschke to J. von Kempski, 1 November 1947.
63. DLA, D: Merkur, Kempski to J. Moras 18 December 1946.
64. A. Vincent, *Modern Political Ideologies* (Malden: Wiley-Blackwell, 2010) p. 9.
65. Paeschke, 'Verantwortlichkeit des Geistes' in *Merkur* 1/1, 108.
66. Ibid., p. 109.
67. E. Kogon, 'Demokratie und Föderalismus' in *Frankfurter Hefte* (6 September 1946) 69–75.
68. Ibid.
69. J.-W. Müller, *Contesting Democracy: Political Ideas in Twentieth-Century Europe* (New Haven: Yale University Press, 2011) p. 130.
70. J. Overhoff, 'Von der Freude an der Vielfalt. Studien zur Kenntnis des Massenzeitalters', in *Merkur* 4/9 (1950) 971–73.
71. See S. Malinowski, *Vom König zum Führer. Soziale Niedergang und politische Radikalisierung im deutschen Adel zwischen Kaiserreich und NS-Staat* (Berlin: Akademie, 2003).
72. DLA, D: Merkur, Paeschke to Leo Matthias, 21 December 1949 and 21 January 1950.
73. DLA, D: Merkur, Kempski to Paeschke 24 December 1947.
74. See H.J. Hennecke, *Wilhelm Röpke: Ein Leben in der Brandung* (Zurich: Schäffer-Poeschel, 2005).
75. W. Röpke, 'Die Nationalisierung des Menschen', in *Merkur* 4/9 (September, 1950) 933–935.
76. Meinecke, *Deutsche Katastrophe*.
77. DLA, A: Merkur, TNL Paeschke, Paeschke, 'Notizen für Aufsätze und Vorträge zur Situation des "Merkur"'.
78. Röpke, 'Nationalisierung des Menschen', in *Merkur* 4/9, 935–39.
79. Ibid.
80. DLA, A: Merkur, TNL Paeschke, 'Zeitgenossen'.

81. G. Ritter, 'Die außenpolitischen Hoffnungen der Verschwörer des 20. Juli 1944', in *Merkur* 3/21 (1949) 1124–137.
82. Lipgens (ed.), *Europa-Föderationspläne der Widerstandsbewegungen 1940–1945* (Munich: Oldenbourg, 1968) p. 161.
83. U. Frevert, 'Europeanizing Germany's Twentieth Century', in *History and Memory* 17.1/2 (2005) 101.
84. J. Elvert, *Mitteleuropa! Deutsche Pläne zur europäischen Neuordnung (1918–1945)* (Stuttgart: Franz Steiner, 1999) p. 303.
85. F. Stössinger, 'Der Schuman-Plan: Ursprünge – Widerstände – Konsequenzen', in *Merkur* 5/39 (1951) 409–28.
86. Ibid., pp. 427–28.
87. L. von Ziegler, 'Imperium Europa', in *Merkur* 2/7 (1948) 117.
88. G. Brunn, *Die Europäische Einigung von 1945 bis heute*, (Bonn: Bundeszentral für politische Bildung, 2004) pp. 54–60; F. Niess, *Die Europäische Idee – aus dem Geist des Widerstands* (Frankfurt am Main: Suhrkamp, 2001) pp. 36–56, 87, 189–223. See also chapters 3–4.
89. H. von Borch, 'Problematisches Europa', in *Merkur* 3/16 (1949) 609.
90. M.E. Reytier, 'Die deutschen Katholiken und der Gedanke der europäischen Einigung 1945–1949: Wende oder Kontinuität?', in *Jahrbuch für Europäische Geschichte* 3 (2002) 163–84.
91. A. Gallus, *Die Neutralisten: Verfechter eines vereinten Deutschlands zwischen Ost und West 1945–1990* (Düsseldorf: Droste, 2001) p. 103.
92. E. Seefried, '"Reich" und "Ständestaat" als Antithesen zum Nationalsozialismus. Die katholische Zeitschrift *Der Christliche Ständestaat*', in Grunewald and U. Puschner (eds), *Le Milieu Intellectuel Catholique en Allemagne, sa Presse et ses Réseaux (1871–1963)* (Berne: Peter Lang, 2006) pp. 413–34.
93. R. Ingram [Franz Klein], 'Amerikas Europäische Politik', in *Merkur* 4/1 (1950) 2–3.
94. H.-P. Schwarz, *Vom Reich zur Bundesrepublik. Deutschland im Widerstreit der außenpolitischen Konzeptionen in den Jahren der Besatzungsherrschaft 1945–1949* (Neuwied and Berlin: Luchterhand, 1966) pp. 223–25.
95. B. Bonwetsch, 'Sowjetunion – Triumph im Elend', in U. Herbert and A. Schildt (eds), *Kriegsende in Europa. Vom Beginn des deutschen Machtzerfalls bis zur Stabilisierung der Nachkriegsordnung 1944–1948* (Essen: Klartext, 1998) p. 55; H.F. Scott and W.F. Scott, *The Armed Forces of the Soviet Union* (Boulder CO: Westview, 1979) p. 142; W. Odom, *The Collapse of the Soviet Military* (New Haven: Yale University Press, 1998) p. 39.
96. Lipgens, *Europa-Föderationspläne der Widerstandsbewegungen*, pp. 15, 23.
97. Weber, 'Zur Gedanken der Neutralisierung Deutschlands', in *Merkur* 3/12 (1949) 1163.
98. M. Hogan, *The Marshall Plan: America, Britain and the reconstruction of western Europe, 1947–1952* (Cambridge: Cambridge University Press, 1987) p. 22; J. Pindar, 'Europe in the World Economy 1920–1970', in C. Cipolla (ed.), *The Fontana Economic History of Europe. Contemporary Economies Part One* (Glasgow: Collins, 1976) pp. 349–50.
99. Willis, *French in Germany*, pp. 61–2; Loth, *Die Teilung der Welt: Geschichte des Kalten Krieges 1941–1955* (Munich: dtv, 2002) p. 172.
100. M. Hochgeschwender, *Freiheit in der Offensive? Der Kongress für kulturelle Freiheit und die Deutschen* (Munich: Oldenbourg, 1998) pp. 119–120, 145–47.
101. B. Russell, 'Das Schicksal des Abendlandes', in *Der Monat* 1/1 (1 October 1948) 8.
102. G. Lundestad, *The United States and Western Europe since 1945: From "Empire" by Invitation to Atlantic Drift* (Oxford: Oxford University Press, 2003).
103. Ingram, 'Amerikas Europäische Politik', in *Merkur* 4/1, 6.
104. Ibid., pp. 7–8.
105. J. von Kempski, Letter to Paeschke, 30 March 1948.
106. DLA, D: Merkur, Lionel Curtis to Paeschke, 14 May 1948.
107. Borch, 'Problematisches Europa', in *Merkur* 3/6, 609.

108. DLA, D: Merkur, Paeschke to Kempski, 20 August 1947.
109. DLA, D: Merkur, Paeschke to Kempski, 25 March 1948.
110. See M. Boveri, 'Rapallo: Geheimnis – Wünschtraum – Gespenst', in *Merkur* 6/9 (1952) 872–88; Paul Scheffer, 'Die Lehren von Rapallo', in *Merkur*, 7/4, (1953), 372–92.
111. DLA, D: Merkur, Paeschke to Kempski, 1 November 1947; Kempski, 'Föderalismus und Unitarismus', in *Merkur* 1/6 (1947/48) 819.
112. On this, see P.T. Jackson, *Civilizing the Enemy: German Reconstruction and the Invention of the West* (Ann Arbor: University of Michigan Press, 2006) 58–62, 150–64.
113. For more on this see R. Granieri, *The Ambivalent Alliance: Konrad Adenauer, the CDU-CSU, and the West, 1949–1966* (New York and Oxford: Berghahn Books, 2003).
114. Willis, *French in Germany*, pp. 25–26.
115. See K. Jarausch, *After Hitler: Recivilizing Germans, 1945–1955* (Oxford: Oxford University Press, 2006) pp. 118–19.
116. Schwarz, *Konrad Adenauer: German Politician and Statesman in a Period of War, Revolution and Reconstruction, vols 1–2* (New York and Oxford: Berghahn Books, 1997) pp. 666–68 (vol. 1) p. 154 (vol. 2).
117. R. Dietl, '"Sole Master of the Western Nuclear Strength"? The United States, Western Europe and the Elusiveness of a European Defence Identity, 1959–64', in Loth (ed.), *Europe, Cold War and Co-Existence 1953–1965* (London: Frank Cass, 2004) pp. 132–51.
118. Granieri, *Ambivalent Alliance*.
119. Loth, 'Adenauer's Final Western Choice 1955–58', in Loth, *Europe, Cold War and Co-Existence*, pp. 23–30.
120. For more on this, see chapters 5–6.
121. M. Conway, 'Democracy in Postwar Western Europe: The Triumph of a Political Model', in *European History Quarterly* 32/1 (January, 2002) 64–66.
122. See W. Kaiser, 'From State to Society? The Historiography of European Integration', in M. Cini and A. Bourne (eds), *Palgrave Advances in European Union Studies* (Houndmills: Palgrave, 2006) pp. 190–208.

Chapter 3

THE *INTERNATIONALER SOZIALISTISCHER KAMPFBUND*
From World Revolution to European Federalism

When setting up their desk and office space most writers do not have to think of how to organize furniture so that they can quickly escape if they return home to trouble. For Fritz Eberhard of the Internationaler Sozialistischer Kampfbund (International Socialist Vanguard) (ISK), who was living in Berlin in the mid 1930s without German citizenship papers, this was his first concern. The room he chose, and which he left only once in four years during daylight, was deemed suitable largely because he could walk through the front door and leave straight through the window, escaping into the fields directly behind.[1] Such precarious conditions were common in the 1930s to many socialists, who, if they avoided the concentration camps, went underground or into exile. This chapter and the next spotlight one such group, the ISK, which flourished in exile and whose leading members went on to be major figures in the post-war SPD.

The group was founded in 1925 out of the International Youth Association (IJB), which sought to train the next generation of socialist leaders and to encourage internationalism in its members. It was one of a number of splinter organizations that formed between the SPD and the Communist Party in Germany (Kommunistische Partei Deutschlands KPD) in the 1920s. Such organizations aimed to overcome the domestic divisions between socialists and communists and the international splits between leftist parties, which had divided along national lines during the First World War and were particularly disunited regarding their relations with the Soviet Communist Party.[2] While the ISK remained distinct from the KPD, its members advocated international socialist revolution and the overthrow of parliamentary democracy throughout the interwar period. Yet, in common with other splinter groups, by the late 1930s, the group's leaders came to advocate a European federation as a means of delivering the sort of economic change that socialists had long believed must be carried out on an international scale and of correcting what they saw as the failed democratization of the European continent that had occurred after 1918.

The ISK was an elite organization only ever intended to train the leaders of a broader political movement. Accordingly, it never had more than between two and three hundred members, and one thousand sympathizers, although these were spread across thirty-two German cities by the end of the Weimar Republic.[3] The group was certainly mocked as an intellectuals' club by the Communist journal *Die kommunistische Internationale*, and if the Gestapo records, court judgements and interviews of 145 members collected by Werner Link are representative then it was indeed primarily made up of white collar and academically trained members.[4] However, the ISK maintained particularly good relations with trade unions, not least international trade unions such as the International Transport Federation (ITF), which gave it access to a mass organization and enabled it, using the ITF's resources, to send propaganda back to Germany when the group's leaders went into exile in the 1930s.[5] Furthermore, the organization worked with other international groups while in exile and was supported by a British sister-organization, the Militant Socialist International (MSI), founded in 1929 (renamed the Socialist Vanguard Group (SVG) in 1941), which became an influential player in left-Labour politics after 1945.[6] The ISK therefore serves as a particularly interesting case study of socialist thought and organization between the interwar and early post-Second World War periods. It also illustrates the impact of transnational encounters on émigré German socialists and, in turn, the impact of exile groups on the post-1945 SPD.

Indeed, such groups as the ISK and the similarly oriented and proportioned Neu Beginnen, founded by former communist Walter Löwenheim in 1929, came to exercise an influence on social democratic politics in exile that was out of all proportion to their size.[7] This was largely because of their elite membership and conspiratorial methods, which made them particularly well suited to an exiled existence in the 1930s, during which time social democracy in Germany ceased to be a mass phenomenon. By 1945, the ISK was the largest German socialist group after the SPD in exile in London, which had become the major exile centre for social democrats. Its leaders such as Willi Eichler, Walter Fliess, Josef Kappius, Minna Specht, Werner Hansen and Otto Bennemann were among the most well-connected and authoritative advocates of social democracy, working closely with SPD leaders Hans Vogel, Erich Ollenhauer and Kurt Schumacher.[8] More broadly, exiles were disproportionately well represented among the SPD party leadership in the early post-war period. Twenty per cent of the social democratic members in the Parliamentary Council (the West German constituent assembly that drafted the Basic Law) and the first two Bundestagen were émigrés, while a full fifty percent of the executive committee of the SPD throughout the 1940s and 1950s had been in interwar and wartime exile.[9] As a consequence, such projects and proposals as the ISK plans for a socialist European federation were able to win enduring influence in exiled social democrat circles and in the early post-war SPD.

The following two chapters use the ISK as a case study to trace the growth in support for European integration that occurred on the Left in Germany between the late 1920s and 1950s and to analyse how this support fitted in with a broader leftist political agenda. The focus is not just on the ISK as a German group but on the transnational connections the group developed in exile, as it advanced conceptions of Europe in conversation with other exiled and host country organizations and via transnational media networks. This chapter picks up some of the themes already addressed, illustrating how interwar dissatisfaction with the post-Versailles settlement and with the practice of parliamentary democracy in Europe motivated the support for European integration that emerged among socialist groups such as the ISK. The narrative also suggests that socialists came to advocate a European community with its heart in Central Europe long before the onset of the Cold War as they became disillusioned with the prospect of building alliances with the Soviets but remained opposed to the adoption of American-style capitalism in Germany and Europe. As will be shown, these socialists believed that a federalization of Europe would make possible an international socialization of the European economies while nevertheless enabling decision making to be devolved downwards within regional federations, rather than being framed by national parliamentarians and bureaucrats. Thus, by focusing on the federalist agenda of socialist groups in the mid twentieth century, we will see how a growing number of socialists sought to move beyond the opposing options of domestic parliamentary reform and international revolution that had split leftists since 1918.[10]

The following section describes how the commitment of socialists to a form of integrated Europe that united East and West had its roots in the politics of post-1918 Europe, when the upheavals in Central Europe convinced socialists that this region must form the nucleus of a future integrated Europe. As will be argued, such *mitteleuropäisch* ideas grew out of a Marxist commitment to international revolution but were refined as the ISK's members went into exile in Western Europe. However, exiled socialists were not simply Westernized by their exile experience; rather in some senses the socialists' plans for European reconstruction became more radical as they sought to offer rival models to the European integration effected by the National Socialist conquests. This argument will offer new context on how socialists came to advocate ideas of a Third Force Europe in the post-Second World War period and why they opposed the European policy of the Christian democrats during this time.

Socialist Internationalism after the Rupture of the First World War

At the end of the First World War, German socialists were isolated from their European colleagues. They were barred from the post-war talks to reconstitute the Second International of socialists that had existed between 1889 and 1914 as a means of promoting cooperation between leftist parties and waging a struggle against economic structures and interest groups that were international in their scope. The German groups were blamed by numerous other national parties for the Second International's collapse, due to their support of the German war effort. This was in spite of the fact that most socialist parties had acted equally nationalistically and voted to support declarations of war between 1914 and 1918. German social democrats went to great lengths to address this problem at a socialist congress in Geneva in July/August 1920 in a talk on 'The Question of Responsibility for the World War', which was designed to clear the way for a reconfigured Second International. Yet even though this organization was reconstituted, it was never really able to establish international preeminence among leftists after the Communist Third International had been inaugurated under Soviet leadership in March 1919.[11]

In spite of their isolation in 1918, we should not simply think of German socialist groups as self-contained, as many historical studies have done.[12] As the case study of the ISK will show, during the interwar period socialist groups continued to work within international organizations and to engage with foreign parties, particularly as they moved into exile. While some studies have spotlighted the interaction that occurred particularly between German groups and Anglo-American labour movements, less attention has been paid to how Central European socialists worked together during the interwar years.[13] This may well be because the Cold War divide separated socialists from Central Europe from one another after 1945 and so our view of their earlier cooperation has been obscured. Yet, Central European socialists did work together before 1945, indeed conceiving schemes for integrating their countries as a means of realizing an international socialist revolution. While such schemes may have become less relevant in the post-Second World War era, they are an important element of mid century socialist internationalist thought and, furthermore, served to animate much of the Third Force sentiment held by German socialists after 1945. They thus provide an important context for the *Ostpolitik* practised by social democrats in the 1960s.

From one perspective, socialists from the new Central European nations had an unprecedented collective strength in the early interwar period, having helped to deliver national republican revolutions in the eight months after October 1918 in Czechoslovakia, Yugoslavia, 'German-Austria', Hungary, Poland and West Ukraine. They were therefore less than eager to agree to the stipulations set out by the Soviets for national organizations wanting to join the Communist-led Third International after 1918. Yet they were equally alienated by the reformist position of the northern parties that sought to reconstitute the Second International at Berne in February 1919.[14] As a result, these groups, alongside other dissident leftist organizations such as the British Independent Labour Party (ILP), the Section française de l'Internationale ouvrière (SFIO) and the Russian Mensheviks, founded the International Working Union of Socialist Parties (IWUSP) in Vienna in February 1921. According to this organization's leading light, the Austrian Socialist Party (Sozialistische Partei Österreichs SPÖ), the body was supposed to function as a working group formed to prepare a future all-embracing International that could lay the groundwork for a future revolution from its centre in Central Europe. However, it only succeeded in uniting all non-Soviet socialists in a Labour and Socialist International or Sozialistische Arbeiter-Internationale (SAI) in May 1923 under the leadership of the Austrian social democrats.[15]

One of the motivations for socialists in Austria to work for an international socialist revolution through such a body was the widespread discontent evident in that country with the post-war settlement. Austria had been reduced from its status in 1914 as a multinational empire of thirty million inhabitants to being, in 1918, a mere rump of six and a half million mostly German citizens, who were cut off from their co-nationals in Germany and in the Sudetenland of the new state of Czechoslovakia.[16] In response, Austrian socialists, indeed more than their main political rivals in the Austrian Christian Socialist Union, advocated an *Anschluss* of Austria and Germany. This, they claimed, would not only fulfil the shattered hopes of the 1848 revolutionaries but bring about the genuine socialist revolution that was terminated in Germany in 1918, yet which could trigger a leftist transformation of *Mitteleuropa*.[17] Indeed even as late as 1926, when the Austrian socialists were formulating their Linz Programme, they were reaffirming their commitment to an *Anschluss* as a necessary step for the completion of the German revolution started in 1918.[18]

Another important factor pushing forward this policy of *Anschluss* was the long-held deference among Central and Eastern Europeans for German socialism. This deference was based on Germany being the most industrialized nation in the region and possessing some of the most important Marxist theorists of the late nineteenth century.[19] However, after 1918, German socialism appeared to be a diminishing force from the perspective of some of the more radical socialist groups in Central Europe. They witnessed with dismay the SPD's post-revolutionary compromise with the bourgeois parties and its reluctance to encourage Austrian plans for an *Anschluss*.[20] Post-war discontent was also evident within Germany. Splinter groups broke away from the Social Democratic and Communist Parties and pursued what was akin to an Austro-Marxist course between the SPD and the KPD, seeking to advance a distinctively Central European socialist revolutionary policy that was equidistant from German reformism and Soviet dictatorship.[21] The ISK was one of these numerous leftist splinter groups that collectively made up a significant movement in the late 1920s and early 1930s and which sought to steer this Third-Way path. Among these groups the largest was the Sozialistische Arbeiterpartei Deutschlands (SAPD or SAP), which boasted a membership of twenty-five thousand in the early 1930s, while Communist splinter groups such as the KPD-Opposition and the Leninbund claimed memberships of three and a half thousand, and five to six thousand respectively.[22]

One of the smaller of the splinter groups, the ISK was founded in Göttingen by Leonard Nelson, an eclectic thinker and educator steeped in the philosophical rationalism of Immanuel Kant and Jacob Fries.[23] Nelson was also a strong opponent of religious organizations, not least the Catholic Church, which appeared to rally so much of the political opposition to socialism in Central European countries in the early post-First World War period. The ISK's leader was a convinced internationalist, advocating a Kantian commonwealth of nations and rejecting the absolute sovereignty of any individual nation.[24] Yet, his commitment to internationalism was by no means unusual among German socialists after 1918, in spite of their initial isolation after the war.[25] Indeed, the German SPD was the only party in Weimar to commit itself to a United States of Europe, with its Heidelberg Programme of 1925. This was formulated by Austrian and Czech theorists Rudolf Hilferding and Karl Kautsky, alongside future German Chancellor Hermann Müller-Franken, who followed an Austro-Marxist line, speaking out against the Versailles settlement and for the 'self-determination of peoples and the rights of minorities', within a European community that was to be administered by federated local and workers' self-administration.[26] This position reflected the authors' Marxist analysis of recent European history. They argued that the war (and the lack of a real peace that followed it) had been prompted by intensifying economic rivalries between European nations as they struggled to maintain their competitiveness against industrial giants emerging in the United States and Asia. Therefore, they contended, by beginning with an economic union in Europe, socialists could reframe the goals of the League of Nations, which would, in any case, remain unfeasible as long as international relations were based on a national right to self-determination which had separated Germans in Central Europe from their co-nationals and made Central Europe less economically efficient.[27]

This document has been regarded as something of an unviable and hazy shift to the left by leading social democrats whose party struggled to integrate *Jungsozialisten* who had joined splinter groups such as the Independent Social Democratic Party (Unabhängige Sozialistische Partei Deutschlands – USPD) rather than submit to the discipline of parliamentary politics and democratic economic reform. Certainly, the programme's plans for Europe were lightly sketched, envisaging an economic union that could simultaneously embrace the British Empire and the Soviet Union.[28] This openness to the Soviet Union, apart from signalling a reappraisal of the seemingly tamed New Economic Policy (NEP)-era Bolshevik party, reflected the conflicted stance of socialists, including the splinter groups. The latter recognized the commanding position gained by the Soviets in the world socialist movement, but nevertheless envisaged working through an International not dominated by the Bolsheviks.[29] In the case of the ISK, its leader, Nelson, explained his regard for Lenin as a political figure who could force through political change without securing support from the majority of the population, in contrast to the humbling compromises made by workers' parties, not least in the post-1918 period.[30] Thus, Nelson, in common with other splinter-group leaders such as Neu Beginnen's Willi Münzenberg (also an influential publisher with ties to Moscow), actually argued for Leninism as a form of international strategy that could supersede the traditional Marxist focus on revolution emanating from the industrialized lands of Western Europe.[31]

By the late 1920s such splinter groups were accordingly looking East rather than West when seeking to shift the political culture in their countries and when looking for allies to bring about a successful revolution in Europe. As we will see in the following section, these groups stiffened their opposition to parliamentary democracy during the interwar period, arguing for international revolution as a remedy for the unsustainable post-war settlement that had created so many new nation-states in Europe after 1918. This context of international revolutionary activity provides the background to the European agenda that ISK members adopted, working in common with fellow Central Europeans during the later interwar and war years.

The ISK: Against Democracy in the Weimar Republic

The ideology of the ISK has generally been described (using the preferred term of the group) as 'ethical socialism', a designation that neatly avoids placing it on a left- to right-wing axis.[32] Certainly, there were ambiguities in the ISK's position, as it, like other splinter groups, sought to profile itself within the ever-widening gap between the social democrats and the communists in interwar Germany. Its founder, Nelson, disagreed with Soviet collectivism and emphasized class less than education as a qualification for revolutionary leadership. Yet, Nelson named the organization's journal, *isk,* after the Bolshevik political newspaper, *Iskra*, and encouraged IJB members to work within socialist and communist youth groups, even after the KPD banned its members from joining the IJB in February 1922.[33] Nelson also intended to work with the SPD, until he was accused of lying at an SPD meeting in 1926, which led to he and his followers' storming out and signalling the end of any cooperation between the IJB/ISK and the SPD.[34]

In terms of style, the organization was run rather more like a Bolshevik cadre than a social democratic party. For instance, under Nelson's leadership, ISK members had to be celibate, vegetarian, teetotal and have renounced any earlier allegiance to a religious denomination. Only then could they receive the *Erziehung zum Führer* or 'Training to be a Leader', that would teach them to lead a successful revolution. Of course, before they could be leaders themselves they had to accept the leadership credentials of Nelson, who trained the members according to, 'elite, anti-democratic leadership principles' to work for a 'dictatorship of education under a single command, over which there should be no external control'.[35] Nelson and his followers were committed to educating their pupils according to progressive methods similar to those advocated by Kurt Hahn, who led the *Landeserziehungsheim* or progressive boarding-school movement and who founded Gordonstoun, a public school established near Elgin in Scotland that has educated British Princes Philip, Charles, Andrew and Edward among others.[36] Closer to home, in 1921 ISK leaders founded their own boarding school at Walkemühle, near Melsungen in northern Hesse, in order to train future political elites. However, in spite of their professed progressivism, the education they advocated was a rather Spartan one, whereby students were offered a cultivation that would set them apart from the corrupting influence of the outside civilization, echoing some of the more conservative attitudes to urban modernity current at the time.[37]

While Nelson's brand of ideology does not fit neatly within any mainstream designation, it is perhaps helpful to contextualize it as one of a variety of critical philosophies emerging from the *Bildungsaristokratie*, or educated aristocracy, in the late nineteenth and early twentieth centuries.[38] Nelson was a tenured academic from an upper-middle-class family of landowners, politicians, lawyers and intellectuals, whose lineage could be traced back to the philosopher Moses Mendelssohn.[39] As such, Nelson fitted squarely within this 'strong class of the population without personal interest in economics', which, claimed Max Weber, 'views more sceptically and criticizes more sharply the triumphal march of capitalism', 'bound by an inner affinity to all the carriers of ancient social *Kultur*'.[40] Nelson offered a critical perspective on the Westernizing forces acting on Germany after 1918, as the *Zivilisationen* of the Western allies sought to reshape German political culture and redraw the map of Europe. Indeed, he favoured building alliances between the farmers of Central Europe and the working class base of the socialist movement in that region and ensured that the party's executive, while being international, was represented by those from Central European lands such as Bulgaria as well as Germany, rather than by members of the Western nations.[41]

After Nelson's death in 1927, the leadership of the organization was taken over by Willi Eichler, Nelson's secretary. Eichler led the ISK until it was dissolved in late 1945, after which time he became a member of the SPD *Vorstand* or executive committee, editor of the *Rheinische Zeitung* (formerly edited by Karl Marx), and one of the architects of the reformist Godesberg Programme of 1959, which turned the SPD away from Marxism after the party had spent more than a decade in opposition.[42] Under Eichler's leadership, the group claimed to be trained as a revolutionary vanguard, but shifted its policy positions as rapidly and unpredictably as most other leftist groups in late–Weimar Germany, inclining alternately to the social democrats and communists.[43] Indeed, in common with most leftist parties in the early 1930s, the ISK proceeded to advocate a united front of those on the left, while continuing to criticize any strategy other than their own. The organization was, however, unusual among leftist groups in that its leaders instructed members to work collaboratively with trade unionists, establishing the Independent Socialist Trade Union (*Unabhängiger Sozialistischer Gewerkschaft* or USG) in association with the ITF, signalling members' recognition that ISK policies would need to attract mass support.[44]

Eichler primarily saw this opening up of the ISK to unions as a means of educating workers according to ISK principles and, through working with the ITF, of creating international solidarities between workers. Representatives of the ISK could, explained Eichler, 'campaign for ideas, that until now were not common in these [German unionist] circles, for instance the idea of an undemocratic elite of functionaries'.[45] In spite of frustrations with mainstream trade unionism and SPD politics, by June 1932 the ISK's leaders sent out an 'Urgent Appeal' for 'a cooperation between the SPD and KPD for [the July 1932] election ... in the form of a common list [of candidates]' that received the endorsements of Albert Einstein, Erich Kästner, Käthe Kollwitz, Heinrich Mann, Franz Oppenheimer and Arnold Zweig among others. Such initiatives were greeted by the SPD, which believed all workers' groups should rally to its cause, as communist-style factionalism, while the KPD regarded ISK activity as doing the 'business of the SPD-leaders'. Once the ADGB (Association of German Trades Unions) told its voters on 16 July to vote for the SPD, the ISK efforts were over.[46]

Such a rejection from the major parties within Germany reinforced the commitment of the ISK leaders, in spite of their participation in electoral politics, to overthrow parliamentarianism, and to seek a European-wide revolution, rather than simply aim for reform within Germany. In this regard the group had much in common with other splinter groups such as the SAP, Kommunistische Partei-Opposition (KPO) and Neu Beginnen, which were already focusing their attention on building international alliances. For instance, the SAP had been created in 1927 in alliance with an Austrian Marxist group and it went on to join the IWUSP, receiving financial support from the Norwegian Workers' Party.[47] Similarly, the KPO was partnered with the Zinoviev-Opposition in the Soviet Union, while Neu Beginnen, a small group of intellectuals that included the influential journalist and academic Richard Löwenthal, was perhaps the most internationally connected of the splinter groups next to the ISK, enjoying good connections to leftists within the British Labour Party, the ILP and to French socialists, who provided financial backing throughout the period of the Blum government.[48]

It should be stressed that the splinter groups' emphasis on building a European opposition to the post-1918 order was shared to a degree by the mainstream social democrats. The latter also doubted whether domestic reform of the parliamentary system would be enough to deliver genuine social democracy in Germany and more broadly in Europe. In the early years of the Weimar Republic, one of the socialist members of the Constitutional Convention of 1919 that formulated the Weimar constitution, Hugo Sinzheimer, claimed that there was a consensus among social democrats 'that political democracy needed alteration'. Nevertheless, other voices within the SPD sought to embed the party within the new German parliamentary democracy, with the authors of the Görlitz Programme of September 1921 even seeking to reorient the SPD from being a workers' party to being a Left *Volkspartei*. The party's leaders went on to realign this position at their next major declaration of policy in the Heidelberg Programme of 1925, which also committed the party to creating a European federation. Although one of its major theorists, Rudolf Hilferding, stressed the fundamental role played by democratic political parties and another, Friedrich Stampfer, argued that social democrats needed to 'learn the art of *winning majorities*', nevertheless, the

Heidelberg Programme explained that winning power within a democracy was only a necessary first step towards achieving the 'socialization of the means of production'.[49] As we have already seen, historians have struggled to situate the Heidelberg Programme. Some saw it as a turn to the left, designed to bring left-wing dissidents back within the fold, while others have argued that its focus on economic measures such as socialization actually signalled a retreat from the language of political revolution and an acceptance that socialists must content themselves with measures of economic reform.[50] Certainly, the ageing leadership of the SPD in Germany was faced with the dilemmas of how to win not only working-class votes but also to attract farmers, the growing white-collar classes and more generally the youth vote.[51] Yet, these considerations were domestic ones. Viewing the Heidelberg Programme from a European perspective, which makes sense, given the Czech and Austrian backgrounds of its leading authors, Kautsky and Hilferding, offers a way of reinterpreting the proposals contained within it. The programme called for a bottom-up socialization of agricultural land, energy resources and industry, which would then be administered through the kind of workers councils' active during the immediate post-First World War period in Austria and Germany. As the Programme made clear, such socializations offered the prospect of overturning the Versailles settlement not primarily through international channels but through local and regional initiatives that would challenge the monopoly of 'constitutionalized' national leaderships and build a European federation from the bottom up.[52]

Socialists were unable to make much progress towards creating this federal Europe at the political level in the interwar period, with local initiatives failing to provide a counterweight to the increasing dominance of the Right in parliamentary politics in Germany and Austria. As a result, groups such as the ISK focused on educating an elite with a European sensibility through the international schools they set up and the journals they published (with Eichler even producing Esperanto versions of his journal, *Sozialistische Warte*, in the 1930s).[53] They, alongside contemporary socialist theorists such as Antonio Gramsci, suggested that an international socialist culture based on the virtues of discussion and self-improvement must be encouraged in civil society before the working classes could become effective political agents.[54] Such civil society ventures would, they maintained, lead to the sort of cultural revolution that the constitutionalized social democratic parties in Germany and Austria could not deliver. This was because such parties had become wedded to the power structures created according to the constitutional and international settlement of 1918/1919, which left-socialists (among many others) never regarded as a durable solution, particularly in the hastily constructed new republics of formerly Habsburg Central Europe.[55]

Socialists in Germany and Austria therefore began to Europeanize their opposition to the prevailing order already before 1933. As has been suggested, this turn towards Europe was rooted not only in the domestic politics of Weimar Germany but reflected the way in which the German state's problems were regarded by groups already working internationally, as the result of a problematic European settlement that they believed required a European solution. As we will see, the international make-up and connections of the splinter groups made them well positioned to take a leading role in formulating a European policy once they moved into exile with the mainstream SPD leadership. Furthermore, as they were forced to watch the neo-imperialist Nazi 'unification' of Europe, they intensified their efforts to offer a model for political revolution that would create an integrated socialist Europe.

1933–1939: Moves towards a *mitteleuropäisch* Revolution?

After the National Socialists had been installed in government, having arrested communist and social democratic deputies and forced through the Enabling Act in 1933, all that was left for the ISK and other socialist groups was underground work or emigration. 'Groups of Five', secretively established by ISK operatives and made up of a variety of anti-fascists, survived in Germany until late summer of 1937. Yet the group was largely forced to conduct its political activity abroad, working to bring down the National Socialist government with foreign political parties and governments.[56] As a result, the problems inherent to the post-1918 settlement were more than ever clearly visible in their European dimensions, to the group's leaders. The leaders of the SPD also fled Germany, travelling to Paris, London, Stockholm, Amsterdam and, chiefly, Prague, forming an 'executive-in-exile' there in 1934.

This SPD executive, renamed Sopade, also came to advance a more radical internationalist programme that echoed the Austro-Marxist agenda pushed forward by the Central European groups that had led the Two-and-a-half International during the 1920s.[57] Such a radicalization and internationalization of social democratic politics was not least due to the cooperation of Sopade leaders with Neu Beginnen operatives, as well as to the influence of Sudeten socialists, who were resisting the demands of the Sudeten German Party for the annexation of the Sudetenland within a Greater Germany.[58] This radicalization was evident in Sopade's Prague Manifesto of 1934, entitled 'The Struggle and Goal of Revolutionary Socialism/The Politics of the German Social Democratic Party', which declared that democracy was merely a necessary route on the way to a socialist revolution, 'a necessity, in order to make the workers' movement again a potential mass movement and … a revolutionary stage towards the seizing of the entire power of the state'.[59] The concrete proposals in this document included the confiscation of property from great landowners and the creation of collectivist agricultural concerns, the socialization of heavy industries without compensation, the nationalization of the *Reichsbank* and other large banks and the breaking up of the centralized state in favour of local self-administration.[60] Yet, this newly radical Prague leadership could not establish its authority among socialist exiles or among the resisters that remained in Germany. It was also constantly under pressure from a nervous Czech government, which was eager not to upset its German neighbour. Consequently, its work had a very limited impact between 1933 and 1938.[61] As we will see, its move into Czechoslovak exile, where it was supported by particularly Sudeten German workers' organizations and joined by émigrés from the SPÖ, did, however, provide the basis for the increased cooperation that occurred among Central European socialists as they moved into exile in France and then Britain.[62]

Indeed, the exigencies of the early to mid 1930s saw a new impetus for parties of the Left to form united fronts, both domestically and internationally. Austrian parties were at the forefront of such efforts, not least because their overthrow in February 1934 illustrated that armed struggle and revolution were apparently their only options. German colleagues who had already worked with Austrian groups since the early post-First World War period, such as the ISK leaders, were influenced by such arguments and stiffened their resolve to seek European-wide revolution rather than mere change within any country. As the ISK leaders explained in their 1934 programme, *Socialist Rebirth*: 'The old argument between the avantgardists and the supporters of mass parties appears to us through experience to have been decided in favour of the former. The avantgarde of the Bolsheviks has taken over and maintained power in Russia, and the large mass organizations of the German, Austrian and Spanish working classes have failed.' For them, the conclusion was clear: '[w]hoever really takes the basis of internationalism seriously must create a world party' and force through revolutionary change on an international scale.[63] Only then would workers across the nations recognize that they 'have only to distinguish themselves in opposition to the upper class, and not, as so often happens in the interests of the ruling classes … together with the bourgeoisie of "their" land and against a different "enemy" land, in which the two [classes] stand equally "united"'. The role of socialist parties in the meantime was to promote a 'recognition that the exploitation proceeds internationally and accordingly must be [internationally] resisted – this was and is appropriate to destroy the theories of national solidarity, national community, the state organism and so on, and thereby to disperse the artificial fog that hinders the proletariat recognising its class position'.[64]

The majority of ISK leaders moved to Paris between 1933 and 1934, rather than Prague, and therefore initially sought to work on a transnational basis from their centre in Western rather than Central Europe. The group's leaders cultivated links to French trade unions through a Swiss member, René Bertholet, and through their connections in the ITF.[65] ISK leaders such as Gerhard Kumleben (who had gone to Britain in the 1920s to establish the sister-organization, the SVG) argued that only through local initiatives such as working in the Paris Popular Front could the enmities that were fostered by those in leadership positions in the communist and social democratic parties be overcome. As he explained: 'The experience in France [the Popular Front] teaches that it is regionally possible to achieve a loyal cooperation between groups who belong to the Second or Third Internationals without an agreement being reached between the leaders of sections or of the International itself.'[66] However, in spite of their ability to fill important positions, for instance providing personnel for the Southern Sector of the Paris Popular Front Movement, ISK members did struggle to work collaboratively in French exile. This was not least because of the hostile presence of Communists who followed the Comintern line of opposing such rival leftists.[67] Nevertheless, their efforts and those of other German socialists to work with their French and British colleagues marked an important development in the Europeanization of a leftist resistance movement. Particularly after former communists such as Willi Münzenberg had broken with the Stalinist Comintern in the late 1930s, they and other leftists sought to create European networks that were independent of Soviet control. For instance, a Franco-German union founded by Münzenberg, after he had left the Communist fold in 1938, fostered reconciliation between French and German groups, the latter of whose members, including Willi Eichler and Anna Siemsen, conversed with their French colleagues and advanced ideas for a future integrated Europe within the pages of Münzenberg's new journal, *Die Zukunft/Ein neues Deutschland: Ein neues Europa!*[68] Such connections bore fruit in the early post-war period, with ISK members Hanna Bertholet and Hilda Monte attending the foundational Geneva Federalists' Meeting in 1943 as a result of their long-standing connections with the left-socialist French and Italian federalist movements, Libérer et Fédérer and Movimento Federalista Europeo.[69]

More generally, ISK leaders sought to stimulate a debate not merely among the German exiles scattered throughout Europe and beyond but among a broad spectrum of European resisters. They did this by maintaining a socialist press, proving to be the most active publisher among the exiled German groups.[70] Their commitment to publishing journals reflected their belief in education and their eagerness to provide a model of a European socialist community, even if this could only exist among exiles. They sought to foster this community by publishing one of the most important journals of the left-wing emigration, *Sozialistische Warte: Blätter für kritisch-aktiven Sozialismus*, which appeared between May 1934 and May 1940, maintaining publication figures of around two thousand and featuring contributions from prominent intellectuals such as Ernst Fraenkel, Leo Trotsky and Thomas Mann among others. The ISK also succeeded, from 1934 onwards, in sending information and propaganda to Germany in the form of political pamphlets known as the *Reinhart Briefe*. They could do this because of a friendship between Eichler and Dutchman Edo Fimmen, General Secretary of the ITF, who arranged for batches of up to a thousand of the pamphlets to be transported illegally into Germany on a regular basis.[71]

By the mid to late 1930s, groups such as the ISK were therefore among the most innovative in terms of developing new forms of international socialist cooperation. Yet, the situation of splinter groups such as the ISK at this time presents a paradox: as they moved into exile in Western countries like France and Britain, they became progressively more estranged from the policies advanced by socialist parties in these countries. As Gerhard Kumleben commented in *Sozialistische Warte,* it was the Western parties still either in power or recognized as a legal opposition who were stifling the potential for radical change in the rest of Europe. He was referring to how proposals from embattled Austrian socialists in 1934 to work with the Soviets through the SAI and the Third International were being blocked by socialist parties in the West, who claimed to represent their national interest as expressed by the majority of the national electorate. These parties thereby handed power to the 'reactionaries' who manipulated democracy in their countries and accordingly made the Socialist International as ineffective as the League of Nations was proving in the mid 1930s.[72] It was no accident, argued Kumleben, that those parties wishing to preserve their independence and block cooperation between revolutionary socialists at the European level also seemed the most keen to advocate parliamentary democracy. As he commented, 'The elevation of sovereignty at all costs that ... hinders [the forming] of a serious League of Nations finds its complement in the founding principle of the Second International, that presents a cumbersome and mostly unrepresentative assortment of parties that want to maintain their independence at all costs'.[73]

The solution for Kumleben was the forming of a genuinely transnational elite that was not subject to the whims of national interest and democratic majorities. He explained: 'It is necessary to build an International that consists not of national parties independent of one another, but of individual members who are united in their fundamental beliefs, and in which the leadership lies in the hands of the most upstanding and capable comrades, without regard for nation, who can conclude binding resolutions concerning all areas of the International.' Kumleben was suggesting that power be handed to an elite that deserved to lead, not because it represented a particularly populous or powerful nation but because it conformed to 'the platonic ideal of the rule of the wise – or less pretentiously put, the rule of the best'. This elite would, argued Kumleben, avoid the 'shortcomings of the despotic "total" state' as well as the 'no less despotic (namely arbitrary) "democratic" state'.[74] Kumleben's comments suggest that by 1934 a distinctive perspective had opened up among some Central European socialists. They became increasingly estranged from the socialists in their host countries in Western Europe, the latter clinging to parliamentary methods on a national level while shying away from defending fellow socialists abroad.

This disillusion with Western socialist parties mirrored a broader disillusion with the Western countries felt by many of the Central European émigrés. For instance, Eichler argued that because of the unwillingness of the Western democracies to stand up to authoritarian regimes such as the Japanese, who had invaded Manchuria in 1932, and the fascists in Italy, who had occupied Abyssinia in 1935/1936, the League of Nations merely offered the same legalistic rubber stamp to acts of violence as the Weimar Republic had done by handing power to the Nazis via the ballot box.[75] Eichler made clear in his journalistic output of the mid to late 1930s that the blame for the failings of international bodies lay with the Western democracies, which had also stood back and allowed Franco's forces to assert their dominance in Spain and went on to approve the *Anschluss* of March 1938.[76] As he declared (around the time that he had to emigrate to Britain), in light of the Munich Agreement, '[t]he most important non-fascist saboteur of collective security was and is Britain. Without Britain's foreign policy there would have been no non-intervention comedy, no prior coddling of Italy and the Third Reich, no annexation of Austria'.[77]

Such arguments about the foreign policy of Western governments and the prospects of German exiles working with Western parties not only divided nationalities from each other but also created divisions within the national socialist groups.[78] For instance, while the mainstream German SPD sought to align itself with the Western parties as it moved into French exile in the mid 1930s, emulating its French counterparts and putting together a German People's Front in February 1936, it marginalized the smaller parties such as the ISK, who aligned themselves instead with Central European colleagues and advanced rival conceptions of a post-Nazi Europe. These rival ideas of Europe focused on an independent, united and revolutionary Central Europe with its core in a Germany whose geographical extent was greater than during the Weimar period.[79] Of course, this commitment to an independent and united Central Europe grew not only out of disillusion with the Western powers but also out of profound disappointment in the Soviets caused by their less than unambiguous support of socialist groups during the Spanish Civil War, the show trials of 1936 and finally the Nazi–Soviet Pact of 1939.[80] Indeed, the actions of the Soviet Union in Spain convinced ISK members that Stalin would probably seek to dominate a revolutionary Germany like an old-fashioned imperial leader, 'without lifting the German masses up through revolution'.[81] Furthermore, as leftist groups retreated into British exile in 1938, the united front of the non-communist groups against the communists – the latter being more populous in Britain by 1944 with three hundred members to the social democrats' 160 – stiffened. This was due not least to the German communists adhering to the Soviet line in 1939/1940 that any German opponents of the Nazi–Soviet Pact be reported to the German authorities as, in Walter Ulbricht's words, 'Fifth Columnists', 'enem[ies] of the German people and abettor[s] of English imperialism'.[82]

By 1938, German socialists were thus showing growing alienation from the Soviets but also reluctance to follow the line of the Western parties.[83] Rather, many exiles started to formulate ideas of a liberated Europe that would be a Third Force, aligned with neither the Soviet Union nor the Western democracies. Heinz Kühn, a figure on the left of the SPD who went on to become the minister-president of North-Rhine-Westphalia from 1966 to 1978, wrote in the *Sozialistische Warte* to explain this position. While he urged socialists in non-occupied countries to work against compromise with the fascist powers, he stressed that exiled politicians, who were less tied to pre-existing governmental structures and international agreements – 'less in thrall to the status quo' – could plan for a new, revolutionary European order from a privileged vantage point.[84] Forced into the 'role of [inactive] observer' and because of their need to keep moving countries, the emigration made them, 'however much they feel primarily obliged to their homeland, all the same into *socialist Europeans*'.[85]

Here it is possible to see one of the roots of the *Dritte Kraft* or Third Force socialism that was put forward by most German socialists early in the post-war period. As the ISK authors put it in 1942: 'today almost every continental Socialist wishes one way or another for a Europe that works together, and outside the dominance of a Great Power to be exact.'[86] Broadly speaking then, by the late 1930s theorists from the splinter groups were contemplating revolutionary change occurring primarily in Central Europe, offering a position dialectically opposed to that put forward by the advocates of *mitteleuropäisch* unity on the Right, such as those featured in the first two chapters. From 1936 onwards, Neu Beginnen authors such as Richard Löwenthal, who later became a close friend of leading British Labour politicians, advanced conceptions of a European revolution that would grow out of a German revolution. His Neu Beginnen colleague, Alexander Schifrin, writing in 1938, further developed Löwenthal's arguments, commenting that the 'way to the reorganization of Europe went via the German revolution'. 'Germany' was, claimed Schifrin, the 'indispensable partner for all European solutions and *Mitteleuropa* would become the most important position for European socialism', with Germany occupying a 'key position', possessing a 'European mission as the mediator between East and West'.[87]

Such statements have led the historian Rainer Behring to identify a *Großdeutschland* ideology emerging from both Neu Beginnen and the ISK, whose members envisaged such an entity as the first of a series of European socialist blocs.[88] However, these ideas were not altogether novel. Instead, they grew out of discussions held between left-socialist groups from Germany, Austria and Czechoslovakia who had been active in international bodies such as the SAI since 1923, who congregated in the exile centre of Prague for much of the 1930s and shared an antipathy for the post-1918 settlement. Indeed, one of Neu Beginnen's major elaborations of policy, *The World War that is Coming*, or *Der kommende Weltkrieg*, was written in 1939 by Richard Löwenthal with Joseph Buttinger, Josef Podlipnig and Karl Czernetz, leaders of the Foreign Delegation of the Austrian Socialists, the representative group of the Austrian socialists in exile in London and New York.[89] This cooperation illustrated the close connections between members of the German splinter groups and Austrian socialists such as Czernetz and Buttinger, all of whom spoke in favour of a Central European federation growing out of the *Anschluss*, instead of advocating an independent Austria as their communist rivals did.[90]

Indeed, ideas for a Central European federation took on a new significance after Nazi incursions into the Sudetenland and Austria in 1938. As Boris Schilmar has illustrated, once the National Socialists appeared to successfully drive through a kind of political and economic integration of Central Europe, socialists increasingly stopped thinking in terms of national categories. Instead, they offered ever bolder European visions, aimed particularly at those masses that had suffered after 1918 and might offer soft support for Hitler's revisionist policies.[91] This seemed particularly urgent once it became clear that Nazi figures such as Carl Schmitt and Alexander Nikuradse were offering their own visions of European integration, based on the division of Europe into various *Lebensräume*, originating with a *mitteleuropäisch Lebensraum* dominated by Germany.[92] Consequently, a certain competition between rival exiled Central European groups broke out. Otto von Habsburg advocated a return to a Danubian monarchy, the Czechoslovak minister-in-exile Hubert Ripka suggested a Central European federation based not on an *Anschluss* but on negotiations between the again independent nations of *Mitteleuropa*, and Sudeten German groups argued for a European federation, against the 'European Nationalism' of Beneš and the Czechoslovak government.[93]

Even within the various German groups, disagreement developed between rival schemes for *Mitteleuropa*. A Sankt Gallen based Neu Beginnen group that formed around Erwin Schoettle in 1938 countenanced a European revolution growing out of the German revolution and stopping East of the Rhine, yet being carried out in collaboration with 'the other great socialist federation of free nations ... with the Soviet Union'.[94] By contrast, the SPD leaders argued against such pro-Soviet theories, advocating instead either a Europe of small states guaranteed by an international organization similar to the League of Nations or the creation of an integrated Europe that was allied with the dominant Western powers of the United States and the United Kingdom.[95] Probably the most important series of exchanges was carried out by those writing in Eichler's *Sozialistische Warte* and those living in the other centre of socialist exile, Scandinavia, from where particularly Willy Brandt debated with Eichler and colleagues in the SAP about plans for European integration. Again, in these discussions, a *mitteleuropäisch* perspective took centre stage. On the one hand, SAP theorists maintained a Marxist reading of Nazism. They argued that the conquests of the Sudetenland and of Austria represented a capitalist rearguard action against the radicalization of left-wing forces that had occurred in this region after the First World War. On the other, figures such as Brandt stressed the importance of racial politics in the region and argued that Germany must offer federation to its Eastern neighbours. This, he suggested, would solve the minorities' problem but also create an international planned economy that would emerge as a viable alternative to the National Socialist neo-imperial system of preferences adopted in the region.[96]

Such discussions might appear rather speculative from a present-day perspective as the borders between Germany, Austria and Czechoslovakia proved to be stable in the post-Second World War era. However, a widespread consensus seemed to emerge during the late 1930s – seemingly confirmed by the Western powers' acceptance of the *Anschluss* and the invasion of the Sudetenland – that an unsustainable post-First World War order was ripe for revision and a struggle for regional hegemony was unavoidable. Thus, the perspective of Central European socialists that they were involved in a revolutionary Central European civil war and must therefore create rival designs for an autonomous Central Europe was widely held, particularly as the possibilities for forming alliances with either the Soviet Union or the Western democracies seemed increasingly remote. I now turn to how such ideas for an integrated Central Europe were developed by Central European socialists in British exile as they witnessed the onset of the Second World War and the rise, once more, of the Great Powers as factors that would decide the future shape of Europe.

The War Years and Exile in Britain: Socialists Reunited as Federalists?

After the German occupation of Czechoslovakia in 1938, Sopade leaders, along with members of the splinter groups based in Prague, fled for Paris. They did not remain there for very long though, due to the outbreak of war between France and Germany. Rather, the majority relocated to Britain, with the promise of some financial support from the British Labour Party.[97] There they joined a variety of German leftists, including Willi Eichler, who had left Paris in April 1938, having probably been denounced by local communists.[98] Over the previous two years the authority of the mainstream SPD had been challenged by a coalition of the various left-wing splinter groups. These groups proved how closely they had become aligned with fellow Central Europeans, uniting under the leadership of their Austrian colleagues, the Revolutionary Socialists of Austria (RSÖ) in 1938, after the Austrian party had tried to include Sopade in a similar cartel in August of that year.[99] The remaining SPD leaders were able to reassert their authority among the émigrés in the following years, taking the leading role in forming the Union of German Socialist Organizations in Great Britain in 1941 that was made up of the SPD, SAP, ISK and Neu Beginnen. Yet, the strength of the SPD leadership at this time should not be overestimated: the party was not only poor but isolated too, with relations between it and the Labour leadership deteriorating rather than improving during the war years. For instance, the National Executive Committee (NEC) of the Labour Party only engaged with the SPD twice during the entire war, reflecting a scepticism of the Germans widely held in Britain at the time and well expressed by William Gillies, the International Secretary of the Labour Party, who wrote to his colleagues that, '[t]he Germans' spirit is not really democratic'.[100]

This relative isolation of the German social democrats from the Labour Party led them to work more closely with their Central European colleagues, with whom they developed the Third Way federalist plans for European integration that they consistently advocated in post-war Germany. For instance, leaders such as Hans Vogel and Erich Ollenhauer, rather than being brought into discussions about reconstruction with the leading British parties, discussed plans for a future Europe with fellow Central Europeans primarily within the setting of the Austrian Labour Club.¹⁰¹ This civil society venture had been initiated as a rival to the Austrian Centre in Paddington that had been formed by Austrian Communists in 1939, and provided a venue for many of the conferences and more informal discussions through which socialists from across Central Europe met and worked on reconstruction plans. Thus, rather than a one-way Westernization occurring among German social democrats as a result of their exile experiences in Britain, we see a more complicated form of cultural exchange being made possible in the exile centre of wartime London.¹⁰² And this exchange, rather than bringing continental and British socialists closer together, may have encouraged continental socialists to develop a distinctive identity and approach to post-war reconstruction and European integration.

By comparison with the exiled SPD leadership the ISK was financially well endowed and well connected in the U.K. The ISK leaders Willi Eichler and Fritz Eberhard secured work with the British Broadcasting Corporation (BBC), the intelligence agencies, the Special Operations Executive (SOE) and the Political Warfare Executive (PWE) on the Sender der Europäischen Revolution (SER) and the Black Propaganda programmes broadcast to Germany from 1940 to 1942. This meant that they were informed about the most important decisions of the War Cabinet and had access to the reports of the information service of the Political Information Department (PID).¹⁰³ Their relative success in working with British political elites may have been due to their establishing a sister-organization in England in 1929 – the SVG – whose members, including Allan Flanders, Edith Moore and Mary Saran, had connections with the International Bureau of the Fabian Society and the Federal Union group of European federalists.¹⁰⁴ Through the Fabians they were able to access labour and intellectual networks via prominent Fabian members such as Harold Laski, who also linked them to leading German academics working at the London School of Economics (LSE), for instance, Franz Neumann and Ernst Fraenkel.¹⁰⁵ As a result, they gained access to the debates about European integration being held by British academics and politicians within institutions such as Chatham House.

Connections with the British were only one facet of the ISK's members' experiences in Britain. Like other German socialists, ISK leaders such as Eichler were particularly keen to establish discussion groups among continental Europeans, believing that the cultivation of a discussion culture among future European elites would lay the groundwork for their future cooperation in post-war Europe.¹⁰⁶ Eichler, for instance, hosted fellow Europeans at SVG member Mary Saran's house in West Hampstead and attended regular meetings at the Austrian Labour Club in London, proving particularly eager to work constructively with East-Central European colleagues.¹⁰⁷ Out of such meetings emerged a European Resistance symposium *Calling All Europe* in 1943, at which federally-minded socialists from across Europe assembled, including the Belgian Jef Rens, Deputy Director General of the International Labour Office; Bernard Drzewieski, a Polish future UNESCO commentator; and Paolo Treves, an Italian Journalist, PSI leader, Fabian Society member and post-war Italian minister.[108] This initiative appears to have been the realization of a plan by the Austrian socialist leader, Oscar Pollak, who published *Underground Europa Calling* in Spring 1942, which argued that Hitler's conquests in Central Europe had actually made a socialist Paneuropa a viable prospect. Eichler and his colleagues from the ISK developed their plans for a federal Europe out of such *mitteleuropäisch* schemes, although they refined them, suggesting, for instance, that Germany itself should be broken up into southern, western and eastern German federations before being integrated into such a Central European community.[109]

Such proposals thus did not simply hearken back to the *Großdeutschland* conceptions of European unity developed by splinter groups before the outbreak of the Second World War. Nevertheless, Eichler, along with many of the leading theorists from Neu Beginnen and the SAP, suggested that the *Anschluss* of 1938 not be reversed but built upon as a basis for a federal union. Similarly, although the SPD leaders in London had already stressed their renunciation of all post-Weimar annexations, the deputy leader Erich Ollenhauer argued that Austrians, Sudeten Germans and Czechs should themselves decide how to redraw their borders within the framework of a federal Europe.[110] Yet, despite these plans for a future *mitteleuropäisch* federation being conceived as a result of discussion with fellow exiles from Eastern and Central Europe, they proved far from appealing to many of these groups. Indeed, the Czech Social Democrat Josef Belina dismissed them as 'Propaganda for Greater Germany in a Socialist coat', as he put it in a letter to William Gillies.[111] Similarly, these schemes were strongly opposed by Austrian Communists, who were eager not to go against the Moscow Declaration of October 1941, which stipulated that Austria must be recreated as an independent entity after the war.[112] This suggests that such *mitteleuropäisch* plans came to be less persuasive among Eastern and non-German Central Europeans once the Soviets had entered the war on the Allies' side, while retaining their attractiveness for Germans who remained committed to revising the seemingly unsustainable interwar *kleindeutsch* settlement.

Interestingly, while such plans for a federal Europe with its heart in a revolutionary and German-led Central Europe failed to win over all of the non-German exiles working with splinter groups such as the ISK, they did serve to unify the latter group with the SPD leadership and its coalition partners. What is more, the members of the socialist working-group agreed that such a federal Europe would be the best way of constraining the domestic and foreign policy of future democracies. Eugen Brehm, who had worked illegally for the SAP in the mid 1930s, had already explained this in an ISK-issued publication, arguing that democracy offered no way out of the demographic diversity of Europe. Instead, it allowed nationalist demagogues to justify military aggression by citing the support of a national or ethnic population.[113] Yet this position was most strikingly explained by Eichler when he was speaking before his European colleagues at the European symposium he convened in 1943. He urged them, '[t]oday people begin to understand that a *State* is no worse off for the abandoning of sovereignty. Perhaps, at some future date, they will also understand that the *people* will be no worse off, once the dogma of the so-called sovereignty of the *people* has been abandoned.'[114] This startling remark illustrates how a federalist agenda came to be interpreted by revolutionary socialists such as Eichler and his ISK colleagues as a means of realizing the revolutionary change they had long advocated, initially via Bolshevik methods. The post-1918 settlement, which had supposedly fostered parliamentary democracy and guaranteed the autonomy of nation-states, had not protected people's freedoms nor nations' sovereignty, argued Eichler. The integrations that had been effected during wartime could, however, provide the basis for a radically new European order put in place by resistance elites, who could reconstruct the economic and political structures of Europe before European populations be granted the right to vote again.

Not only ISK theorists, but a variety of socialists including Willy Brandt argued that any democratic constitution, based on popular sovereignty being exercised by the various nationalities, should be tempered by a European federation. Brandt even suggested that an international authority should possess its own police force in order to enforce its rulings.[115] Yet, part of the promiscuous appeal of European integration in the war years was that it could mean different things to different people. For instance, the plans formulated by ISK theorists for a post-Nazi order fitted in with the agenda of the SPD-led Union in the later war years because the SPD leaders, however committed they were to parliamentary democracy, believed that the German administration needed to be cleaned out and replaced with new structures of local self-administration that would be led by reliable anti-Nazis.[116]

SPD leaders such as Erich Ollenhauer became more sceptical about the prospects of revolution as they witnessed the onset of war, believing instead that meaningful political reforms could only be implemented after the occupation of Germany by victorious Allied forces. Yet they continued to argue, in common with the ISK, that the opportunities of 1918 to bring about real social change in Germany had been squandered. As a result Germany now needed what amounted to revolutionary measures to eliminate the power of the National Socialists.[117] Thus, a manifesto for a post-war German polity formulated by the ISK in October 1943, *Building the Revolutionary German New Order*, that advocated self-government formed out of anti-Nazi work committees, the disbanding of the army and its replacement by soldiers' councils, widespread state ownership of heavy industry and banking, and Third Way European federalism, found its way almost unchanged into the Union's programme for a post-war Germany, *Die neue deutsche Republik*, published in the same month.[118] The SPD may, in this case, have been grateful to profit from the ISK's theoretical work, not least because a Working Group of International Socialists (WIS) in Sweden had sought to establish its authority in the exiled socialist community by publishing 'The Peace Goals of the Democratic Socialists' in March of 1943, an alternative programme for post-war reconstruction that received the endorsement of sixty socialists from twelve countries.[119] However, Eichler genuinely believed that the exiled SPD and the ISK had reconciled important ideological differences by the latter war years. As he reported to members of his organization, 'the Social Democrats, so I believe, have really understood, that with regard to the questions of democracy, the selection of an elite and education we are on a much more rational path than they are'.[120]

When it came to the question of European integration, although a variety of schemes continued to be formulated by socialists in exile, there also appeared to be increasing consensus among the groups around a 'Third Way' federal agenda. This was caused not least by the marginalization of German anti-fascist organizations in the wartime and post-war negotiations among the Great Powers and by the decisions reached at Moscow and Tehran between October and December 1943, whereby Russian plans to annex Poland and the Baltic and partition Germany were accepted by the Western allies.[121] Such an Easternization of Germany and Central Europe prompted even the most formerly pro-American Social Democrats such as Friedrich Stampfer, who was in exile in the U.S., to argue that formerly fascist or warring powers, so long as they were led by socialist parties, could provide a more durable European community than any of the victorious allies. In articles such as 'Frankreich-Deutschland-Italien: Die anderen Drei' and 'Neuer Geist in Frankreich. Georges Bidault und die französischen Sozialisten – Frankreichs Führung zu einem neuen Europa', Stampfer talked of a greater role for France and Italy in post-war Europe as partners of Germany. Together they would belong to the 'anderen Drei', 'the Great Powers from yesterday, the powerless today who have nothing to say', 'in opposition to the Great Three, who today decide the fate of the world'.[122]

Stampfer's position in the latter war years expressed the disillusion of exiled German leftists with the Western allies. It also signalled the position adopted by social democrats in the early post-war period, which was to advocate a European federation that would be independent from both Soviet influence and Anglo-Saxon interference. This position may have, in turn, marginalized German social democrats from the decision-making processes that shaped the early history of the European project, and led to the party leadership being characterized (unfairly) as anti-European and nationalist. However, as this chapter has sought to suggest, the commitment of many leading post-war German Social Democrats to an integrated Europe was long standing and rooted in debates among Central Europeans who had sought to overturn the nationalist political order in Europe since at least 1918.

*****

It may be appropriate to strike an elegiac tone at this point, lamenting the lost united Europe that was formulated in the heads of Central European socialists during the war years and never realized. ISK members, among others, had envisaged radical political change being led by the resistance movements, which would, it was hoped, take a commanding position in a post-fascist and federal European community. As we will see, such hopes were to be frustrated, not least because such a self-selecting European vanguard was, in many ways, regarded as peripheral by national populations and by the Allies, who looked to once more constitute party-based national elites. Furthermore, once the Allies had decided to partition Germany and reconstitute Austria as an independent nation in the Western bloc, while placing much of the rest of East-Central Europe in the Soviet sphere of influence, all talk of creating any sort of *mitteleuropäisch* community seemed naïve and utopian. However, this should not obscure the significance of a Central European perspective that went back to at least 1918 and, indeed, beyond, back to the battles over what form German unification should take and how a tradition of federalism in Germany would be safeguarded in the nineteenth century. Furthermore, as will be suggested, socialist ideas of federalism did not disappear in the post-1945 era. Instead, they motivated the policy of an independent-minded group of local and regional social democratic leaders in the post-Second World War era, which became known as the Bürgermeisterflügel or mayoral wing. This group – whose members also included a number of prominent former exiles – opposed Kurt Schumacher's European policy of the late 1940s and early 1950s, but inspired a later generation of socialist politicians to push forward an *Ostpolitik* that sought to reunify Germany and heal wounds in Central Europe. In what follows, I will outline the position of this Bürgermeisterflügel but also offer a reappraisal of the policy of Schumacher and the post-Second World War SPD leadership, which, I suggest, has been unfairly characterized as favouring German nationalism over European integration.

Just as the interwar and wartime plans for *Mitteleuropa* may seem easy to forget, so too may the interwar anti-democratic sentiment of splinter-group leaders who went on to be leading theorists within the post-war SPD and therefore defenders of the West German federal democracy. Yet, I will suggest that there are lines of continuity between the revolutionary policy of socialists during the interwar years and their post-war commitment to constrain the harmful potential of majoritarian parliamentary politics through a European framework and through the cooperation of local, regional and European-wide socialist groups. As we will see, such a commitment to a European constitutional order and to local and European activism was one of the numerous ways in which groups across the ideological spectrum sought to remedy the seemingly self-destructive nature of interwar democracy. And, as will be argued, it can therefore help to explain why groups from either end of the political spectrum, previously rather sceptical about parliamentary democracy, could reconcile themselves to this form of government in the post-Second World War era.

Notes

1. F. Eberhard [Hellmut von Rauschenplat], *Arbeit gegen das Dritte Reich* (Berlin: Informationszentrum Berlin, Gedenk- und Bildungsstätte Stauffenbergstrasse 3rd ed., 1981) pp. 6–7.
2. Modern Records Centre (MRC), University of Warwick, Socialist Vanguard Group (SVG) Archives, MSS. 173/1/1, 'Surveys on ISK. Background and Information', July 1942: Ten Years Reports (Mary) File.
3. J. Foitzik, *Zwischen den Fronten: Zur Politik, Organisation und Funktion linker politischer Kleinorganisationen im Widerstand 1933 bis 1939/40* (Bonn: Neue Gesellschaft, 1986) p. 29; W. Link, *Die Geschichte des Internationalen Jugend-Bundes (IJB) und des Internationalen Sozialistischen Kampf-Bundes (ISK). Ein Beitrag zur Geschichte der Arbeiterbewegung in der Weimarer Republik und im Dritten Reich* (Meisenheim am Glan: Hain, 1964) p. 141.
4. Link, *IJB und ISK*, pp. 141–2.
5. J. Angster, *Konsenskapitalismus und Sozialdemokratie. Die Westernisierung von SPD und DGB* (Munich: Oldenbourg, 2003) pp. 174, 277.
6. MRC, MSS. 173/18/1, 'Half-Yearly Reports, 1943–1950'.
7. W. Löwenheim (ed. J. Foitzik), *Geschichte der ORG [Neu Beginnen] 1929–1935. Eine zeitgenossische Analyse* (Berlin: Hentrich, 1995).
8. L. Eiber, *Die Sozialdemokratie in der Emigration. Die 'Union deutscher sozialistischer Organisationen in Großbritannien' 1941–1946 und ihre Mitglieder, Protokolle, Erklärungen, Materialien* (Bonn: Dietz, 1998) p. CXXIX.
9. C.D. Krohn, 'Einleitung – Remigranten in der westdeutschen Nachkriegsgesellschaft'; and H. Mehringer, 'Impulse sozialdemokratischer Remigranten auf die Modernisierung der SPD', both in C.D. Krohn and P. von zur Mühlen (eds), *Rückkehr und Aufbau nach 1945: deutsche Remigranten im öffentlichen Leben Nachkriegsdeutschlands* (Marburg: Metropolis, 1997) pp. 14, 105.
10. See G. Eley, *Forging Democracy: The History of the Left in Europe, 1850–2000* (New York: Oxford University Press, 2002) p. 121.
11. R. Steininger, *Deutschland und die Sozialistische Internationale nach dem Zweiten Weltkrieg. Die deutsche Frage, die Internationale und das Problem der Wiederaufnahme des SPD auf den internationalen sozialistischen Konferenzen bis 1951 unter besonderer Berücksichtigung der Labour Party* (Bonn: Neue Gesellschaft, 1979) pp. 6–7.
12. On this, see, among others, D. Groh and P. Brandt, *Vaterlandslose Gesellen: Sozialdemokratie und Nation, 1860–1990* (Munich: Beck, 1992); S. Berger, *The British Labour Party and the German Social Democrats, 1900–1931* (Oxford: Oxford University Press, 1994); M. Donald, 'Workers of the World Unite? Exploring the Enigma of the Second International', in M.H. Geyer and J. Paulmann (eds), *The Mechanics of Internationalism: Culture, Society and Politics from the 1840s to the First World War* (Oxford: Oxford University Press, 2001).
13. On the cooperation between German social democrats and Anglo-American labour movements, see Angster, *Konsenskapitalismus und Sozialdemokratie*. See also C. Holbraad, *Internationalism and Nationalism in European Political Thought* (Houndmills: Palgrave Macmillan, 2003).
14. Eley, *Forging Democracy*, pp. 177–84.
15. Steininger, *Deutschland und die Sozialistische Internationale*, pp. 6–9.
16. T. Kirk, *Nazism and the Working Class in Austria: Industrial Unrest and Political Dissent in the 'National Community'* (Cambridge: Cambridge University Press, 1996) p. 12.
17. See F. Carsten, *Revolution in Central Europe, 1918–1919* (Aldershot: Wildwood House, 1988), pp. 278–96.
18. See *Das Linzer Programm der Sozialdemokratischen Arbeiterpartei (Deutsch)österreichs (1926)*, accessible at: http://www.otto-bauer.net/otto_bauer.html. The relevant passages are in section

VI on 'Die Internationale'. See also N. Leser, *Zwischen Reformismus und Bolschewismus: der Austromarxismus als Theorie und Praxis* (Vienna: Europa, 1985) p. 172.
19. G. Haupt, *Aspects of International Socialism, 1871–1914* (Cambridge: Cambridge University Press, 1986) pp. 52–54, 64–67, 92; I. Wallerstein, *Centrist Liberalism Triumphant, 1789–1914* (Berkeley and Los Angeles: University of California Press, 2011) p. 177.
20. On this, as well as for information on cooperation between Austro-Marxists and the German splinter groups, see M. P. Berg (ed.), *The Struggle for a Democratic Austria: Bruno Kreisky on Peace and Social Justice* (New York and Oxford: Berghahn Books, 2000) esp. pp. 120–27.
21. C. Schorske, *German Social Democracy 1905–1917. The Development of the Great Schism* (New York: Harper Torchbook, 1972).
22. Foitzik, *Zwischen den Fronten*, pp. 24–25.
23. Archiv der sozialen Demokratie (AdsD), Friedrich Ebert Stiftung (FES) Bonn-Bad-Godesberg, IJB/ISK Collection, Box 10, [Eichler speech at] Leonard Nelson Memorial Meeting, 11 July 1942.
24. M. Minion, 'Left, Right or European? Labour and Europe in the 1940s: the Case of the Socialist Vanguard Group' in *European Review of History*, 7/2 (2000) 231.
25. For more on the debates about international politics and specifically about European unity that existed among German socialists in the 1920s, see T. Maync, 'For a Socialist Europe!: German Social Democracy and the Idea of Europe, 1900–1930', University of Chicago PhD Dissertation, 2006. Thanks to Talbot Imlay for drawing my attention to this.
26. See 'XVI. Programm der Sozialdemokratischen Partei Deutschlands, beschlossen auf dem Parteitag in Heidelberg 1925', in D. Dowe and K. Klotzbach (eds, introduction by J. Rau), *Programmatische Dokumente der deutschen Sozialdemokratie* (Berlin and Bonn: Dietz, 1973) p. 224; and F. Niess, *Die Europäische Idee – aus dem Geist der Widerstands* (Frankfurt am Main: Suhrkamp, 2001) p. 23.
27. P. Kampffmeyer (ed.), *Das Heidelberger Programm: Grundsätze und Forderungen der Sozialdemokratie* (Berlin: Vorstand der Sozialdemokratischen Partei Deutschlands, 1925), esp. pp. 26–29, 65–71, 77.
28. See A. Nicholls, *Freedom with Responsibility: The Social Market Economy in Germany, 1918–1963* (Oxford: Oxford University Press, 2003) pp. 81–86; H.A. Winkler, *Der Schein der Normalität: Arbeiter und Arbeiterbewegung in der Weimarer Republik, 1924 bis 1930* (Berlin: J.H.W. Dietz, 1985).
29. B. Schilmar, *Der Europadiskurs im deutschen Exil* (Munich: Oldenbourg, 2004) pp. 47–48; Steininger, *Deutschland und die Sozialistische Internationale*, pp. 6–9.
30. R. Douglas, 'No Friend of Democracy: The Socialist Vanguard Group, 1941–1950', in *Contemporary British History* 16/4 (Winter, 2002) 54; Link, *IJB und ISK*, p. 107.
31. MRC, SVG Archive, MSS. 173/1/10, Leonard Nelson, 'Democracy and Leadership' quoted in Militant Socialist International (MSI), *The Militant Socialist International: Its Aim, Method and Constitution* (London, 1935) p. 23. On Münzenberg's publishing activities, see S. McMeekin, *The Red Millionaire: A Political Biography of Willi Münzenberg, Moscow's Secret Propaganda Tsar in the West* (New Haven: Yale University Press, 2004).
32. For instance, see Douglas, 'No Friend of Democracy', 56 and S. Lemke-Mueller, *Ethischer Sozialismus und Soziale Demokratie. Der politische Weg Willi Eichlers vom ISK zur SPD* (Bonn: Neue Gesellschaft, 1988) p. 73.
33. Link, *IJB und ISK*, p. 107.
34. F. Hasselhorn, 'Göttingen 1917/18–1933', in Rudolf von Thadden (ed.), *Göttingen: Von der preußischen Mittelstadt zur südniedersächsischen Großstadt 1866–1989* (Göttingen: Vanderhoeck und Ruprecht, 1999) pp. 95–96.
35. Eiber, *Sozialdemokratie in der Emigration*, p. CXXVI.
36. S. Schweber, *QED and the Men who Made It: Dyson, Feynman, Schwinger and Tomonaga* (Princeton: Princeton University Press, 1994) p. 487.

37. MRC, SVG Archive, MSS. 173/1/7, 'The School', in 'Surveys on ISK. Background and Information July 1942'; MSS. 173/1/7, '10 Years Reports (Mary)'; MSS. 173/20/8; G. Spencer, *Beloved Alien: Walter Fliess 1901–1985* (Vancouver and Donhead St. Andrew: Geoff Spencer, 1985) p. 11.
38. F. Heidenreich, 'Einleitung: Bildungsideale und -politiken im deutsch-französischen Vergleich', in F. Heidenreich, *Bildung in Frankreich und Deutschland – Ideale und Politiken im Vergleich* (Münster: Lit, 2006) pp. 14–15. Thanks to Ute Frevert for help with this point.
39. P. Pulzer, *Jews and the German State: the Political History of a Minority, 1848–1933* (Detroit: Wayne State University Press, 2003) p. 320.
40. See P. Ghosh, 'Max Weber on "The Rural Community": A Critical Edition of the English text', in *The History of European Ideas*, 31/3 (2005) 327–66.
41. Link, *IJB und ISK*, pp. 124–25, 140.
42. Lemke-Mueller, *Ethischer Sozialismus*, p. 206.
43. Ibid., pp. 97, 90.
44. Foitzik, *Zwischen den Fronten*, p. 86.
45. Angster, *Konsenskapitalismus und Sozialdemokratie*, p. 297.
46. Link, *IJB und ISK*, pp. 159–61.
47. Foitzik, *Zwischen den Fronten*, pp. 23–24, 101.
48. Foitzik, *Zwischen den Fronten*, pp. 25–29; J. Radkau, *Die deutsche Emigration in den USA: Ihr Einfluss auf die amerikanische Europapolitik, 1933–1945* (Dusseldorf: Bertelsmann, 1971) p. 178.
49. Angster, *Konsenskapitalismus und Sozialdemokratie*, pp. 51, 55–56.
50. For the first view, see Nicholls, *Freedom with Responsibility*, pp. 81–83; for the opposite perspective, see W.H. Maehl, *The German Socialist Party: Champion of the First Republic, 1918–1933* (Lawrence: Allen Press/American Philosophical Society, 1986) pp. 109–12.
51. D. Harsch, *German Social Democracy and the Rise of Nazism* (Chapel Hill: University of North Carolina Press, 1993) pp. 28–30.
52. *Heidelberger Programm*, pp. 65–70. I take the notion of the 'constitutionalized' parties from G. Eley in his *Forging Democracy*, pp. 226–38.
53. W. Röder and H. Strauss (eds), *Biographisches Handbuch der deutschsprachigen Emigration nach 1933: Band I, Politik, Wirtschaft, Öffentliches Leben* (Munich: Saur, 1980) p. 148.
54. See Eley, *Forging Democracy*, pp. 210–15.
55. Ibid., p. 226, pp. 237–38.
56. Link, *IJB und ISK*, pp. 177, 224.
57. J.M. Palmier, *Weimar in Exile: The Antifascist Emigration in Europe and America* (London: Verso, 2006) p. 201.
58. G.-R. Horn, 'Radicalism and Moderation within German Social Democracy in Underground and Exile, 1933–1936', in *German History* 15/2 (1997) 203. On the issue of the SdP, see particularly E. Glassheim, *Noble Nationalists: The Transformation of the Bohemian Aristocracy* (Cambridge MA: Harvard University Press, 2005); C.E. Murdock, *Changing Places: Society, Culture and Territory in the Saxon-Bohemian Borderlands, 1870–1946* (Ann Arbor: University of Michigan, 2010).
59. 'XVII. Prager Manifest der Sopade 1934: Kampf und Ziel des revolutionären Sozialismus/Die Politik der Sozialdemokratischen Partei Deutschlands', in Dowe and Klotzbach, *Programmatische Dokumente der deutschen Sozialdemokratie*, pp. 228–31.
60. Ibid.
61. D.E. Barclay, 'Rethinking Social Democracy, the State and Europe: Rudolf Hilferding in Exile, 1933–1941' in D.E. Barclay and E.D. Weitz (eds), *Between Reform and Revolution: German Socialism and Communism from 1840 to 1990* (Oxford and New York: Berghahn Books, 1998) p. 384.

62. H. Mehringer, 'Der deutsche Widerstand im Ausland: Vom antifaschistischen zum antitotalitären Konsens', in Daniel Azuélos, *Lion Feuchtwanger und die deutschsprachigen Emigranten in Frankreich von 1933 bis 1941* (Berne: Peter Lang, 2006) pp. 24–28; Schilmar, *Europadiskurs*, pp. 59–60; see also A. Vatury, 'The SPD Exiles and the Scandinavian Social Democrats, 1933–1956', in J. Brunner (ed.), *Mütterliche Macht und väterliche Autorität: Elternbilder im deutschen Diskurs (Tel Aviver Jahrbuch für deutsche Geschichte 2008)* (Göttingen: Wallstein, 2008) p. 390.
63. Internationaler Sozialistischer Kampfbund (ed.), *Sozialistische Wiedergeburt: Gedanken und Vorschläge zur Erneuerung der sozialistischen Arbeit* (London: International Publishing Company, 1934) pp. 7, 74, 77.
64. 'Neue Wege. Moralischer und politischer Wiederaufbau' in *Sozialistische Warte* 1/1 (May 1934) 4-5.
65. P. Adant, *Widerstand und Wagemut. René Bertholet – eine Biographie* (Frankfurt am Main: Dipa, 1996).
66. Ibid., p. 80.
67. MRC, SVG Archive, MSS. 173/1/7, [Untitled Report], in 'Reports on Work of SVG'.
68. Palmier, *Weimar in Exile*, p. 314; Schilmar, *Europadiskurs*, pp. 152–55.
69. Schilmar, *Europadiskurs*, p. 79.
70. W. Röder, *Die deutschen sozialistischen Exilgruppen in Großbritannien 1940–1945: Ein Beitrag zur Geschichte des Widerstandes gegen den Nationalsozialismus* (Hannover: Verlag für Literatur und Zeitgeschehen, 1968) p. 224.
71. H. Lindner: *"Um Etwas zu Erreichen, Muss Man sich Etwas vornehmen, von dem Man Glaubt, dass es Unmöglich sei". Der Internationale Sozialistische Kampf-Bund (ISK) und seine Publikationen* (Reihe Gesprächskreis Geschichte, Vol. 64, ed. Dieter Dowe. Historisches Forschungszentrum der Friedrich-Ebert-Stiftung) (Bonn: Friedrich Ebert Stiftung, 2006) p. 89.
72. G. Kumleben writing under the pseudonym François Gerard, 'Um die Diktatur des Proletariats. Das ratlose Büro der II. Internationale', in *Sozialistische Warte* 1/3 (July 1934) 77. On Kumleben see L. Black, 'Social Democracy as a Way of Life: Fellowship and the Socialist Union, 1951–9', in *Twentieth Century British History* 10/4 (1999).
73. Kumleben, 'Diktatur des Proletariats', 77. See also G.R. Horn, *European Socialists Respond to Fascism: Ideology, Activism and Contingency in the 1930s* (Oxford: Oxford University Press, 1996) pp. 42–43.
74. Kumleben, 'Diktatur des Proletariats', pp. 78–79.
75. W. Eichler writing under the pseudonym Martin Hart, 'Fern-Ost-Aufgaben' in *Sozialistische Warte* 12/16 (15 August 1937) 361.
76. Hart, 'Spanien als Lehre', in *Sozialistische Warte* 12/12 (15 June 1937) 265–66.
77. Hart, 'Totaler Schock', in *Sozialistische Warte* 13/12 (28 March 1938) 265.
78. Eichler was keen to stress he was not against the 'English' as a whole, being careful to point out that he had learned about the United Kingdom through his English colleagues in the SVG. See AdsD, IJB/ISK Collection, Box 35, Letter from Eichler to Kurt Hiller, 30 March 1938.
79. Link, *IJB und ISK*, pp. 247–51.
80. R. Behring, *Demokratische Außenpolitik für Deutschland. Die außenpolitischen Vorstellungen deutscher Sozialdemokraten im Exil 1933–1945* (Düsseldorf: Droste, 1999), p. 143.
81. P. Ramme [Henry-Harmann], 'Hitler und Stalin', in *Sozialistische Warte* 15/38 (6 October 1939) 893.
82. Röder, *Sozialistische Exilgruppen in Großbritannien*, p. 47. Ulbricht's article and a reply by the working group of non-communist socialist groups in Britain are both quoted in 'Die KPD und die Solidarität der Illegalen', *Sozialistische Warte* 15/7 (28 March 1940) 199–203.
83. Indeed, as Eugen Brehm explained to Eichler in 1938, their advocacy of European federalism was positioned against the imperialism of Western democracies such as Britain. See AdsD, IJB/ISK Collection, Box 34, Letter from Max Herb [Eugen Brehm] to Eichler, 4 February 1938.

84. H. Kühn, writing as Hendrik H. Frans [Heinz Kühn], 'Zur Krise des Internationalismus' in *Freie Sozialistische Tribüne/Sozialistische Warte* 13/51 (December 1938) 1218–19.
85. Ibid.
86. Internationaler Sozialistischer Kampfbund (ed.), *Russland und die Komintern. Gedanken für einen Internationalen Sozialistischen Neuaufbau* (London: Renaissance, 1942) p. 55.
87. Schilmar, *Europadiskurs*, pp. 63–64.
88. Behring, *Demokratische Außenpolitik*, pp. 443, 447
89. Ibid., p. 451.
90. H. Maimann, *Politik im Wartesaal: Österreichische Exilpolitik in Großbritannien 1938 bis 1945* (Vienna: Böhlau, 1975) pp. 49–50, 121.
91. Schilmar, *Europadiskurs*, esp. p. 66.
92. Ibid., pp. 126–37.
93. Maimann, *Politik im Wartesaal*, pp. 135–44.
94. K. Voigt (ed.), *Friedenssicherung und europäische Einigung. Ideen des deutschen Exils 1939–1945* (Frankfurt am Main: Fischer, 1988) pp. 34, 40–41; Behring, *Demokratische Außenpolitik*, p. 451.
95. Schilmar, *Europadiskurs*, p. 55; Barclay, 'Rethinking Social Democracy, the State, and Europe', in Barclay and Weitz, *Between Reform and Revolution*, p. 387.
96. Schilmar, *Europadiskurs*, pp. 141–43, 210–31; M. Herb [Eugen Brehm], 'Bemerkungen zur Aussenpolitik', *Freie Sozialistische Tribüne/Sozialistische Warte* 13/40–41 (October 1938) 954–77.
97. J. Taylor, 'Hans Vogel, the Flight of the Exiled German Social Democrats from France, 1940–41, and the British Labour Party', in A. Grenville (ed.), *German-speaking exiles in Great Britain*, Vol. 2 (Amsterdam: Rodopi, 2000) pp. 123–34.
98. MRC, SVG Archive, MSS 173.1/7 [Untitled Report], 'Reports on the Work of the SVG'.
99. Röder, *Sozialistische Exilgruppen in Großbritannien*, p. 91. Also Lemke-Mueller, *Ethischer Sozialismus*, p. 131; and Link, *IJB und ISK*, p. 261
100. A. Glees, *Exile Politics during the Second World War: The German Social Democrats in Britain* (Oxford: Oxford University Press, 1982) pp. 103, 133; Eiber, *Sozialdemokratie in der Emigration*, p. C.
101. See *Sozialistische Mitteilungen: News for German Socialists in England*, Nr. 44 (December 1942).
102. See M. Conway and J. Gotovitch, (eds), *Europe in Exile: European Communities in Britain, 1940–1945* (Oxford and New York: Berghahn Books, 2001).
103. G. Hirschfeld, 'Deutsche Emigranten in Großbritannien und ihr Widerstand gegen den Nationalsozialismus', in K.-J. Müller and D. Dilks (eds), *Großbritannien und der deutsche Widerstand* (Paderborn: Schöningh, 1994) p. 116. Also see Entries on Fritz Eberhard and Willi Eichler in Röder and Strauss, *Biographisches Handbuch der deutschsprachigen Emigration*, pp. 143, 148.
104. R. Mayne and J. Pindar, *Federal Union: The Pioneers. A History of Federal Union* (London: Macmillan, 1990) p. 84.
105. Angster, *Konsenskapitalismus und Sozialdemokratie*, p. 311.
106. M. Saran, *Never Give Up: Memoirs* (London: Wolff, 1976) p. 89.
107. Saran, *Never Give Up*, p. 89. See also P. Stachura, 'Towards and Beyond Yalta' and Wojciech Rojek, 'The Government of the Republic of Poland in Exile, 1945–92', in P. Stachura (ed.), *The Poles in Britain, 1940–2000. From Betrayal to Assimiliation* (London and New York: Routledge, 2004) p. 12, 33–47.
108. See M. Minion, 'The Labour Party and Europe during the 1940s: the strange case of the Socialist Vanguard Group', 18 at http://www.lsbu.ac.uk/cibs/european-institute-papers/papers2/498.PDF; D. de Bellefroid, 'The Commission pour l'Etude des Problèmes d'Après-Guerre (CEPAG) 1941–1944', in Conway and Gotovitch (eds), *Europe in Exile*.

109. AdsD, IJB/ISK Collection, Box 41, 'Richtlinien eines freien Deutschen für ein Deutschland der Zukunft' [July 1941].
110. [Erich Ollenhauer] 'Protokoll der SPD-Konferenz "Der kommende Friede und das kommende Deutschland" am 10/11 Mai 1941', in Eiber, *Sozialdemokratie in der Emigration*, pp. 502–3.
111. Behring, *Demokratische Aussenpolitik*, p. 428; Eiber, *Sozialdemokratie in der Emigration*, p. 133.
112. Maimann, *Politik im Wartesaal*, p. 171.
113. On Brehm, see J.M. Ritchie, 'Kurt Hiller – A "Stänkerer" in Exile, 1934–1955', in *German Life and Letters* 51/2 (April 1998) 271; M. Herb [Eugen Brehm], 'Sinn und Unsinn des Selbstbestimmungsrechts', in *Freie Sozialistische Tribüne/Sozialistische Warte* 15/1 (4 January 1940), 30
114. MRC, SVG Archive, MSS. 173/17/2, W. Eichler, *Calling All Europe. A Symposium of Speeches on the Future Order of Europe* (London, 1942) p. 12.
115. Schilmar, *Europadiskurs*, p. 221.
116. See Lemke-Mueller, *Ethischer Sozialismus*, pp. 174–77; and Link, *IJB und ISK*, p. 284.
117. See 'Möglichkeiten und Aufgaben einer geeinten sozialistischen Partei in Deutschland. Grundgedanken eines Referates von Erich Ollenhauer in einer Mitgliederversammlung der "Union" in London, 1942', in Dowe and Klotzbach, *Programmatische Dokumente der deutschen Sozialdemokratie*, pp. 241–48.
118. Both programmes can be found in the AdsD, IJB)/ISK Collection, Box 49. See also Lemke-Mueller, *Ethischer Sozialismus*, p. 176.
119. Schilmar, *Europadiskurs*, p. 274.
120. AdsD, IJB/ISK Collection, Box 47, M[onats] A[ntwort] des B[undes] V[orstandes], January 1943.
121. See, for instance, AdsD, IJB/ISK Collection, Box 55, Letter from Hans Vogel to Eichler, 20 March 1945.
122. These articles appeared on 4 December 1943 and 18 November 1944 in the *Neue Volks-Zeitung*.

Chapter 4

THE RISE AND FALL OF A SOCIALIST EUROPE
The ISK and the SPD in Opposition

Amidst the waving of flags and the ringing of bells that signalled the end of the war in Europe, a feeling lingered among many German exiles that there was more fighting to be done. Alongside filing reports on the signing of the armistice in May 1945, journalists for *Die Zeitung*, a German newspaper published in wartime London, pinpointed the prominent Nazis still at large while also highlighting the struggles being made to reeducate Germans. Chronologies of the Nazi aggression, usually counted down in ever decreasing units of time ('after five years, eight months and five days'), seemed to imply that Nazism was a nightmare whose end everyone had eagerly anticipated. However, as these journalists acknowledged, the history of this war and the National Socialist regime did not end in May 1945, nor begin in September 1939 or November 1933, for 'militarism and nationalism ha[d] deeper roots than National Socialism'.[1]

Die Zeitung was a newspaper produced largely by German liberals (with British Foreign Office funding).[2] Its position on the damaging effects of militarism and nationalism was, nevertheless, shared by the German socialists who had been in exile for much of the 1930s and 1940s. Socialists who returned to Germany had long argued that the National Socialists were propelled to power by industrialists, bankers and other architects of monopoly capitalism who sought to cut a deal with Hitler in order to crush the workers' movements.[3] As a result they came back home convinced that there could be no return to Weimar democracy but rather that radical changes to the economic and political structures should be adopted before the German population could exercise any sovereignty.[4] While their analysis was shared by most social democrats in Germany in the early postwar period, their leadership claims were not. Similarly, while their commitment to a socialist integration of Europe was theoretically shared by their fellow social democrats, the early moves towards integration were made by Christian Democratic leaders who were supported by the Western Allies.[5] This meant that exiled socialists' plans for integrating Europe were marginalized among policymakers in the post-war period and that socialists advocated European integration from an oppositional perspective. This chapter traces the trajectory of the ISK group as its members returned to the SPD fold and sought to advocate a European agenda that would redress the problems encountered by parliamentary democracies such as Germany in the interwar period. Particular attention is paid to the enduring transnational connections maintained by the group, and thus to the transnational context within which its conceptions of Europe were advanced.

The argument presented here illustrates how ideas of Europe as an integrated Third Force formulated by ISK members and other exiled socialists became predominant within the post-war SPD. Such conceptions of Europe became particularly persuasive in the early post-war period, as the ensuing division of Germany and Europe appeared to be yet another carving up of a continent that had repeatedly been partitioned and convulsed with war since the growth of nation-states in the nineteenth century. By focusing on the Third Way agenda put forward by formerly exiled socialists, the narrative seeks to nuance the 'Westernization of Social Democracy' thesis as applied to Germany. It suggests that although social democrats may have chosen alliance with the West as a short-term means of resisting Soviet incursions into Germany, they nevertheless sought to change this Cold War status quo, albeit by first accepting that West Germany could work towards creating a neutral, socialist and unified Europe only from a position of strength in the Western bloc.[6]

In case this argument finesses the differences that divided social democrats during the early post-war period too much, it should be made clear that diverging opinions emerged and endured among social democrats. For instance the positions held by the Bürgermeisterflügel (a group of independent-minded mayors introduced in the last chapter) differed from those of the leaders of the national party who clustered around Kurt Schumacher and became the architects of the party's early post-war policy of 'intransigent opposition' to the course taken by the Christian Democrats. This suggests that the legacy of the socialist emigration was a conflicted one. However, it should be stressed that a rhetoric of European integration also served to postpone conflict between socialists. It offered rival groups the promise of revising the status quo and not only fulfilling the internationalist agenda long held by socialist groups but also of overcoming the Cold War division of Germany. This exploration of post-war socialist conceptions of Europe will thus attempt to explain how European integration gained such universal appeal among social democrats and, in turn, became a means by which socialists remained more united than they had been during the interwar period.

The argument advanced accordingly seeks to move us beyond the Schumacher-centric approach of many historians dealing with the SPD's European policy in the early post-war period. It situates the policy of Kurt Schumacher within the context of longer-standing socialist theories of European integration, developed particularly by formerly exiled socialist groups such as the ISK.[7] Furthermore, the argument suggests that socialist Third Force theories of European integration did not end with Schumacher's largely failed policy but reemerged in the *Ostpolitik* initiatives launched in the 1960s by former exiles and advocates of a Third Force Europe such as Willy Brandt. The following section focuses on how former splinter groups such as the ISK were integrated into the post-war SPD and outlines how they were able to advance an oppositional agenda within the SPD, rather than seeking to remain on the margins of parliamentary politics. The focus then shifts to consider how such groups developed the European policy of the SPD and worked within international bodies such as the Socialist International to promote their Third Force agenda.

The Return of the Exiles and the Reforming of the SPD

In December of 1945, Willi Eichler wrote to ISK members to explain that he was to dissolve the group and would encourage its members to rejoin a reconstituted SPD.[8] That the ISK leaders could agree to this decision (in common with other exiled dissident parties in the Union such as Neu Beginnen and the SAP) might appear surprising, given their positions regarding the viability of parliamentary democracy during the interwar and war years. Certainly, the ISK leaders did not leave the United Kingdom altogether convinced of the virtues of parliamentary democracy. Instead, they highlighted their opposition to majoritarianism, complaining that most SPD members in the Union 'had not learned a thing from the time between 1912 and 1945', and wanted 'more elections in order to deepen democracy'.[9] As a result, at the start of 1945 ISK members were expressing their shock that other splinter groups such as Neu Beginnen and the SAP were willing to rejoin the SPD, largely unconditionally. The ISK report for May to December 1944 stated in contrast that the ISK wished to stay true to the Bolshevik principle of building a vanguard to 'clearly represent the founding of socialism as a goal necessitated by Right', and to 'develop and put to the test a leading organization that would be appropriate for this founding' of socialism.[10] Yet, during the course of the year it became clear, at least to Willi Eichler, that the ISK agenda could be furthered within the post-war SPD and, equally importantly, that the ISK was unlikely to thrive as an autonomous grouping in post-war Germany. Eichler travelled around Germany, visiting the cities where there were still ISK members, canvassing their opinions on whether the ISK should ally with the SPD, the KPD or form a new party. He found among these members, as well as among the German and Swiss Social Democrats that René Bertholet and he met on their travels through France, Switzerland and Germany, a great enthusiasm for working within the SPD. 'It was surprising', he wrote, 'how varied the people were who all commit themselves to the SPD. This just confirms our old impression that one cannot merely look on when it comes to working with the SPD but take the movement as a whole … as a fundamentally progressive movement.'[11]

One important cause of Eichler's enthusiasm for the SPD was the encouragement he received from Kurt Schumacher, who became the SPD's predominant figure in the post-war period. Schumacher may not have appeared as the frontrunner for the leadership in the immediate post-war period, given that SPD leaders in the Soviet Zone could be much more active than their Western counterparts, due to the encouragement of renewed political activity from the Soviet authorities compared with the blanket ban on political activism issued in the Western zones. Indeed, by the autumn of 1945, when the American and British authorities allowed political parties to be formed in their zones, the SPD in the Soviet Zone could already boast a membership of between three and four hundred thousand. However, many SPD members in the Western zones and, perhaps more importantly, the Western occupation authorities, suspected that the initial fostering of SPD activity in the East was an attempt by the Russians to lay claim to all of Germany, once a compliant SPD had established its electoral dominance in the country. Thus, Schumacher's strong anti-communism made him appealing to the Americans and British. The latter flew him in a military aircraft to Berlin in February 1946 for a showdown with the leader of the Berlin SPD, Otto Grotewohl, who in 1949 became the first prime minister of the GDR.[12] Furthermore, Schumacher appealed to the majority of SPD rank-and-file who resented the leadership claims of the party's elder statesmen who had fled into exile. Schumacher's record compared favourably, given that he had stayed in Germany and endured a decade of political imprisonment in Dachau.[13]

Indeed, when Hans Vogel, the leader of the London group of exiles, proposed to other members of the Party leadership living outside of Britain in March 1945 that they should reconvene according to their mandate of 1933, not even all of his colleagues from exile agreed. Former Reichstag delegate Siegfried Aufhäuser pointed out that nobody had given the exiled leaders a mandate expecting them to be there twelve years later in such changed circumstances.[14] However, this London mandate was recognized in October 1945 at a national congress hosted in Kloster Wennigsen. This congress was convened by Kurt Schumacher, who was eager to establish his power base in Hanover, particularly vis-à-vis the Berlin SPD, and who thus needed the support of leading exiled socialists.[15]

As part of his reaching out to former exiles, Schumacher also advocated the integration of all the left-splinter groups that had been members of the Union in Britain into the SPD.[16] He went on to make the most of his alliance with the London group, recruiting Erich Ollenhauer (the leading member of the London group after Hans Vogel's death in October 1945) as his deputy leader on the Party Day in May 1946 and eight of the London exiles including Schoettle and Knoeringen from Neu Beginnen as well as Eichler from the ISK as members of the thirty-strong party executive or *Vorstand*.[17] Furthermore, although Schumacher conceded at Wennigsen that, '[t]he Comrades in Germany are not convinced in every case of the necessity for the emigration', this did not mean that the reconstruction plans that exiles had developed while enjoying freedom of expression in Britain were not adopted by social democrats at home. Indeed, as Ludwig Eiber has illustrated, Schumacher's policy programme in 1945 was almost identical to that proposed by the London group.[18]

Eichler's decision to merge the ISK into the SPD was, nevertheless, greeted by other leaders of the group such as Walter Fliess as a 'bombshell'.[19] Eichler justified his decision, arguing that, '[t]he division of the workers' movement was … always regrettable … [but] never so regrettable as it would be now to exist as an individual group, without having fully exploited the opportunities on offer today for unified work'.[20] Here he was recalling what he regarded as Nelson's mistake of 1926, when he gave up the chance to exercise influence within the SPD.[21] The ISK leader may also have been aware of the relative weakness of exiled socialists, whose advice as reeducators was already being shunned by Germans who had not left their country.[22] Nevertheless, addressing the concerns of ISK members, Eichler wrote frankly to Schumacher on the issue of the 'Construction of a Socialist Party' in September 1945, explaining the ISK position that: 'We see the socialist Party as a vanguard that has set as its goal the conquest of state power'. By contrast, 'After the experiences of the socialist struggle in many lands we see in the democratic-parliamentary method no sure means of reaching political power. The Reaction regards democracy only as a facade to camouflage the real power relations … The socialist Party must take account of these facts and … [in] revolutionary situations it must be ready, also without the backing of the majority of the population, to seize power.'[23]

Eichler was addressing the concerns of his colleagues in the ISK that they would have to leave behind their reservations about parliamentary democracy and renounce their vision of a federal Europe reshaped by a revolutionary socialist elite, as they returned to the SPD fold. Instead, while it was true that former ISK members had to work within a party committed to exercising power through the ballot box, the SPD leadership encouraged splinter-group leaders to be the architects of the party's policy of opposition to the early form of democracy practised in the Federal Republic. For instance, when Schumacher and the Bundesvorstand, or federal executive, decided on their policy of 'intransigent opposition' shortly after they lost the first federal elections in August 1949, it was Eichler, in common with other former left-splinter group leaders such as von Knoeringen and Schoettle, who drew up the policy and presented it to a committee of the Bundesvorstand at Bad Durkheim in the same month.[24] This group of former exiles was, furthermore, among the most prominent and vocal supporters of the policy, defending it at the Hamburg Conference of 21 to 25 May 1950 against the accommodationist wing of the party, which was largely made up of the Bürgermeisterflügel.[25]

I will discuss the Bürgermeisterflügel in more detail below; certainly its existence illustrates the conflicted legacy of the socialist emigration on German social democracy after 1945. Nevertheless, for formerly oppositional figures such as Eichler, it appeared that the policy of intransigent opposition they could advocate proved that SPD members had learned from the mistakes of 1918 and Weimar, and were not willing to accept responsibility for policies they did not support in the name of democracy. As Eichler explained in 1947 to his former ISK colleague Fritz Eberhard, justifying the SPD approach:

> The whole SPD belongs decisively in the Opposition in the whole of Germany. Then the accusation that we too have bungled the democracy that the Occupation has tried to build cannot be made … we must go into Opposition so that the others … our opponents are at last exposed. Until now everything harmful that was dreamed up was implemented more or less with the help of Social Democrats. They [our opponents] were protected and … by the main representatives of the German working classes.[26]

By the end of the 1940s, then, formerly revolutionary exiles had not simply aligned themselves with the kind of democracy being put in place by the Western allies and by Chancellor Adenauer's CDU/CSU alliance. However, the SPD leader, Schumacher, proved his willingness not to work within a coalition with the Christian Democrats but to hold true to the socialist vision of German and European reconstruction largely formulated by the exiles, which aimed at a United States of Europe that included a reunified Germany and stretched across the hardening Cold War divide.[27] He therefore resolved to offer 'intransigent opposition', and thereby paradoxically firmed up the identity and the role played by such parties as the SPD within the Federal Republic, institutionalizing opposition within one of the parliamentary parties. Unlike during the Weimar period, oppositional figures such as those from the former ISK, who offered only provisional support for the new German state, were thus not forced to break away from the predominant leftist party in order to elaborate their vision of a radically different Germany. Rather, particularly through their advocacy of a federal, Third Force Europe, they could work within the party towards the future goals of realigning Germany from its current position in the emerging Western bloc and reshaping its political culture.

Developing the SPD's *Europapolitik*

With regard to planning schemes for the integration of Europe, ISK members were similarly encouraged by SPD leaders to advance a socialist vision of a federated Europe quite at odds with the version outlined by Christian Democrats in the early post-war period. As most historians now recognize, in spite of his party's opposition to Germany joining the Council of Europe, the ECSC and the European Defence Community (EDC), Kurt Schumacher was not opposed to European unity. Rather, he rejected the integration of the Federal Republic within a Western European community before either German reunification had been achieved or the Federal Republic had been granted equal status with other European nations.[28] Although he forcefully argued in May 1946 that 'A new Germany would see its highest objective to become a part of the United States of Europe', Schumacher objected to Germany's joining the Council of Europe. He did this because the Saar and the Western zones of Germany were to be accorded associate status whereas he believed that Germany should join only as a full member and that the Saar should be German prior to the federation of Europe.[29] On this issue he was opposed by a significant minority of leading SPD members. This included a number of emigres, such as Max Brauer and Willy Brandt, and (non-emigres) Wilhelm Kaisen, Paul Löbe and Heinz-Joachim Heydorn, most of whom vocally supported the accession of the Federal Republic to the Council of Europe in the Hamburg Conference of May 1950.[30] However, committed advocates of European integration, including exiles such as Eichler, Schoettle and Wehner, alongside those who had remained in Nazi Germany, such as Carlo Schmid, backed Schumacher's policy. They also agreed to the SPD policy of opposing Germany joining the ECSC before the industries of Europe were socialized, so as to ensure they would be administered in a manner consistent with socialist principles, rather than becoming capitalistic cartels.[31]

According to such evidence, we are therefore left with exiles on either side of the European debate within the SPD. In the case of the Bürgermeisterflügel, it appears that mayors such as Max Brauer and Ernst Reuter, and state leaders such as Wilhelm Hoegner, learned to work with coalitions in their jurisdictions and eventually came to prize such coalitions. In some cases, they worked particularly well with coalition partners on aspects of European policy, signalling the convergence of their positions on Europe with those of their colleagues in the Christian and Free Democratic parties, who were often supportive of the integration of a Western *Kleineuropa*. Certainly, in the case of Ernst Reuter in West Berlin, it is relatively easy to understand how he could become eager to integrate West Berlin into a Western alliance, given the exigencies of the post-war situation. West Berliners were being blockaded by the Soviets and Reuter himself was being denied the position of Lord Mayor by the Soviets.[32] Furthermore, the chances that Reuter's long-held commitment to local, communal self-government as a necessary complement to parliamentary democracy would be put into practice were greater within a Western-style pluralist democracy than a Sovietized People's Democracy.[33]

The more difficult question to answer is why other exiles such as Eichler continued to oppose the creation of a Western European economic alliance, at least until the early 1950s. Having argued throughout the years of exile that a Central European (and broader European) community could be created out of the 'integrations' effected by the Nazis, figures such as Eichler, who had developed their schemes for Europe in conversation with colleagues from Central Europe, were unwilling to jettison such plans after 1945, particularly as German and Austrian socialists had become somewhat estranged from the Western socialist parties. The thinking of such socialist theorists of European unity was well summarized in a report written for the London Union of Socialist Parties in 1944 by Walter Fliess, the ISK's foremost economic theorist and a translator for the Committee of the International Socialist Conference (COMISCO) in the late 1940s.[34] In this document Fliess argued that the National Socialist 'integration' of Europe should form the basis from which post-war planners must work.[35] Fliess explained that the admittedly exploitative international corporatist structures that the Nazis had put in place to generate profits for large German companies such as I.G. Farben had laid the groundwork for an integrated European economy. For these businesses, which had enjoyed monopoly status in occupied Europe, could now be socialized, thereby creating publically owned and Europe-wide concerns that would prevent any future capitalist monopolies forming. Similarly, Fliess suggested that the six largest German banks had effectively coordinated the policies of the national banks across occupied Europe. This meant that, although the Nazis had left national currencies in place, they had in reality controlled the currencies of occupied Europe through the Reichsbank. Such a National Socialist integration of the banking system could provide the basis for a 'European Central Banking Institute', which would prevent a return to the interwar situation whereby a 'lack of ... co-ordination ... under the impact of world depression, forced most nations into currency and exchange wars'.[36]

In sum, Fliess advocated the creation of a 'Central European Economic Organization' made up of a 'Central Bank, Investment Control, Coal and Iron Authority' that would effectively be a law unto itself. Indeed, it would be backed up by a European police force 'with powers sufficient to undertake the protection of all the States of Europe, and thus make all national armies superfluous'. Public utilities and communications would be publicly funded and administered in common, with a particular focus on resources that cut across national borders such as the Danube. For Fliess, it was 'also clear that Europe will have to work out a unified foreign policy. Individual States would thus not be able to conclude international treaties without the agreement of the other members of the European Federation'. Although administration within this federation would be centralized, Fliess was keen to stress the possibilities for local and regional self-government within this integrated Europe, harkening back to the *Räterepublik*, as was common for ISK theorists. He explained: 'Within the individual nations bureaucratic and totalitarian tendencies can be combated by far-reaching economic and political self-government ... [which is] the only way in which a people can play a genuine part in determining its own destiny, and thus become educated for participation in a responsible public life'. And similarly, when it came to developing agriculture – a particular concern in Central and Eastern Europe – Fliess offered a different vision to Soviet collectivization. Instead of advocating wholesale nationalization, he promoted the forming of cooperatives, arguing that within an integrated Europe 'the special conditions of agriculture justify the existence of a large class of independent peasant enterprises even in this machine age'.[37]

Fliess thus made the case for a federated Europe that would cut across the early Cold War divide and diverge from the plans of the Western European governments after 1945, not least in terms of how much power should be devolved to local and regional bodies. A still more radical argument against a Western-style political union was made by Fliess's colleague, Hilda Monte, a socialist émigré who had worked with Harold Laski and Franz Neumann, among others, at the LSE. Following through the Marxist argument that Nazism was merely the thuggish face of monopoly capitalism in its stage of crisis, she suggested that there would likely be similarities between the Nazi economic integration of Europe and the post-war integration put in place by the Western allies. As she asked:

> Why has the British Government helped and abetted the Nazis e.g., by the conclusion of the naval agreement of 1935? Why did Britain not prevent Mussolini's conquest of Abyssinia in 1935–6? Why did Britain allow Franco to defeat the Spanish Republic? Why did not Britain, in common with the Soviet Union, guarantee the frontiers of Czechoslovakia in 1938? Any attempt of going to the root causes will inevitably lead to the class interests by which, consciously or unconsciously, the statesmen have been guided in their policy.[38]

Thus, when she spoke of the planned and integrated economy that she regarded as inevitable for post-war Europe, she drew out the elements of continuity between fascist and capitalist corporatism, although she also highlighted their commonalities with socialist planning:

> However immense the difference is between socialism, liberalism, and fascism – in their programmes and in their propaganda they are not always easily to be distinguished. Control and planning, the abolition of unemployment, and international co-operation are advocated by all – though for different purposes ... Just as 'economic collaboration' and 'planning' may have to be translated by 'stabilization of monopoly capitalism', so the 'abolition of unemployment' may translate itself into 'essential works orders' for the benefit of capitalist profit. Even nationalization in the capitalist State does not necessarily mean more than guaranteed profits – or even the nationalization of losses.[39]

Monte's argument was particularly interesting as it, on the one hand, presented a Europe that faced stark ideological choices between capitalism, fascism and socialism, while, on the other hand, it suggested that all ideological parties had reconciled themselves to planned economies, and to integrating them within an international framework. There is certainly evidence to support Monte's analysis in this latter regard. For instance, the dispassionate discussions between Albert Speer, Hitler's corporatist economic advisor and Minister of Armaments and War, and Jean Bichelonne, the French Minister of Production, in 1943 concerning the necessity of a European economic integration provided the basis for the plans that made up Jean Monnet's post-war project.[40] Similarly, as Marshall's European Reconstruction Programme (ERP) went on to show, when it came to American intervention in Europe in the post-war period, Europeans confronted not a laissez-faire superpower but an administrative, planning American state that had reached its high point during the New Deal.[41]

Monte argued that, faced with such rival schemes for European integration, socialists must seize the right to integrate the economies of Europe themselves.

Indeed, she made clear that she (accurately) regarded direct intervention from the United States as the greatest threat to the realization of a socialist Europe. As she explained:

> The USA will constitute the greatest *potential* danger, because she controls the most powerful weapon against revolution – namely: food for the starving peoples of Europe. She knows that nothing is less likely than that starving peoples will revolt against the soup kitchen ... It is essential, therefore, that all those who are aiming at a better order in Europe ... all understand that 'Relief and Reconstruction' are by no means 'unpolitical' subjects.[42]

However, Monte's own rhetoric somewhat undercut her argument. She contrasted how Europe had become 'balkanized' during the interwar period with how the United States under the New Deal had become 'organized' as a single, planned economy. Accordingly Monte advocated an emulation of American planning initiatives such as the Tennessee Valley Authority when she outlined the form that European integration would take, albeit in order to increase European independence from the United States.[43]

Monte died in April 1945, shot as she sought to cross the Swiss–German border, and so did not witness the Marshall Plan, which was supported by Schumacher's SPD and has been interpreted as having revived the 'New Deal' ideology that she had observed in the TVA project.[44] Nevertheless, the arguments that she and fellow exiles advanced about socialist versus capitalist planning and the case she made for a Europe that linked East and West continued to have resonance among SPD politicians throughout the 1950s, in spite of the shift perceptible among American policymakers during this period. Her colleague in British exile, the former Neu Beginnen theorist Richard Löwenthal, adapted her ideas in his influential *Jenseits des Kapitalismus* of 1947. In this text he imagined an integrated Europe as an 'example of democratic socialist planning between the two colossuses' of the United States and the Soviet Union, whose 'European mission' would be 'the greatest historical service that socialism can offer to mankind', yet which could only be realized if Europe remained an independent Third Power not reliant on American capitalism.[45]

Such arguments were picked up and modified by particularly those socialists active in European federalist politics such as Carlo Schmid, who was a leading member of the Council of Europe, and who advocated a 'collective security' arrangement in Europe that cut across Cold War boundaries in 1948.[46] More broadly speaking, the exiles' European conceptions gained traction within the SPD not least because leading members of the ISK such as Eichler and Werner Hansen, the latter having been a prominent figure since the later war years in the German and international trade union movement, were given important roles guiding the policy of the revamped SPD. For instance, Eichler became a member of the Foreign Policy and Cultural Policy Committees of the Party in 1946, and went on to sit on a Commission to shape the Programme of the Party in 1954, along with Hansen.[47] In addition to being an SPD member of the Council of

Europe until 1953, Eichler was also the editor of the first licensed newspaper in the British Zone, the *Rheinische Zeitung*, although he concentrated his efforts more on a theoretical journal, *Geist und Tat*, established by former ISK members, which went on to be one of the most important post-war social democratic publications alongside *Neuer Vorwärts* and *Die Neue Gesellschaft*.[48]

Considering the arguments of such socialist theorists of European integration offers the promise of better understanding the intellectual history behind socialist policy on Europe during the late 1940s and early 1950s. According to much of the political history that has been written on the period, social democrats usually appear as being somehow 'behind the curve' on foreign policy, as having clung on to ideas of a united Germany and not recognizing the realities of the early Cold War as well or as quickly as their Christian Democratic counterparts.[49] However, as the analysis of socialist theories of *Mitteleuropa* and a Third Force Europe presented here has suggested, social democrats thought in equally European terms as their rivals in other parties. Indeed, just as Christian Democrats came to advance a 'magnet' theory of Western Europe which, once consolidated, would attract the countries of Central and Eastern Europe, so too had socialists formulated their own magnet theory. Yet, rather than signalling an embracing of a Western order, this socialist magnet theory maintained a commitment to a Europe that reunited East and West.[50] It was such a commitment to creating a Central European community that ensured that social democrats remained so wedded to recovering a united Germany – for only a united Germany, not shorn of its socialist heartlands in the North and East, could perform such a magnet function for the countries of Eastern and Central Europe, within which socialists had already assumed dominant positions.[51]

This intellectual history background thus refines the pre-existing picture of social democratic foreign policy as being somehow slow to react to realities and excessively shaped by the narrowness of Kurt Schumacher, who, so the story goes, became increasingly out of touch and inflexible due to his decade in a concentration camp.[52] As will be shown in the following section, German socialists were very active in international politics in the post-war period, working hard to revive networks between members of the Socialist International and contributing to the European federalist movement. Nevertheless, the effectiveness of their internationalist efforts was limited by Cold War politics, which gradually constrained the possibilities for international political activity to within the 'small Europe' that became integrated by the Treaty of Rome in 1957.

Allied Plans for Europe, European Socialism and the Disappointments of Victory

As has been illustrated, socialists made the case for an integrated Europe in the later war years in opposition to the plans they believed the occupying forces would implement in the immediate post-war period. Leading figures in the SPD such as Friedrich Stampfer (located in the United States during the war) were, however, initially optimistic that the occupation forces would need to employ reliable (usually leftist) anti-Nazis to rebuild the institutions of governance, to remove all those with ties to the National Socialist regime, and to reestablish trust with European neighbours who had suffered under National Socialist occupation.[53] Such a procedure could, they maintained, be replicated across Europe, with power being turned over to various national resistance movements who had already cooperated with one another by working against the German war effort. What was most promising about this prospect was that many resistance groups with roots in socialist politics (for example Spinelli's in Italy and Ferrat's Franc-tireur movement in France) were committed to European federalism.[54] Thus the prospect of a European federalist movement that could bloodlessly effect a radically different institutional set up across the continent appeared a possible alternative to revolution for ISK members, in common with many others in oppositional groups such as Neu Beginnen and the SAP.

Exiled socialists, many of whom had worked on plans for a post-war Europe, were therefore particularly disheartened by the negotiations concluded between the Allies at the Yalta and Potsdam conferences of 1945. At these conferences, the Allies divided Europe into spheres of influence and shifted Poland's borders westwards into eastern Germany.[55] These negotiations also signalled the marginalization of governments-in-exile such as the Polish, which had worked with the Allies on the post-war reconstruction of their countries.[56] This marginalization of Central Europeans initially convinced socialists like Eichler that they would be more likely to work together for a Third Force Europe, rather than in alliance with any of the Great Powers. For these Great Powers, stated Eichler, had disavowed 'any international order based on rights and ... return[ed] to the old rule of the fist'.[57]

Such plans for a Third Force Europe, conceived in the face of Great Power negotiations, were hampered by the opposition of the dominant socialist parties in wartime and post-war Europe, which were unwilling to work within a reconstructed Socialist International alongside German and other exiled parties. The splits between exiled socialists and those representing the dominant socialist parties in 'free' Europe had been brewing since at least 1939, when the Labour and Socialist International (LSI) – the latest incarnation of the Socialist International – had been reformed so that exile parties became less powerful than parties in the free nations. William Gillies, the International Secretary of the British Labour Party, had argued that the LSI should be reconstituted 'in accordance with the realities of the political situation in the different countries so as to ensure that the real power within the International should be in the hands of the living and active parties'. Gillies had been particularly concerned that Friedrich Adler, an Austrian socialist and secretary of the LSI between 1923 and 1946, would follow a *mitteleuropäisch* agenda and urge socialists to make revolution if war broke out.

Thus, he sought to have power concentrated in the reformist socialist parties of the Western nations and thereby to de-radicalize the Socialist International.[58]

The fears of exiled parties' radicalism expressed by Labour politicians such as Gillies turned into scepticism as realities on the ground in Central and Eastern Europe made the *mitteleuropäisch* plans of German and Austrian socialists appear ever more utopian. For instance, while exiled Germans stressed the possibilities for cooperation among Central Europeans, Hugh Dalton, wartime Minister of Economic Warfare, doubted that countries affected by the Nazi aggression would be eager to cooperate with Germans.[59] He advised the International Sub-Committee of the Labour Party in 1944 that Germans who lived in neighbouring, occupied countries should return because 'in the early post-war years ... there will be a depth of hatred against Germans in the occupied countries, which it is hard for us or for Americans to realize'. Indeed, he suggested that for Germans in Nazi-occupied areas, the choice was quite simply between 'migration' and 'massacre'.[60]

British Labour politicians thus remained suspicious of German socialists, not believing that the latter resembled a Western reformist parliamentary party. Instead, they remained convinced that these exiles advocated a form of *mitteleuropäisch* revolution that no longer appeared viable. The position of Labour politicians regarding German socialists was, of course, of particular significance for European socialists because the LSI during the war depended on the resources and good graces of the British Labour Party.[61] In the post-war period, German socialists continued to be marginalized by the Labour Party, which largely controlled the reconstituted Socialist International and blocked French and Belgian proposals to reform the organization. For instance, when conferences from March 1945 onwards were convened to facilitate the reforming of the International, the German SPD was excluded until 1947 when its members were allowed only 'to give evidence and answer questions', at the Zurich conference in June of that year.[62] This marginalization of German socialists in the International was compounded by other snubs issued by British Labour politicians, who were now in power and shaping the future political order in Germany. For instance, when Denis Healey had tried to get an invitation for the German SPD leaders in the British Zone to come to London to see the Minister of Health, Aneurin Bevan, in 1946 to discuss German issues, he was turned down. Similarly, when the National Council of Labour visited the British Zone in Germany in 1946, it did not call in on the SPD Party headquarters.[63]

If the concept of Westernization is taken to signify more than Americanization, also describing the ways in which Germans were influenced by organizations and parties in other Western countries such as Britain, then the evidence for a Westernization of the German SPD by the British Labour Party is not altogether convincing. However, a rather more negative version of Westernization may have occurred as a result of the estrangement of Central and Eastern European socialist parties from their German counterparts, particularly after the former were subjected to Soviet discipline. For instance, at the fledgling International's Zurich conference of 1947, which signalled a partial rehabilitation of the German SPD, preliminary meetings were held between the Polish delegation and the Czech representation to discuss how they could block the German party from joining a future International. During the conference itself Schumacher endured indiscriminate attacks, not least from the representative of the Polish Party. This fellow socialist declared that Schumacher was 'dangerous for the peace, dangerous for socialism, dangerous for democracy in Germany and for these reasons dangerous for the fate of the Polish people'. He widened his attack on Schumacher to include other German Social Democrats, concluding that 'The SPD is not a force for progress and democracy in Germany'.[64]

By 1947, the bipolar perspective of co-opted socialist parties within the Soviet sphere of influence thus pushed the socialist parties outside of the Soviet bloc closer together.[65] At the Zurich conference, Nordic and British delegates, who, unlike their French and Belgian counterparts, had shown little enthusiasm for a reform of the International in late 1945, now rallied round the Germans and complained that the questioning of Schumacher by Eastern European delegates had been unfair.[66] Indeed, the Western parties came to believe that it was the Eastern European parties, rather than the German SPD – which under Schumacher showed impeccably anti-communist credentials – that should be denied membership of the International, as their subjection to Soviet rule made their cooperation with Western colleagues impossible.[67] Support for the Germans came from many quarters in the Western parties, most movingly from the Jewish SFIO representative, Salomon Grumbach. He urged that there be 'No attack on [German] social democracy … [for] Their opposition was very strong … they were hanged and tortured in concentration camps by the thousands.' The outcome of the conference was that the German SPD was not admitted to the International, even though its application had been accepted by France, the Netherlands, Britain and the Scandinavian states. However, the Western parties continued to support the German cause and harden their opposition to the inclusion of socialist parties from the Soviet bloc in the new International. Indeed, at the next conference in Antwerp in November 1947, the German SPD went on to win the necessary two-thirds majority due to support from the Western parties.[68]

The realignment of the Northern and Western parties with the German social democrats may have largely been due to the Germans' own efforts. The SPD set up foreign representations in Britain, France, Sweden and the Netherlands after 1945 and established a foreign committee to liaise with member parties of the reconfigured International, COMISCO, in 1947.[69] Observing such developments allows us to refine the historiographical orthodoxy which has downplayed the German SPD's contribution to international socialist politics in the late 1940s and early 1950s. These same developments nevertheless show the challenges for German social democrats in creating alliances with parties in either the East or West of Europe. For instance, German social democrats were particularly eager to work with British and Scandinavian parties as they offered alternatives to the Christian Democratic initiatives for integrating Europe that were becoming dominant in countries such as West Germany, Italy and France. Furthermore, these parties also sought to shift the emphasis of European Recovery Program planning from simply increasing productivity towards creating full employment and achieving a greater redistribution of wealth.[70] Yet, the British Labour government rejected a multilateral approach to European integration, preferring to retain as much national sovereignty as possible.[71] And the Labour position was reinforced by the policies of Swedish social democrats, who sought to guard their tradition of neutrality and their welfare statist policies and therefore similarly rejected joining the ECSC.[72]

So, we are confronted with an interesting paradox: that Kurt Schumacher's own 'nationalist' position may well have been reinforced by the international discussions and cooperations engaged in by his party and the Northern and Western socialist parties, which proved less than eager to tie themselves to multilateral bodies.[73] This in turn inverts the typical arguments claiming that Schumacher's prioritizing of German unity and a domestic socialist agenda set the limits to his European commitment: quite the contrary, international politics shaped the kind of domestic political programme proposed by Schumacher.[74]

Of course, it should be remembered that the story of Schumacher's approach to European integration is only one part of the history of the SPD's European policy in the early post-Second World War period. According to recent historiography, another story emerges whereby European federalism was embraced by socialist reformers, and particularly trade unionists, as a way of turning away from Marxism and embedding socialist political activism within the pluralist parliamentary political culture that had been recreated in Western Europe.[75] For instance, when socialists met in COMISCO in December 1948, German delegates agreed to the suggestion by the French representative, Gérard Jacquet, that the 'Socialist Movement for the United States of Europe' should work within the framework of the non-partisan European Movement, based in continental Europe, rather than meeting within the British Labour Party sponsored and controlled COMISCO.[76] This decision may have been due less to a reformist current pulsing through continental socialist parties and more to their disillusion with the leadership of a British Labour Party. British leaders appeared at times isolationist and at others to be pursuing a policy of 'Western Union' that was anti-Communist and either Atlanticist or more genuinely European depending on perspective. They also, in the words of Foreign Secretary Ernest Bevin, appealed to a shared history of fighting against the Germans and for 'common ideals for which the Western Powers have twice in one generation shed their blood'.[77] Nevertheless, when the German section of the 'Socialist Movement for the United States of Europe' formed in November 1950, it was regarded as a collecting point for all the dissenting voices in the SPD, who sought to 'modernize' the party and move it away from its Marxist commitments in favour of seeking to manage capitalism and effect change with the parliamentary system.[78]

Reading the German SPD's policies from the outside in – seeing how foreign policy and international networks drove domestic policy and shaped the complexion of the national party, rather than vice versa – thus gives us a new perspective on the shifts that occurred among German socialists in the 1950s. During this period, many of the former splinter-group radicals and exiles, including Willi Eichler and those who formed the 'Zehner Circle' of social democrats and unionists, became the most reformist voices in the party, pushing it in the non-Marxist direction taken by the Godesberg Programme of 1959.[79] Accordingly, most treatments of the SPD have stressed how a process of reform led socialists to finally reach an accommodation with the institutional set-up predominant in much of the liberal-democratic West. Yet a focus on the European dimensions of the SPD's programme illustrates continuities that suggest how this reformist policy was not a simple turning away from the radicalism of the interwar years. Rather, a European federalist agenda, which stressed how power would be shifted away from national parties and parliaments towards local and sectoral bodies, echoed socialists' efforts to create forms of workers self-administration that went at least as far back as the Heidelberg Programme of 1925 (the first programme to also talk of a United States of Europe). While such federalist reforms might now take place within a pluralist political culture, they nevertheless provided a blueprint of radical change for socialists that hearkened back to an earlier Austro-Marxist agenda. They also anticipated the New Left agenda of the 1960s and 1970s that once again sought to shift the locus of democratic practice from national parliaments to the local community and the factory.[80]

This review of how German social democrats sought to navigate their foreign and domestic policy in the light of international socialist politics after 1945 has therefore offered a picture of them as somewhat ill-fitting members of a Western socialist camp that was itself hardly otherwise united. Furthermore, the role that European federalist politics played was not to further integrate German socialists within a Western bloc but to offer them a future that seemed almost as radically different from the present day as the revolutionary future they had envisaged during the interwar years.

A Westernization of German Social Democracy?

As has been shown, the ISK enjoyed unusually good contacts with British organizations compared with their colleagues in the socialist emigration. Yet, the experience of ISK members working with socialist organizations in Britain was part of a broader encounter of German exiled socialists with the political culture of Britain, which impacted on the positions they formulated while in exile and after they had returned to Germany. For instance, four of the leading ISK members, Walter

Fliess, Otto Bennemann, Werner Hansen and Josef Kappius, were deported to Australia in 1940 as potential fifth columnists.[81] This occurred because of the report written by the Ambassador to The Hague, Sir Neville Bland, on the 'Fifth Column Menace' in May of 1940, which prompted the British authorities to intern many German refugees in camps as far afield as Australia. Walter Fliess, who had been proprietor of the famous Vega restaurant in Leicester Square, as well as being one of the ISK's leading economic theorists, suffered particularly, being put on board the HMS *Dunera* to Australia, allegedly a site of some of the worst British abuses of 'enemy aliens'. On board Fliess's brother, Paul, was reportedly injured, having been struck by the bayonet of a staff member when he got up to use a toilet.[82] Such encounters with the political authorities in Britain may not, then, have conduced toward a simple Westernization of exiled German socialists, but rather may have highlighted certain similarities in disciplinary regimes between Western parliamentary democracies and the fascist powers from which the exiles had fled.[83]

These internment experiences should not be taken to suggest that the German exiles were altogether victimized or ostracized in their daily lives in Britain, even if relations between the British Labour Party and German socialists in the early post-war period certainly complicate the argument that German socialists were becoming Westernized during this period.[84] Looking back at the ISK's experience in Britain, one might, nevertheless, expect the situation of its leaders working with prominent socialists committed to parliamentary democracy, along with the heartening evidence of Labour's rise within a parliamentary system, to account for the ISK's move from advocacy of world revolution to a European federation that need not be exclusively socialist. However, the picture that emerges from the ISK's exile in Britain is rather more variegated.

Whereas ISK leaders were treated with scepticism by the mainstream of British Labour, they were looked up to and supported by their British offshoot, the SVG. This organization, in common with other leftist groups born out of splits in the Labour movement of the 1930s such as the Independent Labour Party and Stafford Cripps' Socialist League, was committed to the infiltration and radicalization of the Labour Party. Its position was well explained by Allan Flanders, a Walkemühle graduate, future editor of *Socialist Commentary* and head of the political branch of the Allied Control Commission for Germany (British section) in the immediate aftermath of the war. He addressed the entryist strategy of the organization, urging his fellow SVG members in 1939 that, 'it is quite possible for militants inside the L.P. to take command of the L.P. machinery and to use this for an agitation' that would serve to radicalize its members from their moderate support of parliamentary democracy.[85]

Flanders's appraisal of the potential for such an entryist strategy proved to be rather too optimistic. In fact, as a result of the radicalism of the British organization, the contact ISK leaders maintained with the SVG initially alienated them from the mainstream of the Labour movement in Britain, while bringing it closer to other, more subversive leftist groups. As Edith Moore and Allan Flanders recognized when they announced the group's change of name from Militant Socialist International to Socialist Vanguard Group to Eichler in 1941: the MSI had 'been sorely hampered by the taunt that we were "strange," a "secret body," a "foreign" body, an un- or anti-democratic body, etc. etc'. What emerged after 1941, however, was not a Damascene conversion to democracy on the part of the English or German groups that suggested a simple process of Westernization. Rather, both groups, along with other leftist splinter groups, moved towards dialogue with the dominant working-class parties, the Labour Party and the German SPD, not least in the hope of radicalizing these larger parties' politics. This Popular Front approach was no doubt also the result of the unusual demands for unity that war seemed to make. However, it offered formerly shunned leftist groups the chance to win places for their members on the Executives of organizations such as the Labour-affiliated Fabian Group and to 'pack' their meetings and thus ensure favourable voting outcomes.[86] As a result it became increasingly possible for these oppositional socialists to (subversively) work for change within, rather than from outside, the existing mainstream political organizations.

Such tactics were not untypical within the British context of the 1940s, where as many as ten Left Labour groups drew support for their more radical policy from the end of the war until early in the 1950s. These groups united particularly around a 'Third Force' European agenda, expressed in the support of 154 Labour MPs for Richard Crossman's amendment to the King's Speech of 1946 that criticized the government for being too pro-American. Many of these MPs went on to form the Keep Left group in 1947, a number of whose members in turn went on to convene the Parliamentary Labour Party Europe Group in December 1947 and the Socialist Europe Group in July 1948, both of which advocated a specifically Third Force agenda.[87] While the entryist strategy long advocated by ISK theorists was only partially vindicated by such developments, they nevertheless convinced elite groups like the ISK of the possibility of winning control of major organizations. This, in turn, suggests a rather more complicated exchange between exiled groups such as the ISK and home-grown socialist movements than a simple cultural transfer from Western democratic socialists to German groups that were previously anti-democratic.

Perhaps most interestingly, these 'subversive' German exiles were then often employed as Westernizing agents, working for the Allied forces on the reconstruction of Germany and the reeducation of the Germans. For instance, after his experience in Australia as a 'dangerous enemy alien', Fliess was appointed by the Foreign Office, on the recommendation of Allan Flanders, to play a leading role in formulating industrial and commercial policy for the Allied Control Commission at the end of the war.[88] Fliess was merely one of many recruits from the ISK made by the British government, whose secret services had already worked with ISK leaders on propaganda broadcasts and who employed Minna Specht, Mary Saran, Bernhard Reichenbach from the ISK, along with Waldemar von

Knoeringen from Neu Beginnen among others, as reeducators for prisoners of war in Wilton Park.[89]

Such a co-opting of British and German left-socialists did not blunt their radicalism, nor encourage them to abandon their plans for a Third Force politics in favour of a Western alignment. For instance, members of the SVG such as Allan Flanders sought to reform the British Labour approach to international politics away from its policy of Western Union.[90] As he explained in 'A Socialist Approach to Western Union', written from the Fabian International Bureau in April 1948: 'Our present economic and military dependence upon the United States is real and inescapable … We rightly prefer it to the alternative, dependence upon Soviet Russia … because it does not mean forfeiting entirely and permanently our independence. Our task is both to increase our independence and to use it to good purpose.' In his analysis an intriguing two-step argument emerged, which acknowledged that Western Europeans were not really independent, but that they would be all the stronger the more they acted together rather than as individual partners of the United States. As he contended:

> If peace should at any time be threatened by Russian aggression in Europe two things are certain: that a Western Union would not be able to offer more than a temporary resistance by virtue of its own armed strength; and that America would come to its assistance. It is this situation, however, that makes it unnecessary for a Western Union to subordinate its policy to that of the United States.[91]

Flanders, in common with many European socialists who conditionally accepted the early moves towards European integration, thus interpreted initiatives such as a Western Union as simply the necessary first steps towards a wider European union that would become increasingly independent from the United States. However, he did this, not by styling this Western alignment as a good in its own right, but – rather as Marxist theory stipulated that a bourgeois revolution must precede a genuine socialist revolution – merely as a necessary stage that would bring about its own overcoming. As his SVG colleague Charlie Buckner explained in a staccato post-war memo called 'Thesis for discussion on "Our attitude to War in an Atomic Age"': 'Need to recognize that sphere of usefulness of direct action becoming narrower. Recognized already in past that tactics of revolution needed revision in the light of development of military technique. Need today to apply same considerations to international sphere.'[92] This way of arguing – that alignment with the United States was merely a short-term and conditional goal and not based on a shared political culture – did not reflect the policy of the British governments of the 1950s. Yet it did speak to the policy of German socialists during the 1950s. They advocated a Third Way vision of Europe, arguing against the creation of the EDC in 1952, opposing the integration of West Germany into the North Atlantic Treaty Organization (NATO) with an anti-militarist 'German manifesto' of January 1955, and devising the 'Germany Plan' in 1959 for an All-German confederation.[93] The evidence from these proposals suggests that the SPD's leaders were eager to move towards a position of neutrality and away from Schumacher's early (and necessary) anti-Communist orientation. Even those social democrats such as Willy Brandt who did support West Germany's incorporation within NATO did so believing that only from a position of strength in the West could they push forward a successful *Ostpolitik*. These developments in socialist thought suggest how socialists such as the former members of the ISK in Germany, and the members of the SVG in Britain, could reconcile themselves to a pluralist parliamentary order and a small Western European community, while nevertheless projecting a future that would supersede it. In the following section I will show how German socialists sought to promote change at a domestic and European level after making such a provisional commitment to the West.

From a European Vanguard to a European Opposition: *Ostpolitik* Foreshadowed?

By 1947, even the most committed proponents of a Third Way Europe such as Denis de Rougemont of the Union of European Federalists (UEF), recognized that the goodwill of supporters of integration could not dismantle the ideological and physical barriers increasingly separating Europeans from each other. As he remarked during his welcoming speech at the first congress of the UEF in Montreux in August 1947: 'Today, there are two positions, two policies, two basic approaches. Not the "Left" or the "Right" that have been almost indistinguishable in their actions. Not socialism or capitalism, from which one wants to be national, the other statist.' Rather, the distinction for him was between: 'totalitarianism and federalism, a threat and a hope. This antithesis dominates our century, it is the real drama, all others will be of secondary importance or illusory.' Rougemont's rhetoric revealed how greatly the early events of the Cold War had shifted the positions of many Western European intellectuals, who now regarded the ideological differences between parties in Western Europe as trivial compared with the threat posed by the totalitarian and un-European superpower of the Soviet Union. Accordingly, it was resolved at Montreux that federalists should begin their work in Western Europe, including western Germany, if a united Germany could not be included within a federal plan.[94] As earlier chapters have suggested, such a focus on Western rather than Central Europe was by no means an easy transition for Christian advocates of European integration such as Rougemont, whose scepticism of Anglo-Saxon culture was undimmed and whose commitment to a Europe that united East and West remained constant.[95] Yet, it seemed unavoidable now that Eastern and Central Europe appeared to have been lost to the Soviets.

German social democrats came to share Rougemont's estimation of the Soviet Union, although not all quite as readily as their leader, Kurt Schumacher, only uniformly lining up behind his anti-Communist policy after the coup in Czechoslovakia in February 1948. As former ISK member Mary Saran explained in an SVG report written in May 1948, many of the early reforms carried out in this Soviet sphere of influence had accorded quite well with the agenda of radical socialists such as the former ISK members. Saran explained that, '[s]upport for the extension of Russian control in Europe, in so far as it came from socialists, rested on the ground that feudal and capitalist regimes were destroyed, land reform carried out, and planning started'. Yet:

> This view was finally shaken by the events of Spring 1948 ... Russian expansion was recognized as a threat ... to the whole 'Western way of life'. Was this, then, the price to be paid for ending feudalism, capitalism and Church domination in Eastern Europe? ... In this case it was impossible to argue that as a socially backward country Czechoslovakia was unfit for free political institutions. Furthermore, unlike Poland, Czechoslovakia was a country whose friendly attitude towards the Soviet Union had never wavered ... The rest of the western [European crossed out] labour movements, by the sheer impact of events, rallied behind the policies of their governments, the Marshall Plan, Western Union and the Atlantic Pact, and thus became placed on the opposite side to Russia.[96]

The reaction of Western European socialists described by Saran is well known. What is perhaps more interesting is that German social democrats tended to row back from this position, at least from the early 1950s after the Stalin Note of March 1952 had given them renewed hope that a unified, neutral Germany could be created. Indeed, in spite of the lack of practical avenues for discussing European integration across the Cold War divide, the SPD under Schumacher's leadership continued to stress their commitment to a reunified Germany and a Socialist International that cut across Cold War boundaries, formalizing this policy in an *SPD-Aktionsprogramm* in 1952.[97] Such a policy was maintained even after the concluding of the NATO military pact between the Western nations and the Warsaw Pact and the Council for Mutual Economic Assistance (CMEA or COMECON) agreements between the Eastern nations, although it provoked intense debate within the SPD.[98] This debate was, in turn, part of a wider European debate among socialists, who rarely lined up uniformly behind national orthodoxies during this period. Most of the historiographical focus on these debates has been on the Atlanticist line adopted by the British Labour Party under Foreign Secretary Ernest Bevin, or on the support shown by French, Italian and Dutch socialists for a Western European federation that would include Britain, contain the new West Germany, and maintain the Western European nations' independence from the United States.[99] Less attention has been paid to the policies of not only the German but also Austrian and Scandinavian parties. They took the least pro-Western line, maintaining their commitment to a reunified Germany and to a 'greater Europe' whose political complexion would be radically more socialist than the ECSC.[100]

Focusing on the policies of these Central and Northern parties should make us alert to the much wider 'neutral' movement that formed within the European socialist parties in the 1950s. This movement only gradually accepted the European institutions created out of the framework of the Schuman Plan as a viable starting point for a more extensive European unity.[101] Furthermore, such a shift towards accepting *Kleineuropa* as a starting point for a greater European union, not least in the German case, provided a platform for the policy of *Ostpolitik*. This policy was not only practised by Willy Brandt in the late 1960s, but had already become increasingly popular in Germany in the late 1950s before the construction of the Berlin Wall hampered attempts to reunite West and East Germany. Indeed, it should be remembered that the period of de-Stalinization in the Soviet bloc ushered in such initiatives as the Rapacki Plan of October 1957, a measure designed to create a de-nuclearized zone between both Germanys and Poland, which seemed to revive the possibility of a neutral Central Europe. This policy, in many ways, resembled those advocated by SPD theorists such as Fritz Erler, a former member of Neu Beginnen and member of the Council of Europe from 1950 who, even after West Germany's entry into NATO and East Germany's into the Warsaw Pact, advocated disengagement and a nuclear-free defence community being formed in *Mitteleuropa*.[102] Furthermore, the Rapacki Plan offered German social democrats hope that the Polish display of political opposition at Poznań in October 1956 and the pushing out of Soviet placemen in favour of the reformist Władysław Gomułka, might in turn signal growing support for a Third Way politics on the part of the East-Central European nations within the Soviet bloc.[103]

It is therefore possible, when observing social democratic foreign policy in the 1950s, to see how thoroughly in flux it was. On the one hand, it is certainly reasonable to focus on the SPD's eventual support for the Rome Treaties agreed in June 1957 and on the announcement made by the Godesberg reformist, Herbert Wehner, committing the Social Democrats to the Western alliance in 1960. Nevertheless, throughout this period the SPD remained committed to a broader version of European integration than that pushed forward by the German CDU. Thus in their pivotal reformist Godesberg Programme of 1959, largely shaped by Willi Eichler, they omitted any explicit commitment to the Western 'small Europe'.[104] Furthermore, even if Willy Brandt's foreign policy inclined first towards the Atlantic Alliance in the early 1960s before he then embarked on the *Ostpolitik* initiatives in the late 1960s, it appears clear that Brandt was committed to a greater Europe throughout the period.[105] He worked not only for reconciliation between the Federal Republic and the Democratic Republic, Poland and the Soviet Union, but also proposed agreements between the European Community (EC) and the Eastern European economic community, the (CMEA or COMECON).[106] Indeed, in some ways, Brandt's policy emulated that of his fellow socialist from Austria and friend from the emigration, Bruno Kreisky. The Austrian Foreign Minister from 1959 to 1966 sought to promote the voices of the neutral countries that were not members of the new European Community, but also tried to keep pathways to the East open. He worked to establish talks between Brandt – when the latter was serving as mayor of Berlin in 1958 to 1959 – and the Soviets, and pioneered an Austrian good neighbour policy or *Nachbarschaftspolitik* in the late 1950s and 1960s that attempted to push more countries in the Eastern bloc towards a Titoist neutrality.[107]

To move into the 1960s and deal with the *Ostpolitik* formulated by the social democrats is to go beyond the parameters of this book. Yet, even the evidence from the 1950s presented here would suggest that any Westernization thesis, with reference to the German SPD, should not be applied with a broad brushstroke. Rather, from what we have seen, there certainly appears to be compelling evidence that German social democrats never stopped looking East, believing that their efforts to overcome the divisions of the Cold War would normalize a highly abnormal political situation in Europe. Furthermore, they did this not only by working to reunite East and West but also by continuously seeking to reform the political culture of Western Europe into a model Third Way community that pointed the way towards a future beyond American-style capitalism and Soviet collectivism.

*****

I have followed the path of ISK members from being revolutionaries within a dissident socialist group in the interwar period to becoming leading members of the post-war SPD. While this story is clearly one of change, the narrative has also drawn out the continuities between the radical positions the leading members adopted in the interwar years, and their apparent embracing of a European West from the mid 1950s onwards. As has been argued, the advocacy of an integrated Europe by socialists within (and beyond) the ISK was an adaptation of a long-standing internationalist agenda shared by left-socialists. They sought to move beyond the twin options of domestic reformism and international revolution and thus to advance a version of socialism that was neither simply Western nor Eastern.

Of course, the *mitteleuropäisch* schemes devised by such groups during the war years became unrealizable after 1945. These groups were left, as members of a reconstituted German SPD, to work with colleagues in Western and Northern Europe rather than with their fellow socialists in the Soviet sphere of influence in East-Central Europe. Nevertheless, German socialists did not lose their commitment to an integrated Europe that cut across the Cold War divide, even if Kurt Schumacher's policy has often been regarded as more nationalist than pro-European. Furthermore, rather than German leftists simply adopting the agenda of the predominant Western socialist party, the largely reformist and isolationist British Labour Party after 1945, some made common cause with more radical organizations such as the SVG, which was committed to an overhauling of British foreign policy and to radical reform of the parliamentary system. More broadly speaking, German socialists also sought to overcome the post-war dominance of the Labour Party in Western Europe by working for integration primarily through the federalist movement, within which continental socialists could advance the kind of Third Way agenda that was being stifled by the Labour Party. Therefore, although the Third Force position taken by German social democrats may have been marginalized in the early post-war decades, it was not marginal either in European socialist politics or among federalist groups. Moreover, it was revived within Germany through the popular policy of *Ostpolitik* that was pushed forward by a later generation of social democratic leaders in the late 1960s. Of course, these leaders promoted *Ostpolitik* as chiefly a form of diplomacy rather than as a revolutionary and transnational agenda for integration. This signalled the greater role that national party leaders would play in integration, instead of it being brought about by the sort of European vanguard imagined by ISK theorists during the war years. Such developments do, therefore, suggest that by the 1960s, European integration had become more of a process negotiated by national players, even if, as in the case of the German SPD, these national players sought to break down the divides between nations and blocs and aim for a different kind of Europe to the pre-existing Western model.

One of the themes that has, nevertheless, emerged through the study of the ISK is how a distinctive European policy was adopted by the independent-minded mayors who often worked in local coalitions and proved particularly influential in terms of pushing forward an integrationist policy within the SPD. I move on now to look at a case study of figures from the Christian Democratic and Social Democratic parties who, while in exile in Switzerland, worked within coalitions. They went on, as regional or national leaders, to promote European integration as a means of safeguarding and enhancing local democracy and regional self-administration. As will be shown, the study of such individuals will bring out certain points of convergence regarding European integration that occurred between groups on the Left and Right from the mid 1920s to the mid 1950s. It will also suggest how groups, for instance in Bavaria, advocated the federalization of Europe as a means of promoting regionalism in Germany and beyond. This will shed light on how a European federalist agenda reinforced federalism within West Germany after 1945, and will help to explain how the regions became more successfully integrated within the West German nation than they had been into the Weimar Republic.

Notes

1. 'Am Ziel', in *Die Zeitung*, 5/427 (11 May 1945), accessible at http://deposit.d-nb.de/online/exil/exil.htm
2. M. Furbach-Sinani, '"Aber meine Feder hat länger gehalten." Walter Trier (1890–1951)', in M. Behmer (ed.), *Deutsche Publizistik im Exil 1933 bis 1945: Personen – Positionen – Perspektiven* (Münster: Lit, 2000) pp. 166–68.
3. J. Herf, *Divided Memory: The Nazi Past in the Two Germanies* (Cambridge MA: Harvard University Press, 1997) pp. 218–48; M. Kessler, *Ossip K. Flechtheim: politischer Wissenschaftler und Zukunftsdenker* (Cologne: Böhlau, 2007) p. 63; H. Grebing and K. Kinner (eds), *Arbeiterbewe-*

gung und Faschismus. Faschismus-Interpretationen in der europäischen Arbeiterbewegung (Essen: Klartext, 1990).
4. See for instance, R. Löwenthal, *Jenseits des Kapitalismus* (Berlin and Bonn: Dietz, 1977); H. Grebing (ed.), *Geschichte der sozialen Ideen in Deutschland* (Wiesbaden: VS, 2005) p. 377.
5. W. Kaiser, *Christian Democracy and the Origins of European Union* (Cambridge: Cambridge University Press, 2007).
6. On this, see chiefly, J. Angster, *Konsenskapitalismus und Sozialdemokratie. Die Westernisierung von SPD und DGB* (Munich: Oldenbourg, 2003).
7. On this Schumacher-centrism, see T. Imlay, '"The Policy of Social Democracy is Self-consciously Internationalist": The SPD's Internationalism after 1945', in *The Journal of Modern History*, forthcoming.
8. 'Rundschreiben des Bundesvorstandes an die Mitglieder über den Eintritt in die SPD und die Auflösung der ISK-Organization vom 10. Dezember 1945', in L. Eiber, *Die Sozialdemokratie in der Emigration. Die "Union deutscher sozialistischer Organizationen in Großbritannien" 1941–1946 und ihre Mitglieder, Protokolle, Erklärungen, Materialien* (Bonn: Dietz, 1998) p. 817. For a later elaboration of Eichler's reasons for dissolving the ISK, see AdsD, Nachlass Eichler, 1WEA000077, Letter from Eichler to Lehmann, 31 March 1946.
9. AdsD, IJB/ISK Collection, Box 55, M[onats] A[ntwort] des B[undes] V[orstandes] No. 4, February 1945.
10. 'Bericht des Londoner Ortsvereins für Mai bis Dezember 1944, Auszug', in Eiber, *Sozialdemokratie in der Emigration*, p. 789.
11. AdsD, IJB/ISK Collection, Box 55, MA des BV, No. 4. London, February 1945, pp. 5–6. See also S. Lemke-Mueller, *Ethischer Sozialismus und Soziale Demokratie. Der politische Weg Willi Eichlers vom ISK zur SPD* (Bonn: Neue Gesellschaft, 1988) p. 187.
12. L. Edinger, *Kurt Schumacher: A Study in Personality and Political Behavior* (Stanford: Stanford University Press, 1965) pp. 94–100.
13. H. Marcuse, *Legacies of Dachau: The Uses and Abuses of a Concentration Camp, 1933–2001* (Cambridge: Cambridge University Press, 2001) p. 142.
14. W. Röder, *Die deutschen sozialistischen Exilgruppen in Großbritannien 1940–1945. Ein Beitrag zur Geschichte des Widerstandes gegen den Nationalsozialismus* (Hannover: Verlag für Literatur und Zeitgeschehen, 1968) p. 244.
15. Röder, *Exilgruppen*, p. 244; E. Matthias, *Mit dem Gesicht nach Deutschland. Eine Dokumentation über die sozialdemokratische Emigration. Aus dem Nachlass von Friedrich Stampfer ergaenzt durch andere Überlieferungen* (Düsseldorf: Droste, 1968) p. 137; A. Glees, *Reinventing Germany: German Political Development since 1945* (Oxford and Dulles VA: Berg, 1996) p. 89.
16. Lemke-Mueller, *Ethischer Sozialismus*, pp. 187–89.
17. Röder, *Exilgruppen*, pp. 244–46.
18. Matthias, *Mit dem Gesicht nach Deutschland*, p. 137. Eiber, 'Verschwiegene Bündnispartner. Die Union deutscher sozialistischer Organisationen in Großbritannien und die britischen Nachrichtendienste', in C.-D. Krohn, E. Rotermund, L. Winckler und G. Paul (eds), *Exilforschung. Ein internationales Jahrbuch. Vol. 15, 1997: Exil und Widerstand* (Munich: Text + Kritik, 1997) p. 66.
19. MRC, SVG Archive, MSS. 173/20/8, G. Spencer, *Beloved Alien. Walter Fliess 1901–1985* (Vancouver and Donhead St. Andrew: Geoff Spencer, 1985) p. 23.
20. AdsD, Nachlass Eichler, 1/WEA000077, Letter from Zurich, 31 March 1946.
21. MRC, SVG Archive, MSS. 173/20/8, Spencer, *Beloved Alien*, p. 23.
22. Krohn, 'Remigrants and Reconstruction', in D. Junker (ed.), *The United States and Germany in the Era of the Cold War, 1945–1990: A Handbook, Vol. 1 (1945-1968)* (Cambridge: Cambridge University Press, 2004) pp. 529–32.

23. Eichler, 'Statement für Dr. Kurt Schumacher über den Aufbau einer sozialistischen Partei vom 4. September 1945. Einige notwendige Voraussetzungen für den Aufbau einer sozialistischen Partei', in Eiber, *Sozialdemokratie in der Emigration*, p. 802.
24. W.D. Graf, *The German Left Since 1945. Socialism and Social Democracy in the German Federal Republic* (Cambridge: Oleander, 1976) p. 137.
25. W.E. Paterson, *The SPD and European Integration* (Westmead: Saxon House, 1974) pp. 38–39.
26. Institut für Zeitgeschichte, Munich (IfZ), Nachlass Fritz Eberhard, ED 117/117, Letter from Eichler to Fritz Eberhard, 8 August 1947.
27. For Schumacher's and the SPD's European policy, see AdsD, Digital Archive, Flugblätter und Flugschriften Collection, 6/FLBL002167, SPD Landesvorstand Bayern (ed.), 'Dr Kurt Schumacher spricht; Die Zeit des Abwartens ist vorüber!', 1946; 6/FLBL004506, SPD Bundesvorstand (ed.), 'Unser Nein ist ein Ja!', 6 September 1953. On Schumacher's preference for going into opposition rather than join a Grand Coalition see J. Klausen, *War and Welfare: Europe and the United States, 1945 to the Present* (Basingstoke: Palgrave, 1998) pp. 182–83; and M. Hughes, *Shouldering the Burdens of Defeat: West Germany and the Reconstruction of Social Justice* (Chapel Hill: University of North Carolina Press, 1999) pp. 84–85.
28. J. Lodge, *The European Policy of the SPD* (Beverly Hills/London, 1976) p. 6; C. Egle, 'The SPD's preferences on European integration: always one step behind?', in D. Dimitrakopoulos (ed.), *Social Democracy and European Integration: The Politics of Preference Formation* (London and New York: Routledge, 2011) p. 26.
29. For Schumacher's position, see eg AdsD, Digital Archive, 6/FLBL001653, SPD Parteivorstand (ed.), *Querschnitt durch die deutsche Politik der Gegenwart* (Hannover; Hannoversche Presse, Druck und Verlagsgesellschaft, 1948); 6/FLBL003079, SPD Bundesvorstand (ed.), 'Volksabstimmung an der Saar', (Hannover: Hannoversche Presse, Druck und Verlagsgesellschaft, 1950); D. Rogosch, 'Sozialdemokratie zwischen nationaler Orientierung und Westintegration 1945–1957', in M. König and M. Schulz (eds), *Die Bundesrepublik Deutschland und die europäische Einigung 1949–2000. Politische Akteure, gesellschaftliche Kräfte und internationale Erfahrungen. Festschrift für Wolf D. Gruner zum 60. Geburtstag* (Stuttgart: Franz Steiner, 2004) p. 292.
30. W. Lipgens and W. Loth (eds), *Documents on the History of European Integration: The Struggle for European Union by Political Parties and Pressure Groups in Western European Countries 1945–1950*, Vol. 3 (Berlin: de Gruyter, 1988) p. 543.
31. Lodge, *European Policy of the SPD*, pp. 9, 12; and Paterson, *SPD and European Integration*, p. 21.
32. D. Zöbl, 'Ernst Reuter und sein schwieriges Verhältnis zu den Alliierten 1946–1948', in H. Reif and M. Feichtinger (eds), *Ernst Reuter: Kommunalpolitiker und Gesellschaftsreformer* (Bonn: Dietz, 2009) p. 270.
33. W. Hofmann, 'Ernst Reuter und der Deutsche Städtetag II 1947–1953', in Reif and Feichtinger, *Ernst Reuter*, p. 286.
34. For more on this work by Fliess, see MRC, SVG Archive, MSS. 173/20/3, MSS. 173/20/4.
35. W. Fliess, *The Economic Reconstruction of Europe* (London: International Publishing Company, 1944) p. 30; W. Paterson, 'The German Social Democratic Party and European Integration in Emigration and Occupation', in *European History Quarterly* 5/4 (1975) 433.
36. Fliess, *Economic Reconstruction*, pp. 36–46.
37. Fliess, *Economic Reconstruction*, pp. 21–55.
38. H. Monte, *The Unity of Europe* (London: Victor Gollancz, 1943) p. 134. Hilda Monte was born Hilda Meisel but was better known by her codename of Monte. She split with the ISK in 1939, arguing that ISK members should attempt to assassinate Hitler. W. Laqueur, *Generation Exodus: The Fate of Young Jewish Refugees from Nazi Germany* (London: I.B. Tauris, 2004) p. 71; Paul Bonart, *But We Said 'No': Voices from the German Underground* (San Francisco: Mark Backman, 2007) pp. 197–99; B. Reinalda, *The International Transportworkers Federation, 1914–1945: The Edo Fimmen Era* (Amsterdam: International Institute of Social History, 1997) p. 194.
39. Monte, *Unity of Europe*, p. 186.

40. D. Dinan, *Europe Recast: A History of European Union* (Boulder CO: Lynne Rienner, 2004) p. 5; S. Hoffmann, 'Paradoxes of the French Political Community', in S. Hoffmann et al., *In Search of France* (Cambridge MA: Harvard University Press, 1963) p. 42.
41. M. Hogan, *The Marshall Plan: America, Britain, and the reconstruction of Western Europe, 1947–1952* (Cambridge: Cambridge University Press, 1987) p. 22.
42. Monte, *Unity of Europe*, p. 194.
43. Ibid., pp. 28, 94, 198.
44. Hogan, *Marshall Plan*, p. 22. Details of Monte's death were reported in a letter by Hanna Bertholet of 25 August 1945 in AdsD, IJB/ISK Collection, Box 59.
45. P. Sering (R. Löwenthal), *Jenseits des Kapitalismus: Ein Beitrag zur sozialistische Neutorientierung* (Nürnberg, 1946) p. 257. For more on this, see T. Imlay, 'SPD Internationalism', *The Journal of Modern History*, forthcoming, which also has further details on the influence of Löwenthal's book. See also H.-P. Schwarz, *Vom Reich zur Bundesrepublik. Deutschland im Widerstreit der aussenpolitischen Konzeptionen in den Jahren der Besatzungsherrschaft 1945–1949* (Neuwied and Berlin: Luchterhand, 1966) p. 569.
46. AdsD, Digitales Archiv, Flugblätter und Flugschriften Collection, 6/FLBL003781, SPD Bundesvorstand (ed.), 'Die SPD und der Generalvertrag!' [Conversation between Carlo Schmid and Rüdiger Proske], 9 May 1952; 6/FLBL003784, SPD Bundesvorstand (ed.), 'Abdruck der Rede Erich Ollenhauers vom 7.2.1952, am ersten Tag der Bundestagdebatte über einen deutschen Verteidigungsbeitrag', 7 Febuary 1952.
47. Angster, *Konsenskapitalismus und Sozialdemokratie* pp. 260–63.
48. F. Boll, 'Jugendbewegung, Widerstand und Exil, Marxismuskritik und Westorientierung. Der Kreis um die Zeitschrift *Geist und Tat*', in M. Grunewald and H.-M. Bock (eds), *Le milieu intellectuel de gauche en Allemagne, sa presse et ses réseaux (1890–1960)*, (Berne: Peter Lang, 2002) pp. 595–602.
49. Schwarz, *Vom Reich zur Bundesrepublik*, pp. 567–71; J. Gaffney, *Political Parties and the European Union* (London and New York: Routledge, 1996) p. 35.
50. See M. Uschner, *Die Ostpolitik der SPD: Sieg und Niederlage einer Strategie* (Berlin: Dietz, 1991) p. 41. On Kurt Schumacher's elaboration of a magnet theory, see R. Fritz-Bournazel, *Europe and German Reunification* (Providence and Oxford: Berg, 1992) pp. 113–14.
51. For a different take on the relationship between European integration and a social democratic magnet theory, see R. Hrbek, *Die SPD – Deutschland und Europa. Die Haltung der Sozialdemokratie zum Verhältnis von Deutschland-Politik und West-Integration (1945–1957)* (Bonn: Europa Union, 1972) pp. 286–90.
52. See, for instance, S. Berman, *The Primacy of Politics: Social Democracy and the Making of Europe's Twentieth Century* (Cambridge: Cambridge University Press, 2006) pp. 188–91; D. Parnass, *The SPD and the Challenge of Mass Politics* (Boulder CO: Westview Press, 1991); W. Carr, 'German Social Democracy since 1945', in R. Fletcher (ed.), *From Bernstein to Brandt* (London: Edwin Arnold, 1987).
53. F. Stampfer, 'Die großen Drei und die Londoner Deklaration der deutschen Sozialisten', in *Neue Volks-Zeitung* 12/48 (27 November 1943).
54. AdsD, IJB/ISK Collection, Letter from Eichler to Spinelli, 23 March 1945; F. Niess, *Die Europäische Idee – aus dem Geist des Widerstands* (Frankfurt am Main: Suhrkamp, 2001) pp. 40–41.
55. O.A.Westad, 'The Yalta Conference and the emergence of the Cold War' and W. Benz, 'Yalta, Potsdam and the emergence of the Cold War: an overview from Germany in the light of the latest research', in R. Stradling (ed.), *Crossroads of European Histories: Multiple Outlooks on Five Key Moments in the History of Europe* (Strasbourg: College of Europe, 2006) pp. 243–50, 279–98.
56. M. Zaborowski, *Germany, Poland and Europe: Conflict, Co-operation and Europeanization* (Manchester and New York: Manchester University Press, 2004) p. 40.

57. Eichler, 'Die Demontage des Friedens', in *Geist und Tat. Monatsschrift für Recht, Freiheit und Kultur*, 11/2 (November 1947) 4.
58. R. Steininger, *Deutschland und die Sozialistische Internationale nach dem Zweiten Weltkrieg. Die deutsche Frage, die Internationale und das Problem der Wiederaufnahme des SPD auf den internationalen sozialistischen Konferenzen bis 1951 unter besonderer Berücksichtigung der Labour Party* (Bonn: Neue Gesellschaft, 1979) pp. 13–15.
59. Steininger, *Deutschland und die Sozialistische Internationale*, pp. 24–25; A. Nicholls, 'Die britische Linke und der 20. Juli 1944', in K.-J. Müller and D.N. Dilks (eds), *Großbritannien und der deutsche Widerstand, 1933–1944* (Paderborn: Schöningh, 1994) p. 125.
60. Steininger, *Deutschland und die Sozialistische Internationale*, pp. 24–25.
61. P. van Kemseke, *Towards an Era of Development: the Globalization of Socialism and Christian Democracy 1945–1965* (Leuven: Leuven University Press, 2006) p. 283
62. For insights into the SPD's hopes for the negotiations occurring within the International, see *Sozialistische Mitteilungen der London-Vertretung der SPD*, eg 96/97, February–March, 1947.
63. Steininger, *Deutschland und die Sozialistische Internationale*, pp. 64–70.
64. Ibid., pp. 76–80.
65. D. Orlow, *Common Destiny: A Comparative History of the Dutch, French and German Social Democratic Parties, 1945–1969* (New York and Oxford: Berghahn Books, 1999) p. 141.
66. Steininger, *Deutschland und die Sozialistische Internationale*, p. 79.
67. Orlow, *Common Destiny*, pp. 140–42.
68. Steininger, *Deutschland und die Internationale*, pp. 81–88; V. Sørensen, *Denmark's Social Democratic Government and the Marshall Plan, 1947–1950* (Copenhagen: Museum Tusculanum Press, 2001) pp. 57–59. Again the *Sozialistischer Mitteilungen* offered a cautiously optimistic appraisal of the events at Zurich, in its hundredth edition from June 1947.
69. Angster, *Konsenskapitalismus und Sozialdemokatie*, p. 245.
70. Sørensen, *Denmark's Social Democratic Government and the Marshall Plan*, pp. 59–60, 75–84; Eichler, 'Die dritte Phase', in *Geist und Tat*, 2/7 (July, 1947) 3–6.
71. Niess, *Europäische Idee*, p. 226.
72. K.M. Johansson and G. von Sydow, 'Swedish Social Democracy and European Integration: Enduring Divisions', in Dimitrakopoulos, *Social Democracy and European Integration*, pp. 160–61.
73. On Schumacher's nationalism see, for instance, J. McAllister, *No Exit: America and the German Problem, 1943–1954* (Ithaca: Cornell University Press, 2002) p. 179.
74. For summaries of such typical arguments see T. Risse and D. Engelmann-Martin, 'Identity Politics and European Integration: The Case of Germany', in A. Pagden (ed.), *The Idea of Europe: From Antiquity to the European Union* (Cambridge: Cambridge University Press, 2002) p. 299; and R. Moeller, 'The German Social Democrats', in Gaffney, *Political Parties and the European Union*, pp. 34–35.
75. See particularly Angster, *Konsenskapitalismus und Sozialdemokratie*, pp. 244-45.
76. Steininger, *Deutschland und die Internationale*, pp. 147, 150.
77. For the Bevin speech on Western Union, see the extract in A.G. Harryvan and J. van der Harst, *Documents on European Union* (New York: St. Martin's Press, 1997) pp. 45–47. For differing interpretations of the policy, see S. Greenwood, *Britain and European Integration since the Second World War* (Manchester: Manchester University Press, 1996) pp. 14–37; and G. Wilks and D. Wring, 'The British Press and European Integration: 1948 to 1996', in D. Baker and D. Seawright (eds), *Britain For and Against Europe: British Politics and the Question of European* (Oxford: Oxford University Press, 1998) pp. 185–88. On the SVG's generally positive reaction to Bevin's policy (and its shift towards a more Atlanticist position), see M. Minion, 'The Labour Party and Europe during the 1940s: The Strange Case of the Socialist Vanguard Group', London South Bank University, Centre for International Business Studies (CIBS), European Institute Working Papers, No.3/1998, 25-27, accessible at: http://www.bus.lsbu.ac.uk/resources/CIBS/european-institute-papers/papers2/498.PDF

78. See R. Hrbek, 'The German Social Democratic Party, I', in R. Griffiths (ed.), *Socialist Parties and the Question of Europe in the 1950s* (Leiden: Brill, 1993) p. 71.
79. Angster, *Konsenskapitalismus und Sozialdemokratie*, p. 398.
80. For more on this New Left agenda, see G.-R. Horn, *The Spirit of '68: Rebellion in Western Europe and North America, 1956–1976* (Oxford: Oxford University Press, 2007) pp. 100–17, 152–57, 206–12; G. Eley, *Forging Democracy: The History of the Left in Europe, 1850–2000* (New York: Oxford University Press, 2002) pp. 341–65.
81. Boll, 'Der Kreis um die Zeitschrift *Geist und Tat*', in Grunewald and Bock, *Le milieu intellectuel de gauche en Allemagne*, p. 611.
82. Spencer, *Beloved Alien*, pp. 31–35. For more on the treatment of German internees on the Dunera, see B. Lan, 'The *Dunera Boys*: Dramatizing History from a Jewish Perspective', in R. Dove (ed.), *'Totally Un-English'? Britain's Internment of 'Enemy Aliens' in Two World Wars: The Yearbook of the Research Centre for German and Austrian Exile Studies (Vol. 7)* (Amsterdam: Rodopi, 2005) pp. 179–92.
83. Spencer, *Beloved Alien*, pp. 42–43. See also M. Seller, *We Built Up Our Lives: Education and Community among Jewish Refugees Interned by Britain during World War II* (Westport CT: Greenwood, 2001) pp. 107, 159.
84. Angster, *Konsenskapitalismus und Sozialdemokratie*, pp. 236–56; A. Lehmann, *Der Marshall-Plan und das neue Deutschland: die Folgen amerikanischer Besatzungspolitik in den Westzonen* (Münster: Waxmann, 2000) pp. 423–24.
85. R. Hyman, 'Flanders, Allan David (1910–1973)', *Oxford Dictionary of National Biography* (Oxford: Oxford University Press, 2004) online edition, October 2009 [http://www.oxforddnb.com/view/article/31112]; R. Douglas, 'No Friend of Democracy: The Socialist Vanguard Group, 1941–50', in *Contemporary British History* 16/4 (Winter 2002) 61–62.
86. MRC, SVG Archive, MSS. 173/18/1, 'Half-Yearly Report November 1943 to May 1944'.
87. Minion, 'Left, Right, or European? Labour and Europe in the 1940s: the case of the Socialist Vanguard Group', in *European Review of History* 7/2 (2000) 230.
88. Spencer, *Beloved Alien*, pp. 28, 57.
89. Boll, 'Der Kreis um die Zeitschrift *Geist und Tat*', in Grunewald and Bock, *Le milieu intellectuel de gauche en Allemagne*, p. 610.
90. L. Black, 'Social Democracy as a Way of Life: Fellowship and the Socialist Union, 1951–9', in *Twentieth Century British History* (1999) 10/4, 526. The SVG continued to exist until 1951, and from then on until 1959 with the new name of Socialist Union.
91. AdsD, Nachlass Eichler, 1/WEA000072, A. Flanders, 'Fabian International Bureau: A Socialist Approach to Western Union', 12 April 1948.
92. AdsD, Nachlass Eichler, 1/WEA000071, undated but catalogued with early post-war documents.
93. H.A. Winkler, *Germany: The Long Road West. Vol. 2: 1933–1990* (Oxford: Oxford University Press, 2007) pp. 151–53, 169–71, 178–81.
94. Niess, *Europäische Idee*, pp. 109–10, 119.
95. N. Naimark, *The Russians in Germany: A History of the Soviet Zone of Occupation, 1945–1949* (Cambridge MA: Harvard University Press, 1995) p. 281.
96. MRC, SVG Archive, MSS. 173/2/3, M. Saran, 'The Socialist Attitude to Russia'.
97. A. Leugers-Scherzberg, 'Von den Stalin-Note bis zum Deutschlandplan: Die deutsche Sozialdemokratie und der Neutralismus in den 1950er Jahren', in D. Geppert and U. Wengst (eds), *Neutralität – Chance oder Chimäre? Konzepte des Dritten Weges für Deutschland und die Welt 1945–1990* (Munich: Oldenbourg, 2005) pp. 52–53.
98. Leugers-Scherzberg, 'Von den Stalin-Note bis zum Deutschlandplan', in Geppert and Wengst, *Neutralität – Chance oder Chimäre*. See also H. Potthoff and S. Miller, *Kleine Geschichte der SPD, 1848–2002* (Bonn: Dietz, 2002).

99. M. Dedman, *The Origins and Development of the European Union, 1945–2008: A History of European Integration* (London and New York: Routledge 2nd ed., 2010) pp. 34–35; P. Jones, *America and the British Labour Party: the 'Special Relationship' at Work* (London: I.B. Tauris, 1997) pp. 68–73; S. Greenwood, 'Ernest Bevin, France and "Western Union": August 1945–February 1946', in *European History Quarterly* 14/3 (1984) 319–38; R. Griffiths, 'European Utopia or Capitalist Trap? The Socialist International and the Question of Europe' and Loth, 'The French Socialist Party, 1947–1954', in Griffiths, *Socialist Parties and the Question of Europe in the 1950s* (Leiden, 1993) pp. 15–23, 32–40.
100. H. Schneider, 'Die österreichische Neutralität und die europäische Integration', and C. Silva, 'An Introduction to Sweden and European Integration 1947–1957, in M. Gehler and R. Steininger (eds), *Die Neutralen und die europäische Integration 1945–1995* (Vienna: Böhlau, 2000).
101. See G. Lundestad, *'Empire' by Integration: The United States and European Integration, 1945–1997* (Oxford: Oxford University Press, 1998); Loth, 'Neutralität im Kalten Krieg', in Gehler and Steininger, *Neutralen und die europäische Integration*, pp. 80–86; Leugers-Scherzberg, 'Von den Stalin-Note bis zum Deutschlandplan', in Geppert and Wengst, *Neutralität – Chance oder Chimäre*, pp. 48–53; H. Soell, *F. Erler – eine politische Biographie* (Bonn: Dietz, 1976); Rogosch, „Sozialdemokratie zwischen nationaler Orientierung und Westintegration', in König and Schulz, *Bundesrepublik Deutschland und die europäische Einigung*, pp. 302–4.
102. A. Gallus, *Die Neutralisten: Verfechter eines vereinten Deutschlands zwischen Ost und West 1945–1990* (Düsseldorf: Droste, 2001) pp. 73-74; C. Bailey, 'The Continuities of West German History: Conceptions of Europe, Democracy and the West', in *Geschichte und Gesellschaft* 36/4 (2010) 586; Leugers-Scherzberg, 'Von den Stalin-Note bis zum Deutschlandplan', in Geppert and Wengst, *Neutralität – Chance oder Chimäre*, p. 55.
103. On this, see D.W. Larson, *Anatomy of Mistrust: U.S.-Soviet Relations during the Cold War* (Ithaca: Cornell University Press, 1997) p. 80; S.J. Brady, *Eisenhower and Adenauer: Alliance Maintenance under Pressure, 1953–1960* (Lanham: Rowman and Littlefield, 2010) p. 222.
104. Vorstand der Sozialdemokratischen Partei Deutschlands, *Grundsatzprogramm der Sozialdemokratischen Partei Deutschlands. Beschlossen vom Außerordentlichen Parteitag der Sozialdemokratischen Partei Deutschlands in Bad Godesberg vom 13. bis 15. November 1959* (Cologne: Deutz, 1959).
105. Uschner, *Die Ostpolitik der SPD*, pp. 53–55.
106. N. Leuchtweis, 'Deutsche Europapolitik zwischen Aufbruchstimmung und Weltwirtschaftskrise: Willy Brandt und Helmut Schmidt', in G. Müller-Brandeck-Bocquet et al., *Deutsche Europapolitik. Von Adenauer bis Merkel* (Wiesbaden: VS 2nd ed., 2010) pp. 70–71.
107. O. Rathkolb, *The Paradoxical Republic: Austria 1945–2005* (New York and Oxford: Berghahn Books, 2010) pp. 175–84.

Chapter 5

'AN ISLAND SURROUNDED BY LAND'
Das Demokratische Deutschland in Switzerland

Impassioned and embattled, speaking out against the violence of the radical Right, Joseph Wirth urged on his listeners with a call to: 'Democracy! But not the democracy that bangs on the table and says: "We are in power!" No, rather the democracy that patiently, in every situation, seeks to serve the cause of freedom in its own, unhappy land ... In this sense all hands and every mouth should be stirred to destroy this atmosphere of murder, strife and poison in Germany.'[1] Wirth was speaking as Federal Chancellor of Germany in the Reichstag, shortly after the murder of Germany's first and only Jewish foreign minister, Walter Rathenau, by ultranationalists in June 1922. Not long before this event, Wirth and Rathenau had worked together on the Rapallo Treaty of April 1922, signed by Weimar Germany and Soviet Russia, which had signalled a rapprochement between the First World War enemies.[2] Wirth was thus well acquainted with entanglements between domestic threats to democracy and tensions in international politics in the aftermath of a European conflict. He went on to try and reconcile the contradictions between tackling extreme nationalism within Germany and representing Germany's national interest abroad, first as a member of the Reichsbanner Schwarz-Rot-Gold, founded in February 1924 by social democrats and centrists to protect the republic from political extremists, and then as Federal Minister for the Occupied Territories from 1929 to 1930, opposing the French annexation of the Rhineland.[3] In spite of his efforts to defend a democratic Germany, Wirth was forced to retreat from the political stage when the Weimar coalitions became progressively more right-wing between 1931 and 1933, and he left Germany after having spoken out against the Enabling Act in the Reichstag in March 1933.[4]

Wirth was part of a significant political emigration, whose members made up around fifteen per cent of the approximately half a million individuals who left Germany, Austria and the German-speaking parts of Czechoslovakia during the period of National Socialist rule. (Most left because they faced racial persecution).[5] He was, nevertheless, unusual in that he was able to remain on the European continent, moving into Swiss exile in 1939, having lived in Paris between 1935 and 1939. One of the few prominent politicians granted the status of a political refugee, he settled in Switzerland, along with a number of his colleagues from Weimar politics, including the Social Democrats Otto Braun, the former Prussian prime minister; Wilhelm Hoegner, the future Bavarian prime minister; and Heinrich Ritzel, the future general secretary of the Europa Union in Germany and member of the Council of Europe. This chapter focuses on these individuals, who formed a working group called Das Demokratische Deutschland in der Schweiz, which met from 1943 onwards and began its official political work in 1945, planning for the reconstruction of Germany and advocating the cause of European integration.

A history of the group illustrates the convergence between certain political groups on the Left and Right that occurred in the war and post-war years concerning questions of democracy and European integration. This convergence emerged, both internationally and at the regional and local levels in Germany. It became an important part of the history of transnational European federalist movements and of the rise of regional politics within post-war West Germany, where states such as Bavaria gained significantly enhanced power and autonomy. Indeed, the European federalist movement, which was ostensibly non-partisan and initially largely linked Social Democrats and leftist Christian Democrats, enabled members to cooperate at a local level across the ideological lines drawn by the national party leaderships. Accordingly, it contributed to ideological conflict not reaching interwar levels once more among politically active citizens. That regional politicians could diverge from their party lines was due not only to the regional and international cross-party coalitions they had fashioned when working for European federalism, however. Rather, as will be argued, a European federalist agenda itself fed off pre-existing federalist sentiment in Germany that had survived the Bismarckian and National Socialist centralizations of power.

I begin this story by tracing how the leading politicians who collected in Swiss exile sought to plan for a reconstruction of a post-Nazi Germany, often in collaboration with the Allied governments and their secret services. On the one hand, the narrative suggests that splits between the wartime allies meant that plans for a reconstructed Germany formulated by exiled politicians refracted the emerging Cold War divisions between the Western Allies and the Soviet Union, even before the end of the Second World War. On the other, it draws attention to how fluid plans for Europe were during the war years. A variety of schemes for reconstituting Germany emerged, including plans for a Greater Germany and for a Danubian federation, which were devised as ways of restraining the Nazi aggression and of reasserting the rights of southern German and Austrian communities that had felt marginalized by a Prussian-led Germany. Such plans may have been sidelined once the faultlines of the Cold War had been established in the late 1940s. Nevertheless, they gave voice to long-standing federalist sentiment in southern Germany and served to rally support for a European federalist agenda, which could address the concerns of southern Germans as well as other victims of German nationalism and persuade the American occupying forces that a 'better' Germany could be constructed.

The narrative thus describes how the group's leaders sought to reconstitute the political culture of Germany and Europe. While they had sought to defend the Weimar republic and were never drawn to the extremist parties that rose in the late 1920s and early 1930s, their proposals for a new democratic order in Germany and a post-war European settlement illustrate how limited a form of democracy even such centrist post-war reformers sought to create. Indeed, for them, European integration was conceived as a means of constraining the practice of parliamentary democracy at the national level by creating international structures that would limit the potential for nationally elected politicians to practice aggressive forms of domestic or foreign policy.

Not least due to the severely restricted environment of Swiss wartime politics, the leading individuals in the organization were not particularly active in Swiss party politics. Instead, they sought to work through civil society organizations such as the Swiss Europa Union and within transnational networks and organizations that were fighting the war effort and planning for a post-war settlement. It is with their work in and through such networks and organizations that the chapter begins.

International Negotiations, Transnational Organizations

Although the leading members of Demokratisches Deutschland often compared Swiss political culture favourably with that of neighbouring nations, the country remained a difficult and largely inaccessible place for most German exiles throughout the late 1930s and early 1940s. Potentially controversial political exiles who threatened to sour relations between the Swiss and the Germans such as the communist poet Erich Weinert and the philosopher Ernst Bloch had their residence permits revoked in 1938, as did other German refugees who published articles critical of Hitler or the Nazi party.[6] Broadly speaking, it was extremely difficult for Germans (or other Europeans) to become political refugees in Switzerland with only 644 persons being granted this status between August 1937 and the end of the war.[7] (To put this into context, one estimate suggests that eight thousand refugees arrived in Switzerland in 1939 alone.[8]) Furthermore, the many Jews fleeing persecution in Germany, Austria and beyond were not regarded as political refugees and were, from 1938 onwards, given special 'J' stamps in passports issued by Berlin, which meant that they could be identified and more easily denied entry.[9] Worse was to come when the borders were completely closed to Jews at a time when they were increasingly under threat in 1942. Even those émigrés who were granted refugee status were banned from working, while the many more who had entered Switzerland and were supposed to 'transmigrate' out of the country but could not, were placed in internment houses and labour camps.[10]

The prominent politicians who would make up the leadership of Demokratisches Deutschland were thus among the most fortunate of the political refugees: apart from obtaining residence permits and being able to move freely around Switzerland, these individuals received the backing of important figures in Swiss public life. Joseph Wirth was aided by prominent fellow Catholics in Lucerne and was financially supported by his colleague in Demokratisches Deutschland, Jakob Kindt-Kiefer, a native of the Saarland who emigrated to Switzerland in 1935 and married the daughter of one of the largest window-frame manufacturers in Zurich.[11] Wilhelm Hoegner – who was well known in leftist circles, as his anti-Nazi Reichstag *Jungfernrede* (maiden speech) of October 1930 had been distributed in millions of copies – was protected and supported by the publisher Emil Oprecht, a leftist figure who emerged out of Willi Münzenberg's Socialist Youth Organization and who sought to advance the career of a number of dissident German authors during the 1930s and 1940s.[12] Even renowned figures such as Hoegner nevertheless struggled to find work or be politically active in Switzerland: Hoegner could only work as a political commentator under the assumed identity of Georg Ritter, posing as a 'Catholic author who rejected and struggled against the total state from the point of view of Catholic dogma'. Indeed, when the editor of the *Volksrecht*, a Social Democratic newspaper in Zürich, published an article under Hoegner's name, rather than his pseudonym, Hoegner was ordered to leave Switzerland within ten months, for having breached the law that forbade émigrés from being involved in political activities in Switzerland. This order was never followed up though, allowing the German social democrat to continue his residence in the country, provided he maintained a relatively low political profile.[13]

By contrast, fellow social democrat and leading member of Demokratisches Deutschland, Heinrich Ritzel, was able to remain politically active. He worked as the General Secretary of the Swiss Europa Union between 1939 and 1947 and authored pro-integration works with the organization's president, Hans Bauer, who was also editor of the left-liberal *National Zeitung* in Basel.[14] The Swiss Europa Union, which was an offshoot of Richard Coudenhove-Kalergi's Paneuropa movement, was based in Basel, where it commanded a membership of around twelve hundred. It spread out across German-speaking Switzerland and the Ticino region from 1934 onwards, producing a monthly journal, *Der Europäer*, and seeking to win support among the political parties for European integration. During the mid-1930s, it became affiliated with the British federalist New Commonwealth Society (nominally led by Winston Churchill) and remained the only continental European federalist organization that was active throughout the war years. After the war it went on to organize the Hertenstein Conference of September 1946, at which the Union Européenne des Fédéralistes (UEF), the most important federalist organization of the post-war period, was formed.[15]

Taken as a group, the leaders of Demokratisches Deutschland thus sought to work against the prevailing order in wartime Europe, by becoming active in associational life and in the media in Switzerland. They also sought to build bridges with the Allies and to revive party political structures among the exile community as ways of, on the one hand, providing the groundwork for a future democratic Germany and, on the other, reestablishing peaceful relations with former enemies as a first step towards European integration. As will be shown, these leaders enjoyed mixed fortunes in their relations with the Allies but proved capable of building lasting alliances with fellow social democrats and Christian democrats, both domestically and within transnational organizations. These alliances provided the foundations for cooperation between parties at local and regional but also international and transnational levels in the post-war years.

Initially, the leaders of Demokratisches Deutschland did not seek to be active within underground transnational resistance movements. Instead they tried to work through elite international channels to bring down the National Socialist government and to plan post-war reforms across Europe. Indeed, while Joseph Wirth kept his distance from resistance movements in Europe, he gained access to elite German oppositional circles and Allied officials, with the Vatican often acting as intermediary. In the late 1930s Wirth was considered to be among the most plausible post-war leaders by the British, particularly should the National Socialist regime be overthrown by a military-led coup. British intelligence deemed the military circle of Admiral Wilhelm Canaris, Carl-Heinrich von Stülpnagel and Carl Friedrich Goerdeler to be the only group capable of removing Hitler, having learned of its putsch plan, formulated before the Munich Agreement in 1938.[16] Yet, whereas military leaders would lack the legitimacy to lead a post-war order, a politician with Wirth's liberal and democratic credentials appeared an ideal figurehead for a democratic Germany.[17]

Between 1939 and 1940, Wirth therefore became a central figure in discussions that ranged between British Foreign Office contacts, go-betweens for Goerdeler and other military leaders, and Catholic prelates based in Rome.[18] Although these talks ultimately proved fruitless, they helped to build a Christian-inspired opposition movement among elites that laid some of the groundwork for post-war cooperation between Christian democratic parties concerning European integration. Furthermore, such oppositional Christian movements were particularly influential in winning the engagement of post-war planners among the allies. This was particularly the case for a number of Christian leaders from a previously more isolationist United States who became increasingly committed to defending a common Western civilization they believed was constituted by the United States and the European nations and based on Christian values.[19]

The willingness of Catholic politicians such as Wirth to work ecumenically with Protestant opponents of the Nazis was particularly important in this regard. Wirth met frequently with Karl Barth in Basel, although the Protestant theologian later came to support the rival Soviet-backed Freies Deutschland movement (discussed below). Similarly, Wirth had meetings with members of Paul Tillich's circle of Protestant opponents of the Nazis, which extended as wide as London, Paris, Belgium and the United States. This enabled Wirth and his circle to establish links to politicians such as future United States Secretary of State John Foster Dulles, who worked on plans for European reconstruction within the (ecumenical although Protestant-led) World Council of Churches (WCC), based in Switzerland.[20] Wirth, alongside Hoegner and Ritzel, was connected with John Foster Dulles' brother, Allen, who led the Office of Strategic Services (OSS, the precursor to the CIA) in Continental Europe from an office in Berne. Indeed, Wirth, who was Agent Number 478 with the OSS, was helped in his efforts to build ecumenical bridges by his OSS connections, thereby being linked to figures such as Willem Visser't Hooft, OSS Agent Number 474, and Dutch Secretary General of the WCC.[21] Visser't Hooft was part of the international anti-war movement and went on to host the meetings of socialist and Christian resistance circles led by Ernesto Rossi and Altiero Spinelli between March and July 1944, at which the early documents of the European federalist movement were drafted.[22]

Wirth's transnational connections were also the product of the growing transnational cooperation that had occurred among Christian politicians and between Christian and social democratic groups in the interwar period. For instance, left-Catholic workers' and peace organizations worked together to found the Secrétariat International des Partis Démocratiques d'Inspiration Chrétienne (SIPDIC), an organization linking Christian parties from France, Belgium, Poland, Germany and Italy that formed in Paris in December 1925.[23] After initial success in the late 1920s, this organization struggled to function as international tensions between nations increased in the early to mid 1930s, with French politicians such as Ernest Pezet seeking to secure the support of Central Europeans for a French alliance policy against Germany. However, when Wirth sought to persuade the Western allies of his connections to the growing conservative and military opposition movement in the late 1930s, it was to such figures as Pezet, who was Deputy Leader of the Foreign Committee of the French National Assembly and with whom Wirth met when he travelled to Paris in April 1940, that he turned.[24]

The Allies remained wary of the motives of the German military and doubted the plausibility of German refugees as post-war leaders of Germany throughout the war years. Yet, the connections made between Christian politicians and Western Allied agencies had a significant impact on the kind of post-war reconstruction planned and implemented by the Americans, British and French. For instance, while Allan Dulles, who was leading the Berne office of the OSS 'concur[red]' with his bosses in Washington, 'that it is not probable that Nazi refugees will take a leading part in the new Germany and they ought not to be "supported" by us', he nevertheless made an exception for the German exiles with whom he had worked in Switzerland. He recommended: 'some of [these] German contacts locally [who] ha[d] kept up close personal association with friends in Germany', believing them to be the only viable alternative to Communist rule in post-war Germany.²⁵ For, as he explained, they represented: 'The only closely knit Bourgeois [sic] element which is not linked up with Nazi ideology ... the Catholic Centrum [sic] element', which was particularly numerous 'in western and southern Germany because the Catholic influence there was anti-dictatorship whether of the communist or Nazi variety'. While singling out the Catholic liberals for particular praise, Dulles nevertheless particularly favoured the kind of ecumenical Christian democratic movement envisaged by the Demokratisches Deutschland leaders, noting also the presence of 'a good element represented in [the] Bekenntnis Kirche [sic Confessing Church] which is prepared to support attempts by Catholics and Socialists to establish a Democratic [sic] system'.²⁶

These initial attempts by oppositional figures from Germany to build bridges with Americans and fellow Europeans across the wartime divide provide context for the successes of the post-war federalist groups. In addition, they help to explain the American commitment to rebuild West Germany and not leave it a pastoralized minor power as envisaged in the Morgenthau Plan of 1944.²⁷ As will be seen, the alliances formed between American post-war planners and European federalists from southern Germany complicate the pre-existing historiographical master narrative that stresses a growing division between European federalists and more Atlanticist national leaders after 1945.²⁸ However, negotiations over post-war planning also revealed the early fissures between Europeans and between the emerging superpowers and thus refracted the early Cold War divisions. It is to these divisions that I now turn.

The Cold War in Microcosm?

Anticipating the spread of communism across Eastern and Central Europe, Allen Dulles reported back to his OSS bosses in Washington DC in 1944, recommending that anti-communist figures such as those building up the Demokratisches Deutschland group be backed by the US. He argued that:

> For the purpose of averting political chaos in Germany which would promote the setting up of a Communist State ... we should give serious thought to whether or not ... we should support those political groups, especially Centrum [sic] and Socialists as a foundation for the establishment of a democratic government ... [for] the Centrum [sic] and Socialist parties alone could be speedily re-formed after the collapse and they are the only ones which may be strong enough to give direction to political life in Germany.²⁹

Dulles may have even encouraged his liberal and social democratic contacts in Switzerland to form their own popular front coalition representing the German community in Switzerland, as well as the wider exile community, once he noted the sponsorship of popular front movements by the Soviets in the later war years.³⁰

Although these exiled leaders were spread out across the Swiss cantons, they needed little encouragement once it became clear in 1943 that another collection of German politicians and intellectuals had organized themselves as a German representation in Switzerland, with the covert patronage of the Soviet Union. The rival group, named Freies Deutschland in der Schweiz, formed part of a broader Freies Deutschland united front movement initiated by the Soviets in Moscow in late 1942. This movement won the support of imprisoned German military personnel and led to the forming of other committees across Europe, not least in France, Belgium and Luxembourg.[31] Yet, it was not only a Soviet initiative; rather, it emerged out of a united-front strategy formulated by Comintern members such as the exiled German communist Wilhelm Pieck, who took the lead in forming imprisoned army members in Moscow into an anti-Hitler coalition.[32]

The Freies Deutschland group proved quite effective at offering political and cultural leadership within broadly based exile organizations. By the summer of 1944, it had selected a Swiss national executive and attracted ostensibly cross-party support, recruiting a number of prominent non-communists among its members. It also styled itself as traditionally nationalist, even dropping the Weimar tricolour for the colours of the nineteenth century imperial empire as its emblem. The group, as seemingly the brainchild of German communists, nevertheless appeared to social democrats and Catholic liberals to be a particular threat to German national interests. These latter groups blamed the communists for strengthening Nazism by their attacks on non-communist leftist critics of the National Socialists both before 1933 and after the Nazi–Soviet Pact of 1939. Such communists also appeared willing to surrender German sovereignty because of their links to Moscow. This caused particular concern once it became apparent that the Soviets would play a major role in shaping the post-war reconstruction. Indeed, after the Potsdam Agreement, in line with Soviet doctrine, Freies Deutschland leaders went on to profess the collective guilt of the German people for the crimes of the National Socialist regime and sought to justify the annexations of German lands in the East by Poland and Russia.[33]

Initially, social democrats such as Braun, Hoegner and Ritzel attempted to reconstitute the SPD as a response to the founding of Freies Deutschland. However, these efforts foundered, partially due to splits within the exiled socialist groups and partly because of the restrictions on political activity enforced by the Swiss authorities and backed up by a nervous Swiss Social Democratic Party (Sozialdemokratische Partei der Schweiz SPS), whose leaders were eager that German socialists receiving financial support respect the legal restrictions placed upon them.[34] By the mid 1940s, social democrats thus came to advocate the forming of a cross-party coalition with Christian democrats. Such a coalition would, in the words of Joseph Wirth, see an end to the 'class spirit' and the 'caste spirit', which he believed had harmed the cause of democratic parties in the Weimar republic.[35] The politicians who formed this coalition went on to establish a membership divided into social-democratic, Christian-liberal and Christian-conservative groupings. They believed that such a division would reflect, and prescribe, the future alignments in German and wider European political life and compel politically active Germans to work together within coalitions. So, a Union deutscher Sozialisten in der Schweiz was formed in March 1945 by leading social democrats including Wilhelm Dittman, a prominent SPD Reichstag delegate, and Anna Siemsen, a pedagogue active in the SPS.[36] It was joined by the Gruppe Christlicher Demokraten assembled by Wirth and Kindt-Kiefer and supported by aristocratic opponents of the NS-regime, and a Liberal-demokratische Vereinigung led by the ex-Deutsche Demokratische Partei (DDP) member Wolfgang Glaesser and Gero von Schultze-Gävernitz, the Germany expert for the OSS.[37] The umbrella organization reached its peak by October 1945 with around twelve hundred members, which slightly eclipsed the thousand or so members that Freies Deutschland could claim earlier that year.[38]

The members of Demokratisches Deutschland came to advocate a European federation as a response to Soviet attempts to weaken a future Germany and to establish communist dominance in Eastern Europe. Indeed, planning one of its first post-war publications, the organization drew up a declaration responding to the Potsdam Agreement and critiquing the proposed annexations of German territories in the East. As the early salvos of the Cold War had not yet been issued by the emerging superpowers, American representatives such as Allen Dulles warned the Demokratisches Deutschland leaders off making such a critical public statement. As a result, the leaders decided to instead send their declaration privately to Western diplomats, although this decision prompted former Prussian Prime Minister Otto Braun to leave the organization's Directorate in September 1945.[39] The leaders nevertheless proposed a reconstruction of Germany within 'a European federation based on the Swiss model' as an alternative to Potsdam, in the organization's first newsletter of September 1945.[40] Thus, their anti-communism led them not to embrace a Westernization of Germany within a U.S.-led bloc but towards European federalism, which they believed would avoid the loss of Germany's East to the newly ascendant Soviet Union's sphere of influence. This suggests that they therefore did not so much advocate federalism as an alternative to a Cold War but as a means of more assertively waging this war.

Braun, although by no means the most committed federalist in the group, had already contemplated Germany's incorporation within a European federation as an alternative to the Allies' plans in his response to the Potsdam Agreement, 'What Must Happen after the War'. In this memorandum, he complained about the annexationist aspirations of Poland and Czechoslovakia, who were laying claim to parts of Silesia, Saxony and Bavaria in the case of Czechoslovakia, and East and West Prussia, Lower Pomerania, the borderland and parts of Silesia in Poland's case.[41] Braun believed that a territorially intact Germany within a European federation would be independent, unlike a diminished Germany that would have to, 'altogether attach itself to the Western states or seek an *Anschluss* of all Germany with Russia as a Soviet state'. This was not least because a Germany subject to all the proposed annexations would lose between a fifth and a quarter of its land, forests, livestock, and vital foodstuffs such as cereals and potatoes.⁴² The southern German leaders of Demokratisches Deutschland shared Braun's aversion to annexations in the East, with Heinrich Ritzel warning the Allies of the threat of a renewed German nationalism in the form of a 'national Bolshevism' should a post-war settlement punish the war's losers too harshly.⁴³

The Demokratisches Deutschland leaders' disillusion was no doubt due to what appeared to be a hasty surrender to the Soviets of much of the German state, as well as large parts of Central and Eastern Europe, by the Americans and other Western allies. For instance, in April 1944, their American contact, Allen Dulles, was urging those in the American government to adopt a 'constructive' policy 'in dealing with the masses of central Europe', because they were proving susceptible to the creative proposals offered by the Soviets. Yet, by October, the OSS Berne chief was cautioning that the Americans:

> [B]e quite realistic … and give our attention primarily to the areas where there is a real prospect that the principles of western civilization can be maintained and developed[:] … France, the Low Countries, Switzerland, Italy, Scandinavia and possibly Greece … [and the] two zones of occupation in Germany where, under the influence of British and American occupying forces, we may be able slowly to reconstruct a social system integrated with the West.⁴⁴

Did this signify then that the members of Demokratisches Deutschland turned to European federalism as a means of rescuing as much of the German state as they could?⁴⁵ In one sense, yes, thus suggesting that these southern and western Germans were not as distinct from other supposedly co-opted German nationalists as their supporters in the OSS might have believed. However, their proposal to incorporate Germany's East within a European federation was not a simple expression of unreconstructed German nationalism. Instead it gave voice to the long-held dissatisfactions of southern and western Germans who had argued since the late nineteenth century against a Prussian-dominated *Kleindeutschland* in favour of a greater Germany that was a more genuinely federal entity.⁴⁶ As Heinrich Ritzel explained in a rallying cry for European integration he wrote for the Swiss Europa-Union with his colleague Hans Bauer in 1945: 'The new Europe under German leadership was nothing other than the continental extension of the Reich that was constructed in 1870 under Prussian predominance and ever more clearly centralized by Berlin until it reached the total "Gleichschaltung"'.⁴⁷

As will be shown in the following section, the opponents of this German *Gleichschaltung* of Europe were concerned with redressing the marginalization of the southern German states in post-1870 Germany and reuniting Germans who were threatened with being partitioned into East and West Germany and a small Austria. Thus, the members of Demokratisches Deutschland may have begun their activities as a group in order to defend German territorial integrity and thereby wage some of the earliest battles in an emerging Cold War against the Soviet Union. Nevertheless, their defence of German sovereignty intersected with a longer-standing agenda of southern Germans who viewed their history not so much in East–West terms as in North–South.

Southern Germany in Central Europe

Among the German exiles who settled in Switzerland during the war years, a significant proportion came from the southern states, not least from Bavaria. These included Michael Freiherr von Godin, a former Dachau internee who became President of the State Police in the post-war period; Hans Nawiasky, a prominent member of the Bavarian People's Party (Bayerische Volkspartei BVP) and future legal advisor for the drafting of the Basic Law; and Alfred Loritz, the future leader of the Economic Reconstruction Association (Wirtschaftliche Aufbau-Vereinigung WAV) political party, and Bavarian State Minister for Denazification.[48] Hoegner worked with a number of such Bavarian politicians when drafting proposals for post-war reconstruction that were written for Allied governments, advancing a distinctive southern German agenda. This agenda proved congenial to American analysts such as Allen Dulles, who interpreted Nazism as a further degeneration of an already aggressive Prussian ideology.[49] For instance, the 'Political Guidelines' that Hoegner wrote with Freiherr von Godin and future Bavarian State Secretary Josef Panholzer (BVP) in August 1944, retained the right for the Bavarian people to become an 'independent European state … or join … another state association'. Such an association would ideally be a 'southern German state union' that would seek 'close economic cooperation' with a Danubian economic community [*Donauraum*], 'if possible … [within] a European economic entity'. However, he and his coauthors stated: 'In the case of the dissolution of the German Empire the reunification of the German people in a federally-organized Reich association, with the inclusion of Austria, without the predominance of one clan or state, remains the highest political goal in the future.'[50] This reflected Hoegner's contention that: 'a renewed and strengthened peaceful Bavarian state could be, along with the other South German states in Central Europe, a strong counterweight to the reemergence of a Prussian predominance and will to conquer.'[51]

As the sometimes tortured syntax of such memorandums attests, they were written for a variety of political masters and with a variety of coauthors and as such are full of compromises.[52] In the case of proposals written by Hoegner and others, they are still an important source, indicating some of the ways in which Germans and other Europeans imagined the reconstruction of Europe before the onset of the Cold War. They illustrate how southern Germans envisaged European integration not simply as a means of creating a future union but of reviving forms of European federal unity that had been lost since the late nineteenth century. Moreover, when it came to envisaging the break-up of Germany, it is interesting to note that Allen Dulles faithfully represented Hoegner's views back to his OSS boss, William Donovan, as late as 1945. Dulles explained that:

> As regards the issue as to whether Germany should be partitioned or not, no decision should be reached at the present time … If the natural tendency of certain areas of Germany is to break away and if, for example, the Rhineland should prefer to join up with France, Holland and Belgium, and Bavaria with the new Austrian state, such movements might be permitted but should not be forced or artificially stimulated.[53]

These plans for strengthening southern Germany and the former Habsburg lands of Central Europe via European integration may have become less relevant in the early Cold War period as Central Europe ceased to exist as any kind of meaningful unit. However, they do illustrate the perspective not just of southern German exiles but a wide range of exiled politicians from across Central Europe, particularly those among the governments-in-exile in London. Such politicians envisaged similar plans and established Danubian and Central European clubs to foster integration between Eastern and Central Europeans.[54] Indeed, these kinds of schemes were proposed not only by exiled politicians but also by Western leaders such as Winston Churchill, who designed his own form of Danubian federation.[55] It should, nevertheless, be noted that the exiled groups were divided over whether a Central European federation would include the southern German states or pointedly exclude them. In fact, Hoegner's plans may well have been designed to counter rival plans such as Churchill's that sought to keep out the southern German states.[56] Regardless, a focus on Central Europe was conceived as an alternative vision to a solely Western European community even after 1945. As an author writing in Demokratisches Deutschland's second bulletin in 1946 commented, Germany would be the 'heart' of a new Central Europe, for, '[n]ot from a transcendental mission, rather as the people of the European centre are we ordained by history to be carriers of *abendländisch* legal values and mediatory figures'.[57]

This conception of Europe as *Abendland* that was neither Eastern nor Western but rooted in a shared Central European history and a political culture that was distinct from interwar parliamentary democracy was by no means unusual among resistance intellectuals in Europe. When in summer 1941 the Confessing Church theologian Dietrich Bonhoeffer drafted a statement on the post-war order to be coauthored with the future federalist Visser't Hooft, he emphasized the distinctiveness of the German tradition when compared with the West, stressing the 'genuine loyalties' of family, *Heimat, Volk* and authority that could counter the 'omnipotence of the state'. Similarly, Adam von Trott, along with others from the Kreisau Circle of elite resisters, sent a memorandum to Stafford Cripps in the spring of 1942 (via Visser't Hooft) that emphasized the non-Western 'fraternity of the *oppressed common* people' of Central Europe. He followed this some time later with another document written shortly before the attempt on Hitler's life, called 'Deutschland zwischen Ost und West', which identified Germany as the centre point between the 'Realprinzip' of the East and the 'Personalprinzip' of the West.[58]

In the case of Hoegner, his commitment to an independent southern Germany within a Central European federation emerged while he was in Switzerland. Indeed, he had spoken out against Bavarian federalism and separatism in 1926, seeing in them monarchist and reactionary tendencies.[59] Even in 1935 in a letter to Waldemar von Knoeringen, a Bavarian member of Neu Beginnen, he was worrying that the war might cut off Bavaria and the Rheinland, leading to, 'a state based on the old estates, with a clerical imprint, like we see in Austria'.[60] Furthermore, by the time he was an elder statesman in the Federal Republic of the 1960s, he was again eager to emphasize his commitment to a Germany that united the northern and southern states.[61] Yet, Hoegner's 'Memorandum on the Future Status of Bavaria in International Law' as it appears in his memoirs, does not correspond with the version found in his papers and referenced above. In the copy recorded in the memoirs, a commitment is made to the German state while the claims for Bavarian sovereignty are not as prominent as in the original document, which promoted either Bavarian autonomy or Bavaria being incorporated within a south German *Staatenbund*, depending on the draft.[62] The various versions of this document thus offer clues into how Hoegner and other southern Germans were eager to refashion rather than simply rescue the German nation-state before a framework for Germany and Europe was decided upon by increasingly antagonistic Superpowers.

The existence of such documents also suggests that southern Germans were encouraged to make the case for their states by their patrons in the OSS. At a meeting in April 1943 between Reinhard Spitzy, a renegade Austrian SS officer, another resistance figure in the Abwehr Erich Kordt, Allen Dulles and Joseph Wirth, Dulles intimated that southern Germany could expect better treatment from the Western Allies than the Prussian parts of Germany.[63] There appear to have been a number of reasons for American planners such as Dulles to favour the southern Germans as the 'better Germans'. Politicians such as Wirth could point to the long tradition of liberalism in southern states such as Baden to portray the people of these states as the long-standing victims of Prussian militarism. According to this narrative, these southern Germans had never been dominated by the great Junker landowners often blamed for the reactionary domestic and aggressive foreign policies of the Prussian state and its successors.[64] However, nor had southern Germany provided the bedrock of the German labour movement, whose early post-war leaders went on to antagonize the American occupying forces with their apparently nationalist and anti-capitalist rhetoric.[65]

By contrast with such labour leaders, the dominant politicians in southern Germany appeared either to be independent-minded social democrats like Wilhelm Hoegner, who proved willing to work across party lines on reconstruction plans, or the Christian politicians who were congenial to Christian American politicians such as Senator James Eastland, who spoke out in December 1945 for the 'civilized, Christian people' in Germany (as opposed to the 'Asian hordes' coming from the East) against the punitive measures envisaged by the Morgenthau Plan.[66] As has already been suggested, not least in the figure of John Foster Dulles, a newly ecumenical perspective linked Christian politicians from the United States with the still predominantly Catholic Christian Democrats in post-war Europe. This development therefore suggests a shift among Catholic politicians from southern Germany away from an unreconstructed *abendländisch* perspective that laid the blame on Protestantism for provoking divisions within a formerly unified Christian Europe.[67]

Such a rapprochement between Protestant Anglo-American leaders and the Catholics of southern Germany and Central Europe appears to have influenced the Allies' policies at least in the later war years. Indeed, at Potsdam, Truman and Churchill were advocating a Great-Southern Germany, made up of Austria, Bavaria, Baden, Württemberg and Hungary. This configuration, as well as breaking up the pre-1945 Germany, offered the potential to check Soviet influence in Austria and Hungary. But it was not without its risks: the southern German states might not so much provide a counterweight as merely a larger resource pool for what might become a Soviet vassal. In light of this Truman did not seek to force a resolution on the Southern State question within the Potsdam Agreement.[68] Questions of recalibrating the balance of power between North and South in Germany and Europe were, thus, subsumed by the sphere of influence politics agreed at Potsdam.

This shift from a North–South perspective to an East–West orientation also became evident among Demokratisches Deutschland leaders. For instance, Heinrich Ritzel had envisaged the creation of a southern German state of '20 million inhabitants' that could play an analogous role to that performed by Austria–Hungary in the nineteenth century and act as a 'counterweight to Prussia–Northern Germany'. Indeed, he contended that a Southern German state in which a healthy political culture developed could even eventually encourage a cultural change in the North and, after a number of generations, lead to a reunified Germany that could then be 'a valuable member of the family of nations'. Yet, after the Soviet–Hungarian Agreement of December 1943, Ritzel imagined the Russians advancing to the heart of Central Europe, and thereafter: '[t]he question of a union with Austria in some form of Southern German Association of States [*Staatenbund*]' already appeared less viable.[69] Hoegner's enthusiasm for a southern German federation within a wider *mitteleuropäisch* community also cooled, once it appeared that Russian dominance in Czechoslovakia and Hungary could not be prevented.[70] However, as the next chapter will illustrate, Hoegner remained committed to a southern renaissance in Germany within the context of an integrated Europe and worked towards this end as Minister-President of Bavaria for much of the late 1940s and 1950s.

Although Germany's position in a Western political community rather than a Central European, neo-Habsburgian federation therefore appeared inevitable soon after 1945, this did not mean that the members of Demokratisches

Deutschland were content to see a western German rump integrated within Western Europe. Instead, they put forward a neutralist perspective for a reunited Germany, having been influenced by their experience in neutral Switzerland. They also argued for a form of democratic political culture that emulated the federal structure of Switzerland, which they believed had served to constrain the practice of parliamentary democracy, chiefly by restraining the dominance of national political parties. In this regard they illustrated the convergence between parties of the Right and Left that occurred concerning how interwar forms of democracy would have to be reworked so as to limit the potential for politicians to again radicalize the masses.

Towards a Democratic Germany?

As their concerns about Soviet influence in Central Europe suggest, the leaders of Demokratisches Deutschland worked to disentangle Germany and its neighbours from the system of alliances that formed as the Second World War ended and the Cold War divisions began to emerge. Unsurprisingly, these exiled German politicians were impressed by the ability of their host nation Switzerland to remain neutral throughout a period of violent ideological conflict in Europe. Indeed, they often described Switzerland as a shining example for a post-war Germany and European community positioned between superpower rivals.[71] Swiss political culture appeared particularly appealing to German exiles, not only because the country had taken a non-ideological approach to foreign policy and thus avoided being drawn into alliances, but because domestically too, Swiss political parties had largely avoided the radicalism that had brought down many of the democratic regimes in the rest of Europe and drawn their successors into a wide-ranging military conflict.

Exiles such as the members of Demokratisches Deutschland who 'after the stormy days in Germany and Austria [had] found peace and quiet in Switzerland', were apt to mythologize the Swiss political system.[72] As Hoegner explained in an article, 'Switzerland, the Model Country', in October 1948, he believed that in Switzerland: '[p]arty politics has not yet poisoned the hearts of the individual citizen who stands above the parties and decides in direct elections over the well-being of the nation and often does not conform himself to the solutions of the parties. In the parliaments there is no verbal tussle of violent demagogues, simply and soberly the peoples' representatives present their reasons and their objections.'[73] Certainly, Hoegner was right in so far as Swiss politicians had managed to conduct politics throughout the generally tumultuous 1930s in a more consensual manner than their colleagues across Europe. However, the lack of violent conflict was largely based on a liberal dominance of politics, and the extreme moderation of the SPS. The social democratic party remained in opposition throughout the interwar period, and only gained one seat out of seven in the

Swiss executive, the Federal Council, despite receiving 28.6 per cent of the vote in 1943 and becoming the largest party in parliament.[74]

Indeed, Switzerland had not been completely immune to the tempestuous political currents sweeping across Europe in the early 1930s. It witnessed street clashes between communists and social democrats in 1932 in Zurich, while a New Right campaign for a conservative renewal of society ended with an unsuccessful move to introduce a more authoritarian constitution by plebiscite in 1935. Yet the SPS committed itself to defending democracy in 1933 and professed its willingness to join in a 'national compromise' in 1935. It renounced class struggle and emphasized its patriotism, gradually reintroducing the Swiss flag at workers' festivals – measures which saw the SPS rewarded with an increased share of the vote in the 1935 National Council elections.[75] Thereafter, the SPS entered a 'sacred union' with the other parties, although, in its 'New Switzerland' programme of 1942, its leaders insisted on pushing through radical social and economic change albeit without raising the threat of revolution.[76] Such an accommodating approach by the SPS appealed to certain social democrats such as Ritzel, who was working with liberals in the Europa Union, and to Hoegner, who was exploring Christian political movements, teaching at the Volkshaus, a cultural centre in Zurich, on Emmanuel Mounier's 'Personalist Manifesto'.[77] However, it was equally disappointing to communist members of Freies Deutschland including Hans Teubner, who in October 1944 supported the founding of a Partei der Arbeit by communists and left social democrats due to the rightwards shift of the SPS.[78]

German politicians such as Wirth, Hoegner and Ritzel were particularly impressed by the non-partisan commitment of Swiss politicians to a 'Spiritual National Defence'. This was a concept largely developed by conservative thinkers such as Gonzague de Reynold, mentor of Federal Councillor Philipp Etter, but embraced by Swiss politicians of all stripes as a rallying cry against National Socialist domination.[79] Again, one would not want to exaggerate the unity of all the Swiss: the 'Spiritual National Defence' was a concept more commonly invoked in German-speaking Switzerland and regarded with some suspicion in the French-speaking region as a 'mystic of unity'.[80] Yet Swiss politicians proved willing to accept the authority of a collegiate and cross-party Federal Council, which ruled equipped with emergency powers.[81] This example of a non-ideological nationalist movement designed to save the national community from internal and external enemies was compelling to German exiles who were fighting the Soviet policy announced at Potsdam to annex large sections of Eastern Germany, and confronting the rival Freies Deutschland movement that appeared well positioned to assume a leading role in a new Sovietized Germany.

The Demokratisches Deutschland leaders illustrated the influence of Swiss political culture on them in their 1945 manifesto, *Das Demokratische Deutschland. Fundamentals and Guidelines for German Reconstruction in a Democratic, Republican, Federalist and Cooperative Sense*. In this document, they outlined how a new Germany would be integrated into a 'Union of European states and a peaceful community of peoples', stressing how it would resemble the more federal structure of the Swiss cantons. Regionalism would be strengthened with provision for a chamber representing the states and representative democracy would be supplemented by local and institutional self-government, which would encourage more autonomy for local communities, businesses, workers, consumers and educational institutions.[82] This raft of measures would constitute an anti-*Gleichschaltung* that would see power travel from the bottom up.

Having worked on European reconstruction plans within the Swiss Europa Union, Ritzel had already developed ideas for reforming German democracy, incorporating elements of the Swiss political system. In a drafted 'Law for the Reshaping of Political Life [in Germany]' that he probably produced for the Western Allied governments, he contended that parties might seem to embody pluralism within a parliamentary democracy. Yet in practice the party dictatorships that had emerged in Italy and Germany were merely the logical conclusion to the party factionalism that had developed within the interwar democracies, in contrast to the non-partisan leadership exercised by the Federal Council in Switzerland.[83] Thus, parties should be permitted in post-war European states but, mirroring the political formations within Demokratisches Deutschland, should be confined to three groupings, reflecting the three currents of opinion the Demokratisches Deutschland leaders rather optimistically believed predominant in Europe. These would be a social democratic party, a liberal democratic party and a social conservative party.[84]

In a document published through the Swiss Europa Union – an organization that sought to create a European federation out of the framework of the Swiss federation – Ritzel had already suggested that bicameral legislatures should be supplemented with other representative institutions, such as economic parliaments. He believed that producers, consumers, owners and workers would work productively together if they were given direct control of the economy rather than trying to gain control by winning political power through national parties.[85] Such institutions, along with enhanced local structures would, he contended, help in 'educating the people to political democracy'. However, such a process of political education would first see a great concentration of power in the hands of regional, national and international elites. Indeed, as Ritzel explained in documents dealing more explicitly with German reconstruction, power should reside in the hands of immoveable leaders until the people had proved worthy of its exercise again:

> In this time of education and until the people can be trusted to exist independently in a renewed political democracy, until one is convinced that the people is mature enough not to sacrifice the political democracy to a charlatan out of its incapacity and lack of critical judgement, governmental structures must be created that for the longer term are independent of the will of the people.

While power should gradually be devolved to first local elected councils, then states and regional unions, throughout this period, a Swiss-style Federal Council of fifteen members should rule a federal German state without requiring the support of the people or the state governments. The risk of a *Führer* or *Duce*-style dictator would be lessened by following the Swiss model and not appointing a federal president; however, there would be no separation of power between legislature, executive and judiciary, and all trade union activity would be conducted within a 'German Work Front'. Such a state of affairs would probably endure for around thirty years, imagined Ritzel, before the German people could be trusted to exercise democratic rights again.[86]

Again, Allen Dulles echoed such views in the recommendations he made to his OSS superiors. In his 'Notes on the German Situation' from 1945, he urged that:

> [t]he rebuilding of political life in Germany prior to the constitution of any central government must begin in the local communities and then in the German states. For example, to take Bavaria as an instance, we should first select trustworthy Burgermasters [sic] for the various Bavarian cities, then we should choose small city and communal councils, then we should allow these bodies to select a central council for the state, thus building up local State government before any attempt is made toward the organization of a central government for the territory that may remain German.[87]

As the Demokratisches Deutschland leaders made clear, such proposals were not only shaped by the positive experiences of German exiles in wartime Switzerland but also by the apparent failure of parliamentary democracy in interwar Germany. Hoegner later explained this position in a speech in early 1946 in Garmisch-Partenkirchen, Bavaria. Despite having himself drafted many constitutions, including the Bavarian, he explained that although, '[t]he Weimar Constitution was certainly, as it claimed, the freest constitution in the world' yet, 'the freeing of a people from a servile spirit cannot be the work of a constitution'. To 'teach the Germans to be free peoples' one had to, instead, start from below. For: 'the communities are older than the state ... the dominance over the state changes repeatedly, but the local administration remains. Thus has local self-government been named the "high school of democracy"'.[88] Accordingly, he believed that parliamentary democracy should be supplemented by elements of direct democracy that worked very well in Switzerland and by the schooling of individuals in local civil society organizations.

Such a belief in direct democracy might imply a great confidence in the will of the people and a wish to bring democracy closer to them. However, Hoegner wanted to see such direct democracy begin at a local level and to work as a potential check on the power of parties to dominate 'parliamentary horse-trading'. For he envisaged that, along with having to be approved by a parliament, constitutional reforms would also have to be supported by a majority of the population in plebiscites. Hoegner's endeavour to limit the power of parties was prompted by a concern that the German youth had become barbarized during the National

Socialist period and was incapable of exercising democratic rights. Thus he also wished to restrict the franchise to those over thirty and to maintain an elite class of political leaders, whose every initiative did not need to be approved by an electorate. As he explained: 'It suffices that the majority decides over the goals and direction of a community, selects its leaders and scrutinizes them. Leadership itself, however, should be the right and duty of the most talented.'[89]

The scepticism of Demokratisches Deutschland leaders with regard to parliamentary democracy and ideologically-profiled parties found its complement in their suspicion of the foreign policies of the democratic Western nations. As the authors argued with regard to the collusion of the Western democracies with National Socialist aggression, confronted with ideologically fanatical party politicians such as Hitler, democratic politicians had been rather reluctant to fight in the defence of democracy.[90] Thus, both internally and at the international level, democracies had proved unable to sustain themselves against ideological parties that sought to undermine the basis of their continued existence. As Ritzel, writing with Europa Union President Hans Bauer, explained, the 'pseudodemocratic constructions' – the nation-states after 1918 – were thus as paper thin as the system of international law created by the League of Nations. The '[s]tates and the community of states ... were [therefore] not the expression of a change of perspective', that is towards embracing democracy, 'much more bloodless phantoms that, due to their terminal weaknesses, were destined to die'.[91]

Accordingly, the Demokratisches Deutschland theorists did not necessarily conceive of a European Union as an association of ideologically united nation-states.[92] Rather, a European federation would play a negative, safeguarding role and limit the power of any national government. As Hoegner explained in a speech on 'The United States of Europe?' given in July, 1946: the 'fundamentals' of such a union would be, (1) ensuring the 'equal rights of all members', (2) guaranteeing that each state could freely choose its own form of government, whether a republic or monarchy, and (3) the protection of 'certain minimum rights of nationals of all the members of the federation such as freedom of conscience, and other human rights, [such as] communal self-government'.[93] Thus, for the leaders of Demokratisches Deutschland, an integrated European community was never intended as a means of ensuring democracy in Europe. Instead, it was conceived primarily as a way of preventing conflict between ideologically different European nations. Such an approach was designed not only to avoid a repeat of the ideological clashes of the interwar period, but also to offer the prospect of a European community that stretched from East to West and which could not be divided by the emerging ideological Cold War.

As can be seen from their writings on the practice of, and prospects for, democracy in Europe, the Demokratisches Deutschland authors did not so much envisage a new democratic era for Europe as plan for the sort of post-post-liberal international order described by Jan-Werner Müller.[94] Such an international order would guarantee the rights of individuals and minorities against national governments but would not stipulate how these governments were formed. What was striking about the authors' proposals was how avowedly un-ideological they were, thereby suggesting that ideological loyalties (and enmities) were to account for the warfare that had broken out across Europe. Such a deemphasizing of ideology was no doubt partially due to the need for Christian and social democrats to make common cause within the Demokratisches Deutschland coalition. However, it also signals that the pose of being post-ideological was not only adopted by *abendländisch* groups on the Right. Rather, it was assumed by regionally based politicians across the ideological spectrum who believed that local communities had been disunited by the polarized party politics practised from a national centre during the interwar years. And yet, as will be seen in the following section, ideological differences did not disappear among members of Demokratisches Deutschland.

The Demise of the Group

The case studies analysed in earlier chapters have illustrated the difficulties faced by émigrés who sought to reestablish themselves as political leaders in post-war (West) Germany. In spite, or perhaps because, of their connections with occupation authorities, such exiles lacked legitimacy among their fellow Germans. Recognizing their remoteness from German life by 1945, political exiles in Switzerland therefore clamoured to occupy a representative role among the 'German colony' living in the cantons and to thereby demonstrate that they could speak for a significant German constituency. The leaders of both Demokratisches Deutschland and Freies Deutschland made rival claims with the Swiss authorities in early 1945 to assume consular duties on behalf of the Germans, as military defeat for the National Socialists appeared increasingly likely. They were, indeed, encouraged and cajoled by the Swiss Foreign Department into working together to facilitate the return home of German refugees and to provide relief aid for needy Germans. Thus, members of both groups met in the *Karl der Grosse* Restaurant in Zurich on 5 May 1945 to agree on an Ambassador who would represent a 'German Resistance Movement'. Wilhelm Hoegner was eventually chosen, with the Communist Leopold Bauer from Freies Deutschland as his deputy, although immediately both groups backtracked from this commitment. The following day, the provisional leadership of Freies Deutschland stated that the Zurich representatives had gone beyond their brief and proposed Bauer for Ambassador instead, prompting the Swiss authorities to close down the German Embassy on 8 May and take over the consulate themselves, while the two groups issued sallies against one another in their rival publications.[95]

The conflict between the groups did not last for much longer, though. By December 1945 Das Demokratische Deutschland was the only remaining representation for the Germans in Switzerland after Freies Deutschland had been instructed to disband by the Soviets.[96] Yet, what should have heralded something of a triumph for the non-communist coalition actually only hastened its demise. Without the threat posed by a Communist front organization the incentive for the leaders to cooperate across party lines weakened. Relations between the social democrat Ritzel and the Christian democrat Wirth had repeatedly been strained and after Ritzel had been elected as Chairman of Demokratisches Deutschland in late January 1946, he sought to pass a resolution of no confidence on Wirth. The latter went on to found an 'Association of Christian Democratic Germans in Switzerland' in March, marking the first stage of the Demokratisches Deutschland parties separating from one another. This was followed by the withdrawal of the social democrat group from the cross-party organization the following month. After this, Wirth came to dominate Demokratisches Deutschland again, along with fellow-liberal Glaesser. The group however never really recovered its role as a forum for debate on Germany's future or as a proponent of European federation. Rather it largely concerned itself with charitable work, sending care packages to Germany and seeking to ease the return of German refugees from Switzerland back to their country of origin.[97]

Such a breakdown in the wartime coalition was perhaps unsurprising as partisan politics began to reemerge in Germany and the Demokratisches Deutschland leaders sought to revive their careers as politicians in the Western zones. Moreover, a basic tension existed between the different roles played by the leaders of Das Demokratische Deutschland. In order to appear plausible as representatives of a new Germany, it was important that aspiring leaders be seen to represent the interests of the German nation and not merely position themselves as the placemen of the occupation forces. Nevertheless, any populist courting of German support risked alienating Allied leadership. Disagreements among the leaders about the balance to be struck between these two roles dogged the organization and led to its demise as a cross-party working group in 1946. For instance, when Braun made a speech in Zurich suggesting that punitive policies on the part of the Allies would bring about another catastrophe, just as an unjust Weimar settlement had radicalized Germans after the First World War, he won much attention from local journalists. Yet, equally, this speech alienated him from his younger colleagues who remained eager to secure employment and political office once the occupying forces had assumed control in Germany.[98] For, as will become evident, the most viable route back to prominence and power in post-war Germany for exiles who lacked a popular base in Germany was to work with the Western allies.

*****

The wartime cooperation between the Western Allies and the Demokratisches Deutschland leaders suggests that these exiles might be counted among the Westernizing agents in post-war German society. Such exiles did not interpret the events of the war, or of the emerging Cold War, with historical innocence though, but viewed them as consequences of longer-standing shifts of power away from local and regional communities towards political centres ruled by partisan elites.

Thus, rather than seek to return to a pre-war normality, they envisaged a more radical post-war reconstruction that would repair the damage wrought by nationalist movements since the nineteenth century.

Such a perspective motivated the transnational federalist movement that emerged in the later war years, not least out of contacts between Catholic politicians from southern Europe. These politicians sought to return power to local communities marginalized by the nation building of the late nineteenth and early twentieth centuries, and to keep European communities out of future ideological struggles such as a Cold War directed from centres outside of Europe. What is striking about such federalist arguments is, nevertheless, how persuasive they proved to American politicians and military planners who acted as sponsors for a number of the exiles they encountered in wartime Switzerland. This appears to have been due to a common Christian democratic perspective that developed among Christian politicians from the United States and Europe who shared a reading of recent European history and felt threatened by the godless Soviet Union. One result of this development was that American planners, who had previously been isolationist or committed to a Western hemisphere detached from a warring Europe, increasingly embraced the idea of a West made up of Europe and the United States.[99] However, this West or *Abendland* was, from the perspective of many German exiles, a community that had its heart in the pre-nationalist communities of Central Europe, which came to be in the Soviet sphere of influence. This meant, as will be shown, that these exiles and the American planners did not always pursue similar policies with regard to constructing a Western bloc in post-war Europe. Rather, federalists continued to pursue a Third Force agenda into the late 1950s.

The arguments for federalism in Germany and in Europe that were advanced by the leaders of Demokratisches Deutschland came to have a significant impact in post-war Germany. They were put into practice by Jakob Kindt-Kiefer, working within in the Geneva Circle of the Nouvelles Equipes Internationales (NEI), by Heinrich Ritzel as General Secretary in the German Europa Union created in 1947 and by Wilhelm Hoegner, who served as Minister-President of Bavaria for much of the late 1940s and 1950s. Hoegner consistently sought to work within coalitions in Bavaria, to defend the local rights of Bavarians against the claims of central government and the central office of the SPD, and to advance the cause of European integration. It is chiefly to his work that the following chapter turns its attention. However, the careers of Heinrich Ritzel, Joseph Wirth and Jakob Kindt-Kiefer are also considered, with a particular focus being trained on the latter's role within the NEI, probably the most important transnational Christian Democratic pressure group of the early post-war period.

Notes

1. Norddeutsche Buchdrückerei und Verlagsanstalt, *Verhandlungen des Reichstags. Stenographische Berichte I. Wahlperiode 1920. Band 356. 236 Sitzung* (Berlin: Norddeutsche Buchdrückerei und Verlagsanstalt, 1922) pp. 8054-058. Accessible at: http://www.reichstagsprotokolle.de/Blatt2_w1_bsb00000040_00023.html
2. See particularly P. Krüger, 'A Rainy Day, April 16, 1922: The Rapallo Treaty and the Cloudy Perspective for German Foreign Policy', in C. Fink, A. Frohn and J. Heideking (eds), *Genoa, Rapallo and European Reconstruction in 1922* (Cambridge: Cambridge University Press, 1991) pp. 49–64.
3. A. Grzesinski (ed. E. Kolb), *Im Kampf um die deutsche Republik. Erinnerungen eines Sozialdemokraten* (Munich: Oldenbourg, 2001) p. 122.
4. H.A. Winkler, *Weimar, 1918–1933: die Geschichte der ersten deutschen Demokratie* (Munich: Beck, 1998) p. 430; I. Ermakoff, *Ruling Oneself Out: A Theory of Collective Abdications* (Durham: Duke University Press, 2008) p. 73.
5. C.-D. Krohn, 'Einleitung', in C.-D. Krohn and P. von zur Muehlen (eds), *Rückkehr und Aufbau nach 1945. Deutsche Remigranten im öffentlichen Leben Nachkriegsdeutschlands* (Marburg: Metropolis, 1997) pp. 8–9.
6. J.M. Palmier, *Weimar in Exile: The Antifascist Emigration in Europe and America* (London: Verso, 2006) pp. 156–57.
7. G. Koller, 'Entscheidungen über Leben und Tod. Die behördliche Praxis in der schweizerischen Flüchtlingspolitik während des Zweiten Weltkrieges', in C. Graf (ed.), *Die Schweiz und die Flüchtlinge 1933–1945* (Berne: Haupt, 1996) pp. 23–24.
8. U. Hörster-Philipps, *Joseph Wirth 1879–1956. Eine politische Biographie* (Paderborn: Schöningh, 1998) p. 536.
9. R. Ludi, 'Dwindling Options: Seeking Asylum in Switzerland 1933–1939', in F. Caestecker and B. Moore (eds), *Refugees from Nazi Germany and the Liberal European States* (New York and Oxford: Berghahn, 2010) p. 95.
10. U. Schwarz, *The Eye of the Hurricane: Switzerland in World War Two* (Boulder CO: Westview, 1980) p. 123; S. Erlanger, 'The Politics of "Transmigration": Why Jewish Refugees had to Leave Switzerland from 1944 to 1954', in *Jewish Political Studies Review 18/1-2* (Spring 2006) 71–85.
11. See 'Verwerflich gehandelt' in *Der Spiegel 38*, from 14 September 1955, 14–15; and Hörster-Philipps, 'Nachkriegskonzeptionen deutscher Politiker im Schweizer Exil. Der Wirth-Braun-Hoegner-Kreis', in C.-D. Krohn and M. Schumacher (eds), *Exil und Neuordnung: Beiträge zur verfassungspolitischen Entwicklung in Deutschland nach 1945* (Düsseldorf: Droste, 2000) p. 91; M. Gehler, 'Begegnungsort der Kalten Krieges: Der "Genfer Kreis" und die geheimen Absprachen westeuropäischer Christdemokraten 1947–1955', in M. Gehler, W. Kaiser and H. Wohnout (eds), *Christdemokratie in Europa im 20. Jahrhundert* (Vienna: Böhlau, 2001) p. 645.
12. G. Ritter, 'Wilhelm Hoegner', in Ferdinand Seibt (ed.), *Gesellschaftsgeschichte. Festschrift für Karl Bosl zum 80. Geburtstag*, Vol. 2 (Munich: Oldenbourg, 1988) p. 341; P. Stahlberger, *Der Zürcher Verleger Emil Oprecht und die deutsche politische Emigration 1933–1945* (Zurich: Europa, 1970) pp. 59–60; Schwarz, *Eye of the Hurricane*, p. 127; D. Holmes, *Ignazio Silone in Exile: Writing and Anti-Fascism in Switzerland, 1929–1944* (Aldershot: Ashgate, 2004) p. 39.
13. P. Kritzer, *Wilhelm Hoegner: Politische Biographie eines bayrischen Sozialdemokrat* (Munich: Süddeutscher, 1979) pp. 113, 125, 129.
14. AdsD, NL Ritzel, *Findbuch*, Vol. I, 'Zur Biographie des Nachlassers', p. II.
15. V. Conze, *Das Europa der Deutschen: Ideen von Europa in Deutschland zwischen Reichstradition und Westorientierung (1920–1970)* (Munich: Oldenbourg, 2005) pp. 219–21; T. Ehs, , '"…as Free and Happy as Switzerland is Today"', in J.-M. Guieu and C. Le Dréau (eds), *Le Congrès de l'Europe à la Haye (1948–2008)* (Brussels: Peter Lang, 2009) pp. 50–51.

16. Hörster-Philipps, *Wirth*, pp. 532–36, 539–41.
17. Hörster-Philipps, *Wirth*, p. 554; K. von Klemperer, *German Resistance against Hitler: The Search for Allies Abroad, 1938–1945* (Oxford: Oxford University Press, 1992) pp. 59–60; H. Küppers, *Joseph Wirth. Parlamentarier, Minister und Kanzler der Weimarer Republik* (Stuttgart: Franz Steiner, 1997) p. 305.
18. Hörster-Philipps, *Wirth*, pp. 539–41, 549–51, 560–61; Klemperer, *German Resistance against Hitler*, p. 58.
19. P.T. Jackson, *Civilizing the Enemy: German Reconstruction and the Invention of the West* (Ann Arbor: The University of Michigan Press, 2006) pp. 99–111.
20. Hörster-Philipps, *Wirth*, pp. 538–80; A. Keim, 'John Foster Dulles and the Protestant World Order Movement on the Eve of World War II', in *Journal of Church and State*, 21/1 (1979) 73–89.
21. R. Immerman, *John Foster Dulles: Piety, Pragmatism and Power in U.S. Foreign Policy* (Wilmington DE: Rowman and Littlefield, 1999) pp. 20–21.
22. J. Heideking, 'Die "Schweizer Straßen" des europäischen Widerstands', in G. Schulz (ed.), *Geheimdienste und Widerstandsbewegungen im Zweiten Weltkrieg* (Göttingen: Vanderhoeck und Ruprecht, 1982) pp. 160–61.
23. W. Kaiser, *Christian Democracy and the Origins of European Union* (Cambridge: Cambridge University Press, 2007) pp. 61–65, 75–77, 86–88; P. D'Agostino, *Rome in America: Transnational Catholic Ideology from the Risorgimento to Fascism* (Chapel Hill: University of North Carolina Press, 2004) p. 167.
24. Kaiser, *Christian Democracy and the Origins of European Union*, p. 111; Hörster-Philipps, *Wirth*, p. 571.
25. A. Dulles, 'Telegram 3800-3806, June 12 1944', in N. Petersen (ed.), *From Hitler's Doorstep: The Wartime Intelligence Reports of Allen Dulles, 1942–1945* (University Park PA: Pennsylvania State University Press, 1996) pp. 307–8.
26. Dulles, 'Telegram 2068-73, February 15 1944', in Petersen, *From Hitler's Doorstep*, p. 220.
27. On the Morgenthau Plan, see J.L. Harper, *American Visions of Europe: Franklin D. Roosevelt George F. Kennan, and Dean G. Acheson* (Cambridge: Cambridge University Press, 1996) p. 105.
28. For more on this, see Conclusion.
29. Dulles, 'Telegram 2068-73, February 15 1944', in Petersen, *From Hitler's Doorstep*, pp. 220–21.
30. See Dulles, 'Telegram 5527, February 19 1945', in Petersen, *From Hitler's Doorstep*, pp. 451–52.
31. H. Schulze, *Otto Braun oder Preussens demokratische Sendung. Eine Biographie* (Frankfurt am Main: Ullstein, 1977) p. 813.
32. H. Bungert, *Das Nationalkomitee und der Westen. Die Reaktion der Westalliierten auf das NKFD und die Freien Deutschen Bewegungen 1943–1948* (Stuttgart: Franz Steiner, 1997) pp. 22, 88.
33. S. Selinger, *Charlotte von Kirschbaum and Karl Barth: A Study in Biography and the History of Theology* (University Park PA: Pennsylvania State University Press, 1998) p. 68; Bungert, *Nationalkomitee und der Westen*, pp. 22–27.
34. H. Wichers, *Im Kampf gegen Hitler. Deutsche Sozialisten im Schweizer Exil, 1933–1940* (Zurich: Chronos, 1994) p. 107.
35. K.H. Bergmann, *Die Bewegung "Freies Deutschland" in der Schweiz 1943–1945* (Munich: Hanser, 1974) p. 116.
36. C. Carstens, 'Für Freiheit, Wahrheit und Glück: Die Pädagogin und Politikerin Anna Siemsen (1882–1951)', in *Berlinische Monatsschrift* 10/2 (February 2001) 58.
37. Hörster-Philipps, 'Wirth-Braun-Hoegner Kreis', in Krohn and Schumacher, *Exil und Neuordnung*, pp. 91–92, 98, 101–08; AdsD, NL Ritzel, Folder 359, 'Mitteilungsblätter der Arbeitsgemeinschaft "Demokratisches Deutschland"', 1/5 (January 1946).
38. Hörster-Philipps, 'Wirth-Braun-Hoegner-Kreis', pp. 108–09. Ritzel told Braun in a letter of 25 August 1945 that the group had around 1000 individual members, not including associated organizations. AdsD, NL Ritzel, Folder 214.

39. AdsD, NL Ritzel, Folder 356, 'Protokoll über die Sitzung des Hauptvorstandes "DD" v. 8.9.45'; NL Braun, Box 6: Material 1940–1950. Braun to Union deutscher Sozialisten u. Gewerkschafter in der Schweiz, 17 October 1946.
40. AdsD, NL Ritzel, Folder 356, 'Report, "Die politische Haltung der deutschen Gruppen in der Schweiz"', 4 July 1945 and '"Protokoll über die Sitzung des Hauptvorstandes "DD" von 8.9.45", 9 September 1945; NL Ritzel, Folder 359, *Mitteilungsblatt der Arbeitsgemeinschaft 'Demokratisches Deutschland'* 1/1, September 1945, esp. J. Kindt-Kiefer, 'Wegworte', p. 2.
41. For some background on the negotiations regarding Czech and Polish annexations, see K. Kaplan, *The Short March: The Communist Takeover in Czechoslovakia 1945–1948* (London, C. Hurst and Co., 1987) pp. 19–30.
42. AdsD, NL Braun, Box 8, Folder 6, Otto Braun, 'Was muss nach Kriegsende geschehen?' [undated, 1945?].
43. AdsD, NL Ritzel, Folder 352, Letter of Heinrich Ritzel to [Curt] Cerf, intended for Mr. Byrnes, American Secretary of State. Dated 4 May 1946. See another copy dated 3.5.46 in Folder 216.
44. Dulles, 'Telegram 2560, April 21, 1944', and 'Document 4-87, Memorandum from Allen W. Dulles to William J. Donovan, New York, 7.10.1944, Notes on the Situation in Europe', in Petersen, *From Hitler's Doorstep*, pp. 272, 383–85.
45. A. Milward, *The European Rescue of the Nation-State* (London and New York: Routledge 2nd ed., 2000) esp. Introduction.
46. M. Umbach, *German Federalism: Past, Present, Future* (Houndmills: Palgrave, 2002) p. 4.
47. H. Bauer and H. Ritzel, *Kampf um Europa. Von der Schweiz aus gesehen* (Zurich:Europa, 1945) p. 20.
48. J.R. Canoy, *The Discreet Charm of the Police State: the Landpolizei and the Transformation of Bavaria, 1945–1965* (Leiden: Brill, 2005) pp. 61–65; M. Berger, 'Michael Freiherr von Godin', in T. Bautz (ed.), *Biographisch-bibliographisches Kirchenlexikon* Vol. 21 (Nordhausen: Traugott Bautz, 2003) pp. 489–505; H. Zacher, 'Hans Nawiasky: Ein Leben für Bundesstaat, Rechtsstaat und Demokratie', in H. Heinrichs, H. Franzki, K. Schmalz and M. Stolleis (eds), *Deutsche Juristen jüdischer Herkunft* (Munich: Beck, 1993) pp. 677–79; H. Woller, *Die Loritz-Partei. Geschichte, Struktur und Politik der Wirtschaftlichen Aufbau-Vereinigung (WAV) 1945–1955* (Stuttgart: DEVA, 1982)
49. Dulles, 'Notes on the Situation in Europe', in Petersen, *From Hitler's Doorstep*, pp. 383–85.
50. IfZ Munich, NL Hoegner, ED 120/20, 'Politische Richtlinien'. See also E. Seefried, 'Schweizer Exilerfahrungen in der Verfassungsgesetzgebung Bayerns 1946', in Krohn and Schumacher, *Exil und Neuordnung*, p. 118.
51. IfZ Munich, NL Hoegner, ED 120/18, W. Hoegner, 'Memorandum über die künftige staatsrechtliche Stellung des Landes Bayern'.
52. See Canoy, *Discreet Charm of the Police State*, pp. 63–64; G. Clemens, 'Remigranten in der Kultur- und Medienpolitik der Britischen Zone', in C.-D. Krohn and A. Schildt, *Zwischen den Stühlen? Remigranten und Remigration in der deutschen Medienöffentlichkeit der Nachkriegszeit* (Hamburg: Hans Christians, 2002) pp. 53–55.
53. E. Peterson, *The American Occupation of Germany: Retreat to Victory* (Detroit: Wayne State University Press, 1977) p. 231; Dulles, 'Notes on the Situation in Europe', in Petersen, *From Hitler's Doorstep*, pp. 386–87.
54. J. Levy, *The Intermarium: Wilson, Madison, and East Central European Federalism* (Boca Raton: Universal-Publishers, 2007) pp. 211–15.
55. K. Larres, *Churchill's Cold War: The Politics of Personal Diplomacy* (New Haven: Yale University Press, 2002) p. 86.
56. P. Kock, *Bayerns Weg in die Bundesrepublik* (Stuttgart: DEVA, 1983) pp. 82–83.
57. R. Barth, 'Gespräch mit England' in *Mitteilungsblätter der Demokratischen Deutschland*, 2/2 (February, 1946) pp. 3–4.
58. Klemperer, *German Resistance against Hitler*, pp. 271–74, 280–81, 373.

59. Ritter, 'Hoegner', in Seibt (ed.), *Gesellschaftsgeschichte*, p. 344.
60. IfZ Munich, NL Hoegner, ER 120/6, Letter from Hoegner, 1 March 1935.
61. W. Hoegner, *Der schwierige Außenseiter. Errinerungen eines Abgeordneten, Emigranten und Ministerpräsidenten* (Munich: Isar, 1959) p. 312.
62. Seefried, 'Schweizer Exilerfahrungen', p. 118; IfZ Munich, NL Hoegner, ED 120/20, Hoegner, 'Gesetz über die vorläufige Staatsgewalt im freien Volksstaat Bayern'.
63. Klemperer, *German Resistance against Hitler*, pp. 324–25.
64. See D. Langewiesche, *Nation, Nationalismus, Nationalstaat in Deutschland und Europa* (Munich: Beck, 2000) pp. 68–72.
65. On this, see, for instance, C. Eisenberg, 'The Limits of Democracy: U.S. Policy and the Rights of German Labor, 1945–1949', in M. Ermarth (ed.), *America and the Shaping of German Society, 1945–1955* (Oxford: Berg, 1993) pp. 60–81.
66. Jackson, *Civilizing the Enemy*, pp. 132–34. On southern social democrats, see E. Wolfrum, *Französische Besatzungspolitik und deutsche Sozialdemokratie. Politische Neuansätze in der 'vergessenen Zone' bis zur Bildung des Südweststaates 1945–1952* (Dusseldorf: Droste, 1991) p. 293.
67. Kaiser, 'Trigger-happy Protestant Materialists? The European Christian Democrats and the United States', in M. Trachtenberg (ed.), *Between Empire and Alliance: America and Europe during the Cold War* (Lanham: Rowman and Littlefield, 2003) p. 68.
68. W. Zorn, *Bayerns Geschichte im 20. Jahrhundert. Von der Monarchie zum Bundesland* (Munich: Beck, 1986) pp. 554–59.
69. IfZ Munich, NL Hoegner, ED 120/15, H. Ritzel, 'Einige flüchtige Gedanken zur Friedenspolitik in Bezug auf Mitteleuropa' and ED 120/8, Ritzel 'Der deutsche Weg zur Demokratie'.
70. IfZ Munich, NL Hoegner, ED 120/18, 'Süddeutschland und Donauraum', various drafts.
71. See W. Lipgens, *A History of European Integration, vol.1, 1945–1947* (Oxford: Clarendon Press, 1982) p. 118.
72. Hoegner, *Schwierige Außenseiter*, p. 142.
73. IfZ Munich, NL Hoegner, ED 120/284, 'Musterland Schweiz', in the *Isarpost*, 5 October 1948.
74. Unabhängige Expertenkommission Schweiz – Zweiter Weltkrieg, *Die Schweiz, der Nationalsozialismus und der Zweite Weltkrieg. Schlußbericht* (Zurich: Pendo, 2002) pp. 64–65; Switzerland (Federal Chancellery), *The Federal Constitution of the Swiss Confederation: September 12, 1848*, (Berne: C.J. Wyss, 1867), p. 25.
75. Expertenkommission, *Die Schweiz, der Nationalsozialismus und der Zweite Weltkrieg*, pp. 70–76; J. Mooser, '"Spiritual National Defence" in the 1930s: Swiss Political Culture between the Wars', in G. Kreis (ed.), *Switzerland and the Second World War* (London and New York: Routledge, 2000) pp. 247–48.
76. A. Lasserre, 'Political and Humanitarian Resistance in Switzerland, 1939–1945', in Kreis, *Switzerland and the Second World War*, p. 224.
77. IfZ Munich, NL Hoegner, ED 120/13, Letter from Hoegner to Kurt Düby and Düby's reply, 26 September 1937.
78. H. Teubner, *Exilland Schweiz. Dokumentarischer Bericht über den Kampf emigrierter deutscher Kommunisten 1933–1945*, (Berlin: Dietz, 1975) pp. 124–25, 276.
79. Mooser, 'Spiritual National Defence', in Kreis, *Switzerland and the Second World War*, p. 240.
80. Ibid., p. 249.
81. Neville Wylie, 'Pilet-Golaz and the Making of Swiss Foreign Policy: Some Remarks', pp. 160–61; and Mooser, 'Spiritual National Defence', p. 246, in Kreis, *Switzerland and the Second World War*.
82. Hauptvorstand der Arbeitsgemeinschaft "Das Demokratische Deutschland" (Joseph Wirth, Otto Braun, Wilhelm Hoegner, Jakob Kindt-Kiefer and Heinrich Ritzel) (eds), *Das Demokratische Deutschland. Grundsätze und Richtlinien für den deutschen Wiederaufbau im demokratischen, republikanischen, föderalistischen und genossenschaftlichen Sinne* (Berne und Leipzig: Haupt, 1945) pp. 8–9.

83. There is some debate among historians as to whether Ritzel's connections were primarily with the British or the French. See Kritzer, *Hoegner*, p. 134 and Schulze, *Braun*, p. 808.
84. AdsD, NL Ritzel, Folder 353, H. Ritzel, 'Gesetz zur Neugestaltung des politischen Lebens'.
85. Bauer and Ritzel, *Von der Eidgenössischen zur Europäischen Föderation* (Zurich and New York: Europa, 1940) pp. 132–3.
86. AdsD, NL Ritzel, Folder 350, H. Ritzel, Untitled document, dated 18 November 1942.
87. Duller, *From Hitler's Doorstep*, p. 386.
88. IfZ Munich, NL Hoegner, ED 120/281, W. Hoegner, 'Rede des bayerischen Ministerpräsidenten am 26. Januar 1946 in Garmisch-Partenkirchen'.
89. IfZ Munich, NL Hoegner, ED 120/58, Hoegner to Nawiasky, 'Denkschrift über die Demokratisierung der Verwaltung', 21 January 1949; Kritzer, *Hoegner*, pp. 152–60; Seefried, 'Schweizer Exilerfahrungen', pp. 122–23.
90. Hauptvorstand Demokratisches Deutschland, *Richtlinien*, pp. 6–7.
91. Bauer and Ritzel, *Kampf um Europa*, p. 12.
92. Bauer and Ritzel, *Eidgenössischen zur Europäischen Föderation*, p. 70.
93. IfZ Munich, NL Hoegner, ED 120/28, W. Hoegner, 'Vereinigte Staaten von Europa?'. Volkshochschule Ulm, 12 July 1946.
94. J.-W. Müller, *Contesting Democracy: Political Ideas in Twentieth Century Europe* (New Haven: Yale University Press, 2011) p. 130.
95. IfZ Munich, NL Hoegner, ED 120/12. Letter of 5 May 1945 from Demokratisches Deutschland and Freies Deutschland to the Eidgenössische Politische Departement in Bern, and 'Niederschrift über die Ergebnisse einer gemeinsamen Sitzung zwischen den Vertretern des "Freien Deutschland" und der Arbeitsgemeinschaft 'Das Demokratische Deutschland', 6 May 1945. See also Hörster-Philipps, *Wirth*, pp. 631–33; and Schulze, *Braun*, pp. 823–25.
96. Hörster-Philipps, *Wirth*, p. 639; AdsD, NL Ritzel, Folder 359, 'Mitteilungsblätter der Arbeitsgemeinschaft "Demokratisches Deutschland"'.
97. Letter from Kindt-Kiefer to Ritzel, 5 February 1946 in AdsD, NL Ritzel, Mappe 358; Hörster-Philipps, *Wirth*, pp. 639–41; Schulze, *Braun*, pp. 833–34.
98. Schulze, *Braun*, pp. 828–29.
99. On this Western Hemisphere perspective, see A. Whitaker, *The Western Hemisphere Idea: Its Rise and Decline* (Ithaca: Cornell University Press, 1954) pp. 2–14.

Chapter 6

'EUROPE OUR FATHERLAND, BAVARIA OUR HEIMAT!'

Das Demokratische Deutschland and the Post-war Trajectories of European Federalism

The exact route taken by the chauffeur, Emmy Rado, who drove Wilhelm Hoegner and Allen Dulles back to Germany in an OSS jeep in June 1945, is not known. Driving from Zurich to Munich, it is nevertheless likely that the group will have skirted around the south-eastern foot of Lake Constance, through the Vorarlberg region. In this western tip of Austria, the High Alemannic dialect spoken, which is difficult for most Austrians to understand, might have confused them into thinking they were still in Switzerland. From there, they will probably have climbed up through the Allgäu Alps, past the drainage basin for the Rhine and Danube rivers that eventually flow into the North and Black Seas. So far, the landscape would have been unimaginably picturesque. Yet, by the time the party would have reached around one hundred kilometres west of Munich, they would have encountered Memmingen, a site of heavy United States Air Force bombing. By this stage in their journey, it is therefore unlikely that they could have avoided the sights of hollowed out townscapes, mass graves and refugees on foot that were characteristics of early post-war Bavaria.[1] With the significant emigration of Germans from the Sudetenland and other eastern parts of Germany's shrinking empire, it may well have felt like Bavaria was assuming new prominence in a new Germany, whose centre of gravity had rapidly shifted from the Prussian heartlands now under Soviet control. Still, seeing the millions of expellees fleeing formerly occupied Central Europe, where they were no longer welcome, it would have required an almost fanatical optimism to imagine that the peoples from this region could peacefully coexist within the kind of European federation conceived by Hoegner and his colleagues while in Swiss exile.[2]

Set against this backdrop of destruction and division between Europeans and the emerging Cold War antagonism between the Western Allies and the Soviets, this chapter examines the efforts of former Demokratisches Deutschland members to work for the reconstruction of Germany and to advance European integration. The contributions made by the Christian democratic members Joseph Wirth and Jakob Kindt-Kiefer to the cause of European integration, through their work in the Nouvelles Equipes Internationales (NEI), has recently been highlighted by historians Michael Gehler and Wolfram Kaiser. They suggest that this organization's record illustrates the value of reconsidering the history of European integration from a transnational perspective.[3] The analysis offered here builds on such research, spotlighting the contribution made by transnational organizations such as the NEI to early Christian democratic campaigns for an integrated Europe. It also suggests that much Christian democratic support for an integrated Europe was not aimed at simply creating a Western *Kleineuropa*, but instead at reclaiming a Europe that united East and West in a broader *abendländisch* community. This episode in the intellectual history of Christian democratic approaches to European integration is an important if perhaps overlooked stage, which highlights the contested nature of Adenauer's policy of *Westbindung*, or alliance with the West, and illustrates the tensions between Christian democratic conceptions of Europe and the logic of a Cold War that divided Europe into East and West.

Moving on from the NEI, I discuss Heinrich Ritzel's work as General Secretary of the cross-party German Europa Union. I analyse how this organization's agenda intersected with the programmes of the political parties in the early Federal Republic. Focusing on such a federalist organization illustrates the role that civil society groups played in securing the 'permissive consensus' behind European integration that was achieved in West Germany and Western Europe.[4] Yet this section also serves to complicate our picture of a European Movement (EM) dominated by such Westernizers as Winston Churchill and his son-in-law, Duncan Sandys, as it shows the continued relevance of a Third Way perspective among grassroots European federalists. It also suggests how the conflict between Westernizing elites and grassroots served to detach the federalist cause from the sources of its support in German localities. This, in turn, sheds light on why European integration came to be seen primarily as a series of negotiations between elites who became increasingly remote from the European populations.

Next to this history of the European Movement, I move on to consider how the European federalist cause intersected with a long-standing federalist agenda in southern Germany. I do this by studying Wilhelm Hoegner's reconstruction work in Bavaria. It will become evident that Hoegner's theoretical work, often developed in tandem with other southern German political groups in Switzerland, provided the basis for the unusual degree of cooperation that occurred between Social and Christian democrats in early post-war Bavaria, particularly regarding questions of democracy and federalism. The argument suggests that a commitment to European federalism provides a crucial, and hitherto lacking, dimension in explaining such political developments. It illustrates how southern German politicians sought to advance arguments for European integration in the early post-war period primarily as a means of redistributing power away from a national centre to the regions and thereby compensating for the weaknesses of parliamentary democracy as it had existed in Weimar Germany. Accordingly, the chapter ends by focusing on a locality, Bavaria, and suggests that much support for European integration in early post-war Germany, rather than being a symptom of a breathless enthusiasm for a universal superstate, was primarily conceived of as a means of protecting local and regional rights.

The Growth of Transnational Christian Democratic Politics, or, The Continued Relevance of Switzerland

As the famous meetings of resistance groups at Willem Visser't Hooft's home in Geneva between March and July 1944 illustrate, Switzerland had served as a wartime refuge where opponents of the National Socialists could meet and prepare for the post-war order.[5] What is less well known is that it continued to provide the setting for Christian Democrats to meet, often covertly, to coordinate their plans for European reconstruction and integration. Perhaps surprisingly, given its small size, the Swiss Conservative People's Party (Schweizerische Konservative Volkspartei SKVP) took the initiative among Christian democrats in early post-war Europe, convening a meeting of primarily Catholic parties from across Europe in Lucerne in early 1947.[6] This informal network of at first primarily Catholic but increasingly inter-denominational Christian politicians was consolidated by the forming of the Nouvelles Equipes Internationales (NEI) later in 1947, an organization made up of national *équipes* that were not supposed to have the factional quality of parties but to comprise a looser collection of Christian politicians dedicated to European integration.[7] The NEI became the most important such grouping of Christian democrats in the post-war period and went on to be reformed as the European Union of Christian Democrats (EUCD) in 1965 and later the European People's Party (EPP) in 1976, one of the major factions in the European parliament.[8] As will be suggested, Demokratisches Deutschland leaders Joseph Wirth and Jakob Kindt-Kiefer played an influential role in the early development of the organization, not least by advancing the left-Catholic agenda they had formulated during the war years in Switzerland.

The NEI primarily operated out of headquarters in Brussels until 1950, when it moved into the Parisian offices of the French Popular Republican Movement (Mouvement Républicain Populaire MRP). However, many of the meetings between its most senior members took place in Switzerland, having been informally organized by the Chairman of the group's Geneva Circle, Jakob Kindt-Kiefer.[9] This circle came to be particularly important as the NEI did not officially invite the emerging German Christian Democratic party (Christlich Demokratische Union Deutschlands CDU) to its early congresses. Nevertheless, German political figures with Swiss connections such as Wirth and Kindt-Kiefer, alongside SKVP politicians, were able to act as go-betweens for German and French Christian Democratic politicians when a more official meeting at NEI congresses could not have taken place due to political sensitivities.[10] Indeed, it was at the informal meetings within the setting of the Geneva Circle that the German Christian democratic leader, Konrad Adenauer, established a working relationship with MRP politicians such as French Foreign Minister, Georges Bidault, which served as a motor of Franco-German rapprochement and early European integration. That such an understanding developed between French and German politicians was, of course, significant for the rehabilitation of (West) Germany among the other European nations. This Christian Democratic connection was particularly important, given the rise of a Gaullist party in France more suspicious of German intentions, which in many ways eclipsed the MRP in the 1950s, but which was not able to dislodge MRP politicians from the Foreign Ministry throughout much of the decade.[11]

The meetings in Geneva were not only significant for the discussions that occurred between Bidault and Adenauer; they also served to reconnect a range of German politicians with their European colleagues. For instance, Germans such as Josef Müller, a leading Bavarian Christian politician, established working relations with Italian federalist and Christian democrat Alcide de Gasperi, on whose recommendation MRP politicians invited him to be the only German observer at their party congress in 1946.[12] Similarly, from mid 1948 onwards, MRP members André Colin, Maurice Schumann, Pierre-Henri Teitgen and Robert Bichet regularly entered into discussions with German colleagues including Heinrich von Brentano, the leader of the CDU/CSU party in the Bundestag and future foreign secretary, Jakob Kaiser, leader of the East German CDU and Fritz Schäffer, the future German finance and justice minister. These discussions served to firm up the good relations that developed between the parties' leaders and were to bear fruit in specific ways such as the combined efforts of Brentano and Teitgen to construct a constitution for the European Political Community (EPC) in the ECSC's Ad Hoc Assembly in 1953.[13]

Another valuable dimension to the discussions that occurred within the Geneva Circle was that politicians could exchange ideas away from the glare of national electorates and party memberships. The advantage of this was clear to Bidault, who, when referring to European policy, commented to his European colleagues that the 'masses have no imagination'. Other more optimistic members believed, by contrast, that such an organization could advance a Christian vision for a federated Europe and thus offer a form of idealistic internationalism that could rival the appeal of Soviet internationalism for Europe's youth. This appeared particularly plausible given the successful mobilization of young people within Christian organizations such as those organized by the Italian Christian Democrats in the early post-war period.[14] Such a perspective was likely also shared by Western secret services, which may well (along with the French Foreign Ministry) have funded the Geneva Circle and certainly, via such organizations as the American Committee on United Europe (ACUE), funnelled money to the EM.¹⁵ Secret services did this in the belief that Western European countries should not simply align themselves within an Atlantic alliance but should first form an intra-European alliance because such a European community would be a more effective magnet for the East than an American-dominated Western bloc.¹⁶

The role played by such exiles as Kindt-Kiefer in the functioning of the NEI was by no means insignificant. Kindt-Kiefer initially proved his worth as a fundraiser, diverting funds to the NEI from a Christian aid organization, Christliche Nothilfe, which he established in May 1946 with Wirth.¹⁷ Such a contribution was particularly valuable for an organization that had to compete with social democratic rivals who benefited from trade union funding.¹⁸ As a result, Kindt-Kiefer was granted access to high-ranking French officials and German Christian democrats, including Adenauer and Victor Koutzine, the French cultural attaché in the French consulate in Geneva, at whose house politicians such as Adenauer and Bidault met from mid 1948 onwards.¹⁹ Along with Koutzine, Kindt-Kiefer carried messages back and forth between Bonn and Paris, even after Adenauer had assumed office in the newly created Federal Republic in May 1949 and could reestablish direct contact with his French counterparts.²⁰

Kindt-Kiefer's prominence behind the scenes was also due to the theoretical work that he and Joseph Wirth had conducted while in Swiss exile, which fitted in well with the left-Catholic agenda popular among Christian Democrats in the early post-war years. This agenda was expressed in such documents as the leftist programmes of the early post-war MRP and in the CDU/CSU's Ahlen Programme of February 1947, which struck an anti-capitalist tone and advocated de-cartelization, the socialization of the coal-mining industry and the extension of cooperatively administered industrial sectors.²¹ Wirth and Kindt-Kiefer had anticipated such plans, issuing a call for a Radical–Social People's Campaign in October 1944. This was designed as a Christian social programme that could compete with reconstruction plans being formulated by socialist resistance groups. It envisaged the appropriation of land from great landowners and its redistribution to create smaller farm settlements, the cultivation and pricing of agricultural produce by cooperatives, a guaranteed minimum wage and full employment, along with a wide-ranging nationalization of energy resources, and credit and insurance companies.²²

On the one hand, such plans for reconstruction were designed to distinguish a form of Christian democracy as it had developed in the south and west of Germany from more authoritarian versions of German conservatism that had supposedly originated in the north and east of the country.²³ On the other, these schemes reflected a personalist perspective common among Christian advocates of European integration. This personalist perspective was distinct from the positions advanced by socialist theorists, not least because of the creative proposals made by personalists for reviving the countryside as a means of countering the potentially harmful effects of urbanization, proletarianization and mass politics in Europe.²⁴ For instance, the late wartime document 'On the Reconstruction', put together by Wirth and Kindt-Kiefer, lamented the growth of European cities, with Kindt-Kiefer claiming that the domestic life of the family was eroded by urbanization as more families divorced and leisure time was spent in the city rather than in the 'quietness' of the village family. Indeed, the city was said to be a place where relationships were instrumental: everyone looked to get what they could, not least the criminals who were more plentiful in urban areas and the 'plutocrats' whose struggle for profits immiserated the workers and led to 'the proletarianisation of inhabitants on the one hand, capitalism on the other'. For Kindt-Kiefer, the unfortunate political consequence of such a process of proletarianization was the creation of the 'mass-person' who, while not 'being connected to his contemporaries by [genuine] bonds', still shared all their characteristics as one of the many who had been *'gleichgeschaltet'* and could be *'moved* by its Führer'.[25]

Kindt-Kiefer's solution was to relocate those who had lost their homes after the bombing of cities in agricultural or semi-agricultural settlements, in which self-government would be practised, rather like the smaller cantons in Switzerland. Yet, this seemed rather too radical in post-war Germany and Western Europe.[26] Such proposals, and the critique of urban spaces that accompanied them, rehearsed the Spenglerian arguments of interwar advocates of a European *Abendland*, who valorized a rural-based *Kultur* and condemned the metropolitan *Zivilisation* supposedly found in Western Europe and the United States. Concerns about the political dangers of urban masses nevertheless did not only hearken back to interwar arguments but continued to exercise Christian thinkers throughout the 1950s – particularly those who sought to revive an *abendländisch* unity in Europe. Indeed, the question of the masses' role in politics proved to be an issue that troubled not only *abendländisch* groups predominantly found in post-war Bavaria, but also Protestant academics and politicians from northern Germany. Many of these Protestants met at conferences from 1952 onwards at the Lutheran Loccum Academy, which was founded near Hannover in 1946 and conceived as a way for the Protestant churches to come to terms with their response to Nazism.[27] At these events, which attracted prominent guests such as José Ortega y Gasset, Theodor Adorno, Walter Dirks, Theodor Heuss and Konrad Adenauer among the 51,000 visitors attending by 1961, Protestant academics worried about the growth of the urban masses and their alienation in the 'modern civilization', which was characterized in the 'technical era' by 'secularization' and 'Promethean pride'.[28] Thus, as they had during the interwar period, *abendländisch* critiques of political and economic modernization continued to provide a source of ecumenical political activity after 1945 and proved able to rally Protestants and Catholics from the Right as well as the Left.[29]

Such sustained antipathy towards urbanization and industrialization from *abendländisch* groups problematizes whether and to what extent German Christian democrats became committed to an Americanized or Westernized economic and political order after 1945. Similarly, the continued commitment of Christian democrats such as Wirth to a European community that reunited East and West suggests that the policy of *Westbindung*, put forward by Adenauer and by French counterparts such as Robert Schuman, was only one among a number of foreign policy positions advocated within these parties in the early post-war years. Certainly, Wirth became an increasingly peripheral figure in the late 1940s and early 1950s: his ever more frequent contact with Sozialistische Einheitspartei Deutschlands (SED) figures such as Otto Grotewohl, the GDR's Prime Minister, to negotiate German reunification, identified him as an unreliable communist stooge in the eyes of Christian Democratic leaders (and won him the Stalin Peace Prize in 1955).[30] Wirth's commitment to overcoming the emerging division of Europe, which he believed to be a continuation of his Rapallo policy from 1922, was not, however, simply peripheral in the CDU/CSU or the liberal Free Democratic Party (FDP) in the early post-war period.[31] Nor was it viewed without sympathy by members of the MRP, even if his increasingly vociferous criticisms of French occupation policy in his native Baden alienated him from the French authorities.[32] Apart from Adenauer's early rival within the CDU, Jakob Kaiser, seeking to reunify Germany as a bridge between East and West, significant numbers of liberals and Christian democrats such as Thomas Dehler, chairman of the FDP and the Federal Republic's first Minister of Justice, and Carl Spiecker, a leading liberal politician and journalist who sought to establish a Union of the Centre (Union der Mitte UdM) in 1949 with Wirth, also advocated a more neutralist course than the first Chancellor of the Federal Republic.[33] Even those further on the Right such as Ulrich Noacke and the Nauheimer Circle of Christian Democrats he founded (which included future Foreign Secretary Heinrich von Brentano), pressed for a neutral Germany within the framework of a non-aligned Central European community.[34]

Wirth and his former associate, Kindt-Kiefer, became marginalized from Christian Democratic leaders by the mid 1950s, which in turn led to the demise of the Geneva Circle as a forum for transnational Christian Democratic debate. Nevertheless, their contribution to the social and European policy of the party appears to have been rather significant.[35] Kindt-Kiefer's activities within the Geneva Circle were of great consequence in cementing the Franco-German alliance that was of such importance in securing early European integration. Yet, such support for European integration under the aegis of Franco-German leadership did not necessarily imply support for a Western 'small Europe' but was conceived as part of a project of reviving a Christian Europe with its heart in Central Europe. Indeed, it was not only German Christian Democrats but also MRP theorists such as Marc Scherer who conceived of a Franco-German rapprochement as a precursor to a wider European *modus vivendi* between nations on either side of the emerging East–West divide.[36]

Paying attention to the European debates within Christian democratic parties might help to explain the apparent shifts in Konrad Adenauer's foreign policy, which was described by Klaus Gotto as having moved from federalist to Atlanticist and then Gaullist phases, rather than being simply pro-Western throughout the 1950s and early 1960s.[37] If, for example, Adenauer's attempts to negotiate with the Soviets before their recognition of the GDR in 1955 and his plans for a neutral Germany formulated in 1956/1957 are considered, it seems that he proved rather more flexible about the shape of a European community than the current historiographical orthodoxy might suggest.[38] As has been suggested, this may well, in turn, have been due to the diversity of opinions over the shape and character of European integration that existed within the Christian democratic compromise, or 'Party-ersatz of the disunited', as Günter Müchler described the grouping.[39]

I will consider Adenauer's foreign policy in the 1950s at a later stage.[40] For now, I move on to consider the Third Way agenda that, as well as being influential among a variety of Christian democratic and *abendländisch* groups, motivated the early cross-party European federalist groups that formed so quickly in early post-war Germany. I do so by focusing on the post-war activities of former Demokratisches Deutschland member Heinrich Ritzel within the German pressure group, Europa Union. Such an analysis of federalist activity will facilitate a better understanding of how political groups converged around an integrationist agenda. It will also help to explain how ideological conflict was felt less acutely in post-Second World War Germany than it had been before 1945, even if federalist groups came to be marginalized by policy-making elites in the 1950s.

The Europa Union: From European Federation to European Opposition

In his capacity as General Secretary for the Swiss Europa Union, Heinrich Ritzel gave a speech to delegates in Berne in November 1945 about Europe's place in the post-war order. He told them that they were witnessing a 'decimation of the standing of Europe in the world' and a 'shifting of the political predominance from Europe to the United States', citing as evidence the location of the United Nations headquarters in New York rather than Geneva. Similarly in the economic sphere, he believed that Europe was losing importance, with only ten European nations being represented at the Bretton Woods meetings of July 1944 and their share of the currency funds making up only 17.45 per cent of the total. Out of such factors 'resulted the pressure for European unity!' urged Ritzel.[41] As he commented in another speech to the Europa Union two years later: 'Europe can and may not rely solely on help from America. Europe has to defend its own history, its tradition, its culture.' If the European nations could reconcile themselves and develop a European consciousness they could 'avert the danger of a colonial existence'. However, were such a European consciousness not to emerge and find institutional validation, then 'Europe in the long run would become the political football of a few world powers'.[42] Or, as Ritzel's colleague in the Swiss Europa Union, Hans Bauer, put it, also writing in the immediate post-war period: 'The world powers are masters not only of Germany but of Europe. The old world has become a kind of protectorate. That is the result of Hitler's "struggle for

Europe" ... America and Asia meet on the Elbe and in Austria ... Only European self-determination ... can save us'.[43]

The leaders of the Swiss Europa Union were outlining a Third Way position for Europe that was advocated by many in the wartime European resistance and which became the orthodoxy among the first generation of European federalists. Such federalist movements mushroomed throughout the Western zones in Germany in the early post-war years and in some areas such as Hamburg, where the reformed Paneuropa Union boasted three thousand members by 1947, they eclipsed the growth of political parties.[44] One of the great appeals for such grassroots activity was the potential for citizens to be politically active without having to sign up to the (often discredited) ideological platforms of one of the political parties. These citizens thereby showed their commitment to a Third Way not only between the United States and the Soviet Union but also between left- and right-wing parties within Europe. For instance, the Europa-Bund that spread across the Western zones declared itself to be 'independent from all party doctrines and party organizations', and was rewarded with a membership of over ten thousand by 1947, having emerged out of a large number of local organizations.[45] This growth of grassroots federalist organizations signalled the revival of the associational life that had been vibrant in both the Weimar Republic and the Wilhelmine Reich. Yet, it also provided a particularly striking instance of the kind of civil society engagement advocated by intellectuals such as the *Merkur* contributors as a means of (re)educating the Germans to be political citizens who were not simply instrumentalized by the political parties.

It should not, however, be assumed that these organizations were simply ideologically neutral or altogether separate from other organized political interest groups. Indeed, the German organizations were influenced by their sister-federalist groups in France, where left-Catholic social teaching had shaped the outlook of the founders. These founders envisaged federalism as a form of decentralized society that could create a humanist, cooperative socialism, which would replace the interwar monopoly capitalism that had been aided by centralist and corporatist states.[46] Such French groups provided much of the backbone to the major umbrella federalist organization, the Union of European Federalists (UEF) created in December 1946, which was led by Alexandre Marc, a personalist and convert to Catholicism from Judaism who had worked with the French resistance.[47] It was not only left-Catholics who were moving closer to their counterparts in the socialist parties though. Socialists like those in the German splinter groups and those active in cross-party organizations such as Demokratisches Deutschland also embraced European federalism as a means of reworking social democratic theory and moving away from centralist state planning to models of workers' self-government. This was certainly true for Ritzel, who, as coauthor of the 'Guiding Principles' of the cross-party Swiss Europa Union explained that: 'the overweening lust for power of the modern state can only be tamed ... the saving of the a*bendländisch Kultur* can only be achieved through the limitation of state sovereignty and the creation of a European federation'.[48]

Ritzel's position again signalled the convergence that occurred between groups on the Left of the Christian democratic movement and particularly those social democratic organizations that were made up of a significant exile contingent. It also illustrated the fluidity in socialist thought before the solidifying of the Cold War borders and before a programme of nationalizations and state centralizations was prioritized by the Schumacher-led SPD. While earlier chapters stressed the difficulties for pro-Europeans working within the Schumacher-led national party, the experience of Ritzel and others illustrate that, at local and regional levels, socialists were able to work for European integration often across party lines. Indeed, the contribution of exiled socialists who had worked in cross-party alliances was recognized by early federalists in post-war Germany, who elected Ritzel and Anna Siemsen to the Presidium of the Europa Union group. This organization had formed in June 1947 out of the many local federalist initiatives that sprang up particularly in the British Zone.[49] Ritzel went on to become the General Secretary of the Europa Union group in Germany as well as representing the Hessian constituency Deiburg-Erbach as a social democrat in the Bundestag from 1949 to 1965.[50] He oversaw the fusing of a number of federalist groups under the Europa Union umbrella, although the initiative came from below in the shape of local organizations, which united in the face of the opposition of many of the national delegates.[51]

The prominence of such socialists within local cross-party federalist bodies no doubt served to soften the partisan hostility that broke out between the parties at the national level. It also helps to explain how politics at the local, municipal and regional level, often conducted through the formation of governing coalitions, could be carried out more successfully than during the interwar period. In spite of the official hostility shown by SPD leader, Kurt Schumacher, for the sort of European integration being pushed forward by the EM once it had been taken over by Winston Churchill's son-in-law, Duncan Sandys, the efforts of such socialist federalists as Ritzel were supported by other leading socialists such as Carlo Schmid, Minister of Justice in Baden-Württemberg from 1947 to 1950, and Vice-President of the Europa Union.[52] As has already been shown, the presence of a social democratic Burgermeisterflügel that was pronouncedly pro-European also helped to maintain a diversity of views within the party. Perhaps because of the presence of leading social democrats within the German Europa Union, the German Council of the EM maintained links with the SPD in Germany, against the opposition of the international leadership of the movement.[53] As a result, other leftist Germans quickly gained positions of authority with Eugen Kogon being elected president of the German EM in 1950.

Despite such encouraging signs that socialists could work for a federalist agenda at the local and regional level, the conservative dominance of the upper echelons of the EM affected how such socialists regarded the cause of European federalism. The inaugural meeting of the EM in the Hague in May 1948 was boycotted by the British Labour Party, the SFIO and the German SPD. With its glittering array of honorary presidents drawn from the ranks of former and future prime ministers this gala event suggested that the federalist movement appeared to be adopting the managed, top-down structure that was said to have compromised the political parties.[54] Thus, many, including the future president of the EM, Eugen Kogon, worried that the complexion of the EM was changing rapidly and that 'genuine European integration' would be replaced by a 'supranational hyperbureaucracy'.[55] This concern was heightened by the pro-Western orientation of the Churchill wing, which sought to set the limits to grassroots federalist activism within the borders of a Western sphere of influence seemingly decided upon by a small coterie of national leaders at Potsdam. Federalists such as Ritzel and his former colleague Hans Bauer thus wanted not only a more radically federalist Europe than that conceived by Churchill and other unionists, but also continued to work for a European unity that cut across Cold War lines. As Bauer explained, in a response circulated to the Central Committee of the Europa Union: while Churchill had put forward a 'very one-sided conception of Europe', the Swiss organization wanted to 'deepen the Swiss idea of neutrality' and to 'insist on a European idea that united East and West'. Indeed, he warned his colleagues to avoid embracing a Western bloc ushered in under the name of Europe just as much as they had rejected Hitler's conception of a 'New Europe'.[56]

The position of the Americans in all of this was interesting, not least because it seemed contradictory. While Westernizers within the German EM started to voice their opposition to Kogon's third-way federalist position in the early 1950s, American financial backers such as the 'American Committee of European Integration' also withdrew their funds.[57] This prompted the organization to shift its orientation and by 1954 to elect the former Swiss exile Ernst Friedlaender to be president. Friedlaender pursued a pro-Western line that supported Adenauer's policies as well as the construction of the ECSC and the EDC. Accordingly, he attracted the support of the Federation of German Industry (BDI), leading to the EM becoming funded by the German Foreign Ministry under Friedlaender's successor, Carl von Oppenheimer.[58] Yet the Americans continued to fund federalist ventures, donating four million dollars to them between 1949 and 1960. Furthermore, American diplomats had already pushed for the more radically federalist leader Paul-Henri Spaak to replace the unionist, Sandys, as president of the EM in 1950. Geir Lundestad's interpretation that the Americans did this in order to prevent Europeans claiming the right to interfere in American affairs as co-members of an Atlantic alliance may be right. Yet, it appears that the Americans did favour intra-European agreements to trans-Atlantic alliances, and therefore sought to maximize Europeans' autonomy. This is evidenced by their initial preference for the exclusively European EDC over the Western European Union (WEU), an organization created in 1954 that put European defence capability under NATO control.[59]

Regardless of such ambiguities in American policy, the integration of federalist organizations into Cold War structures left federalists such as Ritzel feeling alienated and worrying about the 'lack of constructive will and ... the triumph of a new nationalism that takes away the capability of Europeans to see what they share and to overcome what divides them'.[60] As a result, Ritzel was disappointed in his colleagues in the Council of Europe. He rejected the possibility of standing for re-election in 1957, having served in the Council for seven years and having become frustrated, believing it to have achieved little.[61] Ritzel's disillusion suggests that the EM became somewhat estranged from the roots of its early support as national leaders began to dominate and state agencies started to fund it. This helps to explain why historical approaches to European integration that deal with the post-Second World War period tend to focus on the policy-making elites rather than seeking to tell a social history of European integration. Such a dislocation between elites and the grassroots supporters of integration should not, nevertheless, lead historians to minimize the contribution of federalists such as Ritzel. For these federalists oversaw the creation and growth of one of the largest pro-integration groups in the Federal Republic and contributed to a movement for Europe that became genuinely popular in post-war West Germany. They also opened up a transnational network through which they could cooperate and build relationships of trust with other Europeans, from formerly enemy nations.[62]

If federalist groups became a less significant factor in the politics of European integration as the 1950s progressed, it is not the case that issues of European integration simply became remote from the concerns of local or regional political groups. Rather, agendas for European integration were formulated by particularly regional-interest groups and parties as ways of advancing their causes and of seeking to wrest back power from national parties and centralized government institutions. To explore such developments I turn now to the post-war career of Wilhelm Hoegner.

Wilhelm Hoegner: Advancing the Demokratisches Deutschland Agenda in Bavaria

Hoegner was clearly the most successful and influential figure from Das Demokratische Deutschland in the post-war period, occupying the position of Minister-President of Bavaria for long periods during the late 1940s and 1950s. One of the reasons for his success was that he was unusually adept at working within coalition governments in Bavaria, even though he returned from Swiss exile with very clear ideas about post-war reconstruction and indeed with twenty-seven pieces of drafted legislation ready to be enacted. Hoegner served as minister-president from June 1945 to December 1946 and as justice minister from October 1945 until September 1947, when the Bavarian SPD chose to leave the

CSU-led coalition government, against Hoegner's wishes. He returned to the coalition government in 1950 as CSU leader Hans Ehard's deputy and again as justice minister, positions he held until he once more became minister-president in early December 1954, surviving until September 1957 when the CSU won a striking victory in the state elections.[63] Hoegner's ability to work across party lines can largely be explained, as this section will suggest, by his commitment to defend Bavarian autonomy via the construction of a federal Europe, which he shared with members of the centre-right parties.

Such bipartisanship, however, proved something of a novelty in Bavaria. For instance, while conservatives and members of the Bavarian Party's (BP) predecessor, the Bavarian People's Party (BVP), had argued for a State president with stronger constitutional powers and for Danubian federations or Alpine Unions during the interwar period, such proposals were opposed by the vast majority of social democrats including Hoegner.[64] If one seeks to explain Hoegner's untypical willingness to work within coalitions in post-war Bavaria, in spite of the disapproval of his party's leadership, one therefore cannot avoid taking stock of his political work within the cross-party Demokratisches Deutschland, particularly regarding European policy.

Upon returning to Munich, Hoegner revived the relationships he had cultivated across partisan boundaries while in Switzerland. Sharing lodgings with Demokratisches Deutschland colleague Michael Godin between 1945 and 1946, Hoegner socialized with a wide range of monarchists and Bavarian separatists alongside representatives from the major political parties at the political salons that sprang up across Bavaria.[65] Hoegner was moved to work across party lines while in Switzerland, having reflected on the interwar record of the SPD in Bavaria, whose leader, Minister-President Johannes Hoffman, had refused to serve in a coalition government with the middle-class parties after the Kapp Putsch of March 1920. In Hoegner's view such a position had consigned the social democrats to the sidelines and lessened any influence they might have had on those in liberal, middle-class circles.[66] However, Hoegner and social democratic colleagues such as Ritzel had shifted their perspective on social and economic policy more broadly while they were working within Demokratisches Deutschland, and they became more sympathetic to Christian democratic positions than many of their social democratic colleagues in northern Germany. Hoegner acknowledged this when writing to his colleague, Joseph Wirth, in late 1944, in response to Wirth's outlining of a Christian democratic programme for post-war reform. He explained: 'a regard for freedom, humanism and Christianity are the highest cultural values of the *Abendland* and belong to the cornerstones of every *abendländisch* social order. I am firmly convinced that in the decisive moment of European history these values have enabled the opposition of the Anglo-Saxons to the totalitarian states. My party too has to draw out the necessary consequences from this fact.'[67] Hoegner thus advocated a reconciliation between political Christianity and the socialist parties, urging the SPD at its first meeting in Munich on November 1945 to, 'foster the intellectual and ethical values, on which our *abendländisch* culture is based', chiefly Christianity.[68]

Hoegner's frequent references to the *Abendland* set him apart from many of his colleagues in northern Germany and showed how greatly he had been influenced by the *abendländisch* agenda advanced by exiles in Switzerland and advocated by federalist groups in post-war Bavaria. Indeed, such was Hoegner's closeness to *abendländisch* federalists on the Right that even the American military authorities, usually well disposed to anti-centralists from southern Germany, worried he had been duped by Bavarian separatists. For instance, Hoegner's draft of a 'Law for the Provisional State Authority in Bavaria', which stated that 'Bavaria is a democratic republic … Bavaria possesses unlimited state sovereignty', and the Bavarian '*Ministerpräsident* … directs foreign policy', was rejected by OMGUS in late 1945. As the former Yale political scientist Karl Löwenstein, himself a native of Munich and an employee of the Legal Division of OMGUS, commented: 'It is the embodiment of the dream of Bavarian independence nursed for two generations by Bavarian extremists of whom Dr Hoegner permitted himself to become the tool … This declaration of Bavarian independence is a thinly veiled declaration of the secession from Germany.'[69]

Löwenstein's comment perhaps reveals the evolving perspective of an American government that had shifted its plans from consolidating southern Germany in favour of building up a new West Germany that would serve as a magnet during the early years of the emerging Cold War. In fact, Löwenstein may well have misread Hoegner's intentions and overlooked the continuities between Hoegner's position and a long-standing socialist agenda for what amounted to revolutionary change across Germany and Central Europe. Indeed, Hoegner's early proposals can be read more as a plea for a Greater Germany than as making a case for Bavarian separatism. Hoegner argued against the separatist agenda of his colleague Hans Nawiasky, suggesting that: 'Bavaria as a small state … would immediately be the play thing of the Great Powers, and especially become altogether dependent on France'.[70] Suggesting that he favoured a politics of the Danube over a politics of the Rhine (to quote his colleague Ritzel), he argued that the only way to make Bavaria strong was to develop, 'a close means of economic exchange with our neighbours [in Central Europe]', believing that such economic cooperation, 'in the age of the world economy would cause the rigid political boundaries between countries with the same culture to fall' and lead to a 'United States of Europe'.[71]

Although Hoegner's federalist agenda thus emerged from socialist roots, he proved willing to cooperate with the right-wing parties in Bavaria throughout the early post-war years, not least because the latter appeared to have shifted leftwards in their early programmes. Indeed, Hoegner spoke on behalf of the Bavarian SPD, agreeing that an early CSU manifesto, the 'Principles for the Overcoming of the Domestic and External Need of Our People', should form the basis of government work, stating that 'many of [its] articles' such as self-government for local communities 'agreed with our requirements'. Similarly, the CSU, whose members won a strong majority in the constitutional assembly elected in June

1946, did not seek to draw up their own constitution for Bavaria but accepted the draft that was put together by Hoegner (with Nawiasky) first in Switzerland and then refined by the Provisional Constitutional Assembly.[72]

Hoegner continued to follow an unpartisan line with regard to federalism in Germany and Europe. Indeed, he signed the founding document of the Bund Deutscher Föderalisten that formed in Bad Ems in August 1947 and which was largely made up of those on the *abendländisch* Right including Franz Albert Kramer, the editor of the *Rheinischer Merkur*; Johann Wilhelm Naumann, the publisher of a number of right-wing Catholic newspapers; and Heinrich von Brentano, CDU representative and future foreign minister. Although the group also included the more left-Catholic Eugen Kogon of the *Frankfurter Hefte*, most of the social democratic supporters of federalism stayed away. Certainly the SPD's leadership did not approve of Hoegner's cooperation with such a venture. Erich Ollenhauer, the party's deputy leader, wrote to Hoegner in early September to express his displeasure, explaining that no social democrat could work with a group that included two members of the conservative *Rheinischer Merkur* team. Interestingly, he chided Hoegner for committing to a programme that sounded strikingly like the programme advanced by Demokratisches Deutschland, complaining that the group's 'Appeal' called for self-government and a general commitment to the traditions of the *Abendland* such as Christianity.[73]

Faced with such disapproval from the party leadership, Hoegner nevertheless went on to edit a draft programme for the Bund Bayerischer Föderalisten, a regional successor to the Bund Deutscher Föderalisten. Written in late November 1947 in concert with German and European federalists from the Right such as Josef Baumgartner, Franz Weiß and Alois Schlögl, the draft programme stated that:

> [t]he open and disguised advocates of a unitary German state want to dismember Bavaria, limit it to the region south of the Danube and restrict it to being a dependent province of the Reich. For them Bavaria was always a thorn in their side, because it would not let itself be diminished as a simple receiver of orders from an almighty central authority … Bavaria will decline slowly into a colonial land if, in the last hour, this baleful development is not stopped by resolute men.

The programme went on, however, to talk of a positive future for Bavaria were it to become part of a European federation within which it would see an 'extension of communal self-government'.[74] This programme clearly illustrates the frustrations felt by southern Germans who had been encouraged in the later war years to imagine a reconfigured German state whose centre of gravity would be shifted southwards and who believed they would be reconnected with fellow Germans within a European federation. What appeared to be happening in the early postwar years was that political parties with their centre in the north and west of the country were again becoming dominant. This led such political groups in Bavaria to even draft plans for a southern German federation that would embrace at least the American zones in Austria.[75]

Hoegner's proximity to *abendländisch* and Christian democratic circles in Bavaria no doubt makes sense given what is known about his career in Switzerland drafting such plans for a revived southern Germany. Such cross-party loyalties nevertheless made him a 'difficult outsider' within his party, as the title of his autobiography suggests.[76] It may have been significant that the post-war SPD again seemed to be dominated by northerners who had little appreciation for common causes in the South that linked politicians across party lines. Equally significant appears to have been the change in institutional set-up in Germany once the American and British zones fused in January 1947. While the southern states had been provided with governments in September 1945 and had passed constitutions into law by the end of 1946, their autonomy was sharply curtailed when Bizonal institutions were set up in Frankfurt in January 1947. Hoegner's oppositional stance to the new Frankfurt institutions was shared more by the right-wing parties than by the entirety of the Bavarian SPD. Yet, this did not mean that there was no genuinely socialist rationale for objecting to the centralizations effected by the creation of the Bizone. Indeed, when the Americans coordinated their policies with the British, they adopted some of the British Zone's centralist organizations to implement policy across the zones and to veto any plans for socialization advanced at a state level.[77] Therefore, while Hoegner's opposition certainly signalled his disillusion at the shift in American policy from initially encouraging southern German self-government to creating centralized economic ministries at the Bizonal level, it also expressed his opposition as a socialist to the free-market policies being imposed on German states by the American occupation authorities. He could accordingly contrast the prospect of Bavaria existing within a European federation favourably for he conceived of such a federal union, not so much as a unified economic entity, but as a liberal constitutional order that would safeguard the rights of regions against a formerly over-mighty German centre.[78]

From the positions outlined by Hoegner, it is possible to see that his advocacy of European integration developed out of long-standing socialist principles, even if such advocacy appeared at odds with the line adopted by the Schumacher-led SPD in the early post-war period. For instance, the scepticism shown by Hoegner among others regarding the new democratic institutions being established in the Federal Republic echoed the doubts expressed by socialists, since at least the Weimar era, about whether parliamentary democracy would necessarily prove capable of delivering social democracy. Indeed, such scepticism had animated the long-standing internationalism of socialists who believed that the economic forces shaping the political framework and culture of a country were usually transnational, capitalist ones. This internationalist perspective was reworked by socialists in the post-1945 period as they seemingly confronted a democracy being implanted in Germany by foreign occupation forces. As a result socialists were drawn to the increasingly oppositional federalist movement, which proved to be more leftist and more in favour of a Third Way Europe than the Christian democratic and conservative parties that led many of the early post-war governments in Western Europe.

As has been seen from studying Hoegner's early post-war career, socialists in Germany were not uniformly in favour of a programme of nationalizations or of simply strengthening a unitary state. Instead, significant figures in the SPD sought to reconcile federalism with socialism, tying such federalism to a socialist reformist agenda that stressed workers' self-management rather than rule by bureaucracies. This agenda would later become characterized as a New Left agenda; however, it also shared features with the left-Catholicism popular in the early post-war years, which saw in European federalism a way of restoring local community and curtailing the power of centralized party leaderships.[79]

A Europe of the Regions *avant la lettre*?

One of the benefits of a European federation, according to the Demokratisches Deutschland authors, was that it should localize the dominance of any party and, indeed, change the nature of parties as they tailored themselves to fit local and regional needs. Furthermore, such parties would no doubt have to work with dissimilar groupings from different regions within federal European institutions and so hopefully get used to viewing German and European politics in a less sectarian way. Hence, the post-war democracy that these politicians envisaged was much less a party democracy than the interwar version they believed to have been terminally compromised, although potentially being revived in the immediate post-war period. Indeed, referring to his own party, Hoegner (who suffered increasingly bad relations with national SPD leaders) explained his plans in 1948 to reconstitute parties within a new German state, commenting that, '[i]n centrally organized parties the dictatorship of a party apparatus dominates, which itself is dominated by a small clique of men'.[80] Hoegner therefore sought to tie a German federalist agenda into the movement for a European federation, suggesting that party oligarchies would be militated against by the federalizing of national institutions and constrained by European-wide constitutional safeguards. In this regard too, Hoegner was not simply a lonely socialist apostate. He was rather part of the Bürgermeisterflügel discussed earlier, made up of independent-minded big city mayors and regional leaders who had been encouraged to act independently by the occupation forces. This Bürgermeisterflügel proved more eager to form local and regional coalitions than the SPD central party, and supported the early moves towards European integration, in spite of the official SPD line against these initiatives.[81]

As Minister-President, Hoegner nevertheless went further than most members of the Bürgermeisterflügel. He sought to develop a distinctive Bavarian SPD that was no longer a Marxist party of the working class but a more broadly based *Volkspartei*. Speaking at the SPD's first meeting in Munich in November 1945, he used the occasion to praise the Bavarian farmers and to call for social democrats to 'break out of the enclosure of class division' and 'become a People's Party' that would appeal to the 'lower middle classes, the artisans, tradesmen, employees and officials'.[82] Hoegner also expressed more scepticism in majoritarian politics than his party colleagues, supporting a bicameral legislature against the position advocated by his party's leaders, who argued for a single parliamentary chamber. What is more, he handed the strategically important cultural and agricultural portfolios to the Christian-conservative parties and the Work Ministry to the Communists in his first cabinet of 1945.[83] Such moves, which aroused anger in social democratic and trade union circles, illustrated how Hoegner envisaged Bavaria's role in a future German and European federal union. Within this union, regional leaders would not be required to toe a national party line but would be free to fashion alliances in a more ad hoc fashion with the regionally differentiated parties that developed within such a federation.

The regionally based politicians such as Hoegner who made the case for European integration thus argued that they would enjoy much greater power within a European federation than they had exercised within nation-states. This was made clear by a number of Hoegner's conservative colleagues, such as his State Secretary Anton Pfeiffer (CSU) and the then Bavarian Minister-President, Hans Ehard (CSU), who formed the Ellwang Circle in 1947. This discussion group aimed to strengthen federalism in Germany and was linked to reports in *Der Spiegel* of new CDU/CSU plans to create a southern German state federation that would include the French and American zones in Austria.[84] For instance, when prominent members of the Circle, including Heinrich von Brentano and Eugen Kogon, spoke on the issue of Germany in Europe at a meeting in March 1947, they advocated a break from the German democratic tradition 'of the Paulskirche'. They thereby argued that parliamentary democracy would not work within a unitary state but only with a federal nation and integrated Europe, and echoed the scepticism towards parliamentarianism displayed by Demokratisches Deutschland authors. Indeed, Brentano maintained that federal constitutional safeguards must be provided to limit the absolute sovereignty of any national parliament and separate it from an executive, which should be built up of regional leaders rather than national parliamentarians.[85]

One of the interesting elements of the case made by the Ellwang Circle is that it did not necessarily imply the predominantly conservative members taking a hard anti-communist line. Instead, Hans Ehard argued that such a federal arrangement in Germany and Europe would make the apparently inevitable ideological clash between East and West less of a threat.[86] Such a Third Way orientation did not, nevertheless, break down divisions between the Christian democrats and many of the SPD's leaders. Indeed, the latter regarded such discussions by the right-wing parties as endangering the continued survival of a German state. Thus, when Hoegner spoke out in favour of one of the Bavarian Party's directors, Joseph Baumgartner, after the latter launched a *Heimatkurs* that sought to integrate the southern state within a future European federation, he positioned himself at odds with mainstream SPD opinion. This was true even in Bavaria, where the Bavarian state chairman of the SPD, another former exile, Waldemar von Knoeringen, interpreted this policy as a sign of disloyalty to the democratic German state.[87]

Yet, Baumgartner's policy largely echoed the positions advanced by Demokratisches Deutschland leaders. How clearly this was the case can be glimpsed when reading the Bavarian Party's policy as described by Fritz Berthold, a BP representative who wrote to Baumgartner in February 1948 on the topic of 'European Cooperation'. Berthold advocated the slogan: 'Europa our Fatherland, Bavaria our *Heimat*' and urged the 'Overcoming of the National State idea that was Europe's misfortune through the idea of a *Heimat*'. His suggestion entailed 'a common European economy and the division of Europe through the *Heimat*-Idea into cultural entities', which would, he argued, lead Bavarians to seek closer cooperation with 'the other southern German states and Austria'.[88] Reiterating the argument in an article from January 1950 entitled, 'The Ideology of the New Europe', Berthold explained how local self-government would be practised within such a union. It would, he claimed, prevent the populations of Europe descending again into masses by minimizing the role played by national, ideologically profiled parties and encourage loyalty instead to the at once local and universal institution of the Christian [i.e., Catholic] Church, which had served to unite an earlier form of European unity in the Holy Roman Empire. He summarized the programme of the new European ideology thus: 'Christianity – Heimat – Self-Government'.[89]

The obvious similarities between this programme and the agenda put forward by Demokratisches Deutschland authors, not least Wilhelm Hoegner, leaves us with the problem of where to situate the group's leaders in the early post-war era. As has been argued, Hoegner represented an unduly neglected wing of the SPD, which was made up of local and regional leaders who proved willing to work across party lines in coalitions and within federalist organizations and who sought to shift the European policy of the Schumacher-led party. While this argument applies a valuable corrective to pre-existing characterizations of the post-war SPD, it cannot fully explain the extent of Hoegner's apparent ideological cross-dressing in the early post-war period. It would appear that in Hoegner's case, his commitment to European and German federalism was, to a degree, incompatible with following the party orthodoxy of the SPD. Indeed, Hoegner's opposition to state centralism was well known enough among conservative Bavarian politicians that, in late 1948, Amia Gräfin Montgelas invited him to join a People's Movement against the Basic Law that included Fritz Schäffer, the first Minister-President of Bavaria and a founding member of the CSU and Alois Hundhammer, an advocate within the CSU of *abendländisch* thought.[90] Hoegner ultimately voted with his party and against the majority of delegates in the Bavarian State legislature in favour of the Basic Law. Yet, he remained disappointed that it gave the Bundesrat, which was made up of delegates from the state governments, less power than the Bundestag, as this meant that a national majority could again dictate to the regions.[91]

Dissatisfaction with the early moves towards reconstituting a German state in the Western zones continued to animate groups in Bavaria, not least the BP, which attracted support for its advocacy of an independent Bavaria within a European federation until the early 1960s. This suggests a certain tension existing at least within Bavaria between support for the new German democracy and the support shown for European integration. As has become evident, supporters of European integration from southern Germany such as the Demokratisches Deutschland leaders did, indeed, envisage such a tension existing, believing that one of the chief virtues of a European federation would be the diminished role that national parliaments and national parties would play in European politics. Such arguments for Europe were no doubt coloured by the experiences of Demokratisches Deutschland leaders and numerous other southern Germans who found exile in wartime Switzerland. Yet, they also resonated with long-held feelings of marginalization on the part of southern Germans, who in many cases had believed that the end of the war presented a unique opportunity to overturn the *kleindeutsch* settlement put in place in the late nineteenth century.

On the one hand, southern Germans therefore supported European integration as a means of expressing their opposition to the early forms of democracy adopted in West Germany. On the other hand, these southern Germans channelled such opposition into a seemingly greater cause – that of a European unity – which not only offered the prospect of a reunited and enlarged (if decentralized) Germany but also promised to ultimately work against the division of Europe into East and West. As a result, such opposition to the new Republic was contained and became less simply rejectionist than it had been in the interwar period. Indeed, southern Germans were given hope that they could play a special role in the new Germany and the new Europe. Hoegner explained this in his *The Republic Betrayed*, published in 1958. He claimed that, 'Bavaria was the destiny of the German republic' because the 'Bavarian Danube [was] the only German river that did not flow internally but outwards towards the East', meaning that the 'mission of being a transmitter of German culture to the East was ... given to ... those of the Bavarian line'.[92]

*****

The collaboration between Christian and social democratic politicians in Demokratisches Deutschland provides a crucial context for explaining how politicians from different parties could prove willing to work across party lines for the cause of European integration. This group also serves as an important case study that sheds light on the development of organizations such as the Nouvelles Equipes Internationales and the Europa Union, within which leading Christian Democratic politicians and other federalists planned the early stages of European integration. The members of Demokratisches Deutschland played significant roles within these organizations, albeit in both cases representing causes advocated by the grassroots but often abandoned by the leaderships in the 1950s. In this sense, they illustrate the value of recovering a 'lost' form of Third Way pro-integration sentiment, which was marginalized by elites but which often resurfaced in the later 1950s and early 1960s. Turning to the experience of Wilhelm Hoegner, it is possible to see that the agenda he developed to enhance regional self-government within a European federation promoted a convergence between his party and the right-of-centre parties in Bavaria. This, in turn, enabled him to successfully fashion coalition governments in the late 1940s and 1950s, while the mainstream of the national SPD was abstaining from such arrangements.

The support for European integration that united the leaders of Demokratisches Deutschland, and which allied Hoegner with politicians outside of his party in Bavaria, was conceived as a means of shifting power from northern Germany and Europe towards southern Germany and Central Europe and thus of redressing the imbalances supposedly created by the nationalist consolidations (or partitions) of the nineteenth century. This aim of strengthening the position of southern Germany through a revived *Mitteleuropa* linked the members of Demokratisches Deutschland with many of the *abendländisch* groups that formed between the interwar and the early post-Second World War periods. However, such a position also intersected with the agenda of leftist advocates of a Third Way Europe, such as those who had worked within the ISK, who wished to see Germany playing a central role in a new Europe that was a bridge between East and West. Thus, an interesting instance of convergence between leftist and rightist advocates of European integration emerges, not only in Bavaria but across Germany more broadly. This convergence suggests that the Federal Republic's integration within a U.S.-led, Western European bloc was only haltingly accepted as a provisional settlement by a wide spectrum of political opinion in Germany.

As already argued, the support for détente initiatives and *Ostpolitik* not only evident in the later 1960s but also in the late 1950s, should be interpreted in the light of this history of support and activism for a Third Way Europe. For this Third Way European federalism, however marginalized in histories of the European Union, was a significant feature of German political culture in the 1950s. Such support for a Third Way Europe and for *Ostpolitik* suggests that many Germans were never reconciled to a Westernization of Germany but remained committed to Germany being reunified within a broader Europe that united East and West. That Christian Democratic politicians such as Konrad Adenauer were able to push forward a policy of Western European integration at the expense of a reunification between East and West Germany, would appear, however, to be in no small part due to the heritage of southern Germans preferring to be integrated within a loosely integrated Europe, rather than being reintegrated with the parts of eastern Germany that had formed the backbone of the earlier Prussian empire.

It is also interesting to highlight the strength of support for an integrated Europe from southern Germans, when one considers whether European integration signalled the 'rescue of the nation-state'. Such a rescue may have been the goal and achievement of the leading European politicians in the early post-war period. Yet, it seems clear that much of the support for integration in Germany came from groups that were not seeking to preserve the German nation-state created either in 1871, 1918 or 1945, but to enhance the claims of a German region at the expense of the German nation-state as it had existed since the late nineteenth century.

This argument does not aspire to profile advocates of European integration as 'saints'[93] but rather to suggest that the motivations behind European integration, at least in the case of Germans, were not always uncomplicatedly nationalist. Instead, they could emerge out of long held regional loyalties, particularly in areas such as Bavaria, where politicians had sought to mobilize support by highlighting the state's perceived marginalization in a united Germany. Thus, at least in the case of the Federal Republic, European integration constituted as much a rescue of the region as a rescue of the nation-state. Certainly, it strengthened the case for a genuinely federal structure in West Germany and thereby served to ultimately reconcile Germans in southern states such as Bavaria to a future within the German nation, indeed in a way that other regional or breakaway nationalist movements in Europe were often not reconciled in the latter half of the twentieth century.

Notes

1. R. Smith, *OSS: The Secret History of America's First Central Intelligence Agency* (Guilford CT: Lyons, 2005) p. 216; A. Rosmus, *Out of Passau: Leaving a City Hitler Called Home* (Columbia SC: University of South Carolina Press, 2004); J. Lynch, 'The Germanic 48th Parallel: Art, Death and Our Very Own Pop Music in Germany, 1967', in *Tilkal: The Journal of Tol Harndor* 2 (November 2005).
2. P. Ther and A. Siljak (eds), *Redrawing Nations: Ethnic Cleansing in East-Central Europe, 1944–1948* (Lanham and Oxford: Rowman and Littlefield, 2001).
3. M. Gehler and W. Kaiser, 'Transnationalism and Early European Integration: The Nouvelles Equipes Internationales and the Geneva Circle 1947–1957', in *The Historical Journal* 44/3 (September 2001).
4. See L. Hooge and G. Marks, 'A Postfunctionalist Theory of European Integration: From Permissive Consensus to Constraining Dissensus', in *British Journal of Political Science* 39/1 (2008) 1–23.
5. A. Spinelli, 'European Union in the Resistance', in *Government and Opposition* 2/3 (July 1967) 326.
6. T. Gees, 'Successful as a "Go-between": The Conservative People's Party in Switzerland', in M. Gehler and W. Kaiser (eds), *Christian Democracy in Europe since 1945, Vol. 2* (London and New York: Routledge, 2004) pp. 34–39; Gehler and Kaiser, 'Transnationalism and Early European Integration', p. 776.
7. Gehler and Kaiser, 'Transnationale Parteienkooperation der europäischen Christdemokraten: Nouvelles Equipes Internationales und Genfer Kreis 1947 bis 1965', in H. Wohnout (ed.), *Demokratie und Geschichte: Jahrbuch des Karl von Vogelsang-Instituts zur Erforschung der Geschichte der christlichen Demokratie in Österreich* (Vienna: Böhlau, 2000) p. 113.
8. P. Claeys and N. Loeb-Mayer, 'Trans-European Party Groupings: Emergence of New and Alignment of Old Parties in the Light of the Direct Elections to the European Parliament', in *Government and Opposition* 14/4 (October 1979) 461.
9. R. Papini, *The Christian Democratic International* (Lanham: Rowman and Littlefield, 1997) p. 51.

10. B. Salzmann, *Europa als Thema katholischer Eliten: das katholische Europa-Netzwerk der Schweiz von 1945 bis Mitte der 1950er Jahre* (Fribourg: Saint-Paul, 2006) pp. 122–25; Gees, 'Successful as a Go-Between', in Gehler and Kaiser, *Christian Democracy in Europe*.
11. M. Sutton, *France and the Construction of Europe, 1944–2007: The Geopolitical Imperative* (New York and Oxford: Berghahn Books, 2007) pp. 52–53; R. Vinen, *Bourgeois Politics in France, 1945–1951* (Cambridge: Cambridge University Press, 2002) pp. 8–9.
12. Kaiser, *Christian Democracy and the Origins of European Union* (Cambridge: Cambridge University Press, 2007) pp. 193–212.
13. Ibid., pp. 179–80, 242.
14. Kaiser, *Christian Democracy and the Origins of European Union*, pp. 205, 230; P. Ginsborg, *A History of Contemporary Italy: Society and Politics, 1943–1988* (Houndmills: Palgrave, 2003) pp. 168–70.
15. Kaiser, *Christian Democracy and the Origins of European Union*, p. 186; C. Booker and R. North, *The Great Deception: A Secret History of the European Union* (London: Continuum, 2003) p. 43.
16. G. Lundestad, *The United States and Western Europe since 1945. From "Empire" by Invitation to Atlantic Drift* (Oxford: Oxford University Press, 2003) pp. 78–81; R. Dietl, '"Sole Master of the Western Nuclear Strength"? The United States, Western Europe and the Elusiveness of a European Defence Identity, 1959–64', in W. Loth (ed.), *Europe, Cold War and Co-Existence 1953–1965* (London: Frank Cass, 2004) p. 135.
17. H. Küppers, *Joseph Wirth. Parlamentarier, Minister und Kanzler der Weimarer Republik* (Stuttgart: Franz Steiner, 1997) p. 315.
18. Kaiser, *Christian Democracy and the Origins of European Union*, pp. 208–9.
19. AdsD, NL Ritzel, Folder 358, Letter from Grauel to Ritzel, 26 March 1946; Kaiser, *Christian Democracy and the Origins of European Union*, p. 207.
20. Gehler and Kaiser, 'Transnationalism and Early European Integration', p. 780.
21. J.-C. Delbreil, 'The French Catholic Left and the Political Parties', and A. Lienkamp, 'Socialism out of Christian Responsibility. The German Experiment of Left Catholicism (1945–1949)', in G.-R. Horn and E. Gerard (eds), *Left Catholicism 1943–1955: Catholics and Society in Western Europe at the Point of Liberation* (Leuven: Leuven University Press, 2001) pp. 51–52, 204–9.
22. IfZ Munich, NL Hoegner, ED 120/15, see Wirth's proposals for a 'Radikal-Soziales Aktionsprogramm', which were later incorporated into the central document put out by the organization, *Das Demokratische Deutschland. Grundsätze und Richtlinien für den deutschen Wiederaufbau im demokratischen, republikanischen, föderalistischen und genossenschaftlichen Sinne* (Berne and Leipzig: Haupt, 1945).
23. Gehler and Kaiser, 'Transnationalism and Early European Integration', p. 782.
24. L. Passerini, *Love and the Idea of Europe* (New York and Oxford: Berghahn Books, 2009) pp. 174–228.
25. IfZ Munich, NL Hoegner, ED 120/15, J. Kindt-Kiefer and J. Wirth, 'Memorandum *Über den Wieder-Aufbau*', pp. 3–7.
26. IfZ Munich, NL Hoegner, ED 120/15, Kindt-Kiefer and Wirth, *Über den Wieder-Aufbau*, pp. 13–18.
27. V. Conze, *Das Europa der Deutschen: Ideen von Europa in Deutschland zwischen Reichstradition und Westorientierung (1920–1970)* (Munich: Oldenbourg, 2005) p. 125; A. Schildt, *Zwischen Abendland und Amerika: Studien zur westdeutschen Ideenlandschaft der 50er Jahre* (Munich: Oldenbourg, 1999) pp. 120–23.
28. Schildt, *Zwischen Abendland und Amerika*, pp. 123–34.
29. On the growing ecumenism of the *abendländisch* movement in the interwar years, see D. Pöpping, *Abendland: Christliche Akademiker und die Utopie der Antimoderne 1900–1945* (Berlin: Metropol, 2002) pp. 70–93.

30. H. Schulze (ed.), 'Rückblick auf Weimar. Ein Briefwechsel zwischen Otto Braun und Joseph Wirth im Exil', in *Vierteljahreshefte für Zeitgeschichte* 26/1 (1978) 155.
31. A. Gallus, *Die Neutralisten: Verfechter eines vereinten Deutschlands zwischen Ost und West 1945–1990* (Düsseldorf: Droste, 2001); U. Wengst, 'Neutralistische Positionen in der CDU und in der FDP in den 1950er Jahren', in D. Geppert and U. Wengst (eds), *Neutralität – Chance oder Chimäre? Konzepte des Dritten Weges für Deutschland und die Welt 1945–1990* (Munich: Oldenbourg, 2005).
32. AdsD, NL Ritzel, Folder 214, Letter from Braun to Ritzel, 6 October 1945; Letter from Braun to Ritzel, 12 October 1945; NL Ritzel, Folder 225, Untitled Report by Braun on Demokratisches Deutschland Memorandum regarding the Treaty of Potsdam, September 1945; Schulze, 'Rückblick auf Weimar', in *Vierteljahreshefte für Zeitgeschichte*, p. 155; R.E.M. Irving, *Christian Democracy in France* (London: Routledge, 1973) pp. 116–20.
33. 'Fanfare: Sammeln', in *Der Spiegel* 4, 22 January 1949, pp. 3–4; Wengst, 'Neutralistische Positionen in der CDU und der FDP in den 1950er Jahren', in Geppert and Wengst, *Neutralität, Chance oder Chimäre*, p. 41; N. Cary, *The Path to Christian Democracy: German Catholics and the Party System from Windhorst to Adenauer* (Cambridge MA: Harvard University Press, 1996) pp. 208–25.
34. Gallus, *Neutralisten*, pp. 138–59; D. Kisatsky, *The United States and the European Right, 1945–1955* (Columbus OH: Ohio State University Press, 2005) p. 47.
35. H.-P. Schwarz, *Konrad Adenauer: German Politician and Statesman in a Period of War, Revolution and Re-construction. Vol. 2: The Statesman, 1952–1967* (New York and Oxford: Berghahn Books, 1997) pp. 183–85; Kaiser, *Christian Democracy and the Origins of European Union*, p. 209.
36. Irving, *Christian Democracy in France*, p. 117.
37. K. Gotto, 'Adenauers Deutschland- und Ostpolitik, 1954–1963', in R. Morsey and K. Repgen (eds), *Adenauer Studien*, Vol. 3: *Untersuchungen und Dokumente zur Ostpolitik und Biographie* (Mainz: Matthias–Grünewald 2nd ed., 1974) p. 85.
38. For one of the most sophisticated explanations of the concept of *Westbindung* in relation to Adenauer's foreign policy, see R. Granieri, *The Ambivalent Alliance: Konrad Adenauer, the CDU/CSU, and the West, 1949–1966* (New York and Oxford: Berghahn Books, 2003) esp. pp. 1–27.
39. W. Loth, 'Adenauer's Final Western Choice, 1955–58', in Loth, *Europe, Cold War and Co-Existence 1953–1965*, pp. 26–28; Müchler quoted in W. Benz, 'Föderalistische Politik in der CDU/CSU. Die Verfassungsdiskussion im "Ellwanger Kreis" 1947/48', in *Vierteljahrshefte für Zeitgeschichte* 25/4 (1977) 780.
40. For more on this, see the Conclusion.
41. AdsD, NL Ritzel, Folder 367, 'Referat von Zentralsekretär H.G. Ritzel an der Herbst-Delegiertenversammlung der Europa-Union in Berne, 11th November, 1945'.
42. AdsD, NL Ritzel, Folder 367, 'Rededisposition des Generalsekretärs H.G. Ritzel von der Schweizerischen Europa-Union, Basel, 1947'; and NL Ritzel, Folder 367, 'Europa-Union?' [1947? pencilled in].
43. H. Bauer, 'Der Krieg in Europa ist zu Ende – der Kampf um Europa beginnt!', quoted in W. Lipgens, *A History of European Integration: Vol. 1, 1945–1947* (Oxford: Oxford University Press, 1982) p. 121.
44. F. Niess, *Die Europäische Idee – aus dem Geist des Widerstands* (Frankfurt am Main: Suhrkamp, 2001) pp. 85–86; Lipgens, *Die Anfänge der europäischen Einigungspolitik 1945–1950: Erster Teil 1945–1947* (Stuttgart: Ernst Klein, 1997) p. 391.
45. Lipgens, *Anfänge europäischer Einigungspolitik*, p. 599.
46. Conze, *Europa der Deutschen*, p. 294.
47. Niess, *Europäische Idee*, pp. 55–77.
48. AdsD, NL Ritzel, Folder 367, 'Leitsätze der EUROPA-UNION. Schweizerische Bewegung für die Einigung Europas', [undated, 1945–47].
49. Niess, *Europäische Idee*, p. 98.

50. AdsD, NL Ritzel, Findbuch, Band I, pp. II–III.
51. Niess, *Europäische Idee*, pp. 97–100.
52. K.H. Koppe, *Das grüne E setzt sich durch* (Cologne: Europa Union, 1967) p. 23; Lipgens and Loth (eds), *Documents on the History of European Integration*, vol. 3, *The Struggle for European Union by Political Parties and Pressure Groups in Western European Countries, 1945–1950* (Berlin: de Gruyter, 1988) pp. 501–2n.
53. Koppe, *Grüne E*, p. 31.
54. G. Brunn, *Die Europäische Einigung von 1945 bis heute* (Bonn: Bundeszentrale für politische Bildung, 2002) p. 60; and Niess, *Europäische Idee*, pp. 189–92, 221–23.
55. Conze, *Europa der Deutschen*, p. 314.
56. AdsD, NL Ritzel, Folder 367, Letter from Bauer to Zentralvorstand, 29 January 1947.
57. Conze, *Europa der Deutschen*, pp. 312–23; Koppe, *Grüne E*, p. 26.
58. Conze, *Europa der Deutschen*, p. 331; J. Mittag and W. Wessels (eds), *Der 'Kölsche Europäer': Friedrich Carl von Oppenheim und die Europäische Einigung* (Münster: Aschendorff, 2005); Gehler, 'Deutsch-Französische Union oder Achse Berlin – Moskau – Peking? Richard Coudenhove-Kalergi, Fritz Erler, Ernst Friedlaender und die deutsche Frage 1955/56', in M. König and M. Schulz (eds), *Die Bundesrepublik Deutschland und die europäische Einigung 1949–2000. Politische Akteure, gesellschaftliche Kräfte und internationale Erfahrungen. Festschrift für Wolf D. Gruner zum 60. Geburtstag* (Stuttgart: Franz Steiner, 2004) pp. 538–45.
59. Dietl, 'Sole Master of the Western Nuclear Strength?', in Loth, *Europe, Cold War and Co-Existence*, p. 135.
60. H. Ritzel, *Europa und Deutschland – Deutschland und Europa* (Offenbach am Main: Bollwerk, 1947) p. 14.
61. AdsD, NL Ritzel, Findbuch, Band I, p. III.
62. Niess, *Europäische Idee*, pp. 95–100; T. Risse, 'A European Identity? Europeanization and the Evolution of Nation-State Identities', in M. Cowles, J. Caporaso and T. Risse (eds), *Transforming Europe: Europeanization and Domestic Change* (Ithaca: Cornell University Press, 2001) pp. 201–10.
63. K.-U. Gelberg, *Hans Ehard. Die föderalistische Politik des bayerischen Ministerpräsidenten 1946–1954* (Düsseldorf: Droste, 1992) p. 55; Gelberg (ed.), *Die Protokolle des bayerischen Ministerrats 1945–1954. Das Kabinett Hoegner I. 28. September 1945 bis 21. Dezember 1946* (Munich: Oldenbourg, 1997) pp. xxxiv–xxxv, lxi; H. Mehringer, *Waldemar von Knoeringen. Eine politische Biographie. Der Weg vom revolutionären Sozialismus zur sozialen Demokratie* (Munich: Saur, 1989) pp. 314, 319.
64. Conze, *Europa der Deutschen*, p. 125; B. Fait, *Demokratische Erneuerung unter dem Sternenbanner. Amerikanische Kontrolle und Verfassungsgebung in Bayern 1946* (Düsseldorf: Droste, 1998) p. 105; P. Kock, *Bayerns Weg in die Bundesrepublik* (Stuttgart: DEVA, 1983) pp. 29, 33–38.
65. J.R. Canoy, *The Discreet Charm of the Police State: The* Landpolizei *and the Transformation of Bavaria, 1945–1965* (Leiden: Brill, 2007) p. 146; Kock, *Bayerns Weg in die Bundesrepublik*, pp. 165–66.
66. W. Behr, *Sozialdemokratie und Konservatismus. Ein empirischer und theoretischer Beitrag zur regionalen Parteianalyse am Beispiel der Geschichte und Nachkriegsentwicklung Bayerns* (Hannover: Verlag für Literatur und Zeitgeschehen, 1969) p. 46.
67. Hoegner to Wirth, 29 October 1944, quoted in P. Kritzer, *Wilhelm Hoegner: Politische Biographie eines bayrischen Sozialdemokrat* (Munich: Süddeutscher, 1979) p. 139.
68. Hoegner, *Der schwierige Außenseiter. Erinnerungen eines Abgeordneten, Emigranten und Ministerpräsidenten* (Munich: Isar, 1959) pp. 222–23.
69. Kock, *Bayerns Weg in die Bundesrepublik*, p. 107.
70. IfZ Munich, NL Hoegner, ED 120/4, Letter from Hoegner to Gävernitz, 27 April 1945.
71. IfZ Munich, NL Hoegner, ED 120/281, 'Bericht des bayerischen Ministerpräsidenten an den Beratenden Landesausschuss (26.II.1946) [Handtyped version]'; AdsD, NL Ritzel, Folder 357, 'Abschrift, 9 October, 1945'.

72. F. Baer, *Die Ministerpräsidenten Bayerns: 1945–1962. Dokumente und Analyse* (Munich: Beck, 1971) pp. 54–55; J. Balcar, *Politik auf dem Land: Studien zur bayerischen Provinz, 1945 bis 1972* (Munich: Oldenbourg, 2004) p. 136.
73. Kock, *Bayerns Weg in die Bundesrepublik*, pp, 199–203; Kritzer, *Hoegner*, pp. 224–28.
74. See Kock, *Bayerns Weg in die Bundesrepublik*, pp. 205–6. On the link between regionalism and support for European integration see U. Ruge, *Die Erfindung des "Europa der Regionen": kritische Ideengeschichte eines konservativen Konzepts* (Frankfurt am Main: Campus, 2003) esp. pp. 156–70.
75. Benz, 'Ellwanger Kreis', in *Vierteljahrshefte für Zeitgeschichte*, p. 783.
76. Hoegner, *Schwierige Außenseiter*.
77. M. Spicka, *Selling the Economic Miracle: Economic Reconstruction and Politics in West Germany, 1949–1957* (New York and Oxford: Berghahn Books, 2007) p. 55; Kock, *Bayerns Weg in die Bundesrepublik*, pp. 172–3.
78. IfZ Munich, NL Hoegner, ED 120/Vol. 282, 'Vereinigte Staaten von Europa?', Volkshochschule Ulm, 12 July 1946.
79. J. Hellman, *Emmanuel Mounier and the New Catholic Left, 1930–150* (Toronto: University of Toronto Press, 1981) p. 225.
80. IfZ Munich, NL Hoegner, ED 120/284, Hoegner, 'Denkschrift über die politische Gestaltung Westdeutschlands nach dem Scheitern der Londoner Konferenz. January 1948'.
81. A.K. Oeltzen and D. Forkmann, 'Charismatiker, Kärrner und Hedonisten. Die Parteivorsitzenden der SPD', in D. Forkmann and M. Schlieben (eds), *Die Parteivorsitzenden in der Bundesrepublik Deutschland 1949–2005* (Wiesbaden: VS, 2005) p. 69; Schildt, *Max Brauer* (Hamburg: Ellert und Richter, 2002) pp. 90-95; A. Sywottek, 'Max Brauer: Oberbürgermeister – Exilant – Erster Bürgermeister', in Landeszentrale für politische Bildung (ed.), *Hamburg nach dem Ende des Dritten Reiches: politischer Neuaufbau 1945/46 bis 1949. Sechs Beiträge* (Hamburg: Landeszentrale für politische Bildung, 2000) pp. 159–67.
82. IfZ Munich, NL Hoegner, ED 120/280, Rede des bayerischen Ministerpräsidenten Dr. Wilhelm Hoegner in der ersten Versammlung der Sozialdemokratischen Partei München am 25. November 1945.
83. Behr, *Sozialdemokratie und Konservatismus*, pp. 164–65; G. Ritter, 'Wilhelm Hoegner', in F. Seibt (ed.), *Gesellschaftsgeschichte. Festschrift für Karl Bosl zum 80. Geburtstag*, Vol. 2 (Munich: Oldenbourg, 1988) p. 346; Gelberg, 'Einleitung', in Gelberg, *Protokolle des Bayerischen Ministerrats*, pp. xxxiv–xxxvii.
84. Benz, 'Ellwanger Kreis', in *Vierteljahrshefte für Zeitgeschichte*, p. 783.
85. Benz, 'Ellwanger Kreis', in *Vierteljahrshefte für Zeitgeschichte*, pp. 785–86, 794–97; Kritzer, *Hoegner*, pp. 199, 203.
86. Benz, 'Ellwanger Kreis', in *Vierteljahrshefte für Zeitgeschichte*, p. 806.
87. Kock, *Bayerns Weg*, pp. 291–92.
88. IfZ Munich, NL Baumgartner, ED 132/14, Letter from Berthold to Baumgartner, 22 February 1948; Kock, *Bayerns Weg*, p. 149.
89. IfZ Munich, NL Baumgartner ED 132/14, Letter from Berthold to Baumgartner, 3 December 1949, including article 'Europäischer Regionalismus – ein Programmpunkt der Bayernpartei'; IfZ Munich, NL Baumgartner ED 132/14, Letter from Berthold to Baumgartner, 17 January 1950, including draft of 'Die Ideologie des neuen Europa'.
90. IfZ Munich, NL Hoegner ED 120/63, Schäffer to Hoegner, 15 December 1948; Kock, *Bayerns Weg*, pp. 165–66, 293.
91. Ritter, 'Hoegner', in Seibt (ed.), *Gesellschaftsgeschichte*, p. 358.
92. Hoegner, *Die Verratene Republik. Geschichte der deutschen Gegenrevolution* (Munich: Isar, 1958) p. 99
93. See Milward, *European Rescue of the Nation-State*, Chapter 6: 'The Lives and Teachings of the European Saints'.

Conclusion

> She looked over his shoulder
> For vines and olive trees,
>   Marble well-governed cities
> And ships upon untamed seas,
>   But there on the shining metal
> His hands had put instead
>   An artificial wilderness
> And a sky like lead.
>   (W.H. Auden, *The Shield of Achilles*)

Many histories of the European Union or of Europeanization use the familiar format of telling a story '*From* something *to* something', as in 'From Consolidation to Enlargement' or 'From Messina to Maastricht'.[1] This book, by contrast, has suggested that European integration should be analysed not only as a series of events and negotiations that make up a seemingly linear political history from, say, the ECSC to the EU. Instead, it should be studied as a broader and less unidirectional cultural and intellectual history of encounters and cooperations between European peoples, organizations and institutions across the course of the twentieth century.[2] Adopting such an approach makes European history appear less like a smooth runway for the take-off of the European project and more like a crowded landscape within which the meanings of a wide variety of people's activities and discussions have to be carefully deciphered. As has been argued, from the point of view of many Europeans, not least the diverse German-speaking populations of Europe, the early post-Second World War period was not regarded as ushering in the first phase of an unstoppable process of European integration. Rather, it seemed to mark the high point in a process of de-integration that had started in the nineteenth century and accelerated sharply after 1918. Indeed, for many Germans, their nation and the European continent as a whole was stuck in a historical hiatus: Germany itself had become two temporary German states, divided along lines that represented the thinly veiled enmity between the former Allies and which compounded the divisions that had separated Europeans from one another across the twentieth century. Accordingly, intellectuals and politicians often conceived of the post-war German (and by extension European) predicament as something provisional and out of the ordinary, contrasting it with the supposedly more unified past and a hopefully more united future that would constitute a return to normality. Hence the title of this book, *Between Yesterday and Tomorrow*, which tries to capture the mixture of discontent, optimism and nostalgia that motivated many of the arguments for European integration made in the mid twentieth century.[3]

This book has offered a perspective on how integration became an important cause for civil society organizations and how it fitted in with their wider intellectual and political programmes and agendas. These organizations produced widely read journalistic analysis, and helped to revive party political life between the mid 1920s and the early post-1945 period. As groups based around the journal *Merkur* and its predecessors illustrate, the issue of European integration was a central one for many who wished to cultivate associational life between European elites and to develop or revive a free press. They, and organizations such as the ISK and Demokratisches Deutschland, which sought to develop an integrationist policy within socialist and Christian political parties, argued that issues such as the functioning of democracy, the managing of competing nationalisms, the relationship between regions and nations, and the role of religion in politics could only be adequately tackled on a European-wide basis. This book has focused on such arguments, showing how they served to explain and legitimate, but also to critique and rally opposition to, integrationist policies and negotiations among political parties and associations. This intellectual history therefore makes up a significant part of the history behind the series of European treaties that has often been treated as a self-contained narrative of European integration.

Mid-Century Projects for Unifying Europe

Just as many advocates of European integration in the early to mid twentieth century believed that Europe was stuck between Cold War superpowers as well as between a (mythologized) unified past and a hoped-for integrated future, so too has the timeframe for this book cut across more conventional periodizations. By looking across the well established historical markers of interwar and post-war, of pre-1939 and post-1945 histories, the analysis has highlighted that a cultural history of European integration does not necessarily or neatly reflect the chronology of mainstream political histories. Focusing on three quite different organizations, it has illustrated that groups across the ideological spectrum advocated European integration not simply as a means of rescuing the nation-state after the chaos of the Second World War but also as a result of longer-term socialist, Christian democratic and Christian anti-democratic perspectives on reconfiguring the nation-state.

For the *abendländisch* intellectuals and politicians such as those connected with the journal *Merkur* and its predecessors, European integration chiefly meant two things. Once the appeal of a 'post-democratic' integration waned during the 1930s, it meant, first, a series of European-wide constitutional safeguards that would limit the power of democratically elected politicians and parties to wreak the destruction experienced in Germany after 1933. Second, it entailed a re-socialization of European populations and particularly elites through transnational cultural, educational and religious initiatives that would break down post-First World War enmities between nations and revive the transnational connections that had linked earlier generations of leaders in Europe. Such measures would, it was argued, not only address the causes of the developing Cold War and the recently concluded Second World War, but would deal with the deeper roots of ethnic and ideological conflict within and between the European nations.

These predominantly right-wing figures appealed to a pre-1918 European history, seeking to constrain the practice of post-First World War democracy through European integration. They therefore made uneasy members of a CDU-led Westernizing and Westernized elite in the early Federal Republic. Indeed, some on the *abendländisch* Right offered outright opposition to Adenauer's policy of *Westbindung*, while others made only a temporary and provisional compromise with it, advancing their own version of a Third Way politics and even an *Ostpolitik* that would reunite the historical lands of the *Abendland*. Thus, while right-wing groups largely moved within the democratic mainstream after 1945, their advocacy of a united Europe as *Abendland* served to express their opposition to the Western-oriented policy of the CDU leadership and to offer them the prospect of change from the early post-war status quo.[4] Accordingly, rather than describing a one-way process of Westernization, this work has illustrated how many groups, including those on the Right, envisaged European integration as a road that would lead Germany back from its temporary position in the Western camp towards playing a leading role in a reunified Europe.

Socialists, such as the members of the Internationaler Sozialistischer Kampfbund (ISK) and similar splinter groups, whose leaders went on to occupy influential positions in the post-war SPD, also rooted their support for European integration within a longer-standing oppositional internationalist agenda. They interpreted the Second World War as confirmation of the Marxist theory that competing capitalist interests would ultimately resolve their differences through war. Of course, the position of such left-socialists changed between the 1920s and 1950s as the Soviet Union became an unreliable sponsor, or even saboteur, of international revolution, while capitalist and democratic countries ultimately contributed to the defeat of Hitler and to the reconstruction of democracy in West Germany. Accordingly, they came to advocate what amounted to revolutionary change in the form of European integration: they proposed a continent-wide new economic and political order that would begin in a community of non-aligned nations in Central Europe and would eliminate the social preconditions for another war. Even as they reintegrated within the SPD fold in the post-war period and moved towards the political centre ground, these socialists supported a

Third Way integrated Europe that would cut across the Cold War and would be neither communist nor capitalist.

This book, by focusing predominantly on how foreign or European policy shaped the domestic policy of these socialists, rather than the other way around, thus moves us beyond a historiographical orthodoxy that focuses too much on the role of Kurt Schumacher and sees socialists choosing nationalism over internationalism in the early post-war years. Indeed, the argument suggests that socialists' commitment to a Third Way Europe provided a source of the 'intransigent opposition' that the early SPD offered against the CDU/CSU and its Westernizing European policy under Adenauer. This Third Way perspective provided socialists with a vision of a future Germany and Europe that would be radically different to the one created in the early post-war period. It thus informed many of the apparently 'nationalist' and anti-European policies pursued by Schumacher and his colleagues after 1945.

With regard to the socialists and Christian liberals who were largely from southern Germany and represented by the third group, Demokratisches Deutschland, their programme for European integration was conceived, on the one hand, as a response to emergency conditions: the break-up of Germany envisaged at Potsdam. On the other, it developed out of a long-standing federalist agenda put forward by southern Germans who resented the Prussian-led unification (or partition) of Germany into a *Kleindeutschland*. As has been shown, this domestic federalist agenda was Europeanized by the exile experience of the group's leaders, who worked within transnational resistance and federalist movements. In such transnational organizations, the hostility of these individuals to a centralized nation-state fed into a broader agenda for a federal Europe, prompting members to advocate a more radical Third Force form of integration than the national leaders who negotiated the early European treaties or rescue of their nation-states. Yet, in spite of their oppositional stance on European integration, these federalists were able to work successfully at the regional level, often with fellow exiles, to agitate for greater federalism within Germany and to shift the policies of the major national parties. Their experiences therefore illustrate how a European integrationist agenda shaped domestic politics. It reinforced the federalization of West Germany and offered politicians in the regions the prospect for change without having to jettison parliamentary democracy as, for instance, Bavarian separatists had sought to in the interwar period.

Of course, there are limits to the extent to which the integrationist agendas outlined in this book permeated German society. As has become evident, while integrationist groups were very active in terms of local and regional politics and in cultural production, they were never mass movements with memberships that could rival trade unions, for example.[5] Similarly, the kind of projects for Europe explored here were influential within the major political parties but chiefly at the local and regional levels – pushed forward by big city mayors and the Minister-Presidents of certain states. In this regard, they are an important part of the post-war history of the Federal Republic, illustrating one way in which politics between the regions and the centre was negotiated. Nevertheless, the ways in which grassroots agendas for integration were marginalized by national and international leaders is also an important aspect of the history of European integration more broadly. It furthermore highlights the challenges for present-day EU leaders who have looked to encourage civil society engagement as a means of stimulating a European sensibility among citizens and thereby redressing the democratic deficit.[6]

The groups featured therefore do not present a complete picture of the politics of European integration in the mid twentieth century; they do, nevertheless, illustrate the variety of agendas for Europe that existed during the period. Yet, in spite of the clear divergences between the groups, one of the most remarkable features of the post-1945 period was that a certain convergence occurred between Left and Right in Germany, concerning European integration. This convergence occurred around the issues of taming democracy, redefining the role played by religion in politics, federalising formerly unitary nation-states and seeking to extricate an integrated Europe from subordination to one of the Cold War blocs. Such convergence may well have been due to a certain muting of former sentiments on the part of post-war politicians and intellectuals, who were eager to avoid the bitter ideological conflict of the interwar period.[7] It also, nevertheless, constituted a profound change in the political dispositions of elites active in associational life, in intellectual and cultural production and in party politics in Germany. In the interwar period, *abendländisch* intellectuals had argued against the mobilization of masses within political parties and instead advocated their integration within varieties of post-democratic *Volksgemeinschaft* or national community. In contrast, by the post-war years such arguments gave way to an emphasis on defending the constitutional rights of the individual and of local and religious communities at a European level. Similarly, while socialist groups such as the ISK did not simply lose their radicalism after 1945, they shifted their focus away from working towards an international revolution pushed through with the help of a major communist power. Instead, they sought to encourage a Third Way egalitarian and internationalist outlook among the working classes by participating in grassroots federalist movements, often working with Christian political groups. With regard to southern German advocates of federalism, these groups also shifted their perspective. They moved from advancing a rejectionist and separatist interwar agenda towards working (within coalitions) for a Europe of the regions, as a way of maximising the autonomy of these regions within the reconstituted (West) German nation-state.

Such convergences between political groupings might provide further evidence of how and why the 1950s became known as a decade of consensus in which ideology was even said to have died.[8] Yet, the ways in which political attitudes to Europe converged in Germany were precisely due to the unhappy experience of Germans with nation-building and parliamentary democracy before 1945. As has been argued, by the onset of the Second World War, democracy appeared to many to be terminally compromised, having brought about ideological warfare between parties, enmity between radicalized masses and the intolerant dominance of majorities over minorities.[9] Thus, after 1945, Germans across the political spectrum converged around a pro-European agenda as a means not of extending democracy but of containing it. Such a convergence of political attitudes also suggests the discontent with the reconstruction of a nation-state evident among elites in West Germany. Indeed, Germans across the ideological spectrum could embrace European integration because it appeared to offer the prospect of undoing the process of nation-building that had led to the creation of the new West German state. Nevertheless, advancing an agenda for European integration did not only provide a way for individuals and groups to express opposition to the prevailing order in West Germany. It also served to contain this opposition, as these individuals and groups could work for change within a progressive model of an integrating Europe. Thus, the prospect of reforming, say, the new economic system or the new federal institutions in West Germany, or of overcoming the division between East and West Germany, was not simply lost but only postponed, and could be kept alive within the incrementalist European project. In this way, support for European integration allowed groups to develop oppositional visions at the same time as making them less likely to mobilize against the young West German democracy. Alongside the exigencies of the Cold War, the prospect of European integration therefore helps to explain how a variety of political groups (including those formerly opposed to democracy) could reconcile themselves to the practice of democracy in a way that their predecessors had not during the interwar period.

This context of oppositional groups in Germany converging in their support for integration, in turn, suggests that distinctive national approaches to unifying Europe developed and persisted after 1945, even if many of the individuals and groups active in integrationist politics had been exiles and had worked within transnational organizations. While disillusionment with parliamentarianism may have united significant communities of opinion on the Right and Left in some European countries like interwar and wartime France and Germany, this disillusionment was less widespread in others such as Britain. In the latter country, parties of the Marxist left garnered little support; the Labour Party remained committed to parliamentary democracy and the Conservatives dominated a democratically elected National Government throughout the 1930s.[10] This helps to explain why the British Labour Party remained unconvinced of the need to commit Britain to an integrated Europe and why Winston Churchill, even when bringing together European federalists at The Hague in May 1948, regarded European integration as a solution to continental European problems and not relevant to Britain.[11] By contrast, the problems that Germans had experienced in practising parliamentary democracy and managing nationalist movements might explain why a wide variety of political groups could greet early plans for a technocratic ECSC and EEC with approval, compared with the Gaullist approach favoured in mid-twentieth-century France and the much greater scepticism shown by the British public.[12] Similarly, the resilient federalism alive in the German states during the early twentieth century had no real counterparts in Britain or France, where plans for an integrated Europe were not greeted as a means of promoting a domestic federalist agenda.

Ideas of Europe after 1950

While the focus of this book has been on ideas of Europe in the early to mid twentieth century, the legacies of these ideas remained evident in the later twentieth century. For instance, the Third Way conceptions of Europe highlighted throughout the earlier decades went on to animate much of the popular and official support for détente and *Ostpolitik* that became evident, not only in the later 1960s, but also in the mid-1950s, before the construction of the Berlin Wall in 1961 again heightened tensions between the two Germanys. As has already been seen, even within the Christian democratic alliance, Konrad Adenauer's pro-Western orientation did not receive unanimous approval, with leading figures such as Jakob Kaiser, Eugen Gerstenmeier and Heinrich von Brentano offering varying degrees of opposition in the late 1940s and early 1950s.[13] Yet, even Adenauer's pro-Western policy may be due for a reappraisal in light of recent studies of the mid to late 1950s and early 1960s.

Indeed, having initially sought to assure the Federal Republic's sovereignty via integration within a Western alliance, Adenauer made repeated attempts during the mid-1950s to reform the post-war settlement in Central Europe. In spite of the formulation of the Hallstein Doctrine in 1955 by the West German Foreign Ministry, which regarded recognition of the GDR by another power as an unfriendly act (and which could, in any case, be read as a sign of the Christian democratic leadership's commitment to regaining Germany's East), it was not the case that West German leaders were unwilling to envisage an opening up to the countries in the Eastern bloc. From 1956 to 1957, Adenauer sought to respond to the proliferation of plans formulated for a reunified Germany to be created within a demilitarized Central European space. These included the Rapacki Plan designed by the Polish Foreign Minister, and rival schemes announced by George Kennan, the British opposition leader Hugh Gaitskell, and GDR leader Walter Ulbricht. Adenauer devised his own plan for neutralizing Central Europe, imagining the retreat of American and Soviet forces from West Germany and the East-Central European nations respectively.[14] Similarly, he proved amenable to the Norstad Plan put together by the Commander of NATO in 1959, a measure that would have shifted control of the nuclear deterrent away from being the unilateral preserve of the Americans in favour of the Europeans. Perhaps most intriguingly, the German Chancellor also responded positively to de Gaulle's proposals to take an integrated Europe out of NATO in 1963, seemingly shifting his orientation from being Atlanticist to Gaullist and thereby choosing a different form of 'Western' approach.[15] All the while, Adenauer and his colleagues were strengthening trade links between the Federal Republic and the nations of Eastern Europe, which led to the signing of a trade treaty with the Soviet Union in 1958, establishing the Federal Republic as the Soviet Union's major trading partner in Western Europe by 1959.[16] However we interpret Adenauer's 'policy of movement' then, it appears clear that he was either unwilling or unable to simply push forward a policy of ever closer alliance with the United States in the mid to late 1950s. This was not least due to the consistently less pro-Western policy of the CDU's coalition partners, the FDP, the German Party (Deutsche Partei DP) and the League of Expellees and Deprived of Rights (Bund der Heimatvertriebenen und Entrechteten BHE). Indeed, the latter two parties pressed for a return of Germany's eastern lands and advocated recreating a German *Grossraum* throughout the decade.[17]

The abidingly *mitteleuropäisch* perspective of right-wing parties such as the FDP and BHE, both of which voted against the Treaty of Rome in 1957 even though the SPD changed its European policy and supported the treaty, might further confirm how far the commitment of certain groups on the Right to Germany's continued role in Central Europe has been underestimated.[18] Looking further forward into the 1960s, it appears that Germans across the ideological spectrum never stopped looking eastwards or seeking to rescue a German nation-state that was greater than the Western version incorporated within the ECSC and EEC. For instance, the Christian democratic chancellors Ludwig Erhard and Kurt-Georg Kiesinger both spoke about improving diplomatic relations with their neighbours to the East as a step towards realizing a more all-embracing European community. They went on to open trade missions in Warsaw in 1963 and Prague in 1967, which functioned as substitute embassies.[19] Kiesinger went further than his predecessor, accepting the Oder–Neisse border for a future reunited Germany and working with the French on an *Ostpolitik* that would improve diplomatic relations with Romania and Poland and ease relations with the Soviet Union.[20] Thus, any Westernization that occurred among German political leaders in the 1940s and 1950s should perhaps now be seen as the first stage of a longer-term *Ostpolitik* and policy of normalization. And so, to adopt the rationale behind Bahr's and Brandt's *Ostpolitik*, the earlier Western policy should be described as a case of German leaders accepting the status quo of integration in an American-led bloc, in order eventually to overcome this same status quo.

Of course, the authors of *Ostpolitik* as an explicit policy were the leading figures in the SPD, Egon Bahr and Willy Brandt, who were able to make the most significant strides in terms of policy in the late 1960s and early 1970s. While this policy was largely concerned with easing relations between the two German states, it clearly grew out of a longer-standing socialist approach to Europe. And this approach, as Brandt explained in a speech given in The Hague in December 1969, was aimed not at creating a West European bloc but an 'exemplary' community that could serve as a magnet, drawing in all of the European nations.[21] While Brandt (and his successor Helmut Schmidt) was unable to push forward an agenda to make the EC more supranational, particularly as he also sought to bring the unionist United Kingdom into the Community, he nevertheless was able to rally the social democratic parties behind a *Programme for a Social Europe* in 1973. This programme sought to strengthen the social rights of workers and build the EC as a model social democratic community that would appeal to the nations of the Communist bloc.[22]

Such an *Ostpolitik* was not simply the initiative of political leaders but reflected the rapprochement occurring between commercial interest groups, churches and citizens in the German states and their neighbours. For instance, religious leaders sought to effect reconciliation between Poles and Germans in the mid 1960s. Protestant bishops from West Germany stated their recognition of Poland's post-1945 borders and asked for forgiveness for the crimes of the Nazi era, and Polish bishops also sought forgiveness for the forced expulsion of ethnic Germans from Polish lands.[23] Furthermore, the increasing contact between Germans (and other Europeans) may have been as great a stimulus for détente as any official policy – not only were half a million calls made from West German phones to those in East Germany in 1969 (by 1989 the same figure was forty million), but Germans proved willing to send food parcels to Poland in the early 1980s, at the urging of their leader, Helmut Schmidt.[24] Such actions helped to encourage solidarity between peoples who in certain ways came to regard themselves once more as belonging to a shared Central Europe. This 'return of Central Europe' appealed not only to Germans but also to the civil-rights and dissident groups in Czechoslovakia, Poland and Hungary that were playing a vital political role in redefining the political sphere in the Communist bloc.[25] These groups sent each other fraternal letters, travelled to each other's meetings, and invited professors and politicians from Western Europe to their gatherings. Furthermore, they styled all of these initiatives as part of a conversation between fellow Europeans, which attracted widespread attention after the Czech exile, Milan Kundera, issued a call to save *Mitteleuropa* in the early 1980s.[26]

Fears that the Cold War would turn Central Europe into a nuclear and environmental wasteland also encouraged Czechs, Poles, and East and West Germans to seek a united Europe that was independent of the superpowers. Yet, their rediscovery of a shared European community of fate may have provoked a wider reassessment of a shared European history that had been repressed by the logic of the Cold War.[27] For instance, those in the East Central European nations that had expelled their German minorities after 1945 were forced to reconsider the multi-ethnic heritage of their cultures. This, in turn, encouraged them to understand European integration not simply as a marching forward to the future as part of a Western civilization but as a recuperation of a more integrated and multi-ethnic past, as well as entailing a return to Central Europe for the Germans. Similarly, West Germans (and Austrians) were once more reminded that they had not only been separated from their fellow Germans in the GDR but had also become detached from nations that had once included sizeable and influential German minorities.[28]

Such a rapprochement between Central Europeans (and a heightened fear of nuclear war) led to a resurgence in neutralist sentiment across the region in the early 1980s, although this did not affect the policy of Helmut Kohl, who reaffirmed his commitment to alliance with the United States in October 1982. In spite of this renewed show of loyalty to the American-led Western bloc, leaders of the CDU/FDP coalition continued to work to maximize the independence of the EC and to draw in the countries from Eastern Europe. For instance, Hans-Dietrich Genscher, the foreign minister in Kohl's government, worked with his Italian counterpart, Emilio Colombo, to put together a plan for a 'European Act' in 1981. This aimed, among other things, to 'ensure the independence of Europe' and indeed to see Europe playing its 'world-political role' as a united entity.[29] Such an attempt to deepen integration within the EC was complemented by efforts to extend the Community's borders in the late 1980s and early 1990s, with Kohl and his colleagues taking the lead in pushing for the integration of the East-Central European countries into the EC, against the scepticism of their French counterparts. As Kohl emphatically argued, the West European 'torso' should be reconnected to the rest of the European body politic.[30]

As has been shown, the East–West divide was not the only consideration for advocates of European integration throughout the twentieth century. Seeking to preserve and strengthen regional and local autonomy, political parties particularly in the southern states sought to shift power from the North to the South in Germany and Europe. Because of their commitment to a southern renaissance, many southern Germans provided support for a Western European union, believing it might provide the basis for constructing a genuinely federal Europe within which the states of southern Germany would have a greater weight than within the formerly unified Germany. This policy of strengthening federalism domestically through embracing European integration did not appear to pay significant dividends until at least the late 1970s, as national leaders took the leading role in managing the shape of European integration from the end of the 1950s onwards.[31] The late 1970s nevertheless saw the regions making louder demands for autonomy and, after much lobbying, the German states were given the right to consult over the formulation of European policy, although not granted formal policy-making rights.[32] Furthermore, the German states, which were something of a special case in Europe after 1945 in terms of the executive power they wielded within the nation-state, went on to be at the forefront of the moves in the 1980s and 1990s to enhance the role of the regions in the decision-making bodies of the EC/EU and in deciding how European development funds were distributed. This apparent rise of the regions was symbolized by the creating of a Committee of the Regions in 1994 and by the enshrining of the principle of subsidiarity within the EU according to the Maastricht Treaty of 1991.[33]

Whether such developments mean that in recent decades the EU has embarked on a path towards creating a Europe of the regions out of a Europe of nation-states is beyond the scope of this book. However, the shift towards enhancing regionalism has been one of a number of measures, including encouraging transnational civil society organizations, that have been adopted by European policy makers to bring the politics of the EU closer to Europe's citizens and to thereby reinforce the legitimacy of an EU facing a widening 'democratic deficit'.[34] Such measures indicate that EU policy makers recognize that a meaningful integration of Europeans involves more than a series of agreements between national leaders. Yet, as this book suggests, the creating of Europeans, and not just European institutions, is an unstable process, not least due to the different national approaches that persist even in the ways that Europeans conceptualize a Europe beyond national boundaries.[35] Rather than seek to sanitize these historically developed discourses by creating a foundational myth or an 'artificial consensus' among elites about the history of European integration, a recognition of the plurality of understandings and perceptions of Europe may provide a more plausible way of encouraging meaningful discussion and interaction between Europeans.[36] It is hoped that this book might prove to be of some relevance to such future endeavours.

Notes

1. Examples of this format abound, for instance A. Moravcsik, *The Choice for Europe: Social Purpose and State Power from Messina to Maastricht* (Ithaca: Cornell University Press, 1998); G. Brunn, *Die Europäische Einigung von 1945 bis heute* (Bonn: Bundeszentrale für politische Bildung, 2004); L. Herbst, W. Bührer and H. Sowade (eds), *Vom Marshallplan zur EWG. Die Eingliederung der Bundesrepublik Deutschland in die westliche Welt* (Munich: Oldenbourg, 1990); S. Henig, *The Uniting of Europe: From Consolidation to Enlargement* (London and New York: Routledge, 2002); R. McAlister, *From EC to EU: an historical and political survey* (London and New York: Routledge, 1997); D. Sidjanski, *Federal Future of Europe: From the European Community to the European Union* (Ann Arbor: University of Michigan Press, 2000).
2. On this see U. von Hirschhausen and K.K. Patel, 'Europeanization in History: An Introduction', in M. Conway and K. Klaus Patel (eds), *Europeanization in the Twentieth Century: Historical Approaches* (Houndmills: Palgrave, 2010) pp. 1–19.
3. The title is borrowed from the compendium 'German Culture between Yesterday and Tomorrow', J. Moras and H. Paeschke (eds), *Deutscher Geist zwischen Gestern und Morgen: Bilanz der kulturellen Entwicklung seit 1945* (Stuttgart: DEVA, 1954).
4. A. Doering-Manteuffel, *Katholizismus und Wiederbewaffnung: die Haltung der deutschen Katholiken gegenüber der Wehrfrage 1948–1955* (Mainz: Matthias-Grünewald, 1981).
5. Thanks to David Vincent for help with this point.
6. For more on this, see C. Offe, 'Is there, or can there be, a "European society"?', in J. Keane (ed.), *Civil Society: Berlin Perspectives* (New York and Oxford: Berghahn Books, 2007) pp. 169–77.
7. The suggestive metaphor of muted sentiments comes from M. Conway and V. Depkat, 'Towards a European History of the Discourse of Democracy: Discussing Democracy in Western Europe 1945-1960', in Conway and Patel, *Europeanization in the Twentieth Century*, p. 141;

and V. Depkat, *Lebenswenden und Zeitenwenden: Deutsche Politiker und die Erfahrungen des 20. Jahrhunderts* (Munich: Oldenbourg, 2007).
8. The classic account of this death of ideology is D. Bell, *The End of Ideology: On the Exhaustion of Political Ideas in the Fifties* (Cambridge: Harvard University Press, 1962).
9. For more on this, see M. Mazower, *Dark Continent: Europe's Twentieth Century* (New York: Vintage, 2000) pp. 3–40.
10. For a useful three-way comparison of these national approaches to European integration, see T. Risse, 'A European Identity? Europeanization and the Evolution of Nation-State Identities', in M. Green Cowles, T. Risse and J. Caporaso (eds), *Transforming Europe: Europeanization and Domestic Change* (Ithaca: Cornell University Press, 2001) pp. 198–216. For more on France and Germany, see F. Lynch, 'France and European Integration: From the Schuman Plan to Economic and Monetary Union', in *Contemporary European History* 13/1 (2004) 117–21; R. Douglas, *The Labour Party, Nationalism and Internationalism, 1939–1951: A New World Order* (London and New York: Routledge, 2004); R. Mayne and J. Pindar, *Federal Union: The Pioneers – A History of Federal Union* (London: Macmillan, 1990); J. Jackson, *France: The Dark Years 1940–1944* (Oxford: Oxford University Press, 2001) pp. 57–65, 72–81.
11. Brunn, *Europäische Einigung*, pp. 55, 63; G. Lundestad, *The United States and Western Europe since 1945 – From "Empire" by Invitation to Transatlantic Drift* (Oxford: Oxford University Press, 2003) pp. 43, 82.
12. See H.-U. Wehler, *Deutsche Gesellschaftsgeschichte.Fünfte Band Bundesrepublik und DDR 1949–1990* (Munich: Beck, 2008) p. 303; Risse, 'A European Identity?', in Cowles et al., *Transforming Europe*, pp. 198–216.
13. K. Gotto, 'Adenauers Deutschland- und Ostpolitik 1954–1963', in R. Morsey and K. Repgen (eds), *Adenauer Studien, Vol. 3: Untersuchungen und Dokumente zur Ostpolitik und Biographie* (Mainz: Matthias-Grünewald, 2nd ed., 1974) p. 48.
14. W. Loth, 'Adenauer's Final Western Choice,1955–58', in W. Loth (ed.), *Europe, Cold War and Co-Existence 1953–1965* (London: Frank Cass, 2004) pp. 26–30.
15. R. Dietl, '"Sole Master of the Western Nuclear Strength"? The United States, Western Europe and the Elusiveness of a European Defence Identity, 1959–64', in Loth, *Europe, Cold War and Co-Existence*, pp. 141–42. See also R. Granieri, *The Ambivalent Alliance: Konrad Adenauer, the CDU-CSU, and the West, 1949–1966* (New York and Oxford: Berghahn Books, 2003) pp. 1–22. For a rather different reading of how the Atlantic alliance developed during the 1960s, see A. Kempa, 'Reaction to French Withdrawal: The Reconstruction of the Atlantic Alliance, 1966–1968' (DPhil Thesis, University of Oxford, 2010).
16. R. Spaulding, *Osthandel und Ostpolitik: German Foreign Trade Policies in Eastern Europe from Bismarck to Adenauer* (Providence RI and Oxford: Berghahn Books, 1997) p. 3.
17. See K. Larres, 'Britain, East Germany and Détente: British Policy toward the GDR and West Germany's "Policy of Movement", 1955–65', and C. Schukraft, 'Die Anfänge der deutschen Europapolitik in den 50er und 60er Jahren: Weichenstellungen unter Konrad Adenauer und Bewahrung des Status quo unter seinen Nachfolgern Ludwig Erhard und Kurt Georg Kiesinger', in G. Müller-Brandeck-Bocquet et al., *Deutsche Europapolitik. Von Adenauer bis Merkel* (Wiesbaden: VS 2nd ed., 2010) p. 32.
18. Schukraft, 'Anfänge der deutschen Europapolitik', in Müller-Brandeck-Bocquet, *Deutsche Europapolitik*, p. 41.
19. Spaulding, *Osthandel und Ostpolitik*, p. 488.
20. Schukraft, 'Anfänge der deutschen Europapolitik', in Müller-Brandeck-Bocquet, *Deutsche Europapolitik*, p. 58.
21. N. Leuchtweis, 'Deutsche Europapolitik zwischen Aufbruchstimmung und Weltwirtschaftskrise: Willy Brandt und Helmut Schmidt', in Müller-Brandeck-Bocquet, *Deutsche Europapolitik*, pp. 70–71.
22. Leuchtweis, 'Deutsche Europapolitik zwischen Aufbruchstimmung und Weltwirtschaftskrise', in Müller-Brandeck-Bocquet, *Deutsche Europapolitik*, pp. 85–96.

23. T. Garton Ash, *In Europe's Name: Germany and the Divided Continent* (London: Vintage, 1994) p. 299.
24. Garton Ash, *In Europe's Name*, p. 139.
25. J.K. Glenn, *Framing Democracy: Civil Society and Civic Movements in Eastern Europe* (Stanford: Stanford University Press, 2001) p. 25.
26. See J. Wardhaugh, R. Leiserowitz and C. Bailey, 'Creation of European Spaces', in Conway and Patel, *Europeanization in the Twentieth Century*, pp. 32–39; T. Judt, 'The Rediscovery of Central Europe', in *Daedalus* 119/1 (1990) 23–54; P. Ther, 'Milan Kundera und die Renaissance *Zentraleuropas*', in *Themenportal Europäische Geschichte* (2007), accessible at: http://www.europa.clio-online.de/2007/Article=153
27. J. Rupnik, 'Central Europe or Mitteleuropa?', in *Daedalus* 119/1 (1990) 249–78.
28. G. Delanty, *Inventing Europe: Idea, Identity, Reality* (Houndmills: Palgrave, 1995), pp. 132–38.
29. U. Kessler, 'Deutsche Europapolitik unter Helmut Kohl: Europäische Integration als "kategorische Imperativ"?', in Müller-Brandeck-Bocquet, *Deutsche Europapolitik*, pp. 121–23.
30. Kessler, 'Deutsche Europapolitik unter Helmut Kohl', in Müller-Brandeck-Bocquet, *Deutsche Europapolitik*, pp. 132–40, 163
31. On this see A. Milward, *The European Rescue of the Nation-State* (London and New York: Routledge 2nd ed., 2000) esp. pp. 21–45.
32. Leuchtweis, 'Deutsche Europapolitik', in Müller-Brandeck-Bocquet, *Deutsche Europapolitik*, p. 99.
33. J. Anderson, 'The exaggerated death of the nation state', in J. Anderson, C. Brook, and A. Cochrane (eds), *A Global World? Re-ordering Political Space* (Oxford: Oxford University Press, 1995); C. Harvie, *The Rise of Regional Europe* (London and New York: Routledge, 1994); C. Jeffery (ed.), *The Regional Dimension of the European Union: Towards a Third Level in Europe?* (London and New York: Routledge, 1997).
34. This was even as power has been shifted away from bureaucrats on the European Commission towards politicians within the European parliament since Maastricht. http://eur-lex.europa.eu/en/treaties/dat/11992M/htm/11992M.html; J. Steffek and P. Nanz, 'Emergent Patterns of Civil Society. Participation in Global and European Governance', in J. Steffek, C. Kissling and P. Nanz (eds.), *Civil Society Participation in European and Global Governance: A Cure for the Democratic Deficit* (Houndmills: Palgrave, 2007), p. 1.
35. On this, see J. Lacroix and K. Nicolaïdis (eds), *European Stories: Intellectual Debates on Europe in National Contexts* (Oxford: Oxford University Press, 2010).
36. The phrase 'artificial consensus' is taken from M. Freeden, 'On European and Other Intellectuals', in Lacroix and Nicolaïdis, *European Stories*, p. 84.

Bibliography

Primary Sources

Manuscript Collections, Germany

Berlin, Germany
Bundesarchiv, Berlin
   R 56 V Reichschrifttumskammer 1933–1945
Politisches Archiv des Auswärtigen Amts, Berlin
   Inland II A/B
   Inland IIg
Bonn Bad-Godesberg, Germany
Archiv der sozialen Demokratie, Friedrich Ebert Stiftung
   Bestand Internationaler Sozialistischer Kampfbund/Internationaler Jugend Bund
   Digitales Archiv, Flugblätter und Flugschriften
   Nachlass (Papers) Otto Braun
   Nachlass Willi Eichler
   Nachlass Heinrich Ritzel
Marbach, Germany
Deutsches Literaturarchiv, Marbach
Handschriften-Abteilung (Handwritten Documents Section)
   A: Merkur, Teilnachlass Hans Paeschke
   D: Merkur, Redaktionsarchiv aus den Jahren 1946–1978
Munich, Germany
Institut für Zeitgeschichte, Munich
   ED 117: Nachlass Fritz Eberhard
   ED 120: Nachlass Wilhelm Hoegner
   ED 132: Nachlass Josef Baumgartner

Manuscript Collections, France

Colmar, France
Ministères des Affaires étrangères
Archives de l'Occupation en Allemagne et en Autriche
   AC 34/6: Revue Lancelot (1948–1951)
   AC 79/7: Maison d'édition, Lancelot (1949–1951)
   AC 917/3: Merkur, Baden-Baden (1946–1949)
   AC 969/7: Merkur, Baden-Baden (1949–1950)
   AC 972/1: Paeschke Hans: Baden-Baden (1947–1948)
   AC 1097/11: Merkur, Buch Verlag

Manuscript Collections, United Kingdom

Warwick
Modern Records Centre, University of Warwick.
  Socialist Vanguard Group Archive, MSS. 173
Oxford
Bodleian Library, University of Oxford
  Society for the Protection of Science and Learning Papers, MSS. S.P.S.L.

Manuscript Collections, United States

College Park, Maryland
National Archives II, College Park
  RG 226: Records of the Office of Strategic Services 1940–1946
  RG 226: CIA Selected Documents 1941–1947
  RG 260: Office of the Military Government (U.S.), Germany

Interviews

11 July, 2006: Interview with Gene Mater, Media Consultant at the Freedom Forum, Washington D.C. Former member of the U.S. Army in Germany during the Second World War and Head of the News Division of Radio Free Europe.
20 June, 2007: Interview with Kurt Scheel, Assistant Editor, *Merkur: Deutsche Zeitschrift für Europäisches Denken*.

Periodicals

The Atlantic Times, 2007
Bayerische Verwaltungsblätter, 1963
Berlinische Monatsschrift, 2000-2001
Börsenblatt für den Deutschen Buchhandel, 1990
Contemporary British History, 2002
Contemporary European History, 2004
Daedalus, 1990
Europäische Revue, 1925–1944
Europe Speaks, 1942–1946
European History Quarterly, 1975-2004
European Review of History, 2000
Exilforschung: Ein internationales Jahrbuch, 1983–
Foreign Affairs, 1997
Frankfurter Hefte: Zeitschrift für Kultur und Politik, 1946–1948
Freiburger Dioezesan-Archiv, 1981
Freie Sozialistischer Tribüne, 1934–1938
Geist und Tat: Monatsschrift für Recht, Freiheit und Kultur, 1946–1955
German History, 1997-2011
German Life and Letters, 1998
German Studies Review, 1984
Government and Opposition, 1967–1979
The Historical Journal, 2001

History and Memory, 2005
The History of European Ideas, 2005
International History Review, 2009
Internationale Wissenschaftliche Korrespondenz zur Geschichte der deutschen Arbeiterbewegung, 1988
Janata: Weekly Journal of the Indian Socialist Party, 1949
Jewish Political Studies Review, 2002-2006
Journal of Church and State, 1979
Journal of the History of Ideas, 2006
Merkur: Deutsche Zeitschrift für Europäisches Denken, 1947–
Mitteilungsblätter der Arbeitsgemeinschaft 'Demokratisches Deutschland', 1946–1951
Der Monat: Eine internationale Zeitschrift für Politik und geistiges Leben, 1948–1952
Die Neue Rundschau, 1926–1943
News from Germany, 1949
Recherches Germaniques, 1988
Review of International Studies, 2002
Der Ruf: Unabhängige Blätter der jungen Generation, 1946–1950
Schweizer Monatshefte, 1945
Sozialistische Mitteilungen: News for German Socialists in England, 1939–1948
Sozialistische Warte: Blätter für kritisch-aktiven Sozialismus, 1934–1940
Der Spiegel, 1947–
Theory and Psychology, 2001
Tilkal: The Journal of Tol Harndor, 2005
Twentieth Century British History, 1999
Vierteljahreshefte für Zeitgeschichte, 1977–1985
Die Wandlung, 1945–1949
Weimarer Beiträge, 2003

SECONDARY SOURCES

Adant, P. 1996. *Widerstand und Wagemut. René Bertholet – eine Biographie*. Frankfurt am Main: Dipa.
D'Agostino, P. 2004. *Rome in America: Transnational Catholic Ideology from the Risorgimento to Fascism*. Chapel Hill: University of North Carolina Press.
Aldcroft, D. 1977. *From Versailles to Wall Street 1919–1929*. Berkeley and Los Angeles: University of California Press.
Aly, G. 2005. *Hitler's Volksstaat: Raub, Rassenkrieg und nationaler Sozialismus*. Frankfurt am Main: Fischer.
Anderson, J., C. Brook, and A. Cochrane (eds). 1995. *A Global World? Re-ordering Political Space*. Oxford: Oxford University Press.
Anderson, P. 2009. 'A New Germany?', in *New Left Review* 57.
Angster, J. 2003. *Konsenskapitalismus und Sozialdemokratie. Die Westernisierung von SPD und DGB*. Munich: Oldenbourg.
Applegate, C. 1990. *A Nation of Provincials: The German Idea of Heimat*. Berkeley: University of California Press.

Arendt, H. 1963. *Eichmann in Jerusalem: A Report on the Banality of Evil.* New York: Viking Press.

Atack, M. 1989. *Literature and the French Resistance: cultural politics and narrative forms 1940–1950.* Manchester: Manchester University Press.

Aubrac, R. 1997. *French Resistance 1940–1944.* Paris: Hazan.

Auden, W.H. (ed. E. Mendelson) 1994. *Collected Poems.* London: Faber and Faber.

Azuélos, D. 2006. *Lion Feuchtwanger und die deutschsprachigen Emigranten in Frankreich von 1933 bis 1941.* Berne: Peter Lang.

Baer, F. 1971 *Die Ministerpräsidenten Bayerns: 1945–1962. Dokumente und Analyse.* Munich: Beck.

Bailey, C. 2010a. 'The Continuities of West German History: Conceptions of Europe, Democracy and the West in Interwar and Postwar Germany', in *Geschichte und Gesellschaft* 36/4.

———. 2010b. 'The European Discourse in Germany, 1939–1950: Three Case-Studies', in *German History* 28/4.

Baker D. and D. Seawright (eds). 1998. *Britain For and Against Europe: British Politics and the Question of European Integration.* Oxford: Oxford University Press.

Balcar, J. 2004. *Politik auf dem Land: Studien zur bayerischen Provinz, 1945 bis 1972.* Munich: Oldenbourg.

Balfour, M. 1979. *Propaganda in War 1939–1945. Organisations, Policies and Publics in Britain and Germany.* London: Routledge.

———. 1988. *Withstanding Hitler, 1933–1945.* London: Routledge.

Ball, T. and R. Bellamy (eds). 2002. *The Cambridge History of Political Thought.* Cambridge: Cambridge University Press.

Barclay, D.E. and E.D. Weitz (eds). 1998. *Between Reform and Revolution: German Socialism and Communism from 1840 to 1990.* New York and Oxford: Berghahn Books.

Bark, D. and D. Gress. 1989. *A History of West Germany, Vol. 1: From Shadow to Substance 1945–1963.* Oxford: Blackwell.

Bassett, R. 2005. *Hitler's Spy Chief: The Wilhelm Canaris Mystery.* London: Weidenfeld and Nicolson.

Bauer, H. and H. Ritzel. 1940. *Von der Eidgenössischen zur Europäischen Föderation.* Zurich and New York: Europa

———. 1945. *Kampf um Europa. Von der Schweiz aus gesehen*, Zurich and New York: Europa.

Bautz, T. (ed.). 2003. *Biographisch-bibliographisches Kirchenlexikon* Vol. 21. Nordhausen: Traugott Bautz.

Beale, M. 1999. *The Modernist Enterprise: French Elites and the Threat of Modernity 1901–1940.* Stanford: Stanford University Press.

Behmer, M. (ed.). 2000. *Deutsche Publizistik im Exil 1933 bis 1945: Personen – Positionen – Perspektiven.* Munster: Lit.

Behr, W. 1969. *Sozialdemokratie und Konservatismus. Ein empirischer und theoretischer Beitrag zur regionalen Parteianalyse am Beispiel der Geschichte und Nachkriegsentwicklung Bayerns.* Hannover: Verlag für Literatur und Zeitgeschehen.

Behring, R. 1999. *Demokratische Außenpolitik für Deutschland. Die außenpolitischen Vorstellungen deutscher Sozialdemokraten im Exil 1933–1945.* Düsseldorf: Droste.

Beier, G. 1983. *Schulter an Schulter, Schritt für Schritt. Lebensläufe deutscher Gewerkschafter*. Cologne: Bund.
Belitz, I. 1997. *Befreundung mit dem Fremden. Die Deutsch-Französische Gesellschaft in den deutsch-französischen Kultur- und Gesellschaftsbeziehungen der Locarno-Ära. Programme und Protagonisten der transnationalen Verständigung zwischen Pragmatismus und Idealismus*. Frankfurt am Main: Peter Lang.
Bell, D. 1962. *The End of Ideology: On the Exhaustion of Political Ideas in the Fifties*. Cambridge: Harvard University Press.
Beloff, M. 1963. *The United States and the Unity of Europe*. New York: Vintage.
Bengtsson, J.O. 2006. *The Worldview of Personalism: Origins and Early Development*. Oxford: Oxford University Press.
Benn, G., H., Paeschke and J. Moras (ed. H. Hof). 2004. *Briefe Band VII. Briefwechsel 1948–1956*. Stuttgart: Klett-Cotta.
Benz, W. (ed.). 1988. *Neuanfang in Bayern 1945 bis 1949*. Munich: Beck.
Berend, I. 1999. *Central and Eastern Europe 1944–1993: Detour from the Periphery to the Periphery*. Cambridge: Cambridge University Press.
Berg, M.P. (ed.). 2000. *The Struggle for a Democratic Austria: Bruno Kreisky on Peace and Social Justice*. New York and Oxford: Berghahn Books.
Berger, S. 1991. *The Development of Legitimating Ideas: Intellectuals and Politicians in Post-War Western Germany*. New York and London: Garland.
———. 1994. *The British Labour Party and the German Social Democrats, 1900–1931*. Oxford: Oxford University Press.
Berghahn, V. 2001. *America and the Intellectual Cold Wars in Europe: Shepard Stone between Philanthropy, Academy, and Diplomacy*. Princeton: Princeton University Press.
Bergmann, K.H. 1974. *Die Bewegung "Freies Deutschland" in der Schweiz 1943–1945*. Munich: Hanser.
Berman, S. 2006. *The Primacy of Politics: Social Democracy and the Making of Europe's Twentieth Century*. Cambridge: Cambridge University Press.
Bermeo, N. and P. Nord (eds). 2000. *Civil Society before Democracy: Lessons from Nineteenth-Century Europe*. Lanham: Rowman and Littlefield.
Betz, A, and S. Martens (eds). 2004. *Les intellectuels et l'Occupation 1940–1944: Collaborer, Partir, Resister*. Paris: Autrement.
Biller, M. 1994. *Exilstationen. Eine empirische Untersuchung zur Emigration und Remigration deutschsprachiger Journalisten und Publizisten*. Münster and Hamburg: Lit.
Black, L. 1999. 'Social Democracy as a Way of Life: Fellowship and the Socialist Union, 1951–9', in *Twentieth Century British History* 10/4.
Blackbourn, D. 2003. *History of Germany 1780–1918: The Long Nineteenth Century*. Oxford, Blackwell 2nd ed.
Blasius, R. 1989. *Dokumente zur Deutschlandpolitik* First Series, Vol. 3, *1. Januar bis 31. Dezember 1942: Britische Deutschlandpolitik*. Frankfurt am Main: Alfred Metzner.
Blumenwitz, D. et al. (ed.). 1976. *Konrad Adenauer und seine Zeit. Politik und Persönlichkeit des ersten Bundeskanzlers, Bd. 1: Beiträge von Weg- und Zeitgenossen*. Stuttgart: DEVA.
Bock, H.-M. (ed.). 2005. *Französische Kultur im Berlin der Weimarer Republik. Kulturelle Austausch und diplomatische Beziehungen*. Tübingen: Narr

———. 1988. 'André François-Poncet und die Deutschen. Eine biographische Skizze', in *Dokumente: Zeitschrift für den deutsch-französischen Dialog* 44.
Boehling, R. 1996. *A Question of Priorities. Democratic Reform and Economic Recovery in Postwar Germany*. Providence RI and Oxford: Berghahn Books.
Bonart, P. 2007. *But We Said 'No': Voices from the German Underground*. San Francisco: Mark Backman.
Booker, C. and R. North. 2003. *The Great Deception: A Secret History of the European Union*. London: Continuum.
Borchers, H. and K. Vowe (eds).1979. *Die zarte Pflanze Demokratie. Amerikanische Re-education in Deutschland im Spiegel ausgewählter politischer und literarischer Zeitschriften (1945–1949)*. Tübingen: Narr.
Borkenau, F. (ed. with int. by R. Löwenthal). 1981. *End and Beginning: On the Generations of Culture and the Origins of the West*. New York: Columbia University Press.
Borsdorf, U. and L. Niethammer (eds).1976. *Zwischen Befreiung und Besatzung. Analysen des US-Geheimdienstes über Positionen und Strukturen deutscher Politik*. Wuppertal: Hammer.
Bosl, K. (ed. E. Bosl). 1998. *Vorträge zur Geschichte Europas, Deutschlands und Bayerns*. Stuttgart, Anton Hiersemann.
Bourdieu, P. (ed. with int. J.B. Thompson). 1991. *Language and Symbolic Power*. Cambridge MA: Harvard University Press.
——— (ed. with int. R. Johnson). 1993. *The Field of Cultural Production: Essays on Art and Literature*. New York: Columbia University Press.
Brady, J., B. Crawford and S. Wiliarty (eds). 1999. *The Postwar Transformation of Germany: Democracy, Prosperity and Nationhood*. Ann Arbor: University of Michigan Press.
Brady, S.J. 2010. *Eisenhower and Adenauer: Alliance Maintenance under Pressure, 1953–1960*. Lanham: Rowman and Littlefield.
Braun, O. 1940. *Von Weimar zu Hitler*. New York: Europa 2nd ed.
Brecht, A. 1945. *Federalism and Regionalism in Germany. The Division of Prussia*. New York: Oxford University Press.
Brechtefeld, J. 1996. *Mitteleuropa and German Politics: 1848 to the Present*. London: Macmillan.
Bremer, J. 1978. *Die Sozialistische Arbeiterpartei Deutschlands (SAP): Untergrund und Exil, 1933–1945*. Frankfurt am Main: Campus.
Brender, R. 1992. *Kollaboration in Frankreich im Zweiten Weltkrieg. Marcel Déat und das Rassemblement national populaire*. Munich: Oldenbourg.
Brinkley, D. and D. Facey-Crowther (eds). 1994. *The Atlantic Charter*. New York: St.Martin's Press.
Brubaker, R. 1992. *Citizenship and Nationhood in France and Germany*. Cambridge MA: Harvard University Press.
Brunn, G. 2004. *Die Europäische Einigung von 1945 bis heute*. Bonn: Bundeszentrale für politische Bildung.
Brunner, J. (ed.). 2008. *Mütterliche Macht und väterliche Autorität: Elternbilder im deutschen Diskurs (Tel Aviver Jahrbuch für deutsche Geschichte 2008)*. Göttingen: Wallstein.

Bude, H. and B. Greiner (eds). 1999. *Westbindungen: Amerika in der Bundesrepublik*. Hamburg: Hamburger Edition.

Bungert, H. 1997. *Das Nationalkomitee und der Westen. Die Reaktion der Westalliierten auf das NKFD und die Freien Deutschen Bewegungen 1943–1948*. Stuttgart: Franz Steiner.

Burgess, M. 2000. *Federalism and European Union: the Building of Europe, 1950–2000*. London and New York: Routledge.

Caestecker, F. and B. Moore (eds). 2010. *Refugees from Nazi Germany and the Liberal European States*. New York and Oxford: Berghahn Books.

Canoy, J.R. 2005. *The Discreet Charm of the Police State: The Landpolizei and the Transformation of Bavaria, 1945–1965*. Leiden: Brill.

Carsten, F. 1988. *Revolution in Central Europe, 1918–1919*. Aldershot: Wildwood House.

Cary, N. 1996. *The Path to Christian Democracy: German Catholics and the Party System from Windthorst to Adenauer*. Cambridge MA: Harvard University Press.

Casey, S. and J. Wright (eds). 2008. *Mental Maps in the Era of Two World Wars*. Basingstoke: Palgrave.

Ceadel, M. 2000. *Semi-detached Idealists: The British Peace Movement and International Relations, 1854–1945*. Oxford: Oxford University Press.

Charle, C., J. Schriewer and P. Wagner (eds). 2004. *Transnational Intellectual Networks: Forms of Academic Knowledge and the Search for Cultural Identities*. Frankfurt am Main: Campus.

Cini, M. and A. Bourne (eds). 2008. *From State to Society? The Historiography of European Integration*. Basingstoke: Palgrave.

Cipolla, F. (ed.). 1973–1974. *The Fontana Economic History of Europe, Vol. 2*. London: Collins.

Clemens, G. (ed.). 1994. *Kulturpolitik im besetzten Deutschland 1945–1949. Berichte und Dokumente*. Stuttgart.

———. 1997. *Britische Kulturpolitik in Deutschland 1945–1949: Literatur, Film, Musik und Theater*. Stuttgart: Franz Steiner.

Collini, S., D. Winch and J. Burrow (eds). 1983. *That Noble Science of Politics: A Study in Nineteenth Century Intellectual History*. Cambridge: Cambridge University Press.

Conway, M. 2002. 'Democracy in Postwar Western Europe: The Triumph of a Political Model', in *European History Quarterly* 32/1.

Conway, M. and J. Gotovitch. 2001. *Europe in Exile: European Exile Communities in Britain, 1940–1945*. Oxford and New York: Berghahn Books.

Conway, M. and K. Klaus Patel (eds). 2010. *Europeanization in the Twentieth Century: Historical Approaches*. Basingstoke: Palgrave.

Conway, M. and P. Romijn (eds). 2008. *The War for Legitimacy in Politics and Culture 1936–1946*. Oxford: Berg.

Conze, V. 2005. *Das Europa der Deutschen: Ideen von Europa in Deutschland zwischen Reichstradition und Westorientierung*. Munich: Oldenbourg.

Cook, C. and J. Paxton. 2001. *European Political Facts of the Twentieth Century*. New York: Palgrave.

Costigliola, F. 1984. *Awkward Dominion: American Political, Economic and Cultural Relations with Europe 1919–1933*. Ithaca: Cornell University Press.

Cowles, M., T. Risse and J. Caporaso (eds). 2001. *Transforming Europe: Europeanization and Domestic Change*. Ithaca: Cornell University Press.

Daniels, R. (ed.). 1994. *A Documentary History of Communism and the World: From Revolution to Collapse*. Hanover: University of New England Press.

von Dannenberg, J. 2008. *The Foundations of Ostpolitik. The Making of the Moscow Treaty between West Germany and the USSR*. Oxford: Oxford University Press.

Dedman, M. *The Origins and Development of the European Union, 1945–2008: A History of European Integration*. London and New York: Routledge 2nd ed., 2010.

Delanty, G. 1995. *Inventing Europe: Idea, Identity, Reality*. Basingstoke: Palgrave.

Depkat, V. 2007. *Lebenswenden und Zeitenwenden: Deutsche Politiker und die Erfahrungen des 20. Jahrhunderts*. Munich: Oldenbourg.

Diamond, H. and S. Kitson (eds). 2005. *Vichy, Resistance, Liberation: New Perspectives on Wartime France*. Oxford: Berg.

Dimitrakopoulos, D. (ed.). 2011. *Social Democracy and European Integration: The Politics of Preference Formation*. London and New York: Routledge.

Dinan, D. 2004. *Europe Recast: A History of European Union*. Boulder CO: Lynne Rienner.

Döblin, A. 1993. *Schicksalsreise: Bericht und Bekenntnis*. Solothurn und Düsseldorf: Walter.

Doering-Manteuffel, A. 1981. *Katholizismus und Wiederbewaffnung: die Haltung der deutschen Katholiken gegenüber der Wehrfrage 1948–1955*. Mainz: Matthias-Grünewald.

———. 1999. *Wie westlich sind die Deutschen? Amerikanisierung und Westernisierung in 20. Jahrhundert*. Göttingen: Vanderhoeck and Ruprecht.

Douglas, R. 2004. *The Labour Party, Nationalism and Internationalism, 1939–1951*. London and New York: Routledge.

Dove, R. (ed.). 2005. *'Totally Un-English'? Britain's Internment of 'Enemy Aliens' in Two World Wars: The Yearbook of the Research Centre for German and Austrian Exile Studies (Vol. 7)*. Amsterdam: Rodopi.

Dowe, D. and K. Klotzbach (eds). 1973. *Programmatische Dokumente der deutschen Sozialdemokratie*. Berlin and Bonn Bad Godesberg: Dietz.

Duchhardt, H. et al. (eds). 2007. *Europa-Historiker. Ein biographisches Handbuch*, Volumes 2–3. Göttingen: Vanderhoeck and Ruprecht.

Duignan, P. and L.H. Gann. 1992. *The Rebirth of the West: the Americanization of the Democratic World, 1945–1958*. Cambridge MA: Blackwell.

Dulles, A. (ed. N. Petersen). 1996. *From Hitler's Doorstep: The Wartime Intelligence Reports of Allen Dulles, 1942–1945*. University Park PA: Pennsylvania State University Press.

Dyson, K. and K.H. Goetz (eds). 2003. *Germany, Europe and the Politics of Constraint*. Oxford: British Academy/Oxford University Press.

Eberhard, F. 1981. *Arbeit gegen das Dritte Reich*. Berlin: Informationszentrum Berlin, Gedenk- und Bildungsstätte Stauffenbergstrasse 3rd ed.

Eckert, B., G. von Glasenapp and B. Brunn. *Inventar zu den Nachlässen emigrierter deutschsprachiger Wissenschaftler in Archiven und Bibliotheken der Bundesrepublik Deutschland*. Munich: K.G. Saur.

Edinger, L. 1965. *Kurt Schumacher: A Study in Personality and Political Behavior*. Stanford: Stanford University Press.

Eiber, L. (ed.). 1998. *Die Sozialdemokratie in der Emigration. Die "Union deutscher sozialistischer Organisationen in Großbritannien" 1941–1946 und ihre Mitglieder. Protokolle, Erklärungen, Materialien.* Bonn: Dietz.
Eichler, W. 1942. *Calling All Europe. A Symposium of Speeches on the Future Order of Europe.* London.
———. 1962. *100 Jahre Sozialdemokratie.* Bonn: SPD.
———. 1967. *Weltanschauung und Politik. Reden und Aufsätze.* Frankfurt am Main: Europäische Verlagsanstalt.
———. 1970. *Individuum und Gesellschaft im Verständnis demokratischer Sozialisten.* Hannover: Niedersächsische Landeszentrale fur Politische Bildung.
———. 1972. *Zur Einführung in den demokratischen Sozialismus.* Bonn Bad Godesberg: Neue Gesellschaft.
Eisermann D. 1999. *Außenpolitik und Strategiediskussion. Die Deutsche Gesellschaft für Auswärtige Politik 1955–1972.* Munich: Oldenbourg.
Eley, G. 2002. *Forging Democracy: The History of the Left in Europe, 1850–2000.* New York: Oxford University Press.
Elvert, J. 1999. *Mitteleuropa! Deutsche Pläne zur europäischen Neuordnung (1918–1945).* Stuttgart: Franz Steiner.
Ermakoff, I. 2008. *Ruling Oneself Out: A Theory of Collective Abdications.* Durham: Duke University Press.
Ermarth, M. (ed.) 1993. *America and the Shaping of German Society, 1945–1955.* Oxford: Berg.
Eschenburg, T. (ed.). 1983. *Geschichte der Bundesrepublik Deutschland, Vol. I: Jahre der Besatzung, 1945–1949.* Stuttgart: DEVA.
Fait, B. 1998. *Demokratische Erneuerung unter dem Sternenbanner. Amerikanische Kontrolle und Verfassunggebung in Bayern 1946.* Düsseldorf: Droste.
Fink, C., A. Frohn and J. Heideking (eds). 1991. *Genoa, Rapallo and European Reconstruction in 1922.* Cambridge: Cambridge University Press.
Fischer, C. (ed.). 1987. *From Bernstein to Brandt.* London: Edwin Arnold.
———. 2011. *Europe between Dictatorship and Democracy: 1900–1945.* Chichester: Wiley-Blackwell.
Fleury, A., H. Möller, and H.-P. Schwarz (eds). 2004. *Die Schweiz und Deutschland 1945–1961.* Munich: Oldenbourg.
Fliess, W. 1944. *The Economic Reconstruction of Europe.* London: International Publishing Company.
Foitzik, J. 1986. *Zwischen den Fronten: Zur Politik, Organisation und Funktion linker politischer Kleinorganisationen im Widerstand 1933 bis 1939/40.* Bonn: Neue Gesellschaft.
———. 1988. 'Revolution und Demokratie. Zu den Sofort- und Übergangsplanungen des sozialdemokratischen Exils für Deutschland 1943–1945', *Internationale Wissenschaftliche Korrespondenz zur Geschichte der deutschen Arbeiterbewegung, Jr. 24.*
Foot, M.R.D. 1984. *S.O.E. An Outline History of the Special Operations Executive 1940–1946.* London: Greenwood Press/BBC.
Forkmann, D. and M. Schlieben (eds). 2005. *Die Parteivorsitzenden in der Bundesrepublik Deutschland 1949–2005.* Wiesbaden: VS.
Foschepoth, J. and R. Steininger (eds). 1985. *Die britische Deutschland und Besatzungspolitik 1945–1949.* Paderborn: Ferdinand Schöningh.

Fraenkel, E. (eds A. von Bruenneck, H. Buchstein and G. Göhler). 1999. *Gesammelte Schriften. Band 3: Neuaufbau der Demokratie in Deutschland und Korea*. Baden-Baden: Nomos.
Fraenkel, E. 1957. *USA – Weltmacht wider Willen*. Berlin: Colloquium.
Freede, L. 2007. '"Botschafter der Musik": The Berlin Philharmonic Orchestra and the Role of Classical Music in Post-War German Identity', in *Modern Humanities Research Association Working Papers*, 2.
Frevert, U. 2003. *Eurovisionen: Ansichten gute Europäer im 19. und 20. Jahrhundert*. Frankfurt am Main: Fischer.
——. 2005. 'Europeanizing Germany's Twentieth Century', in *History and Memory* 17.1/2.
Friedrich, D. 2011. *Democratic Participation and Civil Society in the European Union*. Manchester and New York: Manchester University Press.
Fritz-Bournazel, R. 1992. *Europe and German Reunification*. Providence and Oxford: Berg.
Gaddis, J. 1997. *We Now Know: Rethinking Cold War History*. Oxford: Oxford University Press.
——. 2005. *Strategies of Containment: A Critical Appraisal of American National Security Policy During the Cold War*. Oxford: Oxford University Press 2nd ed.
Gaffney, J. 1996. *Political Parties and the European Union*. London and New York: Routledge.
Gallus, A. 2001. *Die Neutralisten: Verfechter eines vereinten Deutschlands zwischen Ost und West 1945–1990*. Dusseldorf: Droste.
Gareau, F. 1961. 'Morgenthau's Plan for Industrial Disarmament in Germany', in *The Western Political Quarterly*, 14/2
Garton Ash, T. 1994. *In Europe's Name: Germany and the Divided Continent*. London: Vintage.
Gehler, M. and W. Kaiser (eds). 2004. *Christian Democracy in Europe since 1945, Volume 2*. London and New York: Routledge.
Gehler, M. and R. Steininger (eds). 2000. *Die Neutralen und die europäische Integration 1945–1995*. Vienna: Böhlau.
Gehler, M., W. Kaiser and H. Wohnout (eds). 2001. *Christdemokratie in Europa im 20. Jahrhundert*. Vienna: Böhlau.
Gelberg, K.-U. 1992. *Hans Ehard. Die föderalistische Politik des bayerischen Ministerpräsidenten 1946–1954*. Düsseldorf: Droste.
——. 1997a. *Die Protokolle der SPD-Fraktion in der bayerischen verfassungsgebenden Landesversammlung 1946'*. ZBLG 60.
——. (ed.). 1997b. *Die Protokolle des bayerischen Ministerrats 1945–1954. Das Kabinett Hoegner I. 28. September 1945 bis 21. Dezember 1946*. Munich: Oldenbourg.
Gentile, E. 2006. *Politics as Religion*. Princeton: Princeton University Press.
Geppert, D. and U. Wengst (eds). 2005. *Neutralität – Chance oder Chimäre? Konzepte des Dritten Weges für Deutschland und die Welt 1945–1990*. Munich: Oldenbourg.
Geyer, M. and J. Paulmann (eds). 2001. *The Mechanics of Internationalism: Culture, Society and Politics from the 1840s to the First World War*. Oxford: Oxford University Press.

Ghosh, P. 2005. 'Max Weber on "The Rural Community": A critical edition of the English text' in *The History of European Ideas*, 31/3.
Gienow-Hecht, J. 1999. *Transmission Impossible: American Journalism as Cultural Diplomacy in Postwar Germany, 1945–1955*. Baton Rouge: Louisiana State University Press.
Gienow-Hecht, J. and F. Schumacher (eds). 2003. *Culture and International History*. New York and Oxford: Berghahn Books.
Gilmore, R. 1973. *France's Postwar Cultural Policies and Activities*. Washington DC: Balmare Reprographics.
Ginsborg, P. 2003. *A History of Contemporary Italy: Society and Politics, 1943–1988*. Basingstoke: Palgrave.
Glassheim, E. 2005. *Noble Nationalists: The Transformation of the Bohemian Aristocracy*. Cambridge MA: Harvard University Press.
Glees, A. 1982. *Exile Politics during the Second World War: The German Social Democrats in Britain*. Oxford: Oxford University Press.
———. 1996. *Reinventing Germany: German Political Development since 1945*. Oxford: Berg.
Glenn, J.K. 2001. *Framing Democracy: Civil Society and Civic Movements in Eastern Europe*. Stanford: Stanford University Press.
Göhler, G. and B. Zeuner (eds). 1991. *Kontinuitäten und Brüche in der deutschen Politikwissenschaft*. Baden-Baden: Nomos.
Görres-Gesellschaft (ed.). 1985. *Staatslexikon. Recht, Wirtschaft, Gesellschaft in 5 Banden. Erster Band*. Freiburg im Breisgau: Herder 7th ed.
Graf, C. (ed.). 1996. *Die Schweiz und die Flüchtlinge 1933–1945*. Berne: Haupt.
Graf, W. 1976. *The German Left since 1945. Socialism and Social Democracy in the German Federal Republic*. Cambridge: Oleander.
Gramsci, A., (eds Q. Hoare and G. Nowell Smith).1981. *Selections from the Prison Notebooks of Antonion Gramsci*. New York: International Publishers.
Granieri, R. 2003. *The Ambivalent Alliance: Konrad Adenauer, the CDU/CSU and the West, 1949–1966*. New York and Oxford: Berghahn Books.
Grebing, H. (ed.). 1983. *Lehrstücke in Solidarität. Briefe und Biographien Deutscher Sozialisten 1945–1949*. Stuttgart: DEVA.
———. (ed.). 2005. *Geschichte der sozialen Ideen in Deutschland*. Wiesbaden: VS.
Grebing, H. and K. Kinner (eds). 1990. *Arbeiterbewegung und Faschismus. Faschismus-Interpretationen in der Europäischen Arbeiterbewegung*. Essen: Klartext.
Greenwood, S. 1996. *Britain and European Integration Since the Second World War*. Manchester: Manchester University Press.
———. 1984. 'Ernest Bevin, France and "Western Union": August 1945–February 1946', in *European History Quarterly* 14/3.
Grenville, A. (ed.). 2000. *German-speaking Exiles in Great Britain: The Yearbook of the Research Centre for German and Austrian Exile Studies*, Vol. 2. Amsterdam: Rodopi.
Gress, D. 1985. *Peace and Survival: West Germany, the Peace Movement, and European Security*. Stanford: Stanford University Press.
Griffin, R. 1993. 'Europe for the Europeans: Fascist Myths of the New Order 1922–1992', *Occasional Paper No. 1*. Humanities Research Centre, Oxford Brookes University.
Griffiths, R. 1993. *Socialist Parties and the Question of Europe in the 1950s*. Leiden: Brill.

Groh, D. and P. Brandt. 1992. *Vaterlandslose Gesellen: Sozialdemokratie und Nation, 1860–1990*. Munich: Beck.
Grunewald, M. 1988. 'Deutsche Intellektuelle als Vorläufer des "Geistes von Locarno": Die Neue Rundschau und Frankreich Zwischen 1919 und 1925', in *Recherches Germaniques* 18.
Grunewald, M. and H.-M. Bock (eds). 1996–2001. *Der Europadiskurs in den deutschen Zeitschriften (1871–1955) (Vols. 1–4)*. Berne: Peter Lang.
———. 2002. *Le Milieu Intellectuel de Gauche en Allemagne, sa Presse et ses Réseaux (1890–1960)*. Berne: Peter Lang.
Grunewald, M. and U. Puschner (eds). 2003. *Le Milieu Intellectuel Conservateur en Allemagne, sa Presse et ses Réseaux (1890–1960)*. Berne: Peter Lang.
———. 2006. *Le Milieu Intellectuel Catholique en Allemagne, sa Presse et ses Réseaux (1871–1963)*. Berne: Peter Lang.
Grunewald, M. and F. Trapp (eds).1990. *Autour du 'Front Populaire Allemand', Einheitsfront – Volksfront. Études réunies*. Berne: Peter Lang.
Grzesinski, A. (ed. E. Kolb). 2001. *Im Kampf um die deutsche Republik. Erinnerungen eines Sozialdemokraten*. Munich: Oldenbourg.
Guieu, J.-M. and C. Le Dréau (eds). 2009. *Le Congrès de l'Europe à la Haye (1948–2008)*. Brussels: Peter Lang.
Gunlicks, A. 2003. *The Länder and German Federalism*. Manchester and New York: Manchester University Press.
Harper, J. L. 1996. *American Visions of Europe: Franklin D. Roosevelt, George F. Kennan, and Dean G. Acheson*. Cambridge: Cambridge University Press.
Harryvan, A. and J. van der Harst. 1997. *Documents on European Union*. New York: St. Martin's Press.
Harsch, D. 1993. *German Social Democracy and the Rise of Nazism*. Chapel Hill: University of North Carolina Press.
Harvie, C. 1994. *The Rise of Regional Europe*. London: Routledge.
Haupt, G. 1986. *Aspects of International Socialism, 1871–1914*. Cambridge: Cambridge University Press.
Hauptvorstand der Arbeitsgemeinschaft 'Das Demokratische Deutschland' (eds J. Wirth, O. Braun, W. Hoegner, J. Kindt-Kiefer and H. Ritzel). 1945. *Das Demokratische Deutschland. Grundsätze und Richtlinien für den deutschen Wiederaufbau im demokratischen, republikanischen, föderalistischen und genossensschaftlichen Sinne*. Berne and Leipzig: Haupt.
Hausmann, F.-R. 2004. *'Dichte, Dichter tage nicht!'. Die Europäische Schriftsteller-Vereinigung in Weimar, 1941–1948*. Frankfurt am Main: Vittorio Klostermann.
Heidegger, M. 1993 [1953]. '.'The Question Concering Technology', in *Basic Writings*. New York: Harper and Row 2nd ed.
Heideking, J. and C. Mauch. 1998. *American Intelligence and the German Resistance to Hitler: A Documentary History*. Boulder CO: Westview Press.
Heidenreich, F. 2006. *Bildung in Frankreich und Deutschland – Ideale und Politiken im Vergleich*. Münster: Lit.
Heinemann-Grüder, A. 2002. *Federalism Doomed? European Federalism between Integration and Separation*. New York and Oxford: Berghahn Books.
Heinrichs, H., et al. (eds). 1993. *Deutsche Juristen jüdischer Herkunft*. Munich: Beck.

Hellman, J. 1981. *Emmanuel Mounier and the New Catholic Left, 1930–150.* Toronto: University of Toronto Press.
Henig, S. 2002. *Uniting of Europe: From Consolidation to Enlargement.* London and New York: Routledge.
Henke, K.-D. 1996. *Die amerikanische Besetzung Deutschlands.* Munich: Oldenbourg.
Hennecke, H.J. 2005. *Wilhelm Röpke: Ein Leben in der Brandung.* Zurich: Schäffer-Poeschel.
Herbert, U. and A. Schildt (eds). 1998. *Kriegsende in Europa. Vom Beginn des deutschen Machtzerfalls bis zur Stabilisierung der Nachkriegsordnung 1944–1948.* Essen: Klartext.
Herbst, L., W. Bührer, and H. Sowade (eds). 1990. *Vom Marshallplan zur EWG. Die Eingliederung der Bundesrepublik Deutschland in die westliche Welt.* Munich: Oldenbourg.
Herf, J. 1997. *Divided Memory: The Nazi Past in the Two Germanies.* Cambridge MA: Harvard University Press.
Hirschfeld, G. (ed.). 1983. *Exil in Großbritannien. Zur Emigration aus dem nationalsozialistischen Deutschland.* Stuttgart: Klett-Cotta.
Hirschfeld, G. and P. Marsch (eds). 1991. *Kollaboration in Frankreich. Politik, Wirtschaft und Kultur während der nationalsozialistischen Besatzung 1940–1944.* Frankfurt am Main: Fischer.
Hochgeschwender, M. 1998. *Freiheit in der Offensive? Der Kongress für kulturelle Freiheit und die Deutschen.* Munich: Oldenbourg.
Hoegner, W. 1958. *Die Verratene Republik: Geschichte der Deutschen Gegenrevolution.* Munich: Isar.
———. 1959. *Der schwieriger Außenseiter: Erinnerungen eines Abgeordneten, Emigranten und Ministerpräsidenten.* Munich: Isar.
Hoffmann, S. et al. 1963. *In Search of France.* Cambridge MA: Harvard University Press.
Hogan, M. 1987. *The Marshall Plan: America, Britain and the Reconstruction of Western Europe, 1947–1952.* Cambridge: Cambridge University Press.
Hohls, R., I. Schröder and H. Siegrist (eds). 2005. *Europa und die Europäer. Quellen und Essays zur modernen europäischen Geschichte.* Stuttgart: Franz Steiner.
Holborn, H. 1951. *The Political Collapse of Europe.* New York: Knopf.
Holbraad, C. 2003. *Internationalism and Nationalism in European Political Thought.* Basingstoke: Palgrave Macmillan.
Holmes, D. 2004. *Ignazio Silone in Exile: Writing and Anti-Fascism in Switzerland, 1929–1944* Aldershot: Ashgate.
Holtmann, E. (ed.). 1989. *Wie neu war der Neubeginn? Zum deutschen Kontinuitätsproblem nach 1945.* Erlangen: Erlanger Forschungen.
Hook, D. 2001. 'Discourse, Knowledge, Materiality, History: Foucault and Discourse Analysis', in *Theory and Psychology* 11/4.
Horkheimer, M. and T. Adorno. 1972. *Dialectic of Enlightenment.* New York: Herder and Herder.
Horn, G.-R. 1996. *European Socialists Respond to Fascism: Ideology, Activism and Contingency in the 1930s.* Oxford: Oxford University Press.
———. 2007. *The Spirit of '68: Rebellion in Western Europe and North America, 1956–1976.* Oxford: Oxford University Press.

Horn, G.-R. and E. Gerard (eds). 2001. *Left Catholicism 1943–1955: Catholics and Society in Western Europe at the Point of Liberation*. Leuven: Leuven University Press.

Hörster-Philipps, U. 1998. *Joseph Wirth 1879–1956. Eine politische Biographie*. Paderborn: Schöningh.

Howe, E. 1983. *Die schwarze Propaganda. Ein Insider-Bericht über die geheimsten Operationen des britischen Geheimdienstes im Zweiten Weltkrieg*. Munich: Beck.

Hrbek, R. 1972. *Die SPD – Deutschland und Europa. Die Haltung der Sozialdemokratie zum Verhältnis von Deutschland-Politik und West-Integration (1945–1957)*. Bonn: Europa Union.

Hudemann, R., H. Kaelble, and K. Schwabe (eds). 1995. *Europa im Blick der Historiker*. Munich: Oldenbourg.

Hughes, H.S. 2002. *The Obstructed Path: French Social Thought in the Years of Desperation*. New Brunswick: Transaction.

Hughes, M. 1999. *Shouldering the Burdens of Defeat: West Germany and the Reconstruction of Social Justice*. Chapel Hill: University of North Carolina Press.

Hunt, M. 1987. *Ideology and U.S. Foreign Policy*. New Haven: Yale University Press.

Hüser, D. 1996. *Frankreichs "doppelte Deutschlandpolitik". Dynamik aus der Defensive – Planen, Entscheiden, Umsetzen in gesellschaftlichen und wirtschaftlichen, innen- und außenpolitischen Krisenzeiten 1944–1950*. Berlin: Duncker and Hublot.

Hurwitz, H. 1990. *Die Anfänge des Widerstandes. Teil 1: Führungsanspruch und Isolation der Sozialdemokraten*. Berlin: Wissenschaft und Politik.

Hyman R. 2004. 'Flanders, Allan David (1910–1973)', *Oxford Dictionary of National Biography*. Oxford: Oxford University Press. Online edition, October 2009 [http://www.oxforddnb.com/view/article/31112]

Imlay, T. Forthcoming. '"The Policy of Social Democracy is Self-consciously Internationalist": The SPD's Internationalism after 1945', *The Journal of Modern History*.

Immerman, R.1999. *John Foster Dulles: Piety, Pragmatism and Power in U.S. Foreign Policy*. Wilmington DE: Rowman and Littlefield.

Inglis J. 1998. *Spheres of Philosophical Inquiry and the Historiography of Medieval Philosophy*. Leiden: Brill.

Institut Français Stuttgart, 1987. *Die französische Deutschlandpolitik zwischen 1945 und 1949. Ergebnisse eines Kolloquiums des Institut Français de Stuttgart und des Deutsch-Französischen Instituts, Ludwigsburg, das am 16.–17. Januar 1986 im Institut Français de Stuttgart stattgefunden hat*. Tübingen: Attempto.

Internationaler Sozialistischer Kampfbund (ed.). 1934. *Sozialistische Wiedergeburt. Gedanken und Vorschläge zur Erneuerung der sozialistischen Arbeit*. London: International Publishing Company.

———. 1937. *Die Sozialistische Republik. Das Programm der Internationaler Sozialistischer Kampf-Bund*. London: International Publishing Company.

———. 1942a. *Calling All Europe. A Symposium of Speeches on the Future Order of Europe*. London: Socialist Vanguard Group.

———. 1942b. *Russland und die Komintern. Gedanken für einen internationalen sozialistischen Neuaufbau*. London: Renaissance.

———. 1942c. *Towards European Unity. French–German Relations*. London: Renaissance.

Irving, R.E.M. 1973. *Christian Democracy in France*. London: Routledge.

Jackman, J. and C. Borden. 1983. *The Muses Flee Hitler: Cultural Transfer and Adaptation, 1930–1945*. Washington DC: Smithsonian Institute Press.
Jackson, J. 2001. *France: The Dark Years 1940–1944*. Oxford: Oxford University Press.
Jackson, P.T. 2006. *Civilizing the Enemy: German Reconstruction and the Invention of the West*. Ann Arbor: University of Michigan Press.
Jacoby, W. 2000. *Imitation and Politics: Redesigning Modern Germany*. Ithaca: Cornell University Press.
James, H. 1986. *The German Slump: Politics and Economics 1924–1936*. Oxford: Clarendon Press.
Jarausch, K. 2006. *After Hitler: Recivilizing Germans, 1945–1995*. Oxford: Oxford University Press.
Jeffery, C. (ed.). 1997. *The Regional Dimension of the European Union: Towards a Third Level in Europe?* London and New York: Routledge.
Jeffery, C. and R. Sturm (eds). 1993. *Federalism, Unification and European Integration*. London and New York: Routledge.
Johnson, D. 2001. *Righteous Deception: German Officers Against Hitler*. Westport CT: Praeger.
Jones, P. 1997. *America and the British Labour Party: the "Special Relationship" at Work*. London: I.B. Tauris.
Judt, T. 2005. *Postwar: A History of Europe since 1945*. New York: Penguin.
———. 2011. *A Grand Illusion? An Essay on Europe*. New York: New York University Press.
Jünger, E. 1995. *Strahlungen I/II: 2 Bände*. Stuttgart: dtv/Klett-Cotta.
Junker, D. et al. 2004. *The United States and Germany in the Era of the Cold War 1945–1990: A Handbook, Vol. 1 (1945-1968)*. Cambridge: Cambridge University Press.
Jurt, J. 1993. *Von der Besatzung zur deutsch–französischen Kooperation*. Freiburg im Breisgau: Rombach.
Kaelble, H. (ed.). 2002. 'European Public Sphere and European Identity', Special Issue of *Journal of European Integration History* 8/1.
Kaelble, H. and M. Kirsch (eds). 2008. *Selbstverständnis und Gesellschaft der Europäer. Aspekte der sozialen und kulturellen Europäisierung im späten 19. und 20. Jahrhundert*. Frankfurt am Main: Peter Lang.
Kaelble, H., M. Kirsch, and A. Schmidt-Gernig (eds), 2002. *Transnationale Öffentlichkeiten und Identitäten im 20. Jahrhundert*. Frankfurt am Main: Campus.
Kaiser, W. 2007. *Christian Democracy and the Origins of European Union*. Cambridge: Cambridge University Press.
Kaiser, W., B. Leucht, Brigitte and M. Rasmussen (eds). 2009. *The History of the European Union: Origins of a Trans- and Supranational Polity 1950–1972*. London and New York: Routledge.
Kaiser, W. and A. Varsori (eds). 2010. *European Union History: Themes and Debates*. Basingstoke: Palgrave.
Kampffmeyer, P (ed.). 1925. *Das Heidelberger Programm: Grundsätze und Forderungen der Sozialdemokratie*. Berlin: Vorstand der Sozialdemokratischen Partei Deutschlands
Kaplan, K. 1987. *The Short March: The Communist Takeover in Czechoslovakia 1945–1948*. London: C. Hurst and Co.

Kasten, B. 1993. *Gute Franzosen: die französische Polizei und die deutsche Besatzungsmacht im besetzen Frankreich*. Sigmaringen: Thorbecke.
Katz, B. 1989. *Foreign Intelligence: Research and Analysis in the Office of Strategic Services 1942–1945*. Cambridge MA: Harvard University Press.
Katzenstein, P. (ed.).1997. *Mitteleuropa: Between Europe and Germany*. Providence RI and Oxford: Berghahn Books.
Keane, J. (ed.). 1988. *Civil Society and the State: New European Perspectives*. London: Verso.
——— . 2006. *Civil Society: Berlin Perspectives*. New York and Oxford: Berghahn Books.
Kempa, A. 2010. 'Reaction to French Withdrawal: The Reconstruction of the Atlantic Alliance, 1966–1968'. DPhil Thesis, University of Oxford.
van Kemseke, P. 2006. *Towards an Era of Development: the Globalization of Socialism and Christian Democracy 1945–1965*. Leuven: Leuven University Press.
Kershaw, I. 2002. *Popular Opinion and Political Dissent in the Third Reich, Bavaria 1933–1945*. Oxford: Oxford University Press 2nd ed.
Kessler, M. 2007. *Ossip K. Flechtheim: politischer Wissenschaftler und Zukunftsdenker*. Cologne: Böhlau.
Kettenacker, L. 1977. *Das"Andere Deutschland" im Zweiten Weltkrieg. Emigration und Widerstand in internationaler Perspektive*. Stuttgart: Klett.
——— . 1989. *Krieg zur Friedenssicherung. Die Deutschlandplanung der britischen Regierung während des Zweiten Weltkrieges*. Göttingen: Vanderhock und Ruprecht.
Key, V.O. 1961. *Public Opinion and American Democracy*. New York: Knopf.
Kindleberger, C. 1966. *Europe and the Dollar*. Cambridge MA: MIT Press.
——— . 1973. *The World in Depression 1929–1939*. Berkeley: University of California Press.
Kindt-Kiefer, J. 1944. *Europas Wiedergeburt durch genossenschaftlichen Aufbau*. Berne: Haupt.
Kirk, T.1996. *Nazism and the Working Class in Austria: Industrial Unrest and Political Dissent in the 'National Community'*. Cambridge: Cambridge University Press.
Kisatsky, D. 2005. *The United States and the European Right, 1945–1955*. Columbus OH: Ohio State Press.
Klausen, J. 1998. *War and Welfare: Europe and the United States, 1945 to the Present* Basingstoke: Palgrave.
Klee, E. 2007. *Das Kulturlexikon zum Dritten Reich. Wer war was vor und nach 1945*. Frankfurt am Main: Fischer.
von Klemperer, K. 1992. *German Resistance against Hitler. The Search for Allies Abroad, 1938–1945*. Oxford: Oxford University Press.
Klotz, J. 1983. *Das "kommende Deutschland". Vorstellungen und Konzeptionen des sozialdemokratischen Parteivorstandes im Exil 1933–1945 zu Staat und Wirtschaft*. Cologne: Pahl-Rugenstein.
Klotzbach, K. 1982. *Der Weg zum Staatspartei. Programmatik, praktische Politik und Organisation der deutschen Sozialdemokratie 1945–1965*. Berlin and Bonn: Dietz.
Knipping, F. and J. Le Rider (eds). 1987. *Frankreichs Kulturpolitik in Deutschland, 1945–1950*. Tübingen: Attempto.
Kock, P.-J. 1983. *Bayerns Weg in die Bundesrepublik*. Stuttgart: DEVA.
Koebner, T. (ed.). 1985. *Exilforschung. Ein Internationales Jahrbuch*, Vol. 3: *Gedanken an Deutschland im Exil und andere Themen*. Munich: Text + Kritik.

Koebner, T. and E. Rotermund. 1990. *Rückkehr aus dem Exil. Emigranten aus dem Dritten Reich in Deutschland nach 1945. Essays zu Ehren von Ernst Loewy*. Marburg: Wenzel.
Koebner, T. et al. (eds). 1987. *Deutschland nach Hitler. Zukunftspläne im Exil und aus der Besatzungszeit 1939–1949*. Opladen: Westdeutscher.
König, M. and M. Schulz (eds). 2004. *Die Bundesrepublik Deutschland und die europäische Einigung 1949–2000. Politische Akteure, gesellschaftliche Kräfte und internationale Erfahrungen. Festschrift für Wolf D. Gruner zum 60. Geburtstag*. Stuttgart: Franz Steiner.
Koppe, K. 1967. *Das grüne E setzt sich durch*. Cologne: Europa Union.
Koselleck, R. 1967. *Preußen zwischen Reform und Revolution. Allgemeines Landrecht, Verwaltung und soziale Bewegung von 1791 bis 1848*. Stuttgart: Klett.
———. 1989. 'Linguistic Change and the History of Events', *The Journal of Modern History* 61/4.
Koszyk, K. 1986. *Pressepolitik für Deutsche 1945–1949. Geschichte der deutschen Presse*, Part IV. Berlin: Colloquium.
Kraus, H.-C. (ed.). 2003. *Konservative Zeitschriften zwischen Kaiserreich und Diktatur. Fünf Fallstudien*. Berlin: Duncker und Humblot.
Krauss, M. 2001. *Heimkehr in ein fremdes Land: Geschichte der Remigration nach 1945*. Munich: Beck.
Kreis, G. (ed.). 2000. *Switzerland and the Second World War*. London and New York: Routledge.
Kritzer, P. 1979. *Wilhelm Hoegner: Politische Biographie eines bayerischen Sozialdemokrat*. Munich: Süddeutscher.
Krohn, C.-D. et al. (eds). 1998. *Handbuch der deutschsprachigen Emigration 1933–1945*. Darmstadt: Primus.
Krohn, C.-D. and P. von zur Mühlen (eds). 1997. *Rückkehr und Aufbau nach 1945: deutsche Remigranten im öffentlichen Leben Nachkriegsdeutschlands*. Marburg: Metropolis.
Krohn, C.-D., E. Rotermund and L. Winckler (eds). 1997. *Exilforschung. Ein internationales Jahrbuch. Band 15, 1997: Exil und Widerstand*. Munich: Text + Kritik.
Krohn, C.-D. and A. Schildt (eds). 2002. *Zwischen den Stühlen? Remigranten und Remigration in der deutschen Medienöffentlichkeit der Nachkriegszeit*. Hamburg: Christians.
Krohn, C.-D. and M. Schumacher (eds). 2000. *Exil und Neuordnung: Beiträge zur Verfassungspolitischen entwicklung in Deutschland nach 1945*. Düsseldorf: Droste.
Küppers, H. 1997. *Joseph Wirth. Parlamentarier, Minister und Kanzler der Weimarer Republik*. Stuttgart: Franz Steiner.
Laborie, P. 1990. *L'Opinion française sous Vichy*. Paris: Seuil.
Lacroix, J. and K. Nicolaïdis (eds). 2010. *European Stories: Intellectual Debates on Europe in National Contexts*. Oxford: Oxford University Press.
Landeszentrale für politische Bildung (ed.). 2000. *Hamburg nach dem Ende des Dritten Reiches: politische Neuaufbau 1945/46 bis 1949. Sechs Beiträge*. Hamburg: Landeszentrale für politische Bildung.
Langewiesche D. 2000. *Nation, Nationalismus, Nationalstaat in Deutschland und Europa*. Munich: Beck.

Langewiesche, D. and G. Schmidt (eds). 2000. *Föderative Nation: Deutschlandkonzepte von der Reformation bis zum Ersten Weltkrieg*. Munich: Oldenbourg.

Laqueur W. 2004. *Generation Exodus: The Fate of Young Jewish Refugees from Nazi Germany*. London: I.B. Tauris.

Larres, K. 2002. *Churchill's Cold War: The Politics of Personal Diplomacy*. New Haven: Yale University Press.

Larres, K. and A. Lane (eds). 2001. *The Cold War: The Essential Readings*. Oxford and Malden: Blackwell.

Laska, B. 'Jürgen von Kempski: "Stirner, der so gern Verlachte"' at: http://sammelpunkt.philo.at8080/620/1/kempski.html

Lehmann, A. 2001. *Der Marshall-Plan und das neue Deutschland: die Folgen amerikanischer Besatzungspolitik in den Westzonen*. Münster: Waxmann.

Lemke-Mueller, S. 1988. *Ethischer Sozialismus und soziale Demokratie. Der politische Weg Willi Eichlers vom ISK zur SPD*. Bonn: Neue Gesellschaft.

———. (ed.). 1996. *Ethik des Widerstands. Der Kampf des Internationalen Sozialistischen Kampfbundes gegen den Nationalsozialismus. Quellen und Texte zum Widerstand aus der Arbeiterbewegung 1933–1945*. Bonn: Dietz.

Lenin, V.I. 1966. *Imperialism, the Highest Stage of Capitalism* in Lenin, Vladimir (Christman, Henry ed.) *Essential Works of Lenin: "What Is to Be Done?" and Other Writings*. New York: Dover.

Leser, N. 1985. *Zwischen Reformismus und Bolschewismus: der Austromarxismus als Theorie und Praxis*. Vienna: Europa.

Levy, J. 2007. *The Intermarium: Wilson, Madison, and East Central European Federalism*. Boca Raton: Universal-Publishers.

Lindner, H. 2006. *"Um etwas zu erreichen, muss man sich etwas vornehmen, von dem man glaubt, dass es unmöglich sei". Der Internationale Sozialistische Kampfbund und seine Publikationen*, (Reihe Gesprächskreis Geschichte, Vol. 64, ed. D. Dowe. Historisches Forschungszentrum der Friedrich-Ebert-Stiftung). Bonn: Friedrich Ebert Stiftung.

Link, W. 1964. *Die Geschichte des Internationalen Jugend-Bundes (IJB) und des Internationalen Sozialistischen Kampf-Bundes (ISK). Ein Beitrag zur Geschichte der Arbeiterbewegung in der Weimarer Republik und im Dritten Reich*. Meisenheim am Glan: Hain.

Lipgens, W. (ed.). 1968. *Europa-Föderationspläne der Widerstandsbewegungen 1940–1945*. Munich: Oldenbourg.

———. 1977. *Die Anfänge der europäischen Einigungspolitik 1945–1950. Erster Teil 1945–1947*. Stuttgart: Ernst Klein.

———. 1982. *A History of European Integration since 1914*, vol. 1, *1945–1947*. Oxford: Clarendon Press.

——— 1986. *Documents on the History of European Integration*, vol. 2, *Plans for European Union in Great Britain and in Exile, 1939–1945*. Berlin: de Gruyter.

Lipgens, W. and W. Loth (eds.). 1988. *Documents on the History of European Integration*, vol. 3, *The Struggle for European Union by Political Parties and Pressure Groups in Western European Countries, 1945–1950*. Berlin: de Gruyter.

Liulevicius, V. 2000. *War Land on the Eastern Front: Culture, National Identity and German Occupation in WW1*. Cambridge: Cambridge University Press.

———. 2009. *The German Myth of the East: 1800 to the Present*. Oxford: Oxford University Press.
Lodge, J. 1976. *The European Policy of the SPD*. Beverly Hills and London: Sage.
Lompe, K. and L. Neumann (eds). 1979. *Willi Eichlers Beiträge zum demokratischen Sozialismus*. Berlin and Bonn: Dietz.
Loth, W. 1977. *Sozialismus und Internationalismus: die französischen Sozialisten und die Nachkriegsordnung Europas 1940–1950*. Stuttgart: DEVA.
———. 1991 *Der Weg nach Europa. Geschichte der europäischen Integration 1939–1957*. Göttingen: Vanderhoeck und Ruprecht 2nd ed.
———. 2002. *Die Teilung der Welt. Geschichte des Kalten Krieges 1941–1955*. Munich: dtv.
——— (ed.). 2004. *Europe, Cold War and Co-Existence 1953–1965*. London: Frank Cass.
Löwenheim, W. (ed. J. Foitzik). 1995. *Geschichte der ORG [Neu Beginnen] 1929–1935. Eine zeitgenössische Analyse*. Berlin: Hentrich.
Löwenthal, R. 1977. *Jenseits des Kapitalismus*. Berlin and Bonn: Dietz.
Löwenthal, R. and P. von zur Mühlen (eds). 1982. *Widerstand und Verweigerung in Deutschland 1933 bis 1945*. Berlin and Bonn: Dietz.
von der Lühe, I. and C.-D. Krohn (eds). 2005. *Fremdes Heimatland: Remigration und literarisches Leben nach 1945*. Göttingen: Wallstein.
Lukacs, J. 1965. *Decline and Rise of Europe: A Study in Recent History, with Particular Emphasis on the Development of a European Consciousness*. New York: Doubleday.
Lundestad, G. 1998. *"Empire" by Integration: The United States and European Integration, 1945–1997*. Oxford: Oxford University Press.
———. 2003. *The United States and Western Europe since 1945: from "Empire" by Invitation to Transatlantic Drift*. Oxford: Oxford University Press.
Luthardt, W. and A. Soellner (eds). 1989. *Verfassungsstaat, Souveränität, Pluralismus. Otto Kirchheimer zur Gedächtnis*. Opladen: Westdeutscher.
Lützeler, P.M. 1987. *Plädoyers für Europa. Stellungnahmen deutschsprachiger Schriftsteller 1915–1949*. Frankfurt am Main: Fischer.
Maehl, W. 1986. *The German Socialist Party: Champion of the First Republic, 1918–1933*. Lawrence: Allen Press.
Maimann, H. 1975. *Politik im Wartesaal: Österreichische Exilpolitik in Großbritannien 1938 bis 1945*. Vienna: Böhlau.
Malinowski, S. 2003. *Vom König zum Führer. Soziale Niedergang und politische Radikalisierung im deutschen Adel zwischen Kaiserreich und NS-Staat*. Berlin: Akademie.
Mandel, S. 1973. *Group 47: The Reflected Intellect*. Carbondale and Edwardsville: Southern Illinois University Press.
Mann, K. 1985. *Mit dem Blick nach Deutschland. Der Schriftsteller und das politische Engagement*. Munich: Spangenberg im Ellermann.
Mann, K. and H. Kesten. (eds). 1943. *Heart of Europe: An Anthology of Creative Writing in Europe 1920–1940*. New York: L.B. Fischer.
Marcuse, H. 2001. *Legacies of Dachau: The Uses and Abuses of a Concentration Camp, 1933–2001*. Cambridge: Cambridge University Press.
Marcuse, H. 1998. *Feindanalysen: Über die Deutschen*. Lüneburg: Klampen.

Marquardt-Bigman, P. 1995. *Amerikanische Geheimdienstanalysen über Deutschland 1942–1949*. Munich: Oldenbourg.

Martens, S. (ed.). 1993 *Vom "Erbfeind" zum "Erneurer". Aspekte und Motive französische Deutschlandpolitik nach dem Zweiten Weltkrieg*. Sigmaringen: Thorbecke.

Martens, W. 2009. *Europe: I Struggle, I Overcome*. New York and Heidelberg: Springer.

Matthias, E. (ed.). 1968. *Mit dem Gesicht nach Deutschland. Eine Dokumentation über die sozialdemokratische Emigration. Aus dem Nachlass von Friedrich Stampfer ergänzt durch andere Überlieferungen*. Düsseldorf: Droste.

Mayne, R. 1963. *Die Einheit Europas. EWG, Euratom, Montanunion*. Munich: Prestel.

Mayne, R., J. Pinder, and J. Roberts. 1990. *Federal Union: The Pioneers: A History of Federal Union*. London: Macmillan.

Maync, T. 2006. 'For a Socialist Europe!: German Social Democracy and the Idea of Europe, 1900–1930'. University of Chicago PhD Dissertation.

Mazower, M. 2000. *Dark Continent: Europe's Twentieth Century*. New York: Vintage.

Mazower, M. 2008. *Hitler's Empire: How the Nazis Ruled Europe*. London: Penguin.

Mazower, M. 2012. *Governing the World: The History of an Idea*. London: Allen Lane.

McAlister, R. 1997. *From EC to EU: an Historical and Political Survey*. London and New York: Routledge.

McAllister, J. 2002. *No Exit: America and the German Problem, 1943–1954*. Ithaca: Cornell University Press.

McDermott, K. and J. Agnew. 1997. *The Comintern: A History of International Communism from Lenin to Stalin*. New York: St. Martin's Press.

McMeekin, S. 2004. *The Red Millionaire: A Political Biography of Willi Münzenberg, Moscow's Secret Propaganda Tsar in the West*. New Haven: Yale University Press.

Mehringer, H. 1989. *Waldemar von Knoeringen. Eine politische Biographie. Der Weg vom revolutionären Sozialismus zur sozialen Demokratie*. Munich: Saur.

———. (ed.). 1992. *Von der Klassenbewegung zur Volkspartei. Wegmarken der bayerischen Sozialdemokratie 1892–1992*. Munich: Saur.

Meinecke, F. 1965. *Die deutsche Katastrophe. Betrachtungen und Erinnerungen*. Wiesbaden: Brockhaus 6th edition.

Michel, H. 1972. *The Shadow War: European Resistance 1939–1945*. New York: Harper and Row.

Michels, E. 1993. *Das Deutsche Institut in Paris 1940–1944. Ein Beitrag zu den deutsch–französischen Kulturbeziehungen und zur auswärtigen Kulturpolitik des Dritten Reiches*. Stuttgart: Franz Steiner.

Militant Socialist International. 1935. *The Militant Socialist International: Its Aim, Method and Constitution*. London: International Publishing Company.

Miller, M. 2012. *The Origins of Christian Democracy: Politics and Confession in Modern Germany*. Ann Arbor: University of Michigan Press.

Milward, A. 2000. *The European Rescue of the Nation-State*. London and New York: Routledge 2nd ed.

Minion, M. 2000. 'Left, Right or European? Labour and Europe in the 1940s: the Case of the Socialist Vanguard Group', in *European Review of History*, 7/2.

Minion, M. 'The Labour Party and Europe during the 1940s: the Strange Case of the Socialist Vanguard Group', at: http://www.lsbu.ac.uk/cibs/european-institute-papers/papers2/498.PDF

Mittag, J. and W. Wessels. (eds). 2005. *Der "Kölsche Europäer": Friedrich Carl von Oppenheim und die Europäische Einigung*. Münster: Aschendorff.
Moersch, K. and R. Weber. 2008. *Die Zeit nach dem Krieg: Städte im Wiederaufbau*. Stuttgart: Kohlhammer.
Mommsen, H. 1991. *From Weimar to Auschwitz: Essays in German History*. Cambridge: Cambridge University Press.
Monnet, J. 1978. *Memoirs*. New York: Doubleday.
Monte, H. 1943. *The Unity of Europe*. London: Victor Gollancz.
Moras, J., H. Paeschke and W. von Einsiedel. (eds). 1954. *Deutscher Geist zwischen Gestern und Morgen. Bilanz der kulturellen Entwicklung seit 1945*. Stuttgart: DEVA.
Moravcsik, A. 1998. *The Choice for Europe: Social Purpose and State Power from Messina to Maastricht*. Ithaca: Cornell University Press.
Morsey, R. and K. Repgen. (eds). 1974. *Adenauer Studien*, Vol. 3: *Untersuchungen und Dokumente zur Ostpolitik und Biographie*. Mainz: Matthias-Grünewald 2nd ed.
Moses, D. 2007. *German Intellectuals and the Nazi Past*. Cambridge: Cambridge University Press.
Müller, G. 2005. *Europäische Gesellschaftsbeziehungen nach dem ersten Weltkrieg*. Munich: Oldenbourg.
Müller, J.-W. 2000. *Another Country: German Intellectuals, Unification and National Identity*. New Haven: Yale University Press.
———. 2011. *Contesting Democracy: Political Ideas in Twentieth-Century Europe*. New Haven: Yale University Press.
Müller, K.-J. 1986. *Der deutsche Widerstand und das Ausland. Beiträge zum Widerstand*. Berlin: Gedenkstätte dt. Widerstand.
Müller, K.-J. and D. Dilks (eds). 1994. *Großbritannien und der deutsche Widerstand 1933–1944*. Paderborn: Schöningh.
Müller-Brandeck-Bocquet, G. et al. 2010. *Deutsche Europapolitik. Von Adenauer bis Merkel*. Wiesbaden: VS 2nd ed.
Münkel, D. and J. Schwarzkopf (eds). 2004. *Geschichte als Experiment: Studien zur Politik, Kultur und Alltag im 19. und 20. Jahrhundert. Festschrift für Adelheid von Saldern*. Frankfurt am Main: Campus.
Murdock, C.E. 2010. *Changing Places: Society, Culture and Territory in the Saxon-Bohemian Borderlands, 1870–1946*. Ann Arbor: University of Michigan Press.
Naimark, N. 1995. *The Russians in Germany: A History of the Soviet Zone of Occupation, 1945–1949*. Cambridge MA: Harvard University Press.
Neuss, B. 2000. *Geburthelfer Europas. Die Rolle der Vereinigten Staaten im europäischen Integrationsprozess 1945–1958*. Baden-Baden: Nomos.
Nicholls, A. 2003. *Freedom with Responsibility: The Social Market Economy in Germany, 1918–1963*. Oxford: Oxford University Press.
Niess, F. 2001. *Die europäische Idee: Aus dem Geist des Widerstands*. Frankfurt am Main: Suhrkamp.
Ninkovich, F. 1981. *The Diplomacy of Ideas: U.S. Foreign Policy and Cultural Relations, 1938–1950*. Cambridge: Cambridge University Press.
Norddeutsche Buchdrückerei und Verlagsanstalt. 1922. *Verhandlungen des Reichstags. Stenographische Berichte I. Wahlperiode 1920. Band 356. 236 Sitzung*. Berlin: Norddeutsche Buchdrückerei und Verlagsanstalt. Accessible at: http://www.reichstagsprotokolle.de/Blatt2_w1_bsb00000040_00023.html

Odorn, W. 1998. *The Collapse of the Soviet Military*. New Haven: Yale University Press.

Orlow, D. 1999. *Common Destiny: A Comparative History of the Dutch, French and German Social Democratic Parties, 1945–1969*. New York and Oxford: Berghahn Books.

Pagden A. (ed.). 2002. *The Idea of Europe: From Antiquity to the European Union*. Cambridge: Cambridge University Press.

Palmier, J.M. 2006. *Weimar in Exile: The Antifascist Emigration in Europe and America*. London: Verso.

Papini, R. (trans. by R. Royal). 1997. *The Christian Democratic International*. Lanham: Rowman and Littlefield.

Passerini, L. 2009. *Love and the Idea of Europe*. New York and Oxford: Berghahn Books.

Paterson, W.E. 1974. *The SPD and European Integration*. Westmead: Saxon House.

———. 1975. 'The German Social Democratic Party and European Integration in Emigration and Occupation', in *European History Quarterly* 5/4.

Parnass, D. 1991. *The SPD and the Challenge of Mass Politics*. Boulder CO: Westview Press.

Pells, R. 1997. *Not Like Us: How Europeans Have Loved, Hated and Transformed American Culture Since World War II*. New York: Basic Books.

Peterson, E. 1977. *The American Occupation of Germany: Retreat to Victory*. Detroit: Wayne State University Press.

Petersen N. (ed.). 1996. *From Hitler's Doorstep: The Wartime Intelligence Reports of Allen Dulles, 1942–1945*. University Park PA: Pennsylvania State University Press.

Peukert, D. 1989. *The Weimar Republic: The Crisis of Classical Modernity*. New York: Hill and Wang.

Pfohlmann O. 2003. '"Ein Mann von ungewöhnlichen Eigenschaften": Robert Musil, die "Neue Rundschau"der Expressionismus und das "Sommererlebnis im Jahre 1914"', in *Weimarer Beiträge* 49/3.

Pöpping, D. 2002. *Abendland: Christliche Akademiker und die Utopie der Antimoderne 1900–1945*. Berlin: Metropol.

Poidevin, R. 'Der Faktor Europa in der Deutschlandpolitik Robert Schumans 1948/49', in *Vierteljahreshefte für Zeitgeschichte* 33/3.

Pollet, J.J. (ed.). 1996. *Écritures franco-allemandes de la Grande guerre*. Arras: Artois Presses Universite.

Potthoff, H. and S. Miller. 2002. *Kleine Geschichte der SPD, 1848–2002*. Bonn: Dietz.

Pross, H. 1963. *Literatur und Politik. Geschichte und Programme der politisch-literarischen Zeitschriften im deutschen Sprachgebiet seit 1870*. Olten and Freiburg im Breisgau: Walter.

Pulzer, P. 2003. *Jews and the German State: the Political History of a Minority, 1848–1933*. Detroit: Wayne State University Press.

Pütter, C. 1986. *Rundfunk gegen das "Dritte Reich". Deutschsprachige Rundfunkaktivitäten im Exil 1933–1945. Ein Handbuch*. Munich: Saur.

Quack, S. 2002. *Between Sorrow and Strength: Women Refugees of the Nazi Period*. Cambridge: Cambridge University Press.

Radkau, J. 1971. *Die deutsche Emigration in den USA: Ihr Einfluss auf die amerikanische Europapolitik 1933–1945*. Düsseldorf: Bertelsmann.

van Rahden, T. 2011. 'Clumsy Democrats: Moral Passions in the Federal Republic', in *German History* 29/3.

Raphael, L. and H.E. Tenorth. 2006. *Ideen als gesellschaftliche Gestaltungskraft im Europa der Neuzeit: Beiträge für eine erneuerte Geistesgeschichte*. Munich: Oldenbourg.

Rathkolb, O. 2010. *The Paradoxical Republic: Austria 1945–2005*. New York and Oxford: Berghahn Books.

Reif, H. and M. Feichtinger (eds). 2009. *Ernst Reuter: Kommunalpolitiker und Gesellschaftsreformer*. Bonn: Dietz.

Reimer, A. 2005. *Stadt zwischen zwei Demokratien. Baden-Baden von 1930 bis 1950*. Munich: Martin Meidenbauer.

Reinalda, B. 1997. *The International Transportworkers Federation, 1914–1945: The Edo Fimmen Era*. Amsterdam: International Institute of Social History.

Reitmayer, M. 2009. *Elite. Sozialgeschichte einer politisch-gesellschaftlichen Idee in der frühen Bundesrepublik*. Munich: Oldenbourg.

Reynolds, D. 1997. 'Marshall Plan Commemorative Section: The European Response: Primacy of Politics', in *Foreign Affairs*, 76/ 3. Located at: http://www.foreignaffairs.org/19970501faessay3823/david-reynolds/marshall-plan-commemorative-section-the-european-response-primacy-of-politics.html

Reytier, M.-E. 2002. 'Die deutschen Katholiken und der Gedanke der europäischen Einigung 1945–1949: Wende oder Kontinuität?', in *Jahrbuch für Europäische Geschichte* 3.

Richardson, J. 2006. *European Union: Power and Policy-Making*. London and New York: Routledge.

Ritzel, H. 1947. *Europa und Deutschland – Deutschland und Europa*. Offenbach am Main: Bollwerk.

———. 1949. 'Europäischer Frühling?', in *Europa: Organ der Europa Union* (in der Schweiz).

Röder, W. 1968. *Die deutschen sozialistischen Exilgruppen in Großbritannien 1940–1945. Ein Beitrag zur Geschichte des Widerstandes gegen den Nationalsozialismus*. Hanover: Verlag für Literatur und Zeitgeschehen.

Röder, W and H. Strauss (eds). 1980. *Biographisches Handbuch der deutschsprachigen Emigration nach 1933: Band I, Politik, Wirtschaft, Öffentliches Leben*. Munich: Saur.

Rogosch, D. 1996. *Vorstellungen von Europa: Europabilder in der SPD und bei den belgischen Sozialisten 1945–1957*. Hamburg: Krämer.

Röpke, W. 1945. *Die deutsche Frage*. Zurich: Rentsch.

Rosenberg, E. 1982. *Spreading the American Dream: American Economic and Cultural Expansion 1890–1945*. New York: Hill and Wang.

Rosmus, A. 2004. *Out of Passau: Leaving a City Hitler Called Home*. Columbia SC: University of South Carolina Press.

Ross, C. 2008. *Media and the Making of Modern Germany: Mass Communications, Society, and Politics from the Empire to the Third Reich*. Oxford: Oxford University Press.

Rougeyron, A. 1996. *Agents for Resistance: Inside the French Resistance 1939–1945*. Baton Rouge: Louisiana State University Press.

Ruge, U. 2003. *Die Erfindung des "Europa der Regionen": Kritische Ideengeschichte eines konservativen Konzepts*. Frankfurt am Main: Campus.

Rupieper, H.J. 1993. *Die Wurzeln der westdeutschen Nachkriegsdemokratie. Der amerikanische Beitrag*. Opladen: Westdeutscher.

Salzmann, B. 2006. *Europa als Thema katholischer Eliten: das katholische Europa-Netzwerk der Schweiz von 1945 bis Mitte der 1950er Jahre*. Fribourg: Saint-Paul.
Saran, M. 1941. *European Revolution*. London: International Publishing Company.
———. 1976. *Never Give Up: Memoirs*. London: Wolff.
Saran, M. et al. 1945 *Remaking Germany*. London: International Publishing Company.
Scharf, C. and H.-J. Schroeder (eds). 1983. *Die Deutschlandpolitik Frankreichs und die französische Zone 1945–1949*. Wiesbaden: Franz Steiner.
Schildt, A. 1999a. *Ankunft im Westen: ein Essay zur Erfolgsgeschichte der Bundesrepublik*. Frankfurt am Main: Fischer.
———. 1999b. *Zwischen Abendland und Amerika. Studien zur westdeutschen Ideenlandschaft der 50er Jahre*. Munich: Oldenbourg.
———. 2002. *Max Brauer*. Hamburg: Ellert und Richter.
Schildt, A. and A. Sywottek (eds). 1993. *Modernisierung im Wiederaufbau. Die westdeutsche Gesellschaft der 50er Jahre*. Bonn: Dietz.
Schiller, K. and C. Young. 2010. *The 1972 Munich Olympics and the Making of Modern Germany*. Berkeley, University of California Press.
Schilmar, B. 2004. *Der Europadiskurs im deutschen Exil, 1933–1945*. Munich: Oldenbourg.
Schlie, U. 1994. *Kein Friede mit Deutschland: die geheimen Gespräche im Zweiten Weltkrieg*. Munich: Langen Müller.
Schneider, H. 1977. *Leitbilder der Europapolitik 1. Der Weg zur Integration*. Bonn: Europa Union.
Schoelzel, S. 1996. *Die Pressepolitik in der französischen Besatzungszone 1945–1949*. Mainz: Hase und Koehler.
Schoendube, C. and C. Ruppert. 1964. *Eine Idee setzt sich durch. Der Weg zum vereinigten Europa*. Hangelar bei Bonn: Heinrich Warnecke.
Schorske, C. 1972. *German Social Democracy 1905–1917: The Development of the Great Schism*. New York: Harper Torchbook.
Schot, J. and V. Lagendijk. 2008. 'Technocratic Internationalism in the Interwar Years. Building Europe on Motorways and Electricity', in *Journal of Modern European History* 6/2.
Schot, J. and T. Misa. 2005. 'Inventing Europe: Technology and the Hidden Integration of Europe', in *History and Technology* 21/1.
Schulz, G. (ed.). 1982. *Geheimdienste und Widerstandsbewegungen im Zweiten Weltkrieg*. Göttingen: Vanderhoeck und Ruprecht.
Schulz, W. 'Vom "Sonderweg" bis zur "Ankunft im Westen": Deutschlands Stellung in Europa' at: http://www.historicum.net/fileadmin/sxw/Lehren_Lernen/Schulze/Vom_Sonderweg_bis_zur_Ankunft_im_Westen.pdf
Schulze, H. 1977. *Otto Braun: oder, Preußens demokratische Sendung. Eine Biographie*. Frankfurt am Main: Ullstein.
Schumacher, K. 1949. 'Our Place in Europe', in *News from Germany* 2/3.
Schwarz, F. 1971. 'Literarisches Zeitgespräch im Dritten Reich: Dargestellt an der Zeitschrift *Neue Rundschau*', in *Börsenblatt für den deutschen Buchhandel* 27/51.
Schwarz, H.-P. 1966. *Vom Reich zur Bundesrepublik. Deutschland im Widerstreit der außenpolitischen Konzeptionen in den Jahren der Besatzungsherrschaft 1945–1949*. Neuwied and Berlin: Luchterhand.

———. 1997. *Konrad Adenauer: German Politician and Statesman in a Period of War, Revolution and Re-construction*. Vols. 1–2. New York and Oxford: Berghahn Books.
Schwarz, U. 1980. *The Eye of the Hurricane: Switzerland in World War Two*. Boulder CO: Westview.
Schweber, S. 1994. *QED and the Men Who Made It: Dyson, Feynman, Schwinger and Tomonaga*. Princeton: Princeton University Press.
Scott, H. and W. Scott. 1979. *The Armed Forces of the Soviet Union*. Boulder CO: Westview.
Seemann, H. (ed.). 2008. *Europa in Weimar. Visionen eines Kontinents*. Göttingen: Wallstein.
Seibt, F. (ed.). 1988. *Gesellschaftsgeschichte. Festschrift für Karl Bosl zum 80. Geburtstag, Band II*. Munich: Oldenbourg.
Selinger, S. 1998. *Charlotte von Kirschbaum and Karl Barth: A Study in Biography and the History of Theology*. University Park PA: Pennsylvania State University Press.
Seller, M. 2001. *We Built Up Our Lives: Education and Community among Jewish Refugees Interned by Britain during World War II*. Westport CT: Greenwood.
Shore, C. 2000. *Building Europe: The Cultural Politics of European Integration*. London and New York: Routledge.
Sidjanski, D. 2000. *Federal Future of Europe: From the European Community to the European Union*. Ann Arbor: University of Michigan Press.
Siegel, W. 1978. *Bayerns Staatswerdung und Verfassungsentstehung 1945/46*. Bamberg: Bayerische Verlagsanstalt.
Skiera, E. 2010. *Reformpädagogik in Geschichte und Gegenwart: eine kritische Einführung*. Munich: Oldenbourg.
Smith, A. 1986. *The Ethnic Origins of Nations*. Oxford: Blackwell.
Smith, B. 1983. *The Shadow Warriors, OSS and the Origins of the CIA*. New York: Basic Books.
Smith, H.W. 1995. *German Nationalism and Religious Conflict: Culture, Ideology, Politics, 1870–1914*. Princeton: Princeton University Press.
Smith, J.E. (ed.). 1974. *The Papers of Lucius D. Clay: Germany, 1945–1949*. Bloomington IN: Indiana University Press.
Smith, R. 2005. *OSS: The Secret History of America's First Central Intelligence Agency*. Guilford CT: Lyons.
Soell, H. 1976. *Fritz Erler – eine politische Biographie*. Berlin and Bonn: Dietz.
Söllner, A. 1982. *Zur Archäologie der Demokratie in Deutschland. Analysen politischer Emigranten im amerikanischen Geheimdienst*. Frankfurt am Main: Europäische Verlagsanstalt.
———. 1996. *Deutsche Politikwissenschaftler in der Emigration: Studien zur ihrer Akkulturation und Wirkungsgeschichte*. Opladen: Westdeutscher.
Sørensen, V. 2001. *Denmark's Social Democratic Government and the Marshall Plan, 1947–1950*. Copenhagen: Museum Tusculanum Press.
Spalek, J., K. Feilchenfeldt and S. Hawrylchak (eds). 2002. *Deutschsprachige Exilliteratur seit 1933, Band 3, USA, Teil 3*. Berne und Munich: Franke.
Spaulding, R. 1997. *Osthandel und Ostpolitik: German Foreign Trade Policies in Eastern Europe from Bismarck to Adenauer*. Providence RI and Oxford: Berghahn Books.
SPD Parteivorstand (ed.). 1948. *Querschnitt durch die deutsche Politik der Gegenwart*. Hannover; Hannoversche Presse, Druck und Verlagsgesellschaft.

Spencer, G. 1985. *Beloved Alien: Walter Fliess 1901–1985*. Vancouver and Donhead St. Andrew: Geoff Spencer.
Spengler, O. 2006. *Der Untergang des Abendlandes. Umrisse einer Morphologie der Weltgeschichte*. Munich: dtv 17th ed.
Spicka, M. 2007. *Selling the Economic Miracle: Economic Reconstruction and Politics in West Germany, 1949–1957*. New York and Oxford: Berghahn Books.
Stachura P. (ed.). 2004. *The Poles in Britain, 1940–2000. From Betrayal to Assimiliation*. London and New York: Routledge.
Stahl, E. 'Merkur im freien Fall', at: www.satt.org/gesellschaft/03_12_merkur.html
Stahlberger, P. 1970. *Der Zürcher Verleger Emil Oprecht und die deutsche politische Emigration 1933–1945*. Zurich: Europa.
Steffek, J., C. Kissling and P. Nanz, Patrizia (eds). 2007. *Civil Society Participation in European and Global Governance: A Cure for the Democratic Deficit?*. Basingstoke: Palgrave.
Steininger, R. 1979. *Deutschland und die Sozialistische Internationale nach dem Zweiten Weltkrieg. Die deutsche Frage, die Internationale und das Problem der Wiederaufnahme des SPD auf den internationalen sozialistischen Konferenzen bis 1951 unter besonderer Berücksichtigung der Labour Party*. Bonn: Neue Gesellschaft.
Stirk, P. (ed.). 1994. *Mitteleuropa: History and Prospects*. Edinburgh: Edinburgh University Press.
———. 1996. *A History of European Integration since 1914*. London: Pinter.
Stonor Saunders, F. 1999. *Who Paid the Piper? The CIA and the Cultural Cold War*. London: Granta.
Stradling R. (ed.). 2006. *Crossroads of European Histories: Multiple Outlooks on Five Key Moments in the History of Europe*. Strasbourg: College of Europe.
Sutton, M. 2007. *France and the Construction of Europe, 1944–2007: The Geopolitical Imperative*. New York and Oxford: Berghahn Books.
Switzerland (Federal Chancellery). 1867. *The Federal Constitution of the Swiss Confederation: September 12, 1848*, Berne: C.J. Wyss.
Szende, S. 1975. *Zwischen Gewalt und Toleranz: Zeugnisse und Reflexionen eines Sozialisten*. Frankfurt am Main: Europäische Verlagsanstalt.
Tent, J. 1982. *Mission on the Rhine. Reeducation and Denazification in American-Occupied Germany*. Chicago: University of Chicago Press.
Teubner, H. 1975. *Exilland Schweiz. Dokumentarischer Bericht über den Kampf emigrierter deutscher Kommunisten 1933–1945*. Berlin: Dietz.
von Thadden, R. (ed.). 1999. *Göttingen: Von der preußischen Mittelstadt zur südniedersächsischen Großstadt 1866–1989*. Göttingen: Vanderhoeck und Ruprecht.
Ther, P. 2007. 'Milan Kundera und die Renaissance *Zentraleuropas*', in *Themenportal Europäische Geschichte*. Accessible at: http://www.europa.clio-online.de/2007/Article=153
Ther, P. and A. Siljak (eds). 2001. *Redrawing Nations: Ethnic Cleansing in East-Central Europe, 1944–1948*. Lanham and Oxford: Rowman and Littlefield.
Trachtenberg, M. (ed.). 2003. *Between Empire and Alliance: America and Europe during the Cold War*. Lanham: Rowman and Littlefield.
Turner, H. 1985. *German Big Business and the Rise of Hitler*. Oxford: Oxford University Press.

Umbach, M. (ed.). 2002. *German Federalism: Past, Present, Future*. Basingstoke: Palgrave.
Unabhängige Expertenkommission Schweiz – Zweiter Weltkrieg. 2002. *Die Schweiz, der Nationalsozialismus und der Zweite Weltkrieg. Schlußbericht*. Zurich: Pendo.
Urwin, D. 1995. *The Community of Europe: A History of European Integration since 1945*. London: Longman 2nd ed.
Uschner, M. 1991. *Die Ostpolitik der SPD: Sieg und Niederlage einer Strategie*. Berlin: Dietz.
Vaillant, J. (ed.). 1984. *Französische Kulturpolitik in Deutschland 1945–1949*. Constance: Universitätsverlag Konstanz.
Viehoever, V. 2004. *Diskurse der Erneuerung nach dem Ersten Weltkrieg: Konstruktionen kultureller Identität in der Zeitschrift* Die Neue Rundsschau. Tübingen: Francke.
Vincent, A. 2010. *Modern Political Ideologies*. Malden: Wiley-Blackwell 3rd ed.
Vinen, R. 2002. *Bourgeois Politics in France, 1945–1951*. Cambridge: Cambridge University Press.
Visser't Hooft, W. 1972. *Die Welt war meine Gemeinde*. Munich: Piper.
Voigt, K. (ed.). 1988. *Friedenssicherung und europäische Eingung. Ideen des deutschen Exils 1939–1945*. Frankfurt am Main: Fischer.
Vorholt, U. 1991. *Die Sowjetunion im Urteil des sozialdemokratischen Exils, 1933–1945: eine Studie des Exilparteivorstandes der SPD, des Internationalen Sozialistischen Kampfbundes, der Sozialistichen Arbeiterpartei und der Gruppe Neu Beginnen*. Frankfurt am Main: Peter Lang.
Vorstand der Sozialdemokratischen Partei Deutschlands. 1959. *Grundsatzprogramm der Sozialdemokratischen Partei Deutschlands. Beschlossen vom Außerordentlichen Parteitag der Sozialdemokratischen Partei Deutschlands in Bad Godesberg vom 13. bis 15. November 1959*. Cologne: Deutz.
Wagner, H.-U. (ed.). 2000. *Rückkehr in die Fremde? Remigranten und Rundfunk in Deutschland 1945 bis 1955*. Berlin: Vistas.
Wagnleitner, R. 1994. *Coca-Colonization and the Cold War: The Cultural Mission of the United States in Austria after the Second World War*. Chapel Hill: University of North Carolina Press.
Waller, J. 1996. *The Unseen War in Europe: Espionage and Conspiracy in the Second World War*. London and New York: I.B. Tauris.
Wallerstein, I. 2011. *Centrist Liberalism Triumphant, 1789–1914*. Berkeley and Los Angeles: University of California.
Walser Smith, H. 1995. *German Nationalism and Religious Conflict: Culture, Ideology, Politics, 1870–1914*. Princeton: Princeton University Press.
Weber, M. 2001. *Gesammelte Werke und Schriften*. Berlin: Infosoftware.
Wehler, H.-U. 2008. *Deutsche Gesellschaftsgeschichte*, Vol. 5: *Bundesrepublik und DDR 1949–1990*. Munich: Beck.
Welch Larson, D. 1997. *Anatomy of Mistrust: U.S.-Soviet Relations during the Cold War*. Ithaca: Cornell University Press.
Wendt, B.-J. (ed.). 1992. *Vom schwierigen Zusammenwachsen der Deutschen. Nationale Identität und Nationalismus im 19. und 20. Jahrhundert*. Frankfurt am Main: Peter Lang.
Wengst, U. 1985. *Auftakt zur Ära Adenauer: Koalitionsverhandlungen und Regierungsbildung 1949*. Düsseldorf: Droste.

Werner, E. 1982. *In Dienst der Demokratie: die bayerische Sozialdemokratie nach der Wiedergründung 1945*. Munich: Münchner Post/Neue Bayernzeitung.
Werner, M. and B. Zimmermann. 2006. 'Beyond Comparison: Histoire Croisée and the Challenge of Reflexivity', in *History and Theory* 45/1.
West, N. 1992. *Secret War. The Story of SOE, Britain's Wartime Sabotage Organisation*. London: Hodder and Stoughton.
Whatmore, R. and B. Young (eds). 2006. *Palgrave Advances in Intellectual History*. Basingstoke: Palgrave.
Whitaker, A. 1954. *The Western Hemisphere Idea: Its Rise and Decline*. Ithaca: Cornell University Press.
Wichers, H. 1994. *Im Kampf gegen Hitler. Deutsche Sozialisten im schweizer Exil, 1933–1940*. Zurich: Chronos.
Wiener, A. and T. Diez (eds). 2004. *European Integration Theory*. Oxford: Oxford University Press.
Wiesen, J. 2004. *West German Industry and the Challenge of the Past, 1945–1955*. Chapel Hill: University of North Carolina Press.
Wilke, J. 2000. *Grundzüge der Medien- und Kommunikationsgeschichte. Von den Anfängen bis ins 20. Jahrhundert*. Cologne: Böhlau.
Willis, F.R. 1962. *The French in Germany 1945–1949*. Stanford: Stanford University Press.
Willis, F.R. 1965. *France, Germany, and the New Europe: 1945–1967*. Stanford: Stanford University Press.
Wilson, P. 1999. *The Holy Roman Empire, 1495–1806*. Basingstoke: Palgrave.
Winkler, H.A. 1985. *Der Schein der Normalität: Arbeiter und Arbeiterbewegung in der Weimarer Republik, 1924 bis 1930*. Berlin: J.H.W. Dietz.
———. 1998. *Weimar, 1918–1933: die Geschichte der ersten deutschen Demokratie*. Munich: Beck.
———. 2000. *Der lange Weg nach Westen. Zweiter Band. Deutsche Geschichte vom "Dritten Reich" zur Wiedervereinigung*. Munich: Beck.
———. 2007. *Germany: The Long Road West. Vol. 2: 1933–1990*. Oxford: Oxford University Press.
Winkler, H.A. and H. Kaelble (eds). 1993. *Nationalismus – Nationalitäten – Supranationalität*. Stuttgart: Klett-Cotta.
Wistrich, E. 1994. *The United States of Europe*. London and New York: Routledge.
Wohnout, H. (ed.). 2000. *Demokratie und Geschichte: Jahrbuch des Karl von Vogelsang-Instituts zur Erforschung der Geschichte der christlichen Demokratie in Österreich*. Vienna: Böhlau.
Wolfe, R. (ed.). 1984. *Americans as Proconsuls. United States Military Government in Germany and Japan, 1944–1952*. Carbondale: Southern Illinois University Press.
Wolfrum, E. 1991. *Französische Besatzungspolitik und deutsche Sozialdemokratie. Politische Neuansätze in der "Vergessenen Zone" bis zur Bildung des Südweststaates 1945–1952*. Düsseldorf: Droste.
Woller, H. 1982. *Die Loritz-Partei. Geschichte, Struktur und Politik der Wirtschaftlichen Aufbau-Vereinigung (WAV) 1945–1955*. Stuttgart: DEVA.
Yergin, D. 1980. *Shattered Peace: The Origins of the Cold War and the National Security State*. Harmondsworth: Penguin.
Young, J. 1993. *Britain and European Unity, 1945–1992*. Basingstoke: Macmillan 2nd ed.

Zaborowski, M. 2004. *Germany, Poland and Europe: Conflict, Co-operation and Europeanisation*. Manchester and New York: Manchester University Press.

Zanoli, M. 2003. *Zwischen Klassenkampf, Pazifismus und geistiger Landesverteidigung: die Sozialdemokratische Partei der Schweiz und die Wehrfrage 1920–1939*. Zurich: Forschungsstelle für Sicherheitspolitik der ETH.

Zauner, S. 1994. *Erziehung und Kulturmission. Frankreichs Bildungspolitik in Deutschland 1945–1949*. Munich: Oldenbourg.

Ziemke E. 1975. *The U.S. Army in the Occupation of Germany, 1944–1946*. Washington D.C.: Centre of Military History, United States Army.

Zimmer, A. 1987. *Demokratiegrundung und Verfassungsgebung in Bayern. Die Entstehung der Verfassung des Freistaates Bayern von 1946*. Frankfurt am Main: Peter Lang.

Zorn, W. 1986. *Bayerns Geschichte im 20. Jahrhundert. Von der Monarchie zum Bundesland*. Munich: Beck.

INDEX

A

Abendland (Occident)
  abendländisch academies, 9, 177
  abendländisch groups in Bavaria, 177, 185–86, 190
  abendländisch groups in civil society, 16, 80
  abendländisch journals, 9, 14, 31, 74
  and anti-Bolshevism, 9, 74
  as alternative to Europe in Western bloc, 9, 77, 200
  and borders of Europe, 11, 39, 173
  and Catholicism, 14, 61
  and Christian democracy, 179, 184–85
  and contrast between *Kultur* and *Zivilisation*, 177
  definition of *Abendland*, 9
  and democracy, 14, 31, 67, 202
  and ecumenism, 14, 158, 177
  and Europe as Third Force, 16, 24, 80, 200
  and federalism within Germany, 80
  and Holy Roman Empire, 13
  and *Mitteleuropa* /Central Europe, 24, 156, 166, 192
  and modernization, 180–81
  and resistance to Americanization, 74, 77
  Untergang des Abendlandes, 14
  and the West, 9, 166
  and Westernization of FRG, 9, 177
Abetz, Otto, 45, 63
Adenauer, Konrad
  Franco-German rapprochement, 175–76
  membership of Europäischer Kulturbund, 30
  Ostpolitik, 204–205
  policy of *Westbindung*, 6, 74, 76, 79, 173, 178, 200, 204
  relation to federalists, 8, 77
  revival of party democracy in West Germany, 65
Adorno, Theodor, 23, 25, 43, 61, 177
Americanization, 8–9, 62, 74, 77, 127
Anschluss
  opposition to *Anschluss* of 1938, 100, 102
  right-wing support for idea of *Anschluss*, 38, 43
  socialist support for idea of *Anschluss*, 90, 101, 105
anti-republicanism, 31, 33, 40, 46, 74, 78
aristocracy
  in decline after 1918, 40, 42
  as different kind of elite to democratic, 30, 35, 42, 68, 69
  relation to New Right, 42, 68
  role in Bundesrat, 13
  role in Europäischer Kulturbund, 31
  role in Holy Roman Empire, 9
  role in military, 40, 46, 48, 153
  as transnational, 35, 68
Asia, 11, 32–33, 91, 158, 180
associations
  in civil society, 5, 62, 199
  federalist associations (see also federalism), 79, 180
  in interwar Germany, 16
  in post-war West Germany, 24, 62
  relation to cultural production, 6, 42, 199
  relation to democracy, 6–7, 24, 42
  transnational associations, 39, 55, 66
Austria (Österreich)
  as Catholic state, 31
  and heritage of Holy Roman Empire, 66
  as marginalized part of Germany, 4, 14, 38, 154
  as multinational empire, 36

as part of Central Europe/*Mitteleuropa*, 10, 38, 102, 127, 136–37, 206–207
as part of Greater Germany, 37, 38, 43, 105, 155
as southern German state, 156–58, 186, 189–90
as Western nation in post-war period, 108, 135
as WW1 loser nation, 32, 36, 38, 90
Austro-Marxism, 90–91, 96, 130

B

Bauer, Hans, 148, 154, 163, 179, 182
Baumgartner, Joseph, 186, 189–90, 197
Bavaria (Bayern)
    Bavarian separatism, 185, 201
    German exiles from Bavaria, 155, 185
    federalists in Bavaria, 146, 155, 157, 177, 185, 189
    intersection of European federalism and German federalism within Bavaria, 138, 174, 184–87, 189–91
    as marginalized southern German state, 38, 186, 192–93
    opposition to centralizations of power in FRG, 65, 166, 187, 189
    as part of 'better', southern Germany, 155–58, 191
Bayerische Partei/Bavarian Party (BP), 184, 190–91
Bayerische Volkspartei/Bavarian People's Party (BVP), 155, 184
Belgium, 10, 31, 37, 71, 150, 152, 156
Benn, Gottfried, 25, 42, 52
Bergstraesser, Arnold, 26, 30, 40, 45, 59, 63
Bertholet, René, 97, 112, 117
Bevin, Ernest, 56, 129, 135, 142, 144
Bidault, Georges, 107, 175–76
Bizone/Trizone, 6, 187
Blum, Léon, 22, 94
Bolshevism
    anti-Bolshevism, 9, 32, 60, 154
    ISK understanding of, 91–92, 97, 106, 117
Borch, Herbert von, 44, 59, 63, 73, 77
Bosch, Robert/Bosch Corporation 31, 60
Brandt, Willy
    Ostpolitik, 117, 134, 136, 205
    as part of Bürgermeisterflügel, 121
    Programme for a Social Europe, 206
    writings on European integration, 102–103, 106

Braun, Otto, 146
    attitude to annexations of Germany's eastern states, 153–54
    relations with Allied powers, 153, 165
Brentano, Heinrich von
    on Adenauer's policy of *Westbindung*, 79, 178, 204
    on federalism within Germany, 186, 189
    work within NEI, 175
Briand, Aristide, 7, 29, 41
Briand Plan, 24, 37, 63
Britain, 28, 33–34, 46, 63, 72
    British attitudes to European integration, 29, 135, 203–204
    as exile centre, 97, 98, 100, 103, 118, 130–31
    foreign policy in run-up to WW2, 44, 100, 123
    German socialists' attitudes to, 100, 104, 123, 131
    as part of Western *Zivilisation*, 9, 36
    press in Britain, 23
    role in Western bloc, 135
    socialist groups in, 97, 98, 100, 103, 118–19, 127
    as WW2 victor nation, 74
Brussels Defence Pact, 3, 79
Bundesverband der Deutschen Industrie (BDI), 60–61, 182
Bürgermeisterflügel, 108, 116, 119
    position on European integration, 121, 181, 188

C

Canaris, Admiral Wilhelm, 46, 53, 149
capitalism, 26, 134
    Christian critiques of, 25, 177, 180
    leftist critiques of, 93, 123, 135
    relationship to rise of Nazism, 115, 123
    social democratic accommodation with, 130
    and United States, 25, 33, 88, 124, 137
Catholicism (see also *Abendland*, Christian democracy, personalism)
    Catholic Academic Association (CAA), 31
    Catholic publications, 31, 74, 186
    Centre Party, 31, 151
    ecumenism, 14, 149, 174, 177
    Kulturkampf, 30–31
    left-wing Catholic groups, 25, 59, 67, 150, 174, 176, 180
    opposition to Catholic Church, 90

relation to Protestantism, 14, 58, 61
right-wing Catholic groups, 40, 45–46, 61, 177, 180
role in Holy Roman Empire, 36, 74, 190
role of Vatican in transnational negotiations, 149
and southern Germany, 18, 151, 158, 186
transnational cooperation between Catholics, 166, 174
Central Europe (*Mitteleuropa*), 24, 30, 207
Allied plans during wartime, 107, 127, 151, 154, 158
economic integration of, 36–37, 185
ethnic mix, 10
exiled groups from, 97, 99–100, 102–103, 126, 156
German-speaking populations, 4, 10, 91, 172, 205
Germany's role, 12, 17–18, 36–39, 155–56, 185, 192, 206
Habsburgs' role, 38, 55, 95
minorities, 38–39
Nazi incursions, 72, 101–102, 105
as neither Eastern nor Western, 156
neutralism, 79–80, 126, 136, 178, 200, 204
Ostpolitik, 77, 136, 204–205
plans for German-led *Mitteleuropa*, 10, 36, 38–39
relation to *Kultur*, 9
return of, 10, 206–207
revolutions in, 89–90
right-wing plans for integration of *Mitteleuropa*, 36–39, 77
socialist plans for integration of *Mitteleuropa*, 15, 72, 88–90, 100–105, 121, 125–26
Soviet presence, 108, 134, 136–37, 158–59, 166, 172
Central Intelligence Agency (CIA), 150
as funder of cultural production, 25, 58–59, 75
Chatham House, 63, 76, 104
Christian democracy (see also personalism, Catholicism)
American attitudes to Christian democracy, 151–53, 166
approach of national Christian democratic leaders to integration, 73, 173, 175–76, 178, 192, 204–205
convergence between Christian and social democrats, 181, 184, 187

ecumenism, 151
role in federalist movements, 146, 149, 173, 191
role of liberal Catholicism, 151–53, 158, 176
scepticism of Christian political groups about democracy, 15, 158, 199
socialist opposition to Christian democratic policy on integration, 88, 116, 120, 125, 129
and Third Way Europe, 179, 189
transnational organizations , 3, 149, 166, 173–76, 178, 191
and Westernization, 177–78, 204–205
Christianity
as forming values on which European culture based, 185
as safeguard against totalitarianism, 184
as unifying force in Europe, 14, 190
Christlich Demokratische Union/Christian Democratic Union (CDU), 17
Ahlen Programme, 176
connections to MRP, 174–75
connections to SKVP, 174–75
debates about *Westbindung*, 74, 79, 178, 200
European policy of coalition partners, 178, 205
proponents of European integration, 16, 189
Christlich Soziale Union/Christian Social Union (CSU)
Bavaria's role in FRG, 189–90
debates about *Westbindung*, 79
electoral record in Bavaria, 183–85
relations with SPD in Bavaria, 185–86
support for federalism, 189
Churchill, Winston
critiques of his European policy, 182
ideas on European integration, 156, 158, 203
role in EM, 73, 148, 173, 182
civil society, 4–5, 7
civil society elites, 19n, 68, 80
civil society groups in Eastern Europe in 1970s and 1980s, 5
debates about European integration, 3, 202, 208
definition, 5
Gramsci on civil society, 95
groups active in EU, 19n, 202
in interwar period, 24, 28–29, 31, 45, 47

in post-war period, 47, 55, 63, 80
media and civil society, 5–6, 23–24, 28, 44, 55
and National Socialism, 69
as opinion former, 5, 44, 55, 58–59, 173
relation to democracy, 6, 28, 47, 58, 66–67, 80, 95, 162
relation to nation-state, 35, 38–39, 62
relation to political parties, 28, 64, 66, 180
socialist ideas of, 95
transnational civil society, 5, 29, 38–39, 47, 64, 80, 95, 208
civilization, see *Zivilisation*
coalitions, 17
 Allied policy towards, 65
 in Bavaria, 183–84, 192
 of Christian and social democrats, 152–53, 164–65
 critiques of coalitions, 41
 of exiled socialist groups in Britain, 103, 105
 in FRG, 121, 181, 188, 205, 207
 regional versus national coalitions, 121, 146, 166, 181
 role in democracies, 121, 152, 181, 202
 Schumacher's decision not to join Grand Coalition, 65, 120
 in Weimar Germany, 31, 37, 41, 145
Cold War (see also *Ostpolitik*)
 Cold War borders in Europe, 1, 3, 55, 75, 159, 173, 199
 Cold War division of Germany, 116, 120, 135, 153–54
 cultural Cold War, 25, 58, 134
 Eastern bloc in Europe, 75, 127–28, 135, 206
 Europe as Third Force, 14, 17–18, 35, 73, 88, 116, 124, 182, 201–202
 neutralism, 73, 133
 splits between Allies during WW2, 17, 146
 Western bloc in Europe, 9, 73, 79
Comintern, 33, 98, 152
Committee of the Socialist International Conference (COMISCO), 121–22, 128–29
Communism
 Communism as mass rule, 35
 Communist bloc in Eastern Europe, 206
 Communist threat in Europe, 33
 Communists in government in Bavaria, 189
 ex-Communists, 25, 87, 98
 fall of Communism, 5

KPD, 86
KPD-O/KPO, 90
Leninbund, 90
Popular Fronts, 97, 152
 in Soviet Union, 86
 splits between communists and socialists in Weimar Germany, 86, 90, 92–94
 splits between exiled communists and socialists (for those in Switzerland see entries on Demokratisches Deutschland and Freies Deutschland), 98, 100–101, 103–105
 spread of Communism across Eastern Europe, 151, 153
 in Switzerland, 160
 Third International, 89
Confessing Church [*Bekennende Kirche*], 60, 151, 156
Congress for Cultural Freedom (CCF), 25, 58
conservatism
 conservative attitudes to democracy (see also entries under Abendland and democracy), 80, 176
 conservative Franco-German groups, see Franco-German associations
 conservative intellectuals, 25, 29, 45
 conservative opposition to National Socialism, 60, 69, 71, 150
 conservative revolution, 15, 42
 conservative version of *Ostpolitik*, 55
 Conservatives in Britain, 203
 conservatives in EM, 181
 inner émigrés, 26, 62, 71
 relationship between conservatives and National Socialists, 10
 Swiss Conservative People's Party (SKVP), 174
constitutions
 Basic Law, 68
 Bavarian constitution, 162, 185–86
 changes to constitutions by plebiscite, 160, 162
 constitutional nationhood, 13
 constitutional rights of the individual, 202
 constitutional settlement in Germany in 1871, 13
 democratic constitutions after 1918, 6, 42
 democracy enshrined in constitutions, 65, 106
 Europe as constitutional order, 187–88, 200
 Weimar constitution, 41, 94, 162

Coudenhove-Kalergi, Richard, 7, 28–29, 38, 45, 60, 148
Council for Mutual Economic Assistance (CMEA or COMECON), 135–36
Council of Europe, 120–21, 124, 136, 183
Cripps, Stafford 131, 156
Culture. see *Kultur*
Curtius, Ernst Robert, 43, 45, 61
Customs Union, Austro-German, 37
Czechoslovakia
  borders, 102, 123, 153
  coup of 1948, 135
  dissident groups, 206
  German occupation of, 103
  minorities, 39
  trade with Germany, 10, 37
  revolution, 89
  Sudetenland, 90

D

Danube, 172, 185–86, 191
  Danubian clubs, 156
  Danubian federation, 122, 146, 155–56
  Danubian monarchy, 74, 102
Dawes Plan, 32, 34
de-integration in Europe, 13, 47, 198
democracy, see Christian democracy, liberal democracy, parliamentary democracy, social democracy
democratic deficit, 5, 202, 208
democratization, 5, 13, 62, 86
Demokratisches Deutschland (Das Demokratische Deutschland)
  anti-Communism, 153
  as coalition, 151, 164, 186, 191
  conceptions of democracy, 162–63, 180, 188–89, 191
  effect of exile in Switzerland, 159–62, 191
  federalism, 153–54, 180, 186, 191
  links to Allied governments, 149, 153
  neutralism, 159
  opposition to Potsdam Agreement, 153–54
  rivalry to Freies Deutschland, 17, 164
  southern German revival, 158, 186, 191
  tensions within, 165
denazification, 55–56, 155
Deutsch-Französische Gesellschaft, 29, 45, 57
Deutsch-Französisches Studienkomitee, 31, 63
Deutsche Verlagsanstalt (DEVA), 60–61
dictatorship, 13, 55
  different versions of dictatorship, 67–68
  National Socialist dictatorship, 55, 73–74
  party dictatorships, 161, 188
  Soviet dictatorship, 68, 90
Döblin, Alfred, 28, 54
Dulles, Allen
  as OSS chief, 150–51
  relationship to Demokratisches Deutschland, 150–51, 153, 156, 172
  views on Germany, 150–51, 155–57, 162
  views on post-war order in Europe, 154
Dulles, John Foster, 150, 168

E

East Germany, see GDR
Eastern Europe (see also *Ostpolitik*)
  agriculture, 72, 122
  Council for Mutual Economic Assistance (CMEA/COMECON), 136
  democratization, 5
  Eastern bloc, 64, 76
  Easternization, 74–75, 107
  ethnic minorities, 33
  expulsion of Germans from, 127
  post-communist, 5
  redrawing of map at Versailles, 27
  revisionism, 27
  revolutions, 135
  Soviet influence, 76, 127–28, 135, 153
  Western Europe as magnet, 125, 205–207
Eberhard, Fritz [Hellmut von Rauschenplat], 86, 104, 120
education, 92–93
Ehard, Hans, 184, 189
Eichler, Willi
  analysis of Soviet foreign policy, 101
  Bolshevism, 106
  criticism of British foreign policy, 100
  as editor and journalist, 93, 95, 102, 125
  European policy of post-war SPD, 119, 121
  exile in Britain, 104
  exile in France, 98, 103
  Godesberg Programme, 17, 136
  as leader of ISK, 93
  as leading member of socialist cartel in exile, 87
  as leading social democrat in FRG, 87, 118, 124, 130
  League of Nations, 99
  position on *Anschluss*, 105
  relation to SVG, 132
  relations with trade unions, 93, 98

return to SPD fold, 107, 117–19
SPD policy of intransigent opposition, 119–20
support for Third Force Europe, 126
transnational civil society groups, 98, 104–105
views on democracy, 105–106
elites
EM elites, 173, 179, 183
EU elites, 5, 183, 192, 208
French-German elites, 29, 31, 35, 55, 57, 78
national elites, 108
party political elites, 165
role of elites in democracies, 35, 40, 42, 58, 68, 78, 80, 203
socialist elites, 92–93
transnational elites, 31, 35, 62, 66, 68, 104, 199–200
Ellwang Circle, 189
Europa-Bund, 64, 180
Europa Union (Germany), 3, 166, 173, 179, 181, 191
Europa Union (Switzerland), 147–48, 154, 160–61, 163, 179–80, 182
Europäische Revue, 24, 26–27, 32, 43, 62, 66
discussions of minorities, 39
ideas of *Mitteleuropa*, 36, 77
links to big business, 60–61
links to other Catholic publications, 31
National Socialist influence, 44
as predecessor to *Merkur*, 24, 26–27, 43, 59–60
readership, 31, 35, 47
relation to Europäischer Kulturbund, 29–30, 45
views about Soviet Union and United States, 34
Europäische Schriftsteller Vereinigung (ESV), 45
Europäischer Kulturbund, 29–30, 40, 43, 47
European Coal and Steel Community (ECSC), 3, 175, 198, 203, 205
BDI opposition to, 60–61
European socialist parties' position on, 129, 135
federalists' position on, 182
SPD opposition to, 120–21
European Community (EC), 1, 136, 206–207
European Defence Community (EDC), 79, 120, 133, 182

European Economic Community (EEC), 203, 205
European Movement (EM)
American financing of, 175–76, 182
conflicts between federalists and unionists, 73–74, 173, 181, 183
relation to political parties, 129, 137, 146, 181–82
roots in wartime resistance movement, 7, 73, 75, 150
European Nationality Congress, 38
European Parliament (EP), 3, 174
European Recovery Programme (ERP), see Marshall Plan
European treaties, 8, 199, 201
European Union (EU), 3, 207–208
histories of EU, 192, 198
relationship between EU institutions and interest groups, 5, 19n, 208
European University Institute (EUI), 1
exiles (see also Demokratisches Deutschland and ISK), 2, 4, 7, 47, 74, 102, 130
differences among exiles, 102–103, 106–107, 121, 146, 152, 156, 190
exile press, 98, 102, 115
exiled socialist groups, 17, 86–89, 96–98, 100–101, 105
exiles forming coalitions, 152–53, 181
exiles in Scandinavia, 106–107
governments-in-exile, 75, 126, 156
hostility to exiles, 62, 118–19, 126–27, 164–65
influence in transnational networks, 176, 182, 201, 203
influence on American agencies, 150–51, 166
London as exile centre, 103–105, 115, 156
remigrants, 54, 74, 87–88, 108, 115–19, 124, 130, 183, 185
restrictions on exiles, 147–48
splits between exiled and host nation socialist, 126–27
as Westernizers, 8–9, 25, 88, 98–100, 107, 116, 120, 131–32, 160, 165

F

Fabian Society, 104–105
family, role of, 5, 67–68, 156, 177
fascism
similarities to socialism and capitalism, 123
support expressed in *Europäische Revue*, 40–43, 45

Federal Council (of Switzerland), 160–62
Federal Republic of Germany (FRG), West
  Germany, 24–25, 47, 60, 157, 173,
  176, 178
  American support for, 151, 185
  democracy, 80, 119–20, 191, 202–203
  institutions, 6, 187, 202
  relations with Eastern Europe, 18, 116,
    204, 206
  relationship with GDR, 18, 136, 154
  role in integrated Europe, 79, 121, 175,
    183, 192–93
  role in Western alliance, 12, 79, 120,
    133–36, 192, 200, 204–205
federalism (see also European Movement)
  cross-party nature of federalist groups, 129,
    180–81, 186, 202
  European federalist groups, 1, 3, 63, 98,
    104, 126, 148, 173, 180
  federalism within Germany, 13, 17, 65,
    146–47, 157, 202
  federalists' role in integrating Europe, 7–8,
    73, 134, 137, 146, 150, 175, 182–83,
    191, 201
  historiography of federalism, 7–8, 183,
    192
  intersection of domestic German and
    European federalism, 17–18, 74, 80,
    108, 138, 154, 173, 185–86, 188–89,
    201, 204, 207
  popularity of federalist groups in Germany,
    180–81
  Third Way federalism, 14, 73, 77, 80, 88,
    103, 106, 130, 137–38, 151, 153, 166,
    173, 179, 182, 187–88
First World War
  changes to European map, 2, 33–34, 102
  decline of Europe, 32
  fall of empires, 2
  French-German reconciliation, 27–28
  revolutions, 15, 95
  rise of nationalism, 38
  Soviet-German relations, 145
  splits in international socialist
    organisations, 88–89
Flanders, Allan, 104, 131–33
Fliess, Walter, 87, 119, 132
  being deported to Australia on the *Dunera*,
    130–31
  ideas for integrating Europe, 121–23

France
  anti-Republicanism, 32–33, 40, 46–47, 63
  Catholicism, 35–36, 46–47, 180
  Christian democracy, 129, 150, 180
  as enemy of Germany, 27–28, 44, 72, 123,
    145
  Franco-German reconciliation, 26, 28–30,
    46, 55–58, 78
  French Revolution, 35–36, 74
  French Zone of Occupation, 16, 26,
    54–58, 78, 178, 189
  Gaullism, 56, 175, 178, 203–205
  as host nation for exiles, 17, 97–98, 100,
    103
  as market for Germany, 10, 37, 72
  as member of Western bloc, 128, 154, 175
  as occupied nation, 54
  Vichy, 32, 47, 56, 63
  as WW2 victor nation, 74, 78, 150
  as *Zivilisation*, 9, 36, 154
Franco-German associations,
  Christian democratic groups, 150, 174–76
  cultural organizations, 23–31, 57–58
  socialist groups, 77, 98
Frankfurter Hefte, 25, 59, 64, 67, 186
Freie Demokratische Partei/ Free Democratic
  Party (FDP)
  opposition to CDU's European policy, 79,
    178, 205
Freies Deutschland (see also Demokratisches
  Deutschland), 17, 149, 152–53, 160, 164

G
Gasperi, Alicide de, 8, 175
Gasset, José Ortega y, 35, 61, 64, 177
de Gaulle, Charles, 47, 78
Gaullism, see France
Geist und Tat, 125
German Democratic Republic (GDR), East
  Germany (see FRG, *Ostpolitik*), 118,
  178, 204
  Berlin Wall, 136
  division between Germans, 193, 206–207
  Hallstein Doctrine, 204
  member of Warsaw Pact, 136
  Soviet recognition of, 80, 179
German national identity, 4, 10
Gide, André, 28, 45, 61, 63
Gillies, William, 103, 105, 126–27
Gleichschaltung, 42, 154, 161
Godesberg Programme, 17, 93, 130, 136

Goebbels, Josef, 43, 45–46
Goerdeler, Carl, 60, 71, 149
Gramsci, Antonio, 58, 95
Great Depression, 122
Greater Germany, *Großdeutschland*
  Austrians' support for, 38, 43, 64
  Nazi version, 43, 74
  socialist conceptions, 96, 101, 105
  southern German case for, 146, 154, 185
Gruppe 47, 25

H

Habsburg, Otto von, 74, 102
Habsburgs
  Habsburg Empire, 74, 95, 156
  Habsburg Monarchy, 10
  Neo-Habsburgian plans for integrating Europe, 38, 55, 64, 158
Heidegger, Martin, 24–25, 71
Heidelberg Programme (SPD), 91, 94–95, 130
Hertenstein Conference, 148
Heuss, Theodor, 44, 61, 177
historiography of European integration, 3, 7–10, 17, 129
Hitler, Adolf
  business support for, 115
  foreign policy revisionism, 102, 163
  military opposition, 46, 54–56, 71, 149, 152
  plans for European Empire, 10, 105, 179–80, 182
  right-wing opposition, 31, 69
Hoegner, Wilhelm
  anti-centralism, 65, 186–87, 189–90
  as Bavarian Minister-President, 146, 166, 183–84
  conflict with post-war SPD leadership, 186–88
  connections to OSS, 150, 156, 172
  defence of Bavarian autonomy, 155, 157, 185
  drafting of constitutions, 183, 185–86
  ideas about democracy, 159, 162–63, 189
  influence of Switzerland on his political ideology, 157, 159–60
  memorandums for post-war reconstruction, 155–56, 185
  openness to Christian political movements, 160, 184
  relationship to southern German federalists, 185–86, 189
  as socialist reformer, 187–90
  strengthening of southern Germany, 17, 155, 157–58, 187, 191–92
  struggles in Switzerland, 148
  support for European federalism, 157, 163
  working within coalitions, 121, 157, 160, 166, 184–86, 189–90, 192
Holy Roman Empire
  attempts to recreate, 9, 38, 66, 74
  federal structure, 13, 66, 77
  geographical dimensions, 12
  nostalgia for, 13
  role of Christianity in, 14, 74, 190

I

ideology
  and civil society, 58, 64
  democracy as ideology, 69, 74
  end of ideology, 202
  and foreign policy, 2, 15, 33, 44, 74, 159, 163, 166
  ideological convergence over European integration, 72, 121, 138, 146, 159, 181, 192, 202–203
  ideological shifts among socialist groups, 17, 101, 107
  National Socialist, 69, 71, 151, 155
  political parties and ideology, 14, 61, 64, 68, 146
  press and ideological alignment, 24–26, 28
  suspicion of ideology, 6, 12, 14, 24–25, 44, 61–62, 64, 66, 159, 163–64, 180
imperialism, 15, 72, 100
industrialists
  as anti-Communists, 60
  as opponents of National Socialism, 31
  as supporters of National Socialism, 31, 45, 115
  role in promoting European integration, 30, 60–61
inner émigrés, 26, 45, 62, 71
intellectual history, 7–8, 47, 73
  intellectual history of socialist internationalism, 125
  intellectual history of Christian democratic approaches to integration, 173
  as part of social and cultural history, 11, 198
International Transport Federation (ITF), 87, 93, 97–98
International Working Union of Socialist Parties (IWUSP)/Two and a Half International, 89–90, 94, 96

Internationaler Jugend-Bundes/Internationaler Sozialistischer Kampfbund (IJB/ISK)
    advocacy of revolution, 86, 88, 94, 97, 106, 137
    anti-Catholicism, 90–91
    attitude towards Bolshevism, 91–92, 97, 100, 106, 117, 135
    broadcasting propaganda, 132
    connections in Britain (see also Socialist Vanguard Group), 104, 130–33
    dissolving of group, 117–19
    exile years, 17, 88, 96–98, 131
    ideas about democracy, 92–94, 105–106, 117, 119, 199
    importance of education, 87, 90, 92–93, 95
    internationalism, 91, 95
    leadership structure, 92
    links to trade unions, 87, 93–94
    National Socialist repression, 86, 96
    publishing activities, 6, 98, 105
    relationship with KPD, 86, 92–94
    relationship with other splinter groups, 86–87, 90, 93
    relationship with SPD, 6, 17, 86, 92–94, 107, 116–19
    sister-organization, see Socialist Vanguard Group
    transnational connections, 17, 88–89, 94, 98, 104–105
    Third Way socialism, 101, 106–107, 192, 202
    Westernization, 99–100, 130–34
    working with other exiled socialist groups, 103, 105–106
intransigent opposition (of the SPD), 116, 119–20, 201
Italy
    agriculture, 72
    campaign in Abyssinia, 44, 99
    Christian democracy, 129, 150
    fascism, 29, 40–41, 161
    federalist movements, 126
    as 'good European', 44
    as part of 'Western civilization', 154
    as post-war leader in Europe, 107

J

Jacobinism, (see French Revolution), 68–69
Jaspers, Karl, 23–24, 45, 64
Jünger, Ernst, 25, 55–56, 71

K

Kempski, Jürgen von, 66, 68, 78
Kindt-Kiefer, Jakob, 148
    anti-urbanism, 176–77
    as Christian democrat within Demokratisches Deutschland, 153, 176
    as fundraiser, 176
    in Geneva Circle of NEI, 166, 173–74, 176
    as go-between for French and German Christian democrats, 174–76, 178
    Radical-Social People's Campaign, 176
Kleindeutschland, 154, 201
Kleineuropa, 121, 136, 173
Knoeringen, Waldemar von, 118–19, 132–33, 157, 190
Kogon, Eugen
    editor of *Frankfurter Hefte*, 25, 58, 64, 67
    member of federalist groups within Germany, 186, 189
    president of German EM, 181–82
Kohl, Helmut, 12, 207
Kommunistische Partei Deutschlands (KPD) (see also ISK – relationship with KPD), 86, 90, 92
    rivalry with SPD in Weimar Germany, 94
    support of Nazi-Soviet Pact, 100
Kreisau Circle, 156
Kreisky, Bruno, 136–37
Kultur, 9
    Germans as *Kulturvolk*, 39
    as opposed to *Zivilisation*, 36, 93, 177
    revival of European *Kultur*, 62, 181
Kulturkampf, 30–31
Kumleben, Gerhard, 97, 99

L

Labour Party (Britain)
    approach to European integration, 129, 137–38, 182, 203
    as dominant post-war European socialist party, 73, 127
    left-Labour groups, 87, 89, 131–32
    policy of Western Union, 129, 133, 135
    reforms of Socialist International, 126–27, 129
    relationship with German socialist groups in exile, 101, 103, 126–27, 130–31, 137–38
Laski, Harold, 104, 123
Lasky, Melvyn, 25, 58

League of Nations, 37, 102
  Briand Plan, 7, 29
  criticism of, 44, 99, 163
  ISK proposals for reform, 91
Lebensraum (living space), 34, 44, 102
Lenin, Vladimir Ilyich, 91
liberal democracy, 12
liberalism, 26, 61, 67, 123, 157
Lipgens, Walter, 7–8
Little Entente, 37
Locarno Treaties, 24, 27, 32
  'spirit of Locarno', 28
Loccum Academy, 177
Löwenthal, Richard
  ideas for integrating Europe, 101, 124
  links to Austrian socialists, 101
  links to British socialists, 94, 101
Loth, Wilfried, 1

M

magnet theory, 28, 125, 176, 185, 206
majorities
  dominance of national majorities over minorities, 12, 35, 203
Mann, Heinrich, 28
Mann, Thomas, 28
  journalism, 98
  as member of Europäischer Kulturbund, 30
  as prominent exile, 62
Marshall Plan/European Recovery Programme
  ISK support, 135
  Organization for European Economic Cooperation (OEEC), 3
  promoting Franco-German reconciliation, 75
  SPD support, 124
  support in *Merkur*, 75
  support of BDI, 60
  Westernization, 8, 77
Marxism (see also Austro-Marxism), 64, 93, 129
masses
  in cities, 176–77
  civil society in mass societies, 67–68
  as consumers, 61
  creation of masses by nationalist movements, 14, 35
  and democracy, 69, 159
  elitism about masses, 35, 61, 175
  mass parties, 12, 61, 67, 80, 97, 202
  mass rule, 12, 55
  Massenmachiavellismus, 65
  radicalization of masses, 12, 14, 67, 203
  rise of the masses, 34
  The Revolt of the Masses, 35, 61
  and revolution, 100
  socialism as mass movement, 96
  United States and Soviet Union as polities dominated by the masses, 14, 16, 34–35
  and xenophobia, 69
media, 9
  censorship, 27, 30, 58, 63, 148
  cultural journals, 16, 23–26, 28, 35, 48, 57–58, 64, 67
  press, print media, 23, 27, 47, 55, 65, 79, 98, 199
  propaganda, 27, 43, 45, 87, 98, 104, 132
  radio, 104, 132
  role of Allies, 58, 65
  role of associations, 5, 28, 47, 73
  transnational media, 47, 88
Merkur, 6–7, 16, 24
  assessments of, 25–26
  contributors, 24–25, 63–64, 67–69, 76–78
  federalism, 73
  founding of, 26–27, 55, 58
  French-German reconciliation, 57–58
  French government role as censor, 26, 57
  funding of, 59–62
  ideology, 25–26, 55, 59–64, 66–69, 76
  links to *Europäische Revue*, 24, 27, 42–45, 199
  links to *Neue Rundschau*, 24, 27, 42–43, 199
  position on National Socialism, 71–73
  Third Way Europe, 76–78, 80
Militant Socialist International (MSI) (see Socialist Vanguard Group)
Milward, Alan, 3–4, 7–8, 80
minorities
  European Nationality Congress, 38–39
  German minorities, 36, 38, 206–207
  Minorities Statute, 39
  nations with sizeable minority populations, 15, 33, 43, 102
  rights of minorities, 12, 91, 163
Mitteleuropa, see Central Europe
modernization, 4, 177
Monat, Der, 25, 59, 76
Monnet, Jean, 8, 123

Monte, Hilda [Hilde Meisel]
  links to British academic circles, 123
  as member of transnational federalist circles, 98
  writing on planning and European integration, 123–24
Moras, Joachim
  as editor of *Europäische Revue*, 27, 42
  fundraising for *Merkur*, 59–60
  links to business circles, 60
  role as intellectual in National Socialist Germany, 45
  views expressed in *Europäische Revue*, 44–45
  views on German national identity, 63–64
Moravcsik, Andrew, 3, 8
Mounier, Emmanuel, 63, 160
Müller, Josef, 175
Munich Agreement, 100, 149
Münzenberg, Willi, 91, 98

N

National Socialism
  attacks on civil society, 67
  censorship of media, 27, 42–44, 46
  centralizing policies, 146
  conservative opponents, 26, 46, 60, 62, 71, 149
  electoral success, 41, 99
  as form of Prussianism, 43, 69, 154–55
  as ideology, 69, 71, 74, 102
  intellectuals in National Socialist Germany, 45, 71
  National Socialist Empire as forerunner of integrated Europe, 71, 96, 100–103, 121–24
  National Socialist plans to integrate Europe, 7, 10, 43, 71–73
  negotiations with Soviet Union, 100, 152
  negotiations with Western governments, 163
  occupations of European countries, 32, 101, 127
  as political religion, 15, 74
  propaganda, 43
  racial politics, 146
  reasons for its rise, 74, 115, 122
  relations between military and NS Party, 46, 55–56, 71, 149
  relations between NS Germany and Switzerland, 147
  repression of opponents, 96, 146
nationalism, 6
  economic nationalism, 70
  ethnic v constitutional versions, 13, 74
  federalism as reaction to, 102, 199
  German nationalism from perspective of southern Germans, 147, 154
  Kurt Schumacher as nationalist, 108, 201
  link to imperialism, 44
  nationalism after 1945, 70, 183
  rise of nationalism in Europe after 1918, 28, 33–34, 40, 115, 145
  rise of nationalism in Europe in the nineteenth century, 38, 115
nationalization of resources, 70, 96, 122–23, 176, 181, 188
nation-state
  birth of nation-state in Germany, 14
  critical perspectives on nation-state after 1945, 55–56, 70–71, 199, 203
  federalist proposals to reform nation-states, 80, 163, 189, 193, 201–202, 207
  growth of nation-state in nineteenth century, 2
  hostility to new nation-states after 1918, 6, 16, 33, 40, 47
  minorities within nation-states, 38–39
  political leadership in nation-states, 35
  rescue of nation-state after 1945, 2, 8, 192–93
  role of nation-state in socialist thought, 15, 92, 106, 116, 199
Naumann, Friedrich, 10, 28, 36
Nawiasky, Hans, 155, 185–86
Nazi-Soviet Pact, 100, 152
Nelson, Leonard, 90
  attitude towards Bolshevism, 91–92
  break from SPD, 92, 119
  as educator, 92–93
  internationalism, 90, 93
  leadership style, 92
  opposition to Catholic Church, 90–91
  philosophical influences, 90, 93
neo-realism, 7–8
Netherlands, 10, 31, 128
Neu Beginnen
  founding of, 87
  reuniting with SPD, 117
  role of leaders within post-war SPD, 118–19, 136
  role within exiled socialist cartels, 96, 103
  strategy, 91

theories of European revolution, 101–102, 105, 126
Third Way support for European integration, 124, 126
transnational connections, 94, 101
Neue Rundschau,
  changing character during National Socialist years, 43
  fears of Soviet Union and United States, 32, 34, 36
  links to civil society associations, 28
  Paeschke as editor, 42–43, 46
  as predecessor to *Merkur*, 27
  as venue for debates on European integration, 27, 32–33
  as venue for Franco-German dialogue, 24, 28
neutralism (see also federalism – Third Way federalism)
  support for neutral Germany after 1945, 73–74, 159, 178, 207
newspapers, print media, see media
North Atlantic Treaty Organization (NATO), 133–36, 157, 182, 204
nostalgia, 13–14, 199
Nouvelles Equipes Internationales (NEI), 3, 173–74, 191
  Geneva Circle, 166, 174–75

O

Occident, see *Abendland*
Office of Military Government, United States (OMGUS), 65, 185
Office of Strategic Services (OSS)
  Berne Office, 150
  links to federalist movement, 150
  policy on southern German states, 156–57
  role in advising US policy on European reconstruction, 150–51, 154, 156, 162
  role of German exiles, 150–51, 153, 172
  warnings on spread of Communism, 151, 154
Ollenhauer, Erich, 87, 103, 105–106, 118, 186
Organization for European Economic Cooperation (OEEC), 3, 60
Ostpolitik
  in the 1950s, 18, 77, 79, 136, 192, 204
  in the 1960s, 18, 79, 137–38, 192, 204–205
  Brandt's policy, 134, 136, 205

Ostpolitik as initiative promoted by civil society groups, 206
right-wing plans for, 55, 200
socialist plans for, 89, 108, 117

P

Paeschke, Hans
  activities during National Socialist period, 46
  analysis of National Socialism, 69, 71
  assessment of his role as *Merkur* editor, 26
  connections to French officers during Occupation, 26–27, 54–55, 57
  on émigré intellectuals, 62
  on *Europäische Revue*, 27, 42–44
  on funding of, and control over, *Merkur*, 58–62
  on German traditions, 26, 63–64, 69
  on Germany's role in Western bloc, 77
  on ideological leanings of *Merkur*, 26
  on *Neue Rundschau*, 27, 42–43
  as participant in transnational civil society, 64
  as promoter of Franco-German rapprochement, 46–47, 57–58
  on role of elites in democracies, 68
  on role of media in civil society, 24, 58–59, 62, 64
  role in Deutsch-Französische Gesellschaft, 29, 45, 57
  role in Germany military during WW2, 26, 54
  understanding of democracy, 66–67
Paneuropa Union, 7, 29, 180
parliamentary democracy, 4, 9
  alternative forms of parliaments, 161–62, 189
  antiparliamentarian groups, 32
  constraining of, 12, 147, 159, 161
  interwar versions, 13, 31, 33, 41, 92, 106, 156, 162
  scepticism of, 13, 31, 33, 40–41, 48, 67–68, 88, 92, 117, 119, 156, 161, 163, 189
  socialist attitudes to, 15, 17, 86, 88, 92, 94, 99, 106, 108, 117, 119, 121, 129–31, 134, 137, 187
  Swiss version of, 159–60, 162
peace
  interwar peace, 27, 32, 74, 91, 150
  peace during Cold War, 133, 178

plans for post-war peace, 56, 71, 78, 106–107, 149, 160–61, 172
role of civil society in creating and maintaining peace, 24
PEN (Poets, Essayists and Novelists) International, 29, 45
permissive consensus, 4, 173
personalism, 15, 63, 160, 176, 180
plebiscites, see referenda
political geography, 11, 35
political parties
  coalitions between leftist parties, 97–98, 100, 103–104
  coalitions between parties in exile, 152–53, 164–65
  coalitions between parties in FRG, 121, 181, 183–87, 191–92
  coalitions between parties in Weimar Germany, 37
  critiques of mass parties as too moderate, 95, 97, 99
  European integration as an issue for parties, 11, 15–17
  function of parties in parliamentary democracies, 6–7, 35, 66–67, 94–95, 107, 159, 161–62, 188–89
  international party alliances, 88–89, 98–100, 121, 126–30, 149–50, 174–75
  as major actors in history of European integration, 16, 73, 80
  parties in Switzerland, 159–60
  reintroduction of parties in FRG, 65–67, 117–18, 151, 188
  relationship between local and national parties, 183–84, 186, 188
  relationship between parties and civil society organizations, 6–7, 28, 59, 64–65, 67, 80, 103–104, 148, 173, 180, 187–88
  religious make-up of parties in Germany, 30–31, 152–53
  role of parties in FRG, 6, 120
  role in promoting international conflict, 13–14, 35, 163, 190
  role in radicalizing masses, 12, 14, 41, 61, 67–69, 80, 152, 161, 163, 190
  splits between socialist parties along national or bloc lines, 86, 126–30, 135–36
Popular Fronts
  between exiled socialist groups, 132

in France, 46
local Popular Fronts, 97–98
Soviet-sponsored Popular Fronts among German exiles, 17, 151
Potsdam Agreement
  bloc building, 14, 126, 158, 182
  division of Germany, 78, 153, 158, 160, 201
  marginalisation of resistance movements and governments-in-exile, 75, 126, 153
Prussia
  dismemberment of, 153, 157, 172
  federalist reaction to Prussian predominance, 13–14, 17, 146, 154, 158, 192
  National Socialism as form of Prussianism, 43, 69, 155, 157
  opposition of Prussian military elites to National Socialism, 46
  as predominant German state, 4
  Prussian-led unification of Germany, 38, 201
public opinion, 5

R
Rapacki Plan, 80, 136, 204
Rapallo, Treaty of, 77, 178
reconstruction, post-war
  Allies' plans, 17, 54–55, 126, 132, 150, 152–53, 155
  Christian democrats' plans, 174–77
  exiles' plans, 9, 17, 126, 132, 146, 150, 152–53, 155, 160–62, 166, 173, 176–77, 183
  German military opposition's plans, 71
  role of Marshall Plan, 8, 75, 123
  socialists' plans, 88, 103–104, 106–107, 118–24
referenda, plebiscites, 1, 5, 41, 160, 162
regionalism
  as abiding sentiment in Germany, 13, 164–65, 186–87, 193, 202
  in Bavaria, 186, 189–91, 201
  Bürgermeisterflügel practising form of, 108, 188
  'Europe of the regions', 17, 80, 188, 206–207
  relationship to European federalism, 7, 13, 72, 80, 122–23, 138, 146, 161, 173–74, 181, 183, 189, 192–93, 201, 206

religion (see also *Abendland*, Christianity, Catholicism), 11, 14–15, 199, 202
  political religion, 15
reparations, 28, 32, 34, 75
resistance movements
  as core of European federalist movement, 7, 47, 73, 126, 180
  marginalization in reconstruction plans of Allies, 75, 126
  post-war cooperation between resistance movements, 56, 126, 180
  wartime cooperation between resistance movements, 98, 104–106, 150, 156, 174
Reuter, Ernst, 121
revolution, 11, 160
  conservative revolution, 15, 42, 74
  cultural revolution, 95
  European integration as form of revolutionary change, 15, 89, 101–102, 105–107, 126, 185, 200
  fascist 'youthful revolution', 41
  French Revolution, 36, 41
  German revolution of 1918, 33, 89–90, 106
  ISK theories of, 86, 88, 92, 94, 97, 99, 106, 131, 137, 202
  opposing options of reform and revolution, 88, 97, 119, 137
  role of Leninist vanguard, 91–92, 119
  Sender der Europäischen Revolution (SER), 104
  Socialist International and its position on reform versus revolution, 126–27
  Soviet Union and revolutions in Europe, 33, 200
  SPD's attitude towards revolution, 90, 95–96, 106, 120
  WW1 and revolutions, 31, 33, 89–90, 92
Revolutionäre Sozialisten Österreichs (RSÖ), 103
Reynold, Gonzague de, 63, 160
Ritzel, Heinrich, 146
  break-up of Demokratisches Deutschland, 165
  connections to Allied secret services, 150, 154, 161
  ideas about democracy, 161–63
  plans for German reconstruction, 161–62
  promoting of southern German agenda, 154, 158
  role in founding Demokratisches Deutschland, 152
  role in Council of Europe, 146, 183
  role in German Europa Union, 166, 173, 179, 181–82
  role in Swiss Europa Union, 148, 154, 163, 179–81
  working across party lines, 160, 181
Rochelle, Pierre Drieu la, 32–33, 35
Röpke, Wilhelm, 63
  on masses and xenophobia, 68–69
  on relationship between nationalism and socialism, 69–70
Rohan, Karl Anton
  calls for German-led Central European community, 37–40
  on cultivating a new European elite, 40–42
  as founder of Europäischer Kulturbund and *Europäische Revue*, 30
  on minorities in Central and Eastern Europe, 39
  opposition to interwar democracy, 42
  position on Italian fascism, 40–41
  as promoter of Franco-German reconciliation, 35–36
  relations with National Socialists, 43–44
Romier, Lucien, 32–33, 35
Rossi, Ernesto, 7, 150
Rougemont, Denis de
  as European federalist, 134
  as interwar anti-liberal, 63
  as personalist, 63
Ruf, Der, 25, 57, 64, 73
Ruhr, controversy over French control of, 27–28
Russia, (see also Soviet Union)
  as Cold War superpower, 118, 133
  as imperial power in Eastern Europe, 39, 76, 107, 118, 135, 158
  as part of Europe, 64
  shifts in its borders, 75 , 107, 118, 152–53
  as threat to Europe, 32–33, 60, 118, 135, 152–53, 158
  as un-European, 32–33, 39

S

Saenger, Samuel, 28, 36
Saran, Mary
  as member of SVG, 104
  as reeducator for the British Occupation, 132–33

on Soviet expansion in Eastern Europe, 135
Scandinavia, socialist groups in, 102
  WIS as rival to SPD-in-exile in London, 106–107
Schmid, Carlo, 57
  as member of CCF, 58
  as member of Council of Europe, 124
  position on Schumacher's European policy, 121
Schmitt, Carl
  critique of interwar democracy, 41
  as member of Europäischer Kulturbund, 30
  and National Socialist versions of European integration, 102
  pupils of Schmitt, 65–66, 68
Schoettle, Erwin, 102, 118–20
Schreyvogl, Friedrich, 31
Schumacher, Kurt, 116, 125
  anti-communism, 118, 128, 134
  attacks from Eastern European socialists, 128
  eagerness to reconstitute political parties in post-war Germany, 65
  European policy, 77, 108, 116–17, 120–21, 135, 137, 181, 187, 190, 201
  nationalism, 17, 76–77, 108, 129, 137, 181, 201
  policy of 'intransigent opposition', 119
  reasons he became first post-war leader of SPD, 118
  relationship with socialist exiles, 87, 118–19
  Schumacher-centrism, 116, 139n, 201
  support for Marshall Plan, 124
Schuman Plan, 3, 72, 136
Schuman, Robert, 8, 178
Schweizerische Konservative Volkspartei/Swiss Conservative People's Party (SKVP), 174
Second International
  before and after WW1, 88–89
  shortcomings of, 99
Second World War, 3, 75
  as context for post-war European integration, 2, 103–105, 199–200
  collaboration during WW2, 47, 73, 123, 146
  ideas for integrating Europe formulated during WW2, 10, 105
  immediate aftermath, 23, 27, 47

Marxist interpretation of, 200
precursors to future Cold War divide during WW2, 146, 159
secret services (see also OSS)
  exiles' links with, 132–33, 146
  funding of European federalist ventures, 175–76
  propaganda work, 104, 132–33
Secrétariat International des Partis Démocratiques d'Inspiration Chrétienne (SIPDIC), 150
Seipel, Ignaz, 31
self-determination of peoples (see also majorities, minorities)
  and de-integration of Europe after 1918, 12–13, 32–33, 35
  as form of Americanization, 62
  and minorities as problems, 38
  and rise of the masses, 35
self-determination of European peoples, 179–80
socialist support for self-determination of peoples within a European federation, 91
Siemsen, Anna
  and French-German pro-integration groups, 98
  as leading member of the Europa Union, 181
  political activities in Switzerland, 153
Social Democratic Party of Germany (SPD), 6, 17, 76
  attitude of SPD politicians to parliamentary democracy, 94–95, 108, 120
  attitude of SPD towards Soviet Union, 102, 118
  in Bavaria, 185–90, 192
  Bürgermeisterflügel, 108, 119, 121, 188
  and Cold War, 118, 128, 133–37
  in Eastern and Western Zones, 118
  internationalism, 17, 128–29, 200
  as major player in politics of European integration, 16, 138
  and Marxism, 93
  and *Ostpolitik*, 204–205
  policy of 'intransigent opposition', 120, 201
  policy of SPD in exile on European integration, 105–107
  policy on German reunification, 135

post-war policy on European integration, 17, 116, 121, 129–30, 132, 136–37, 181, 188, 205
reaction to Adenauer's policy of *Westbindung*, 79, 135–36
reformism, 90, 94–96, 106, 126, 129–30, 188
relations between SPD and other European socialist parties after WW1, 88–90
relations between SPD and splinter groups, 86, 90
relations between SPD in exile and splinter groups, 87, 96, 103, 105–107
relations between SPD in exile and Western governments, 100, 103, 124, 126–27, 132, 137
relations with Communists in Weimar Germany, 94
role of exiles in post-war SPD, 87, 116–19, 181, 186, 188–90, 200–201
role of ISK members in post-war SPD, 86–87, 93, 116–20, 124–25, 137
role in post-war Socialist International, 127–28
support for European integration in interwar period, 91
socialism (see also SPD)
and democracy, 96–97, 106, 108, 129–30
as inherently nationalist, 69–70, 188
and internationalism, 80, 88–89, 97, 102
as reformist or revolutionary, 15, 90, 96–97, 99, 101, 106, 108, 117, 129, 133, 137, 188
relationship between socialism and federalism, 102, 108, 129, 180–81, 187–88
relationship to rival ideologies, 64, 123, 134
role of a socialist party, 117
socialist theories of civil society, 95
socialist theories of Europe, 15, 88
Third Way socialism, 88, 101, 124, 137
Socialist International, (see also Second Intenational, Sozialistischer Arbeiter Internationale, SAI/LSI), 117, 125
plans to reform Socialist International during WW2, 126–27
problems in 1930s, 99
SPD plans to revive Socialist International after WW2, 135
Socialist Vanguard Group (SVG)

attitude towards Western Union, 133–34, 137
change of name to Socialist Union, 143n
entryism, 131–33
founding (as Militant Socialist International), 87, 97
as intermediary between ISK exiles and British Labour contacts, 104
relation to other left-socialist groups in Britain,
role in facilitating meetings between exiled European socialists, 104
Sopade
cooperation with splinter groups, 96, 103
move from Prague to Paris, 103
radicalization of SPD policy in exile, 96
Soviet bloc
democratization, 5, 206
de-Stalinization, 136
lack of freedom, 76
and *Ostpolitik*, 204, 206
role of culture in Soviet bloc, 64
socialist parties from Soviet bloc in Socialist International, 128
Titoism, 137
Soviet Union (see also Russia)
appeal of Soviet Union to splinter groups, 91, 100, 102
as authoritarian, 25
and Cold War, 9, 14, 146
disillusion of splinter groups with Soviet Union, 100, 103, 123, 135, 200
as godless, 14, 166
as imperial power, 14–15, 153
as mass polity, 35
and *Ostpolitik*, 77, 136, 205
and policy on GDR, 79
SPD policy towards, 134–36
sponsorship of Freies Deutschland, 152
as threat to Europe, 32–34, 74, 134
as threat to united Germany, 151–54
as un-European, 36, 134
as WW2 victor nation, 74
Sozialdemokratische Partei der Schweiz (SPS)
connections to German socialists exiled in Switzerland, 152
moderation of SPS during interwar and war years, 159–60
Sozialistische Arbeiterpartei Deutschlands (SAP(D))
attitude towards interwar democracy, 94

exile in Scandinavia, 102
international links with socialist groups, 94
as largest splinter group, 90
Marxist analysis of Nazism, 102
as member of exiled socialist cartel in Britain, 103
position on *Anschluss*, 105
rejoining post-war SPD, 117
Sozialistische Einheitspartei Deutschlands (SED), 178
Sozialistische Partei Österreichs (SPÖ)
in exile in Czechoslovakia, 97
as leading member of IWUSP/SAI, 89
Sozialistische Warte, 98–100
contributors, 98
Esperanto version, 95
as forum for debate between socialists in exile, 102
Sozialistischer Arbeiter Internationale (Labour and Socialist International) SAI/LSI
British Labour Party dominance during WW2 and post-war period, 127
founding of, 90
opposition to Third International, 99
reform during WW2, 126
Spengler, Oswald, 14, 177
Spinelli Group, 1
Spinelli, Altiero, 7, 126, 150
Stampfer, Friedrich, 94, 107, 126
Sternberger, Dolf, 24, 44
Stunde Null (Zero Hour), 4
Sudetenland
annexation to Greater Germany, 96, 101–102
as home to German minorities in Czechoslovakia, 90
post-war emigration of Germans from, 172
Switzerland
Catholicism, 31
conditions for refugees, 146–48
democracy, 159–62
European federalist organizations in, 148
as exile centre, 17, 138, 148, 150–51, 155, 164–65, 173, 184–86, 191
German authors from, 63
as home to German communities, 4, 164–65
interwar politics, 160
as meeting-point for federalists, 174–75
as model for Demokratisches Deutschland leaders, 157, 159, 177
neutralism, 159
OSS Berne Office, 150
as part of Western civilization, 154
Spiritual National Defence, 160
World Council of Churches (WCC), 150

T

technocrats, 1, 3–4, 203
Tehran, Conference, 107
teleology, 2
Third Force/Third Way, Europe as Third Force/Third Way
exiles' support for Europe as Third Force, 100–101, 126, 133
federalists' support for Third Way Europe, 65, 134, 166, 173, 179–80, 182, 187–88, 192, 201
ideas of Third Way Europe in Eastern Europe, 136
left-socialist British groups' support for, 132–33
and *Ostpolitik*, 18, 89, 117, 138, 192, 204
post-war SPD's advocacy of Third Way Europe, 116–17, 120, 133–34, 137–38, 200–201
pre-Cold War roots of Third Way sentiment, 14, 35, 72–73, 76, 80
right-wing support for Europe as Third Force, 16, 24, 74, 76
socialist splinter groups' advocacy of Third Way Europe, 90, 120, 202
SPD in exile's support for Third Way Europe, 103, 106–107
Third Force ideas advanced in print media, 73–74
and Westernization thesis, 116, 192, 200
Third International, 89, 98–99
Tocqueville, Alexis de, 6
trade unions
critiques of their role in democracies, 66, 70
as funders of social democratic parties, 176
links to ISK, 87, 93–94, 97, 124
as mass-membership organizations, 201
as reformists within post-war SPD, 129
transnationalism
federalism as transnational movement, 146–47, 166, 178, 183, 201
history of European integration from a transnational perspective, 173
transnational civil society organizations, 24, 55, 63–64, 66, 146–47, 200, 208

transnational debates between right-wing advocates of European integration, 47–48, 55, 63
transnational debates between socialists, 17, 87–88, 97–98
transnational economic interest groups, 15, 187
transnational elites, 35, 66, 68, 99, 200
transnational empires, 35
transnational media networks, 88
transnational resistance movements, 149
transnational party alliances, 3, 6, 16, 80, 97–98, 116, 149–50, 166, 173, 178
Trizone, see Bizone
Trott, Adam von, 156

U
Ulbricht, Walter, 100, 204
Union of European Federalists/Union Européenne des Fédéralistes (UEF)
  forming of, 148
  leaders, 134, 180
  membership figures, 3
United States
  as capitalist, 25, 124
  as Cold War combatant, 14, 58, 76, 133
  as cultural patron, 58
  and cultural transfer, 8–9
  as democratic polity, 9, 33, 68
  as donor to Europe after WW2, 75, 124
  as European culture, 36, 64
  as exile centre, 26, 126
  as godless, 14
  as imperial power, 14, 32–33
  as industrial giant, 91
  as land of the future, 33
  as mass polity, 35
  as part of Western civilization, 149, 158, 166
  as post-WW1 creditor nation, 32, 34, 75
  as victor nation after WW2, 74, 78, 179
  and Westernization, 8–9, 76–77, 133, 135, 205, 207
  as *Zivilisation*, 9, 36, 177
urbanization, 33–34, 176–77

V
Versailles Treaty
  abendländisch opposition, 9, 34, 40
  alterations to, 27, 44
  and Americanization, 34
  and democracy, 34, 42
  growth of nation-states, 2 , 34
  socialist opposition, 91, 95
Vichy, 32, 47, 56, 63
Visser't Hooft, Willem
  as anti-war activist, 150
  as federalist, 156, 174
  as OSS agent, 150
Vogel, Hans, 87, 103, 118

W
Wall Street Crash, 29, 34, 37
Wandlung, die, 24, 59, 64
war (see also First World War, Second World War, Cold War)
  economic causes of, 91, 200
  as Europeanizing experience, 2, 10, 71, 122
  and relation to revolution, 126, 154
  veterans, 40
  wars between nations, 34, 116
  World Wars as part of European Civil War, 102–103
Warsaw Pact, 135–36
Weber, Alfred, 24, 32
  as funder of *Merkur*, 59
  as member of Europäischer Kulturbund, 30
  on United States and Europe, 32, 75
Weimar Republic
  associational life, 180
  constitution, 13, 41, 68, 94, 162
  generational conflict, 42
  hampered by international settlement after WW1, 165
  interest groups, 36–37
  National Socialists' electoral successes, 99
  and parliamentary democracy, 33, 41, 115, 174, 187
  party politics, 93–94, 120, 145, 152
  print culture, 27, 47
  relations between regions and national centre, 13, 138
West Germany, see FRG
Westbindung
  Adenauer's policy of *Westbindung*, 6, 79, 192
  opposition to Adenauer's policy, 77, 173, 178, 200
Western bloc (see also *Abendland*, Third Force/Third Way, Europe as Third Force/Third Way)

and anti-Communism, 9
US dominance in, 9, 77, 79, 176, 207
West Germany's role in, 9, 116, 120, 166, 192
Western Europe (see also *Abendland*, Third Force/Third Way, Europe as Third Force/Third Way, Western bloc)
   and democracy, 99–100, 129, 135
   distinctiveness of socialist perspective in Western European countries, 99–100, 129–30
   as independent from United States, 135, 176, 182
   as industrialized part of Europe, 91, 177
   as magnet, 125
   origins of post-war Western Europe, 2, 73, 77, 121
   as part of greater Europe, 12, 18, 77–78, 120, 134, 156, 159, 207
   as part of Western bloc, 133, 135
   Western Europe as cultural entity, 75–76, 134–35
Western European Union (WEU), 182
Westernization of Germany (see also *Abendland*, Third Force/Third Way, Europe as Third Force/Third Way), 8–9, 35, 78, 153, 192, 200, 205
   as distinct from Americanization, 8, 77, 127, 130–31
   émigrés as Westernizers, 8–9, 62, 131–32, 137
   relation to democratization, 12
Westernization of intellectuals, 75–76

Westernization of social democracy, 104, 116
Wilhelm II, Kaiser, 10
Wilson, Woodrow
   as author of interwar settlement in Europe, 12–13, 33–34
   and self-determination of peoples, 32–33, 38, 62, 74
Wirth, Joseph
   as Catholic politician, 148
   as Chancellor in the Weimar Republic, 145
   as defender of democracy, 150, 152, 176–77
   as ecumenical Christian democrat, 149–50, 166, 173–76, 184–85
   exile in Switzerland, 147–48
   influence of Switzerland on, 160
   as OSS contact, 150, 157
   as promoter of southern Germany, 157
   relation to wartime resistance movements, 149
   relations with Allies, 149–50, 157
   as supporter of neutralism, 177–78
   working in coalitions, 148, 152–53, 165
   working in transnational networks, 150, 166, 173–76, 178

Y

Yalta Agreements, 71, 74–75, 126
Young Plan, 34

Z

Ziegler, Leopold, 62, 72
Zivilisation (see also *Kultur*), 9, 36, 93, 177

www.ingramcontent.com/pod-product-compliance
Lightning Source LLC
Chambersburg PA
CBHW072148100526
44589CB00015B/2136